T0329736

TRUE STORY

TRUE STORY

How a Pulp Empire Remade Mass Media

SHANON FITZPATRICK

HARVARD UNIVERSITY PRESS

Cambridge, Massachusetts & London, England

2022

Publication of this book has been supported through the generous provisions of the
Maurice and Lula Bradley Smith Memorial Fund

First printing

Library of Congress Cataloging-in-Publication Data
Names: Fitzpatrick, Shanon, author.
Title: True story : how a pulp empire remade mass media / Shanon
Fitzpatrick.
Description: Cambridge, Massachusetts : Harvard University Press, 2022. |
Includes bibliographical references and index.
Identifiers: LCCN 2021053974 | ISBN 9780674268012 (cloth)
Subjects: LCSH: Macfadden, Bernarr, 1868–1955. | Sensationalism in
journalism—United States—History—20th century. | Mass media—United
States—History—20th century. | Pulp literature,
American—History—20th century. | Health in mass media—History—20th
century. | Physical fitness—United States—History—20th century.
Classification: LCC PN4784.S4 F58 2022 | DDC 070.5092
[B]—dc23/eng/20220217
LC record available at https://lccn.loc.gov/2021053974

*Dedicated to
Ruthann Meyer, Emily Rosenberg,
and Timothy Merlis*

Contents

Introduction

On a breezy August afternoon in 1952, high above Orly Field outside Paris, a wiry old man wearing red flannel pajamas hurled himself out of a plane. Hundreds of feet below, news crews, police guards, curious factory workers, and a bevy of women in bikinis craned their necks to watch. A few tense seconds passed; then, right on time, a parachute billowed open. The skydiver's plan was to descend gently into the river Seine, where the bathing beauties would fish him out, but strong winds blew him fifty yards off course. Skirting elm trees and power lines, he crash-landed in a dusty watermelon patch, to which the reporters rushed to find him unscathed. The following day, newspapers in France and the United States described the unusual way the American fitness entrepreneur and former publishing mogul Bernarr Macfadden had celebrated his eighty-fourth birthday.[1]

If you have never heard of Macfadden, it is not your fault. But to be fair, it is not his fault either. When the sprightly octogenarian made his Paris jump, it was just the latest episode in a long career spent courting fame through dramatic acts of self-promotion and bodily spectacle. In fact, the man had once released three different illustrated biographies about himself *on the same day,* all telling the remarkable story of how a poor and sickly orphan pulled himself up by his bootstraps to become a legendary bodybuilder, health guru, writer, editor, and magazine publisher. Even more remarkably, much of this story was true.

Long before he started skydiving for attention, Macfadden worked his way up from poverty to found the Physical Culture Publishing Company, a publishing house specializing in health and fitness; after the First World War, this company expanded into Macfadden Publications Inc., a prolific purveyor of mass-market magazines whose success made its founder fabulously wealthy. Ultimately, the Macfadden publishing house became one of America's most influential media companies—a sensational "pulp empire" of muscles and magazines, known for its interactive content, broad reach, and massive circulations. This book tells the *True Story* of Macfadden's transformative pulp empire and how it remade mass media during pivotal decades of US ascendency and globalization.

• • •

The history of the Physical Culture Publishing Company/Macfadden Publications inextricably intertwines with the unlikely rise—and later descent into obscurity—of its eponymous founder, whose biography remains one of the stranger stories in the crowded American rags-to-riches canon.

The future Bernarr Macfadden was born into poverty in Missouri's Ozark mountains in 1868. During a hard-scrabble childhood, he lost both his parents, leaving him orphaned at the young age of eleven. Next, the boy was taken in by relatives in St. Louis, where a few years later he suffered a mysterious illness. Everyone assumed he would die, but Macfadden fought back through "physical culture," a health reform movement popularized in the late nineteenth century that promoted exercise and natural healing. By working out, lifting weights, and experimenting with different diets, he not only regained his health but morphed into a paragon of muscular manhood.

Macfadden struck out into the world to evangelize—and make a profit from—health and fitness. In New York in 1899, he founded the Physical Culture Publishing Company, a small publishing house dedicated to disseminating his ideas about perfecting the human body. In its inaugural years, the company distributed books and periodicals mostly written and edited by Macfadden himself, who filled them with photographs of his own muscular physique. Its flagship publication was *Physical Culture*, a magazine whose eclectic mix of articles, opinion pieces, and physique photographs attracted a diverse audience of health seekers and others interested in the body beautiful, even as censors sought to shut it down. Simultaneously with writing, editing, and running his publishing house, Macfadden invented exercise devises, held physique competitions, established a physical culture training college in Chicago, and opened vegetarian restaurants and health homes, building up an iconoclastic personal brand. By the

1910s, Macfadden, the Physical Culture Publishing Company, and its sensational media circulations had achieved widespread renown—or notoriety, depending on whom you asked.

In 1919, as the United States was entering a new era of prosperity and global influence following the Great War, Macfadden transformed his niche publishing house into a bigger enterprise. Inspired by the letters fans had been sending to *Physical Culture,* he developed *True Story,* a pioneering "confession" magazine that purported to be written by regular people, including its own readers. An immediate success, *True Story* connected with broad popular audiences, included many young women, working-class laborers, and immigrants who were ignored or maligned by other publishers. With its formula of emphasizing audience participation and catering to non-elite audiences, Macfadden Publications, as the company would hereafter be called, introduced a slate of new magazines, covering subjects as diverse as romance, detective and true crime, news, film and radio fandom, and pulp fiction, in addition to physical culture. With its products flooding newsstands in the United States and circulating abroad in several foreign markets, the company came to boast the "Largest News Stand Sale in the World."

The meteoric rise of Macfadden Publications made its founder rich and famous, but he never rested on his laurels. Keeping a tight grip on the public spotlight, Macfadden fathered a large Physical Culture Family; branched out into newspapers, film, and radio; founded a philanthropic institution; ran health resorts; and got involved in both Democratic and Republican politics. Recognizing the publisher's influence during the Great Depression, Franklin Delano Roosevelt (FDR) invited him to the White House and Eleanor briefly edited one of his magazines before Macfadden moved rightward politically in the mid-1930s. Abroad, the leaders Benito Mussolini and the pope made room in their schedules to meet with him, and foreign entrepreneurs licensed his writings and publications. Beloved by fans and disdained by critics, Macfadden and his unusual media company embodied much about America's kinetic, sensational, expansive, and politically flexible popular culture that mushroomed during the interwar period.

Macfadden remained president of his eponymous publishing house until 1941, the year that the United States entered the Second World War and rival publishing mogul Henry Luce (*Time, Life*) forecasted the dawn of an "American Century." Going forward, the company would concentrate on its true story and women's periodicals, branching out into paperbacks and even serving as an international distributor of American comic books. Meanwhile, Macfadden spent his senior years promoting bodybuilding

Fig.I.1 Some Macfad-
den Publications
magazines in the
1920s
Media History Digital
Library

competitions, courting energetic women, and skydiving on his birthdays. "I feel damned good!" he assured reporters after his 1952 jump, confident he would have many more decades to cement his legacy as an unforgettable American icon of strength and success.[2]

Much like parachutes, however, legacies can be unpredictable and hard to control. As it turned out, Macfadden died just three years after his Paris jump, in 1955, at the respectable but ultimately unexceptional age of eighty-seven. And while a slew of obituaries memorialized the "tycoon of magazines and muscles" who had revolutionized modern fitness culture and mass periodical publishing, he was quickly replaced in public consciousness by a new generation of muscle builders, health gurus, and media entrepreneurs, many of whom had been influenced by his works.[3] A similarly anticlimactic denouement beset Macfadden Publications, which passed on through a series of corporate mergers in the 1960s. Looking back now to Macfadden's flight over the Seine, it can seem as though the old man plunged straight down into the ash bin of history—which is certainly where most of his former company's books, periodicals, and business records ended up.

The Macfadden publishing house constitutes an important chapter in American media history that deserves to be remembered better. As this book will show, for over five decades, Macfadden and the company he built popularized new understandings of health, fitness, and the body beautiful; contributed to the democratization of periodical reading and writing; and pioneered media genres, content formulas, modes of production, and marketing strategies that became ubiquitous elements of popular entertainment and consumer culture in the United States and the world in the twentieth century. Thus, the true story of Macfadden's pulp empire of muscles and magazines offers insights into the historical development and flexible cultural politics of a media landscape that remains in evidence today—one that is sensational, body obsessed, interactive, confessional, and globalized.

• • •

Considering the enduring familiarity of so many of the Macfadden publishing empire's contributions—fitness publications, confession magazines, participatory media genres that invite audiences to create content—it may seem mysterious that the Macfadden name is not more well known. There are several explanations for this. One obvious place to start is with the inconvenient reality that there is no central Macfadden archive, as neither the man nor the company bequeathed an organized trove of business records, personal papers, and other collected materials to posterity. There is also the compounding factor that the Macfadden company's publications were not designed to last. Like other cheap print media, they broke down on contact with the elements, got bleached by the sun, and were readily "pulped"—that is, destroyed, thrown away, or recycled and turned into other things.

Perhaps counterintuitively, the publisher's thirst for celebrity likely worked against the durability of the Macfadden name in the long run as well. Throughout his career, the Father of American Physical Culture rarely missed an opportunity to draw attention to himself, highlight his importance, or get others to do this work for him. Within the physical culture movement where he got his start, superlatives were the name of the game, and Macfadden expertly deployed both pen and camera to assert his singularity. However, with the passage of time, and the forces of aging and gravity doing their work, such proclamations lost their resonance, especially as fresh health and fitness icons entered the scene.

The sensational nature of Macfadden's publications, combined with the publishing house's commercial success, had implications for the Macfadden legacy as well. From the beginning, Macfadden, his company, and its products evoked disdain and criticism. Initially, moralistic censors and medical professionals objected to the Physical Culture Publishing Company's dissemination of scantily clad bodies and unscientific health advice. After the Great War, the ascent of Macfadden Publications Inc. and its attention-seeking president ignited debates about the nature of mass culture and consumer capitalism. Because its rise was so closely linked to the patronage of non-elites—especially immigrant and young women readers—the Macfadden publishing empire was accused of corrupting literature, culture, politics, and the traditional public sphere. Detractors at home and abroad framed the company as a symbol for the vacuity and voraciousness of what would pejoratively become known later as the United States' "culture industry."[4]

This strain of antipathy toward Macfadden Publications, rampant among educators and intellectuals, persisted into the second half of the twentieth century, lingering long after Macfadden's death. During the post-WWII decades of national growth and corporate prosperity, critical distaste for Macfadden's boastful persona, sensational media, and non-elite readership was enhanced by the Cold War imperative to counter stereotypes portraying American mass culture as gauche and feminized. In this context, Macfadden Publications and its cheap print products, especially those associated with female audiences, were not enshrined in an emerging canon of historically important US corporations and celebrated vernacular media and entertainment forms. Indeed, when a professor at the Missouri

School of Journalism named William H. Taft started work on a biography of the publisher in the late 1960s, an eminent Ivy League historian admonished him that "Macfadden was not worth writing about and no serious writer should waste his time researching the subject."[5] Tellingly, Taft never finished his book.[6]

Of course, academic gatekeepers do not hold a monopoly on preserving or transmitting the past. In various quarters beyond the ivory tower, Macfadden and his publishing house remained memorable and influential. For instance, many weightlifters and fitness buffs around the world maintained devotion to Macfadden and his publications over the years, even as the use of anabolic steroids and hormone injections among bodybuilders came to render the Father of American Physical Culture's antique physique increasingly unimpressive to outsiders. Relatedly, Macfadden's longtime promotion of clean eating, natural healing, and outdoor exercise meant that his publications retained relevance for healthy living and alternative medicine enthusiasts, including vegetarians and anti-vaccination activists. Beyond physical culture, Macfadden Publications' confession, romance, and true crime magazines held persistent appeal for detective and romance story aficionados, leading to some preservation efforts. The same goes for the company's movie magazines, which to this day command high prices from collectors. Furthermore, queer audiences that cohered around both physique culture and pulp media constitute another network in which some of Macfadden's output remained familiar and in circulation. In sum, the very qualities that made the Macfadden media empire forgettable or deplorable to some made its products especially memorable and relevant to others.

This dynamic, along with broader intellectual and cultural trends, has influenced when and how the Macfadden publishing empire has been studied. Accompanying the growth in popularity of social and cultural history, the linkages between Macfadden's publishing house and historically marginalized social groups, subcultures, and consumer markets sparked growing curiosity about the company and its founder in the final decades of the twentieth century. As a result, the Macfadden name drifted back into greater focus in the academy and among mainstream journalists, with profiles introducing the publisher to a younger generation appearing in places such as *American Heritage* and new biographies offering thoughtful analyses of his career and accomplishments.[7] With the bodybuilding, aerobics, self-help, and alternative healing industries booming, scholars revived Macfadden's reputation as an "apostle of strength and fitness" and a "reformer of the feminine form," reflecting growing theoretical interest in "the body" as a locus of identity and power relations.[8]

Meanwhile, professors of American Studies and related disciplines turned the brittle pages of Macfadden Publications' magazines looking for insights into the experiences of working-class people, the development of US consumer society, and other topics.[9] Indicative of this development is literary scholar Ann Fabian's conclusion that Macfadden's publishing house shaped the "peculiar mixture of the physical and the sensational, the sexual and the commercial" that characterized US mass media and popular culture in the twentieth century.[10] More recently, in 2009, the writer Mark Adams titled an engaging biography of Macfadden *Mr. America*.[11] If the publisher was still alive, he'd likely appreciate this moniker, for it captures his own Herculean efforts to be seen and remembered as an epic national icon.

A century and a half after the birth of the Father of American Physical Culture and over one hundred years since the debut of *True Story* magazine, whether Macfadden is "worth writing about" seems no longer in question. Nevertheless, it remains the case that the publisher has attracted merely a fraction of the attention paid to figures like William Randolph Hearst, Henry Luce, and other print media moguls who were his contemporaries. Despite their influence and wide reach, Macfadden's media products remain remarkably underexamined as well, especially when compared to middlebrow magazines or movies. The same goes for the history of the Macfadden corporation. *True Story* pushes far beyond biography to construct a multifaceted history of the Macfadden publishing house spanning more than half a century, foregrounding its imbrications in, and contributions to, modern mass media and popular culture, empire, globalization, and consumer and corporate capitalism.

• • •

The following chapters proceed roughly chronologically, reconstructing the history of the Macfadden publishing company and analyzing its media, circulations, and transformations. Chapter 1 begins by revisiting the oft-told story of Macfadden's early years, showing how the world of fitness in the late nineteenth-century US Midwest in which he came of age set the stage for his career as a physical culturalist and publisher. Next, Chapter 2 follows the rise of the Physical Culture Publishing Company, situating its origins within a transatlantic boom in health and fitness entertainment and consumer culture. The third and fourth chapters track the company's growth during the 1900s and 1910s, an era marked by mass immigration, imperial expansion, Progressivism, and the First World War. Together, these first four chapters show how Macfadden's business became one of the world's most prolific purveyors of physical culture publications while shaping the development of a "body-centric" and interactive modern media and consumer culture headquartered in the United States.

The second half of this book focuses on the transformation of Macfadden's business into the media corporation Macfadden Publications. The creation of *True Story* in 1919 and the publisher's subsequent meteoric ascent is discussed in Chapter 5, which situates this growth within the context of the expansion of American consumer society in the 1920s. The history of the company during the Great Depression is the subject of Chapter 6, which examines how the economic and political upheavals of the 1930s presented new opportunities for expansion and consolidation as Macfadden Publications sought to influence public affairs and the relationship between populism and corporate capitalism. Voyaging abroad, Chapter 7 explores foreign editions and international circulations of the company's magazines during the interwar period. Chapter 8 then discusses the publishing house's operations immediately before, during, and after the Second World War, during which it parted ways with its founder and thereafter focused on women's periodicals; pulp paperbacks; and other cheap print media, including comics. Finally, reflecting upon the enduring legacies of Macfadden's publishing house, the conclusion explores how the historical significance of this pulp empire lies not only in its singularity and iconicity but also in its tendencies toward multiplicity and reconfiguration.

While *True Story* builds on other works about Macfadden and his company, these chapters cover new ground geographically, methodologically, and thematically, producing a *longue durée* account of Macfadden's publishing empire—and what this publishing empire can tell us about the broader mass-mediated cultural landscape it reflected and helped to shape—that has not previously been told. First, this book insists that the history of Bernarr Macfadden and Macfadden Publications, which has in the past been cast as an American story, is more truthfully told as a global and transnational one as well. Characterizations of Macfadden as a national icon and his publishing house as an exceptionally "American Phenomenon" stretch back a long time.[12] The publisher's self-publicity and promotional materials, as well as criticisms of his company's success, centered what the publishing house reflected or indicated about the United States. Subsequent scholarship has maintained a similar scope of analysis. However, the arenas in which previous biographers and historians have emphasized the publisher's national impact—including health reform, sports and athletics, and mass media and consumer culture—had wider global dimensions, and so too did Macfadden's publishing empire.

As we will see, Macfadden and his company were influenced by global events and foreign influences, including travel, migration, war, trade, and various dimensions of globalization. Border-crossing movements of people, ideas, money, and power shaped every stage of the company's development—from its turn-of-the-century origins as a transatlantic business through its adoption of an explicitly American corporate identity after the First World War. At the same time, the company's products proved superlatively able to traverse boundaries of various kinds, often reaching audiences far from their point of origin. Foregrounding the Physical Culture Publishing Company/Macfadden Publications' global influences and transnational circulations de-exceptionalizes some aspects of its history while revealing ways in which it was uniquely American.[13]

Second, this study emphasizes the enormous significance of immigrants to the development of the Physical Culture Publishing Company/Macfadden Publications. It was, as we will see, Central European immigrants who introduced physical culture to young Macfadden in the Midwest. Next, the publisher lived for a time on both sides of the Atlantic while establishing his company in the early years of the twentieth century. Meanwhile, migrant laborers who came to or passed through the United States often served as audiences for and then formal or informal distributors of his publications. The meteoric growth of Macfadden Publications that took place during the interwar period was fueled by readers, writers, and other cultural workers who were frequently foreign-born or second-generation Americans, as attested by memoirs, sociological studies, early market research, and the company's own self-publicity. While the corporation eventually packaged its audience to advertisers as a vast market of assimilated "wage earners," the diverse backgrounds and immigrant identities of those who interacted with Macfadden's publications indelibly shaped the form and contents of this American media empire and its meanings.[14]

Next, this study connects the history of Macfadden's publishing house to America's expanding role in the world during the first half of the twentieth century through the lens of empire. Crucially, Macfadden's career and the trajectory of his publishing house intertwined with specific colonial and imperial processes. The acceleration of US military conquest and commercial expansion during this era played an important role in shaping the reach of Macfadden-brand publications overseas, as did British imperial and neocolonial networks that offered additional paths to English-reading customers from diverse backgrounds. In terms of content, the publishing house's popular physical culture and entertainment media helped construct gendered and racialized understandings of bodily difference, fitness, and modernity that reflected and reinforced imperial ideologies and overseas empire-building projects, as well as formations of what has been called internal colonialism. That Macfadden's metaphorical publishing empire was a product of US military and market empire, as well as a purveyor of imperial culture domestically and abroad, is a central argument of this book.[15]

Foregrounding the imperial in the transnational history of Macfadden's publishing house raises some important questions about how and why different audiences engaged with its media and what the terms of this engagement were. This is especially the case because of the popularity of the company's publications among readers who could be described as racially, economically, or geopolitically marginalized. For instance, *Physical Culture* appealed to athletes living under colonial regimes as well as African American men building their bodies in an age of segregation and racial terrorism; *True Story* was pitched to new immigrants and "working girls" struggling to make ends meet and carve out a place for themselves in American cities; and the company's books and magazines circulated abroad in societies wary of cheap US exports and the perceived voraciousness of American mass culture. Imperial ideologies and forces of marginalization and subjugation were often bolstered by American popular culture, including Macfadden's media empire; and yet, many of the texts the company circulated and the modes of production and consumption it modeled provided resources for the formation of alternative forms of identity, connection, and empowerment, including those that explicitly challenged or fostered resistance to colonial relationships and imperial worldviews.[16]

Therefore, fourth, to investigate the cultural politics of Macfadden's metaphorical publishing empire, this study decenters Bernarr Macfadden's subjectivity and intentions and examines what the company's media meant to such differently positioned consumers, combining broader discussions of historical and geographic context with close readings of specific media texts and biographies of actual readers and cultural workers. In this way, it acknowledges the expansive scale of Macfadden Publications and its imbrications in imperial and hegemonic processes of various kinds without falling back on outmoded models of cultural colonialism or media power that fail to account for the complexities of participatory media production and reception.[17]

The following chapters highlight, for instance, how forms of audience engagement encouraged by Macfadden's periodicals not only blurred distinctions between producers and consumers but amplified polysemy and fostered especially active ways of relating to the printed page, other readers, and related cultural industries taking shape. Within the Macfadden publishing empire, transnational and non-elite circulations combined with interactive modes of content creation to produce media forms that were cacophonously multivocal and easily wedded to a range of political ideologies and agendas, even as they tended to reinforce evolving tenets of racial, consumer, and corporate capitalism that contributed to exclusionary formations of "Americanization" at home and foundational pillars of US hegemony.[18] Analyzing Macfadden's publishing house and its circulations thus elucidates complex interactions between mass-market media, globalization, print capitalism, and cultural power that developed during pivotal decades of US and world history spanned by the company's rise and disintegration.

· · ·

Which brings us to a final contribution of this study: its conceptualization of Macfadden's publishing company as a *pulp empire*. While this phrase may seem like it is composed of contradictory terms—one connoting an expansive presence and influence, and the other marginality and impermanence—it is meant here as a productive juxtaposition. It is intended to connect the Macfadden publishing company's story to a kaleidoscopic arena of mass-mediated popular culture and systems of cultural production that have operated to shape America's expansive mass consumer society and the US's complex role in the world.

Pulp, of course, is a word with multiple meanings. As a noun, it most commonly refers to a "wet mass of material"; a type of cheap paper product; or a sensational media aesthetic or text, especially "sensational writing that is generally regarded as being of poor quality."[19] These definitions are related genealogically. In the mid-nineteenth century, cheap "pulpwood" paper made from fibers extracted from wood, rather than rags, became an important commodity that lowered the cost of printing, providing raw material for the democratization of publishing and reading. With its access to papermaking ingredients, comparatively high literacy rates, subsidized postal service, and large population hungry for information and communication, the post–Civil War United States, in which Macfadden came of age, proved an especially fertile field for new publishing ventures. The result was an explosion of cheap books and periodicals that were marketed beyond elites to the middle class and then juvenile and working-class audiences, whose rising purchasing power shaped the creation of new forms and genres of mass-market print culture. In turn, new "imagined communities" of readers and writers emerged, contributing to the formation of the world's first mass-mediated, multiethnic, consumer capitalist society, whose evolution and expansion would shape and be shaped by the Macfadden publishing company.[20]

From the start, cheap publications aimed at non-elite audiences provoked moral outrage, critical disdain, and censorship. "Pulp" thus became not only a material description but also an aesthetic classification used to describe the sensational content and perceived low quality of mass-produced media in relation to hierarchical conceptualizations of taste, culture, and social order.[21] Entrepreneurs in the United States pioneered several waves of such pulp media during the late nineteenth and early twentieth centuries. Initially, there were "story papers" and dime novels, which helped to spread the hobby of leisure reading and propelled the domestic and international popularity of genres such as the Western. It was in this milieu that Macfadden came of age, developed his reading and writing habits, and started his own publishing house. Another influential era followed the Great War, when cheap pulp fiction magazines flooded newsstands with serialized detective, crime, adventure, and romance-themed stories. This trend coincided with the dramatic growth of Macfadden Publications, whose own periodicals contributed to the development of these genres. Subsequently, around the Second World War, comic books and pocket paperback novels exploded in popularity, with the Macfadden company participating in these sectors too as a publisher and international distributor.[22]

The Physical Culture Publishing Company/Macfadden Publications was too long-lived and its products too diverse to fit squarely within any one of these individual pulp genres or moments; yet its story, remarkably, intersects with them all. It therefore offers a uniquely apt metonym, or stand-in, for an expansive realm of fleshly, sensational, and interactive mass-mediated popular culture that took shape in the early twentieth-century United States and then evolved over ensuing decades of national transformation and globalization in tandem with various projects of Americanization. Through the case study of the Macfadden pulp empire, then, this book spotlights a dynamic of cultural power that might itself be called pulp empire due to the material and aesthetic properties of its apparatus, and in recognition of its concurrent tendencies toward proliferation, disintegration, and reconfiguration.

CHAPTER ONE

Decades of Fitness in
the Dynamic Midwest

B EFORE BERNARR MACFADDEN, there was only Bernard McFadden. This was the name William and Mary McFadden gave their first child, a boy born on August 16, 1868, in Mill Spring, Missouri, a small outpost on the Black River in the Ozark mountains about 130 miles south of St. Louis. It was not an auspicious time or place to start a family. When Bernard entered the world, remnants of the recent Civil War still marked the surrounding landscape. Debts were high, soldiers' bodies remained unburied, and political tensions and racial violence simmered throughout the region.

Like many of his generation, Bernard's father had seen the carnage of war up close. Drafted into the Union Army, he fought in the nearby Battle of Pilot Knob, where 1,500 soldiers in blue resisted 10,000 Confederate troops on their way to St. Louis in the autumn of 1864. William survived the war but would continue to battle his own demons. Having originally come west to breed horses, he ended up more interested in betting on them at the racetrack. William lost money, drank heavily, and likely abused his wife, who gave birth to their second and third children, both daughters, in 1870 and 1873. The family of five lived together in a two-room, dirt-floored farmhouse until Bernard's mother reached the end of her rope. Following the birth of her youngest, Mary left with the kids and sued for divorce. Not long after this separation, William succumbed to delirium tremens, an illness triggered by ethanol withdrawal. The corn whiskey he lived for had finally killed him.

A resourceful woman, Mary worked herself to the bone to keep her young family fed and clothed. But sadly, she took ill as well. Suffering the dual ravages of poverty and tuberculosis, a disease known as "consumption" for the way it devoured its victims, she struggled to care for Bernard and his sisters. When an attempt to inoculate her son against smallpox backfired, the boy's long convalescence added to her woes. Mary was forced to send away her eldest, first to an institution, and then to relatives in Illinois who wanted help running their small hotel, which was where Bernard was at the age of eleven when his mother died. Orphaned, penniless, and separated from siblings he barely knew, the boy was still grieving when his guardians fostered him out to a farmer looking for cheap labor. For the next two years, he lived with the farmer's family, drudging through church services and outdoor chores and growing increasingly discontent with his meager wages. Finally, he ran away. The railroad lines transforming the nation's landscape offered free transport for those who were adventurous or desperate, or in this case, both.

Next, Bernard went to live with relatives in St. Louis, the "Gateway to the West," where he met his Uncle Harvey, a bookkeeper who had previously taken in one of his sisters, and his maternal grandmother. Among these more supportive kin, Bernard settled in nicely, getting a job as a route boy for a credit agency and then moving on to work in the office of a grocery. After years of hardship and loneliness, he had finally found a sense of belonging and stability. But alas, another misfortune struck. Seemingly out of the blue, the boy's health flagged. Headaches, nausea, and a racking cough left him weak and fatigued. The doctor who was called prescribed medications, but they only made the patient sicker. Bernard had apparently inherited a weak constitution, and it was assumed he would be joining his parents soon beyond the grave.

Then, in the "blackest hour" of Bernard's sickness, when "the badge of death seemed already on him," a path to salvation appeared.[1] Guided by snippets of newspaper coverage he had seen about a health and life reform movement called "physical culture," Bernard embarked on a self-directed quest to build up his sickly body through fresh air, diet, and vigorous exercise. When doctors prescribed drugs, he refused to take them. Instead, he bought dumbbells and lifted them in the basement. Quitting his urban office job, he fled to the countryside, performing odd jobs and refueling his body with hearty, unprocessed foods. When Bernard finally returned to St. Louis a few years later, he joined a gymnasium. What followed was a journey of bodily recovery and personal transformation. Through physical culture, the lonely Ozark orphan morphed into a strapping paragon of physical fitness and manly independence, ready to take on the world.

Later, Bernarr Macfadden and his various biographers would recount the tale of his childhood travails and adolescent transformation with gusto. According to the stories they told, the boy's journey was a lonely, uphill one, undertaken against great odds. Carrying the burden of a poor health inheritance from his dead parents, he had had to dodge misguided doctors, doubtful relatives, slothful urban living, and society's widespread ignorance about the miraculous powers of physical culture to transform individuals and whole societies. Indeed, as Macfadden became a public figure in the twentieth century, his humble past and personal battles to overcome poverty and sickness would become a well-known origin story, repeated ad nauseam by journalists and integrated into his publishing company's brand identity. This *bildungsroman* framed Macfadden as a self-made man and revolutionary historical figure, a boy who "built his own body up from weakness threatening death, into throbbing, pulsating healthfulness" and then inaugurated physical culture's "triumphal march in America."[2] The sickness-to-health, rags-to-riches melodrama ultimately made for an irresistible and lasting "mythography," one that mapped nicely onto larger narratives about US recovery and growth following the Civil War.[3]

This is not the only story that can be told about Bernarr Macfadden's early life, however. Analyzing his own memoirs, biographies, and other historical sources reveals a theme absent from later self-centered accounts: the central role played by transnational currents of people, ideas, and products in shaping his coming-of-age in the American Midwest and the impacts of these years on his subsequent career. Bernard certainly overcame tough luck and bad circumstances, but he did not battle a society entirely hostile to the physical culture ideals, practices, and products on which he would found his personal celebrity and media empire. Nor was the story of physical culture parthenogenesis, in which brand-new ideas about health and fitness sprung fully formed from his head, a true one.

Instead, Bernard McFadden came of age in years when interest in reforming, strengthening, displaying, comparing, and commodifying human bodies flourished simultaneously in many areas of the world. And while he would later characterize his younger self as a "Missouri hillbilly," his birth region was in fact a locus of development, globalization, and cross-cultural encounter. Here, transnational currents of health reform, fitness, and bodily display intersected and recombined to produce new configurations of culture, identity, and commerce.[4] It was through this late nineteenth-century world of health and fitness in the dynamic Midwest that the man who would become Bernarr Macfadden—and therefore, the publishing company that would eventually become Macfadden Publications—took shape.

Decades of Fitness

The disintegration of the McFadden family over the post–Civil War decade following Bernard's birth was likely experienced by its members as an intensely private chain of events. Yet their encounters with illness, poverty, itineracy, and death—and Bernard's reported childhood longings for revival—reflected broader patterns. In the second half of the nineteenth century, anxieties about social degeneration became a central feature of public discourse in many places around the world at once, producing anxious conversations about how personal and social ills might be healed in tandem to produce stronger bodies, societies, and nations.

In the United States, a "widespread yearning for regeneration" that "was variously spiritual, moral, and physical" swept over the nation during the Reconstruction period.[5] This yearning inspired national reforms, including changes to the Constitution, continued pushes for industrial growth and economic centralization, and the promotion of westward settlement into the territories of Indigenous nations. Meanwhile, many Americans came to believe that healing the body politic required paying greater attention to improving the actual physical bodies of its members. Politicians, moralists, scholars, religious figures, medical professionals, healers, and entrepreneurs advocated for the national cultivation of physical fitness. Together, they produced cacophonous therapeutic discourses and devised plans devoted to improving, disciplining, and shaping human bodies, and through them, modern society itself. So pervasive were these efforts that the years between the end of the Civil War and the turn of the century have been described as "decades of fitness."[6] This was the background against which Bernard Mc-Fadden's adolescent "discovery" of physical culture took place.

During these decades of fitness, Americans' yearnings for regeneration created new connections between the realms of medicine, public health, religion, and popular culture, and between reformers in the United States and those in other parts of the world. The national rivalries and wars, campaigns of colonial conquest and resistance, and various experiences of economic modernization and demographic flux that characterized the nineteenth century made managing and improving the fitness of bodies and populations widely important. For instance, this period saw the emergence of national military training programs in many countries, as well as new efforts to engineer greater public health. Campaigns to improve personal and collective bodies easily spilled over and between borders of all kinds, contributing to the proliferation of a multifaceted, international physical culture movement that celebrated the achievement of stronger, healthier, and more beautiful bodies. New ideas regarding bodily health and social renewal reached the American heartland from other places in the nation and abroad; at the same time, the Midwest also became a center of health reform and physical culture.[7]

Dramatic changes in the realms of medicine ensued. In the postwar era, physicians and medical reformers worked to advance science-based medicine and strengthen their authority and role in constructing a healthier body politic. Among a population that remained widely suspicious of doctors and surgeries, the fledgling American Medical Association (AMA) worked to make a medical profession and improve its public image. Looking to Europe, where medical degrees brought higher social standing, the AMA helped American doctors police the boundaries of their profession, establish more respectable public personas, and define what constituted modern medical practice.[8] From their headquarters in Chicago, the organization supported stricter educational and licensing requirements for practitioners and publicized new understandings of antisepsis, pharmacology, and disease control. As a result, Americans increasingly turned to credentialed doctors for help healing sick bodies and achieving a fitter nation.[9] While the identity of the man who attended Bernard McFadden when he fell ill in St. Louis is unknown, his family's decision to call in a doctor who prescribed "medicine after medicine" reflects this professionalization of doctoring and growing trust in pharmacological cures.[10]

Young Bernard's alleged rejection of his doctor's orders, however, was also in line with the times, as enthusiasm for physical culture produced competing visions of how bodies and nations might best be healed. For decades, a range of voices had advocated more holistic prescriptions for health that emphasized the interrelatedness of the body, mind, and soul. The growth of scientific modern medicine fueled contentious debates that grew louder across the last decades of the nineteenth century. What caused disease? Did pharmacological and surgical interventions help or hinder the body's own curative abilities? Was true medical knowledge derived from tradition and experience, from universities and laboratories, or from God? Attitudes of "medical pluralism" persisted and even gained strength and depth in the face of the professionalization of doctoring.[11] The blending of modern medical methods with traditional practices spawned multifaceted natural living movements, religious doctrines, and an influential alternative medicine industry that was centered in the Upper Midwest yet remained always in conversation with developments abroad. This pluralist strain of healing determined the tenor of US physical culture discourse during Bernard's youth.

In the United States, the alternative and holistic medicine industries were characterized by particularly American formations of Christianity and entrepreneurship. Powered by an evangelical ethos that framed human society (or at least certain communities of believers) as perfectible, "hygienic utopianism" swept across the nation.[12] Prominent religious and intellectual leaders argued that physical health was essential to spiritual health, and they sought to make America a holier nation by reforming the diet, exercise routines, and dress of individuals.[13] With midcentury roots in the Bavarian Alps, an international health resort and sanatorium movement, which aimed to cure diseases like tuberculosis through holistic regimes of exercise, rest, nutrition, and electric and hydrotherapies, took strong root in the United States, where healers often emphasized the body-soul connection. For example, James C. Jackson's Health Resort in Dansville, New York—which Macfadden would later take over in 1931—emerged as a beacon of alternative healing during the decades of fitness. Advertised as the lofty "Home on the Hillside," Jackson's center specialized in treating consumption through vegetarianism, sexual temperance, and vigorous exercise. Among those Jackson influenced was Ellen G. White, the Seventh-day Adventist leader and founder of the Adventists' Western Health Reform Institute in Battle Creek, Michigan, who contended that bodily improvement was a precondition for spiritual transcendence. Claiming that God had opened "the great subject of health reform" before her in vision, White presented a divinely sanctioned plan for nutritious eating and natural living that eschewed mainstream physicians and their treatments.[14] Another Seventh-day Adventist, John Harvey Kellogg, presided over the Battle Creek Sanitarium, preaching a range of holistic cures for modern ailments and feeding patients the whole-grain cereals that would make Kellogg's a household name. A mix of evangelical rhetoric, nature worship, holism, experimentation, and capitalism came together in the American arm of the transatlantic sanatorium movement that was flourishing around the time Bernard McFadden experienced his teenage physical culture conversion.

Americans during the decades of fitness sought not only to cure diseases of the body and soul but to reverse the degenerative effects of modern life itself. In the United States, the mechanization of farm labor and food manufacture, accompanying financial panics, the growth of cities, migrations from abroad, and the perceived attrition of an imagined Western "frontier" sparked anxieties about the nation's future. The rapid modernization of the Midwest and the internationalization of its economy propelled such fears, as cities like St. Louis and Chicago incorporated farm families, immigrants, and small businesses with bewildering rapidity. The conditions in which Americans lived, labored, and consumed in this modernizing landscape triggered alarm about whether the nation was adequately fit. Reformers, doctors, and other experts decried the effects of sedentary labor, crowded urban living, and even prepared foods on the vitality and reproductive capabilities of men and women, especially white, middle-class citizens whose birthrates were dropping.[15]

In this context, "nature"—particularly the rugged landscapes of the West—seemed to offer a rich resource for reviving individual constitutions and national strength. Nature tourism businesses, land prospectors, and small-town boosters joined sanatorium advocates in publicizing the invigorating powers of escaping the city.[16] Newspaper ads published throughout America and overseas advertised midwestern and western lands, jobs, and leisure activities to people seeking health. After recuperating from illness his first winter in St. Louis, teenaged Bernard participated in a modest way in this trend. Saying goodbye to his St. Louis family, he crossed Missouri by rail and foot, heading for McCune, Kansas, where he built up his physique through manual labor, fresh air, and exercise before returning to St. Louis some time before his seventeenth birthday.

While Bernard's quest for vitality led him to farming and odd jobbing in Kansas, some of his contemporaries participated in more violent projects of western conquest undergirded by gendered ideals of rebirth and rejuvenation. In the years following the Civil War, clashes between Indigenous nations and settlers backed by US soldiers flared across the American Plains and Southwest. Settling on Indian lands and fighting in the so-called Indian Wars offered some American men a way to reconstruct and strengthen their own bodies and careers while shoring up national imperial power.[17] An ethos of regenerative violence also undergirded the era's various anti-immigrant movements and the growth of the Ku Klux Klan, which aimed to redeem white southerners' masculine power through disenfranchising and terrorizing African Americans.[18] The brutality of such campaigns caused some Americans to criticize the ascendant martial ethic that presented acts of population destruction as the path to a stronger body politic.[19] Nevertheless, projects of military conquest and political domination were widely celebrated in political and popular culture as arenas where American masculinity could be strengthened and the settler colonial nation cleansed of unharmonious or disruptive elements. Circulating alongside public health and medicine reform and visions of hygienic utopianism, this gendered and racialized martial ethic was a central part of the wide spectrum of attempts to reverse the degenerative effects of modern life that saturated American culture while Bernard McFadden was growing up in the decades of fitness.

Spectacular Bodies in Print and Performance

The rising mania for health, fitness, and strong bodies was also evident in popular print and entertainment culture. Circulations of informational and entertainment reading materials, along with traveling amusements like the circus, provided a window onto discussions about health reform, methods of physical regeneration, and celebrations of athleticism. Through America's expanding realms of mass-mediated entertainments, Bernard encountered a wide world of physical culture where fit and dynamic human bodies—especially white male ones like his own—symbolized expertise, opportunity, and mobility.

Later in life, when Bernarr Macfadden was eager to burnish his reputation as a self-made man, he would remember encountering only "brief casual newspaper stories" on physical culture as a youth.[20] In fact, the physical culture ideas that saturated public discourse during the decades of fitness were discussed at length in every form of print media. Rather than being forced to grasp at elusive textual threads for information on sickness and health, young Bernard had access to an abundance of health and fitness-related print culture.

The decades of fitness in the United States corresponded with a revolution in publishing that turned Americans into a nation of readers. By the time Bernard was ten, literacy rates were around 90 percent for native-born, white adults.[21] American book, newspaper, and periodical publishers ramped up production after the Civil War, expanding not only their offerings but also their target audiences. A deluge of print media offered consumers new intellectual horizons and cultural connections, sources of information and entertainment, and opportunities for work and profit.[22] This reading and publishing revolution reached Bernard McFadden, who, despite his presumably spotty school attendance, became a voracious consumer of the printed word from an early age.

First, dime novels were his boyhood reading material of choice, and after he was orphaned at the age of eleven, it was to these he turned for companionship and solace.[23] In his love of cheap fiction Bernard was not alone, as mass-produced dime novels and "story papers" were proliferating throughout the United States and Europe. With their affordable prices, easy-to-understand style, and sensational and melodramatic plots, they became "unequalled in mass appeal by any other form of literature."[24] Bernarr Macfadden would later look back with some horror at the sedentary nature of this childhood habit. Yet while fiction-reading may not have directly strengthened his young body, the transnational dime novel industry played an important role in popularizing physical culture discourse and demonstrating the marketability of affordable reading material that cele-brated strong bodies.

Although there is no record of the specific dime novels Bernard Mc-Fadden acquired, he likely encountered certain titles and topics. Across the various subgenres of dime novels aimed at boy readers on both sides of the Atlantic, characters and plots that glorified physical fitness, endurance, and competition predominated. The first dime novel publishers discovered that stories pitting bold young protagonists against the world were pop-ular, so this plot was reproduced in endless configurations. Dime novel heroes embark in these books on physically demanding adventures, con-stantly setting off to soldier, sail the Seven Seas, ride the rails, or join the circus. Along the way, they demonstrate their close-yet-masterful relation-ships with untamed lands, complicated urban environs, and socially and racially foreign peoples. The prolific output of author Horatio Alger Jr. during Bernard's youth best illustrates this trend. In books such as *Julius, or, The Street Boy Out West* and *The Young Circus Rider,* the physical prowess, discipline, and "clean living" of Alger's protagonists lead to per-sonal betterment and social mobility. Concurrently, a more rough-and-tumble world of cheap fiction centered on the exploits of cowboys, frontiersmen, scouts, outlaws, mountaineers, adventurers, and soldiers. Bernard likely heeded the call of publisher Beadle & Adams's popular *Boy's Library of Sport, Story and Adventure* series, which included the *Adventures of Buf-falo Bill from Boyhood to Manhood.* Along with Buffalo Bill, other tough "real-life" characters like Kit Carson and Calamity Jane, featured in con-temporaneous dime novels, go off on their own daring adventures, show-casing the importance of athleticism, agility, and wilderness skills in navigating the world and its dangers.[25]

As American frontier stories and Westerns traveled overseas, American readers also devoured imported stories penned by foreign, mostly British, writers, with the lack of clear copyright protections prior to the Interna-tional Copyright Agreement of 1891 ensuring that stories popular across the Atlantic were quickly pirated and imitated on the other side. Bernard almost certainly sampled "school stories," a category of children's fiction pio-neered in Great Britain in which schoolboys demonstrate their worth through athletic achievement. The British writer Thomas Hughes entertained young readers on both sides of the ocean for decades with his enormously suc-cessful *Tom Brown's Schooldays* (1857), a tale of "boyhood perfected on playing fields."[26] Likely before he encountered any of the prescriptive health literature of his day, Bernard lay awake into the night following the adven-tures of dime novel heroes whose strong and healthy bodies brought them adventure, love, popularity, fame, and fortune.

Dime novels and story papers achieved such ubiquity in the United States that many of the nation's leading intellectuals and reformers became alarmed. When Bernard was ten, the Yale sociologist William Graham Sumner published "What Our Boys are Reading" in *Century* magazine, an exposé on juvenile reading material. Sumner lamented that such books were "spiced to the highest degree with sensation" and sent the message that "[t]he first thing which a boy ought to acquire is physical strength for fighting purposes."[27] Similar concerns were echoed by Anthony Comstock, the powerful US postal inspector who headed the New York Society for the Suppression of Vice. Comstock's 1883 book *Traps for the Young* devoted an entire chapter to dime novels and story papers. Satan himself, the author declared, was responsible for "lining the news-stands and shop-windows along the pathway of children" with cheap stories designed to corrupt young minds.[28] While critics such as Sumner and Comstock aimed to halt the pernicious influence of cheap fiction, their testimonies underscore the extent to which dime novels promoted a fun and empowering form of sensational physicality that appealed to popular audiences, including boys like Bernard.

The booming late nineteenth-century dime novel industry created new business opportunities in the realm of transatlantic mass-market print culture. Many of the cheap stories Bernard likely consumed as a boy were produced by Beadle & Adams and Street & Smith, America's two most successful dime novel publishers. The former dated back to the pre–Civil War era, when the brothers Erastus and Irwin Beadle began issuing series of ten-cent, paper-covered novels shipped to readers on a regular schedule: "Books for the Million." Street & Smith, Beadle's main competitor, was founded in New York in 1855 by Francis Scott Street and Francis Shubael Smith, men with backgrounds in newspaper and magazine production. By the late nineteenth century, these publishing houses had evolved into prolific "fiction factories" that applied new methods of mechanization and standardization to the business of literary production.[29] Fiction factory writers, paid by the word, utilized formulaic plotlines and stock characters in order to churn out titles at a breathless rate. Production was helped along by the lack of international copyright protection, which facilitated the easy transfer of already-written stories from Europe, as well as by US firms' growing power to attract talent from abroad. American dime novel publishers demonstrated that sensational print media, drawn from a variety of sources and aimed at a mass audience, could mean big business. Furthermore, these large publishing houses also illustrated the potential global mobility of mass-market reading material originally created for diverse US audiences, as American Western, detective, and romance dime novels of this era were eagerly consumed overseas. Though young Bernard McFadden would have been more captivated by dime novels' exciting contents than the business models that propelled their success, the late nineteenth-century cheap fiction industry offered important lessons about what it took to succeed in the expanding, competitive marketplace of popular print culture.

Bernard's childhood love of dime novels eventually paved the way for more serious reading. Upon his move to St. Louis at the age of twelve, a new world of printed pages revealed itself in the form of the St. Louis Public Library, which had opened its doors to the public for on-premises reading and reference in 1874. Young Bernard made extensive use of the library's dictionaries, encyclopedias, and books. He became particularly interested in advice literature, tapping a vein of writings aimed at helping sick or anxious readers recover vitality and improve their strength. This genre was not new—it had flourished since before the boy could read, its ubiquity a defining characteristic of the decades of fitness. In 1871, for instance, a prominent national magazine had observed that physical culture ideas had become "so popular with nearly all classes of people" that "books on bodily strength will find abundant favor."[30] This was certainly the case for Bernard, who after overcoming his major illness began spending more and more time in the stacks.

According to Macfadden's memoirs, it was at the St. Louis Library that Bernard first encountered William Blaikie's 1879 tome *How to Get Strong and Stay So,* a book that would have a profound influence on his intellectual and physical development and future career. While other contemporary health reformers courted elite and middle-class Americans, Blaikie presented, in easy-to-understand language, programs of exercise centered on aerobic activities and small dumbbell routines that were affordable to the working masses. The chapter "Home Gymnasiums" declared, "All that people need . . . is a few pieces of apparatus which are fortunately so simple and inexpensive as to be within the reach of most persons."[31] It was after reading this that Bernard purchased his first pair of dumbbells.

By the 1870s, a wide-ranging literature described health and strength-building philosophies and techniques that were popular in other parts of the world. In his frequent trips to the library, Bernard would have come across information on an array of practices—including hydrotherapy, vegetarianism, temperance, physical education, dress reform, gymnastics, and bodybuilding—that were part of foreign and transnational reform movements. Blaikie's *How to Get Strong* drew heavily on the tenets of German gymnastics as well as British school athletics programs, for example. Bernard may also have read works by Dr. George Herbert and Charles Fayette

Taylor, brothers who traveled to Europe during the 1850s in order to study Pehr Henrik Ling's Swedish Movement Cure. Upon returning to the United States, they published *Theory and Practice of the Movement Cure* and *An Exposition of the Swedish Movement Cure* (1860).[32] The movement cure, also known as kinesiotherapy, influenced a wide range of American health and fitness reformers, including domestic science expert Catherine Beecher, homeopath Dr. Dio Lewis, and others who wrote about exercise.

Although most of the literature in the United States about physical culture focused on European and American practices, it is likely that Bernard also encountered some descriptions of Middle Eastern or South Asian fitness regimes in his reading. In his memoirs, Macfadden recalled traveling across the Midwest with a pair of wooden Indian clubs in tow. These bowling-pin-shaped wooden clubs, which were lifted and swung in strength-building and calisthenic exercises, became a fad during Bernard's youth. According to historians, the martial art of club swinging flowed for centuries through networks of Islamic conquest before arriving in America from India by way of imperial Great Britain.[33] After gaining popularity among British colonial soldiers stationed abroad, Indian club use migrated to Europe in the mid-nineteenth century, where it was integrated into various European physical education and gymnastic systems. An American entrepreneur named Simon Kehoe, an early purveyor of gymnastic equipment, then wrote *Indian Club Exercises* (1866), which was largely responsible for introducing American audiences—perhaps including Bernard—to the originally South Asian form of physical culture. This manual also helped redefine how Indian clubs looked and the ways in which they were used. Whereas club-swinging in India usually involved very heavy clubs that would be lifted by strong men, in the United States, Kehoe's lighter clubs became associated with choreographed calisthenic drills that could be performed by almost anyone, including children.[34] Their history illustrates a pattern of transnational geographic transfer and adaptation common to many physical culture products and body-centric print media that Macfadden encountered in his youth.

Macfadden would later emphasize the long hours he spent educating himself in the public library, yet Bernard surely spent most of his time out in the world. Beginning from a young age, he earned his living, and the working-class milieu of St. Louis hosted its own lively print culture. For instance, if Bernard stopped at a saloon, hotel, or barbershop on his way home from work or the library, he might have encountered a very different kind of physical culture writing in the sports pages of tabloids such as the *National Police Gazette*. Too notorious for libraries and even for some newsstands, the *Police Gazette,* published in New York and available in male-dominated spaces throughout America, was edited by a flamboyant Irish immigrant named Richard K. Fox. In addition to its lurid crime stories and pictures of showgirls, one of the paper's main draws was its coverage of the sporting world. Unlike more elite publications, the *Police Gazette* expansively defined athletics to include blood sports, prize fighting, and various other competitive amusements associated with workers, and particularly immigrants. In its pages, native-born, Anglo-American athletes shared space with fighters and wrestlers from different backgrounds who reflected the diversity of American popular sporting culture at the end of the century. The success of the *Police Gazette*'s formula influenced metropolitan dailies around the country, resulting in a steady growth of printed sports coverage. McFadden may have kept up with the world of sport through consuming the racy *Police Gazette* and the sporting pages of local newspapers.[35]

Although Bernarr Macfadden would choose to downplay the physical culture resources available to him as a child, allusions throughout his memoirs to acts of reading provide a fragmentary glimpse of the importance that circulations of available print culture played in his early development. By the 1880s even a working-class youth with limited schooling had access to a diverse array of physical culture literature and printed representations of strong and healthy bodies. Furthermore, the widespread popularity of fitness and regeneration, the mobility of doctors and health reformers, lax international copyright law, and public libraries' accessible collections made the media that McFadden encountered global in scope. Early on, Bernard likely gained a familiarity with health advice from cosmopolitan doctors and alternative practitioners, British boarding school athletic programs, various European gymnastic systems, and exercise equipment from the Middle East and South Asia—all through the printed page.

The reading revolution of the nineteenth century coincided with the growth of other leisure pursuits that promoted physical culture, including a boom in live entertainments that focused on the display and commodification of spectacular bodies. Bernard McFadden grew up during the "golden age" of the American circus, when advances in railroad transportation brought amazing collections of performers and acts to the Midwest.[36] Throughout the century, savvy self-promoting impresarios such as P. T. Barnum, Carl Hegenbeck, Adam Forepaugh, and James A. Bailey collected people and animals from all over the globe, creating fantastic traveling shows that were heavily advertised from city to country.[37] These transnational, "body-centric" entertainments presented real-life versions of the strong characters, daring exploits, and disciplined physiques about which Bernard was so fond of reading.

Bernard attended his first circus as a boy, probably sometime during 1883 when Barnum's show visited St. Louis. On the program for this season were a flying trapeze act, Roman gladiators and feats of strength, Caledonian sports, scientific fencing demonstrations by members of the French army, a variety of rope tricks, collar and elbow wrestling, gymnastic and scientific boxing, double horizontal bar acts, and Japanese wire-walkers—a list that demonstrates how the circus turned various national sporting and exercise traditions into international attractions. More than any other act, Bernard was particularly enthralled by the acrobats: "Strength and a perfect body were what he craved; and here were men who glorified in both," making him want to become an acrobat himself.[38] Around the time Bernard visited "The Greatest Show on Earth," he may have also attended Buffalo Bill and Doc Carver's "Wild West, Rocky Mountain, and Prairie Exhibition," which encamped in St. Louis the following year.[39]

One of the main draws of the late nineteenth-century circus was the diverse mélange of spectacular human bodies from different places and cultures it brought together. In how they chose members, orchestrated acts, and publicized events, circuses offered viewers narratives about the world that were linked to practices of bodily display and performance. For example, Barnum and Bailey's, drawing on conventions developed in other live entertainments of the era, introduced an "Ethnological Congress of Savage and Barbarian Tribes" the year Bernard likely saw his first show. If Bernard inspected this congress, then he saw people labeled Wild Men from Borneo; Soudan Nubians; Wild Sioux Indians; Genuine Zulu warriors; and Australian Cannibals and Boomerang, described as the "lowest of the human race."[40] Show organizers placed these foreign peoples not under the Big Top but near the animals in the menagerie.[41] Another year, Barnum advertised his circus's "Peerless Prodigies of Physical Phenomena and Great Presentation of Marvelous Living Curiosities."[42] This slogan indicates how the circus bifurcated human bodies into hierarchical racial and evolutionary categories. While "prodigies of physical phenomena" swung from trapezes, performed acrobatic stunts, wrestled, fenced, and engaged in other feats of mobility, a subset of dark-skinned circus bodies were shown as passive "living curiosities"—relics of a wild and barbarous past who were excluded from the circus's iconic three rings.[43] Certain foreign bodies—however strong—were marked as too primitive to be displayed by the modern circus as paragons of physical culture.

While popular entertainment culture racially sorted between spectacular bodies and those relegated to sideshows, the circus's identity as a transnational space simultaneously highlighted the possibility for slippage between these categories. Under the Big Top, performing men and women (as well as some nonbinary persons) from diverse backgrounds with malleable backstories exhibited highly skilled and flexible bodies that seemed to transcend the laws of nature. Circus stars enacted constantly shifting identities and defied audience expectations about what their bodies should and could do.[44] Through intense physical training, along with careful costuming and scripting, some circus performers moved between roles and identities like they moved between towns and countries. As an orphan from the Ozarks, Bernard's childhood awe at the circus, and intense longing to become an acrobat, suggests that he grasped the transformative potential of physical culture for a marginal body like his own.

At the Gymnasium

Bernard McFadden did not remain content merely reading about the blossoming world of health and fitness culture and watching spectacular performing bodies from the sidelines. Instead, he longed to become a physical culture expert and athletic performer himself. Luckily for him, St. Louis had become a physical culture mecca of sorts. Rather than having to attend a fancy school or run away to the circus to achieve his dreams, Bernard could begin by joining the nearby Missouri Gymnasium, a bustling athletic facility and social club founded and frequented by members of the city's sizable German American population.

When Bernard first arrived, St. Louis was on its way to becoming America's fourth-largest urban center. Along with rural transplants, recent immigrants to the United States made up a substantial portion of this growth, with St. Louis forming, along with Milwaukee and Cincinnati, one corner of the "Golden Triangle" of German immigration. In 1860, almost a third of the city's 160,000 residents were German-born, and in the 1880s German immigration to the United States reached its zenith.[45] Unlike some other groups in the United States, German Americans were not contained to firmly bounded ethnic neighborhoods or ghettos, and their culture and traditions permeated St. Louis.[46] After moving to the city, Bernard came into frequent contact with German people, their language and customs, and their institutions; if he attended school there (it is unclear whether he did), he would have had to learn some German, a required subject in the city's public education system until 1888.

St. Louis's German community acquired a national reputation as one of the most cultured immigrant groups in America.[47] Among the most formidable institutions they established were *Turnvereins*, also known as gymnasiums, which became centers of German American culture and social life. In Germany, *Turnvereins* and an associated Turner movement had sprung up in the wake of Napoleon's defeat of the Prussian army in 1806. Founded by Friedrich Ludwig Jahn, the Turner movement posited that a national program of vigorous physical exercise inspired by patriotic ideals was needed to revitalize a struggling society and prevent future military defeat.[48] Germans who left for the United States after the outbreak of the Revolution of 1848 brought the Turner tradition with them. Transplanted across the Atlantic, Turner societies continued their tradition of mixing politics and physical culture by framing physical preparedness as a means of defending liberty and democracy. Many Turner groups in the Northeast and Midwest mobilized to oppose slavery and nativism, and more than two-thirds of Turners in America eventually served in the Union Army. Early in the Civil War, German Turners in St. Louis became heroes when they defended the federal arsenal and captured nearby Fort Jackson from a pro-Confederate militia.[49]

As interest in physical culture grew in the United States after the war, *Turnvereins* drew increasing attention. Because they served as multipurpose social halls that hosted political meetings and athletic displays of German nationalism, they were sometimes condemned by nativists and moral reformers campaigning for alcohol prohibition and stricter immigration laws. In response, savvy German American community leaders presented Turner Halls and the physical culture traditions they hosted as evidence of German Americans' desirable physical and intellectual qualities.[50] By the late-nineteenth century, the appeal of the Turner movement in America had expanded well beyond the German community. In 1880 the national membership was approximately 13,000; over the next decade this figure more than tripled.[51] Between 1883 and 1890, the years that Bernard lived with his uncle and grandmother, the Executive Committee (called the *Vorort*) of the growing North American *Turnerbund* was located in St. Louis, and the city was widely regarded as the center of Turner activity in the Midwest.

Much of this growth was due to continued German immigration and the success of German communities within the United States, but it also stemmed from the interest of non-German Americans in physical culture. After recovering from his childhood illness, Bernard became captivated by the possibilities of building up his body in a *Turnverein*. Initially, this dream was beyond his means, as he could not afford the subscription fee, but eventually he managed to pay for a membership.[52] Inside the Missouri Gymnasium, Bernard discovered a wondrous world. There were reading rooms, dressing rooms, spaces for meetings and socializing, and even impressive modern bathrooms with hot and cold water. But it was the main floor gym and its equipment that held the strongest appeal. Here, men in sleeveless shirts and tights worked out, building up their musculature, agility, balance, and strength. Bernard immediately began spending most of his free waking hours at the gym. In this sweaty Eden, as Macfadden would later view it, he was initiated into a brotherhood of fellow health enthusiasts and athletes who helped him finally feel at home. Through the German American community's Missouri Gymnasium, Bernard became part of a flesh-and-blood physical culture community that provided him with the equipment, advice, and companionship that facilitated his transformation from searching adolescence into muscular manhood.

Membership in the gymnasium introduced Bernard to new people and possibilities for his future. One friend, a specialist on the horizontal bars, proposed that they pair up and start a circus stunt and tumbling act. The routine they put together was booked by a local variety theater, allowing Bernard to realize his childhood dream of becoming an acrobat before a foot injury ended the act. Wrestling, a popular pursuit at the Missouri Gymnasium, proved to be a more lasting and lucrative endeavor. In his time at the gym, Bernard became a close friend and training partner of George Baptiste, a man known in local sporting circuits as "Young Hercules." Born in St. Louis to Greek parents, Baptiste was an accomplished bodybuilder and heavyweight wrestler, specializing in the Greco-Roman style practiced around the Mediterranean and recently popularized in the United States.[53] As Macfadden's biographer later described, Bernard and Baptiste developed an intense routine: "Day after day the two friends warmed up together in callisthenic drills and other gymnasium activities, and they set their supple bodies to the violent joys of wrestling. They would end a hard set-to dripping with perspiration. A short run together, to cool down; a warm shower . . . a cold shower . . . and they felt like the young kings they were."[54]

Bernard's membership at the Missouri Gymnasium and his friendships with men like Baptiste drew him into the sporting world. Beginning in his late teens, Bernard competed in wrestling competitions for cash prizes, becoming a bit of a name on the heavily immigrant Midwestern wrestling circuit. In his years competing as an athlete, Bernard's success depended as much on dramatic flair and savvy financial calculations as on rigorous physical training. Lacking the height and bulk of athletes like Baptiste, Bernard specialized in long, grueling matches that drove his opponents to exhaustion. He also experimented with severe diets to gain and lose the pounds necessary to perform in multiple weight classes. Perhaps his most impressive achievement came when he trained down to 135 pounds and then proceeded to challenge—and defeat—both lightweight *and* heavyweight champions in Chicago.

Bernard's interest in wrestling coincided with a more general rise in popularity of athletics and spectator sports around the world. As playing and watching sports gained wide appeal as leisure pastimes, individual events often attracted divergent audiences, giving rise to overlapping yet distinct sporting cultures. In the United States, for instance, the onlookers who frequented Ivy League football games were not the same crowds that flocked to socialize and gamble at the wrestling and boxing matches that McFadden attended; in these matches "[t]here was a pagan delight in display of muscle, in the strongman stunts, the braggadocio, and even scanty costumes . . . that offended the nice people, those who . . . promoted Victorian team sports in public."[55] Later in life, Macfadden would brag at length about his wrestling accomplishments, but in a way that emphasized the respectability of his athletic pursuits. "It must never be forgotten that the editor and publisher . . . was, for some years, a wrestling champion in the central United States, with all that that implies of rigid training and desperate striving," his authorized biographer would solemnly proclaim.[56] But the reality of wrestling in the late nineteenth century was a more boisterous and colorful one.

The kinds of popular athletic events that Bernard competed in and promoted were nationally and ethnically diverse.[57] Sports reporters from the 1880s and 1890s described a realm of manly spectacle filled with German, Irish, English, Greek, Italian, Japanese, and African American wrestlers practicing an array of wrestling styles from various parts of the globe. Top wrestlers traveled widely, seeking prizes and glory through international competitions and foreign tours. For example, in one of the few defeats to which Macfadden ever admitted, at the age of eighteen, he was thrown by a middle-weight named Matsada Sorakichi, who had come to the United States in 1884, publicly resolving "to vanquish all comers."[58] Bernard's match with a visitor known as the "Cyclone of Japan" indicates the diversity of the working-class sporting culture that educated and sustained him as a young man, as well the ways this arena could serve as a proving ground for its members. For instance, while competing in the United States, Matsada Sorakichi used his skills to fight off a mob of men hurling racist insults at him, leading the *Chicago Tribune* to declare in its report on the incident that "a Japanese will hereafter be highly respected."[59]

The competitive sports that flourished in the American Midwest, aided by increasing attention from news media, provided opportunities for personal and economic mobility through physical prowess and showmanship. For his part, Bernard was quick to translate his wrestling and promotion skills into cash and publicity. After matches, he began giving physical culture lectures and wrestling demonstrations that drew from his reading and training experiences and allowed him to show off his hard-won muscula-ture. Working outside the ring as a fight promoter for wrestling and boxing, he earned hundreds of dollars. From these experiences, he learned important lessons, among them that physical competitions featuring the showy exploits of muscular athletes could be lucrative endeavors. Ulti-mately, through immersing himself in the immigrant milieu of the Mis-souri Gymnasium and the transnational sporting circuits of the American Midwest, Bernard began building not just health and strength but also a livelihood.

In his early twenties, Bernard found himself casting about for a more per-manent career, however. Improving his own body was no longer enough—he wanted to proselytize the wonders of physical culture to wider audiences and make money while doing so. Bernard thus attempted to start his own business. With his savings, he rented an apartment in St. Louis and set up headquarters for a health and fitness training studio. Outside he hung a sign announcing the services of "Bernard McFadden, Kinistherapist." Unfortu-nately, rather than attracting clients, the placard simply baffled passers-by and the business flopped. According to Macfadden's biographer, "[o]f course, no one . . . knew that the third word [on the sign] meant 'healer of disease, by use of movements,'" for Bernard had allegedly coined the term *kinistherapist* by cobbling together Greek root words, plucked from the dic-tionary he carried in his pocket.[60] In this story, repeated in many biogra-phies, Bernard's ideas were so revolutionary that they required their own neologism. A more realistic interpretation is that Bernard borrowed (and perhaps unintentionally misspelled) his title from "Kinesiotherapy," the Swedish system of kinetic healing that had been popular for decades among health reformers in the United States.[61]

Next, Bernard accepted a job as athletic director at a nearby military school. In addition to teaching wrestling and football, he started writing a novel. The result was *The Athlete's Conquest: The Romance of an Athlete*, a work that combined elements from health reform literature, bodybuilding manuals, Victorian romance, and dime novels. The protagonist is "a strong, athletic, well-made fellow" named Harry Moore, who is a "walking ency-clopedia of health laws" with "the courage and strength of a lion." The plot follows Harry's pursuit of a beautiful, athletic woman who has vowed to devote her life to women's health reform. Along the way, he fights off a gang of ruffians, wins a race, throws an arrogant wrestling champion, and convinces a friend to start exercising, before finally winning the hand of his shapely dream woman. Circulation of the self-published first edition of this novel was limited mainly to loyal student athletes at the military school. Yet in its didacticism, melodrama, and overt physical culture themes—a combination reflecting the print media genres Bernard had most enjoyed in his youth—*The Athlete's Conquest* foreshadowed a winning formula to which its author would later return.

The Chicago World's Fair

In 1893, when Bernard was twenty-five, the Midwest was thrown into the international limelight when the World's Columbian Exposition opened in Chicago. Over the nineteenth century, world's fairs had grown increasingly elaborate as vehicles to promote trade, national identity, and cross-cultural exchange, and the Columbian Exposition was the grandest one to date. In addition to marking the quadricentennial of Christopher Columbus's transatlantic journey, it celebrated American modernity, the importance of the Midwest, and the city of Chicago's meteoric rise.[62] With its 600 acres of exhibits and entertainments, the fair was heralded as a not-to-be-missed extravaganza, the event of the century. Full of curiosity and ambition, Bernard headed to the Windy City.

Visitors to the Columbian Exposition felt like they had been transported into a veritable dream world, and Bernard was no exception. Arriving in Chicago, he approached the exposition via boat. The Peristyle, a one-hundred-foot-tall structure adorned with Grecian-style nudes, was the disembarkation point for an ornate plaster city manufactured expressly for the fair. The White City, as it was called, housed official displays from participating countries, states, organizations, and industries. The juxtaposition of its symmetrical neo-Classical architecture, built amid Chicago's ultramodern landscape, was designed to signify the arrival of the United States as a the modern heir to Classical civilization and an up-and-coming world power.[63] Set amid grandiose buildings and misty lagoons, sculpture played an important part in conveying this narrative.[64] Casts of muscular male and female physiques covered the White City, thrilling Bernard and many others with their dazzling whiteness and ideal forms.

Adjacent the main exposition was the Midway Plaisance, a mile-long strip dedicated to amusements, concessions, and quick profit, where human bodies were also on central display. Whereas the White City presented ideal human forms meant to educate and awe, savvy entrepreneurs turned the Midway into a large-scale ethnological amusement park complete with ethnic villages, reconstructions of distant city streets, and zoo-like enclosures of foreign people. Visitors paid individual admission fees to see different human "types" quartered in their simulated "natural" habitats. The Midway's exhibits of cultures labeled foreign, exotic, and primitive had been arranged with the help of anthropologists from the Smithsonian Institution to convey a linear narrative of civilization built upon notions of racial incompatibility and evolutionary hierarchy.[65] The picturesque German Village sat closest to the White City, while the Midway's various African, Pacific Islander, and Indigenous groups were placed at the outermost margins of the fair. Midway promoters accentuated and eroticized physiological differences between fairgoers and those on display, as seen with the navel-bearing "Oriental" dancing girls who made the "Street in Cairo" a smashing success.[66] Predictably, such flesh-baring exhibits enraged moral reformers who thought that the fair should uplift, not titillate. African American leaders, already protesting forms of segregation and exclusion in the White City, criticized the Midway's exploitative portrayals of non-white bodies as well.[67] Nevertheless, amusement-seekers continued to throng the Midway, making it the most popular site at the fair.

The Columbian Exposition and the Midway, sites of transnational encounter in which human bodies often took center stage, contributed to a larger cultural and intellectual milieu in which human physiques were continuously being measured, compared, displayed, interpreted, and mediated in ways that emphasized differences between peoples. As the African Americans who protested the fair understood, such bodily spectacles could help exacerbate and justify social and geopolitical hierarchies, including racism and American exceptionalism. Yet while the Columbian Exposition was designed to depict America as a strong and united nation, and Anglo-Americans as the fittest leaders of modern civilization, this narrative was by no means seamless.[68] Anxieties about the health of the national body politic and its members, characteristic of the decades of fitness, shadowed the event. For instance, when the American Historical Association met in Chicago during the fair, they listened to the historian Frederick Jackson Turner discuss how the supposed closing of the American frontier would affect the US body politic.[69] Other visitors expressed more immediate concerns about what they perceived as Chicago's unhealthy mix of teeming crowns, urban crime, and overstuffed factories, slaughterhouses, and tenements.[70]

Bernard found at the fair fertile ground for promoting physical culture. Through an acquaintance named Alexander Whitely, he secured a job on the Midway demonstrating the Whitely Exerciser, a home exercise device with adjustable settings the whole family could use. With his well-honed musculature and deep knowledge of physical training regimes, Bernard was a natural demonstrator and salesman. Day after day he took up his position in the Whitely booth, flexing, posing, and discussing the transformative power of exercise. Having originally intended to visit Chicago for two weeks, he extended his stay to six months. An international fair where exposed human bodies figured so prominently in the decor and entertainment provided an exceptional opportunity to cash in on the toned physique and accompanying body of knowledge he had built.

Fortuitously, Bernard's stint on the Midway coincided with the Chicago debut of an emerging bodybuilding legend. On August 1, 1893, a young Florenz Ziegfeld Jr., the ambitious son of a noted German American Chicago nightclub owner who had been appointed musical director of the fair, presented his first vaudeville star: the strongman Eugen Sandow. Born in Königsberg in 1867 as Friedrich Wilhelm Müller, Sandow was nearly the same age as Bernard, and though born 4,000 miles apart, they had shared some similar life experiences. Allegedly an underdeveloped child, Sandow discovered physical culture as a youth at his local Turner hall, where he developed remarkable bodybuilding skills. Independent and adventurous, he then became a wrestler and acrobat, joining an East Prussian circus before striking out on his own as a strongman. In Europe, he attracted the attention of a New York talent agent who brought him to New York. Playing a statue-come-to-life in an operetta called *Adonis,* the Prussian strongman was scouted by Ziegfeld, who booked him for Chicago.[71]

Advertised as "The World's Strongest Man" and a "Modern-Day Hercules," Sandow catapulted to stardom during the Columbian Exposition, dazzling audiences with theatrical displays of his superhuman strength, regal bearing, and good looks. During his shows, he struck aesthetically pleasing poses to orchestral accompaniment and lifted heavy weights, including a "human barbell" consisting of two grown men. Accentuated by makeup, mirrors, and strategic lighting, his bulging physique impressed and titillated viewers, reportedly sending overwhelmed socialites into breathless tizzies. During a fair overflowing with art, technology, educational exhibits, and ethnographic attractions, Sandow presented a stripped-down human body, shaped by the global physical culture movement, as perhaps the most marvelous achievement of all.[72]

Whether Bernard McFadden saw the Great Sandow's show at the Trocadero Theater is unknown. But he surely encountered Ziegfeld's publicity campaigns and related media coverage, as well as the popular photographs and "cabinet cards" sold after shows. At a time when "the distinctions between weightlifting, bodybuilding, wrestling, and circus-strongman performances" were still blurry, the Prussian strongman embodied a kind of consummate physical culturalist that Bernard wanted to become, one who wedded transnational health and fitness ideals with an entrepreneurial spirit and flair for showmanship.[73] The statuary and exhibits of the White City were certainly wondrous, yet it was the crowded Midway and nearby commercial attractions, including Sandow, that seem to have left the deepest impressions on Bernard McFadden during his long stay at the Chicago world's fair.

• • •

By the time the Whitely Exerciser booth closed for the season, Bernard had seen and learned much at the fair that would be useful to him going forward. Bodily displays, entertainment, and commerce were intertwining in complex and lucrative ways within mass-mediated popular culture. Representations of the body beautiful (or its antithesis) were provoking widespread fascination as symbols of racial and civilizational identity, while also circulating as spectacular products meant to be consumed and emulated. If Bernard wanted to take his career to the next level, and make a better living from physical culture, he would need to achieve wider exposure.

To this end, back in St. Louis, Bernard sought out a prolific local photographer named Fitz W. Guerin. In 1894, Guerin produced a series of photographs titled "Prof. B. McFadden in Classical Poses." In these images, twenty-five-year-old Bernard explicitly imitates the Great Sandow's own publicity stills, posing nude as Ajax, Atlas, Hercules, and Sampson

Fig. I.I An image from the 1894 series *Prof. B. A. McFadden in Classical Poses*, by the St. Louis photographer Fitz W. Guerin. Prints and Photographs Division, Library of Congress, LC-USZ62-89851

under bright lights against a dark backdrop. Bernard's muscles, honed by years of exercise, sport, and strategic fasting, were smaller than Sandow's, but they boasted remarkable symmetry and definition.

With photographic proof that he had mastered the art of physical culture and a celebrity strongman's techniques of bodily display, Bernard once again felt the familiar tug of restless ambition. The World's Columbian Exposition, it seems, had expanded his horizons beyond the Midwest. Gathering his paltry life savings, he packed his bags, bought a train ticket, and headed east. Originally aiming for Boston, he eventually landed instead in New York City, where, within five years, he would put the images of his physique taken in St. Louis to use illustrating his first magazines.

CHAPTER TWO

The Transatlantic Birth of the Physical Culture Publishing Company

WHEN THE AMBITIOUS BODYBUILDER STILL known as Bernard McFadden arrived in New York in the mid-1890s, the city was undergoing dramatic expansion and transformation. Despite the lingering effects of the Panic of 1893, the worst depression in the nation's history, New York remained a beacon of opportunity on the world stage. Immigrants, mostly Catholics and Jews from eastern and southern Europe, streamed in daily through new processing centers on Ellis Island, beneath the newly erected Statue of Liberty. While some fanned out westward, many settled in New York's enclaves of swelling tenements and boardinghouses. In a busy neighborhood inhabited by native-born Americans, Irish, Germans, Russians, and Poles, Bernard rented two rooms on East Twentieth Street and set up a physical culture studio.[1] To mark the beginning of this new stage in his life, he also changed his name. *Bernarr Macfadden,* as he would thereafter be known, was a more memorable appellation. Rolling off the tongue like a growl, it conveyed strength and distinction, setting him apart from the city's hordes of Irishmen. For good measure, he also bequeathed himself the title of Professor.

Thus remade, Professor Bernarr Macfadden began advertising his services as a personal trainer. In his studio, he taught corpulent businessmen and aspiring actors seeking instruction in weight lifting and calisthenics. He also gave public lectures on healthy eating and strength building, which led him to begin penning articles on these subjects. When his training business slowed in the heat of summer, Macfadden returned to demonstrating the Whitely Exerciser, soon partnering with a local sporting goods business to create the Macfadden Exerciser, an elastic band-and-pulley weight training system that attached to household doors. Drawing on the skills honed back in Chicago, Macfadden hawked his invention up and down the East Coast, using his own body to evidence its promise.

In retrospect, this might be seen as a period of gestation for Macfadden, but its primary yield at the time was frustration. Attendance at the studio waned and the business that manufactured the Macfadden Exerciser failed. Worst of all, no matter how many ungrammatical jeremiads Professor Macfadden wrote about physical culture, no publisher wanted them. Nearing thirty, yet still lacking a stable livelihood, he turned again to his trusty strategy of leaving town and trying to make it somewhere else. Now, however, Macfadden had a shining polestar to guide his travels: Eugen Sandow, the bodybuilder who had captivated audiences during the Columbian Exposition.

Since Chicago, the Great Sandow's career had taken off. Still managed by Florenz Ziegfeld Jr., he followed his run at the 1893 World's Fair with an extended American tour that kicked off in New York at Broadway and 34th Street. While in the city, he posed for Napoleon Sarony, a premier theater photographer whose wildly popular pictures of the strongman helped cement Sandow's reputation as a globally renowned bodybuilder-celebrity. The Great Sandow's physique was also immortalized on celluloid in Thomas Edison's nearby New Jersey studio, where the performer starred in one of the first motion pictures. By the time Macfadden arrived on the East Coast, customers at the city's newfangled kinetoscope viewing parlors could pay to look into a box to see forty seconds of flickering film of the Prussian Adonis flexing his muscles. Those who were impressed by what they saw could purchase *Sandow on Physical Training: A Study in the Perfect Type of Human Form*, a lavishly illustrated, ghostwritten autobiography published there in 1894. Considering his interests, Macfadden was probably an eager consumer of these products. His first Manhattan apartment was near the music hall where Sandow headlined, and in 1896, he, too, posed for Sarony, likely wanting similar portraits of his own.

With his image now in widespread circulation, Sandow embarked on a national tour, hitting music halls across the country and appearing in more moving pictures. Eventually, however, the novelty of his act, as well as his relations with his controlling manager, attenuated. Faced with dwindling audiences and looming exhaustion, Sandow departed America in 1896 to begin a new phase of his career in Great Britain. In 1897, Bernarr Macfadden packed up his exerciser, gathered his unpublished fitness screeds, and booked passage on a Cunard liner bound for Liverpool. Within three years, both men would begin publishing pioneering physical culture magazines.

There is no evidence that Bernarr Macfadden ever met Eugen Sandow. Always keenly attuned to competition, the American even neglected to mention the world's most famous strongman when he wrote his first memoirs in the 1910s. Nevertheless, Sandow undoubtedly exerted a vast and long-lasting influence on Macfadden, with both men's careers becoming temporarily intertwined in the years around the turn of the century, an "age of reform," when various parallel and intersecting improvement impulses sparked widespread interest in physical culture, thereby propelling Sandow's and Macfadden's respective movements into publishing.[2] Tracing points of convergence between their careers illustrates how transnational reform cultures, Atlantic crossings, British colonial and neocolonial networks, and widening spheres of US power in the world shaped the birth and formation of the publishing house that would eventually become the pulp empire Macfadden Publications.

Atlantic Crossings

When Macfadden bought a second-class ticket on a Cunard ocean liner in 1897, he was participating in a transportation revolution that was shrinking space and time. Once costly and burdensome, transoceanic travel was becoming faster and more affordable. Working-class passengers willing to quarter with others in windowless cabins could now reach a new continent in under two weeks.[3] Macfadden might not have appreciated this fact as he vomited relentlessly from New York to Liverpool, but crossing the Atlantic was easier than ever.

By the time the seasick American stumbled onto the foreign shore, Eugen Sandow had already established a new chapter of his career there. Before coming to America, Sandow had worked in Britain, competing against beefy weightlifters with names like Sampson, Goliath, and Cyclops. During his time in the United States, he had also married an Englishwoman with whom he purchased a home in London, much to the disappointment of his many American admirers. As Sandow already knew—and Macfadden would soon discover—Britain offered fertile ground for physical culture enterprises because it had long been a central node in numerous health and fitness reform movements.

Importantly, England was the intellectual birthplace of "muscular Christianity," an ideology that sought to regenerate the church and the nation in tandem by improving the physical and spiritual strength of Anglo men.

Advocating for more robust displays of spirituality and evangelism, proponents of this ideology, such as university professor Reverend Charles Kingsley, advocated for the "divineness of the whole manhood," which could be strengthened by sport, athleticism, and active engagement with the outdoor world. By the end of the nineteenth century, British ideals of virile religiosity had been popularized through print culture and organizations like the Young Men's Christian Association (YMCA), which spread the gospel of physical culture near and far with missionary zeal.[4]

The gendered religious ideal of muscular Christianity developed in tandem with discourses of imperial manhood that linked male physical fitness to empire-building. In Britain's "Imperial Century," the Crown added huge swaths of territory and millions of people to its dominion. In this context, physically strong "soldier heroes of adventure," real and fictional, joined muscular Christians as ideal citizens whose bodily fitness increased national vitality and imperial strength.[5] For instance, when Queen Victoria celebrated her Diamond Jubilee in 1897, the year Macfadden arrived, military regiments from throughout the empire, led by white commanders, paraded the streets, showcasing the empire's power and reach. Such racially demarcated displays were meant to communicate that British imperialism brought health and order to the world.[6]

The influential discourses of muscular Christianity and imperial manhood helped fuel the popularity of sports and athletics. British schools were leaders in emphasizing fitness education and team sports, a phenomenon reflected in Thomas Hughes's *Tom Brown's School Days* and other didactic children's literature about schoolboy athletes popular across the Anglophone World in the second half of the nineteenth century.[7] Among adults, sporting events traditionally associated with the leisure stratum became common pastimes, leading to a sporting mania that transcended class lines. Though some elites fretted about the increased accessibility of sport, others considered athletics to be an excellent means of disciplining the bodies of children, the poor, and imperial subjects.[8] Sport also served the causes of national and United Kingdom unity. When the first modern Olympic Games were held in Greece in 1896, the United Kingdom of Great Britain and Ireland sent ten athletes to compete, and their performances were followed closely back home.[9] And though men and boys held center stage at sporting events, health and educational reforms resulted in increased support for physical activities for girls and women. Pastimes deemed appropriately feminine—such as tennis, badminton, and calisthenics—were more circumscribed than the range of competitive sports popular among men and boys, but by the late nineteenth century, physical culture was considered desirable for both sexes in Britain.[10]

Banking on physical culture's growing appeal as a way of life in addition to entertainment spectacle, when Sandow reestablished himself in London, he did not merely resume his strongman shtick. Instead, he quickly set about organizing a multifaceted health and fitness business. Using the profits generated by his American success, and applying publicity methods learned from Ziegfeld, he established his own Institute for Physical Culture in 1897. Located in Piccadilly, the institute included a state-of-the-art gymnasium and training school supervised by the strongman himself. The fitness classes it offered for both men and women took place in fashionable and comfortable surroundings bedecked with Persian rugs, privacy curtains, and the latest sporting goods equipment. Here, bodybuilding was made respectable and even a bit glamorous.

Keeping himself in the public eye, Sandow also returned to the stage, performing in select theaters and music halls. Now an expert showman, he used his good looks, regal bearing, and penchant for theatricality, including costume changes between tops-and-tails to pink tights and gladiator sandals, to create memorable performances. By January 1897, Sandow was being hailed by the press as "the attraction of the moment." Most musclemen were considered "an offense" to good taste; however, the handsome and talented Sandow proved himself a noteworthy exception. As one reviewer enthused, "London has not seen a more presentable strongman."[11]

In addition to performing and running his institute, Sandow also contributed to a "flurry of physical culture publishing" that blanketed England in the mid-1890s.[12] His second book, *Strength and How to Obtain It* (1897), brought together bodybuilding instructions with biographic anecdotes, anatomical drawings, testimonials from pupils, and attractive photographs of the author. Its printing coincided with other pamphlets, almanacs, and bound tomes that articulated ideas about health reform and the body beautiful.[13] Next, in 1898, Sandow debuted a magazine. Initially christened *Physical Culture,* then renamed *Sandow's Magazine of Physical Culture* in 1899, and finally shortened to *Sandow's Magazine,* the strongman's new periodical marked an important moment in the development of modern health and fitness media and consumer culture. Its pages combined didactic fitness advice with illustrations and photographs of impressively muscular bodies, particularly the strongman's own. Recurring article topics included detailed bodybuilding exercise instructions; health improvement advice; correspondence columns; and ads for bodybuilding courses, health foods, clothing, and exercise apparatuses. Men were the magazine's primary audience, but physical culture for women, children, and even animals was discussed. Sandow authored some of the content himself, while other pieces were commissioned from athletes, entertainers, and writers. Articles like "American v. English Univ. Athletics" and "Hints to Girl Golfers" exemplify the magazine's genteel flavor.

As Sandow's publishing efforts were helping to grow his reputation and business, Macfadden was wandering abroad in the strongman's sizable shadow. Partnering with a local sporting goods company, he toured the British Isles promoting sales of the Macfadden Exerciser. In each town, he stopped to model his body, striking poses against a black cloth backdrop, a tried-and-true strongman technique that produced dramatic visual contrast on the cheap. Lecturing post-performance, he instructed audiences on how to achieve their own muscular results. With typical self-regard, Macfadden saw this tour as a "triumphal march" among appreciative audiences who wanted to hear more about his ideas.[14] And so, Macfadden, too, decided to start his own magazine. According to the story he would later tell, he was distributing a folder containing advertisements for his exerciser and articles he had penned regarding health and fitness—the ones no publisher had wanted—when audiences mistook the materials for a periodical and attempted to subscribe. Inspired by their eagerness, Macfadden looked around for a publishing partner and found Hopton Hadley, a British bicycle entrepreneur. The two men collaborated on a journal originally called either *Macfadden's Magazine* or *Health and Strength*.[15] But quickly thereafter, perhaps in recognition of Sandow's overshadowing popularity in Britain, Macfadden parted ways with Hadley and returned home to pursue a new publishing business.

Once back in New York, Macfadden rented an office near his old neighborhood where he laid the plans for a new magazine titled *Physical Culture*. First printed in March 1899—eight months after Sandow's publication of the same name debuted—the cover of its inaugural issue featured "Professor B. Macfadden in classical poses," an image from the 1893 series of photos in which the obscure St. Louis wrestler and entrepreneur imitated bodybuilding poses more famously struck by the Great Sandow. Inside were articles penned by Macfadden under various pseudonyms on health-related topics. And just like that, an obscure publishing house run on the cheap by a restless bodybuilder and health crank who wrote faster than he could spell was born: the Physical Culture Publishing Company.

Progressing Businesses

Macfadden's and Sandow's movements into publishing took place during an age of reform that would later come to be known as the Progressive Era. Made up of "shifting, ideologically fluid" movements characterized by the impetus to promote positive change, progressivism was a transnational phenomenon.[16] On both sides of the Atlantic, enthusiasm for reform amplified interest in physical culture among many groups at once. Not entirely unrelated, this era also witnessed the growing popularity of periodicals, with a plethora of new publications emerging to deliver regular doses of information and edification to curious readers. At the confluence of these contexts, health and fitness related periodicals began appearing in many countries around the turn of the century. While most were journals put out by organizations dedicated to promoting health reform or sport, commercial markets for physical culture periodicals also emerged.[17]

In their nearly simultaneous creation of publications titled *Physical Culture,* Sandow and Macfadden showed the optimal suitability of the magazine format, which collected articles and features by multiple authors on disparate topics, for mediating physical culture's ideological diversity and multifaceted nature and selling audiences on its benefits. The economics of starting a magazine also made sense. Publishing paper-bound media required a relatively small initial investment, so issues could be sold for five or ten cents (or two pence) apiece, widening the audience of potential customers. More portable than books, yet also less flimsy and time-sensitive than newspapers, magazines could be shipped efficiently and cheaply, especially when they qualified for subsidized mailing rates, as they did with the US Postal Service. Furthermore, by the turn of the century, advances in printing had made it possible to include ample illustrations and photographs in magazines.[18] Such images were an essential draw for bodybuilding enthusiasts, as well as those harboring more libidinal interests in seeing unadorned human forms.[19]

Sandow and Macfadden managed to make their own publications particularly successful, widely read, and influential. Both men were charismatic communicators and gifted entrepreneurs who seamlessly combined didactic health advice with entertainment and commerce. In a single issue of one of their magazines, for instance, it was common for audiences to encounter illustrated exercise guides and anatomical diagrams; portraits of strongmen and other superlatively developed performers; poems and fiction; and articles on sports teams, military training, morality, disease and sanitation, diet regimens, and the mind-body-spirit connection. Reflecting his own broad conceptualization of physical culture, Macfadden cast an especially wide net for subjects and contributors. Under his own name and various pseudonyms, he wrote about bodybuilding, sports, the body's capacity for natural healing, the perils of processed foods, and many other topics. Guest contributors from different walks of life—including generals, socialists, bodybuilders, feminists, professors, actors, healers, politicians, public health advocates, beauty experts, and religious figures—jostled to define, defend, and proselytize their visions for personal and social improvement in *Physical Culture*. While some authors focused on narrow topics, such as the right way to lift barbells or how to consume enough intestinal roughage, others linked physical culture to broader political projects and utopian visions. For his part, Macfadden easily toggled between these scales. By combining nuts-and-bolts instruction with lofty rhetoric that celebrated health, strength, beauty, happiness, progress, and success—things everyone wanted—Macfadden presented physical culture as a general interest topic with wide applicability to audiences interested in enacting progressive personal and social changes of various kinds.

While constantly soliciting contributions, Macfadden left readers very clear about who was in charge by establishing himself as the central editorial and authorial presences in his magazine, as did Sandow. In this respect, both men appear to have taken a page from contemporary newspaper moguls like Joseph Pulitzer and William Randolph Hearst in America and George Newnes and Alfred Harmsworth in England. Throughout their respective magazines, Sandow and Macfadden made liberal use of editorials and other modes of addressing readers to grow their personal celebrity as editors and entrepreneurs. Sandow, who had learned the utility of distinguishing himself from the lowbrow world of musclemen from whence he came, used his magazine to enhance his reputation as the "gentleman strongman." Adopting the staid motto *Mens sana in corpore sano* ("a healthy mind in a healthy body"), he addressed his audience politely, conveying an authoritative yet genial tone as he conversed about physical culture and the ways his readers could achieve stronger and more wholesome selves.[20] Macfadden, in contrast, struck more strident and messianic chords. His "great purpose in life," as he informed readers in his second issue, was "to preach the gospel of health, strength, and the means of acquiring it"; at the same time, "Weakness is a Crime" so "Don't be a Criminal," he barked, coining what would become *Physical Culture*'s first motto.

Of course, these two editors were not just disembodied voices connecting to readers through words. Both Sandow and Macfadden peppered their magazines with photographs of themselves stretching, exercising, posing in costume, and performing feats of strength. Sandow favored formal studio portraits of himself, tending to don Classical costumes in physique photographs and interspersing these flesh-heavy images with staid domestic portraits where he was accompanied by his wife and daughter. Such images communicated his identity as a respectable family man who linked physical culture to bourgeois values. Macfadden, often lacking the traditional accoutrements of manly respectability such as money or a permanent wife in

Fig.2.1 The November 1899 issue of Macfadden's *Physical Culture* magazine, featuring a photograph of the strongman Eugen Sandow on its cover. Terry and Jan Todd Collection/H.J. Lutcher Stark Center for Physical Culture and Sport

these early years, crafted a more stripped-down and intimate aesthetic, offering readers a constant stream of images of his taut, nearly nude body, photographed from every angle. There were some formal business portraits, yet his floppy mop of hair and haphazard grooming lent even these a decidedly candid quality. Both Macfadden and Sandow excelled at selling themselves along with their publications while projecting different demeanors and visual sensibilities.

The sense of connection that Sandow and Macfadden fostered with their readers through direct address and bodily exposure was not a one-way street. In both their magazines, they instituted a distinctive participatory dynamic that would remain a common feature of physical culture media and the defining hallmark of Macfadden's subsequent periodicals. Again building on techniques established in the popular press, both publishers conducted advice columns. Their magazines also devoted considerable space to reprinting letters and photographs submitted by readers, which frequently blurred the line between correspondence and testimonial advertising. "The Editor would like to hear from those who, like himself, have been brought from extreme weakness to health and strength through physical culture," Macfadden wrote. Below this solicitation, an illustrated letter from a man described as "Once an Invalid, Now an Athlete," provided a model testimonial. Perhaps hoping to assuage doubts about the truthfulness of the correspondence he printed, Macfadden encouraged controversy as well. "Criticise, criticise—the more the better," he instructed.[21] Readers complied by debating the editor's advice on diet and fasting and complaining about the number of nude images printed in the magazine (too many for some, not enough for others). Like the seasoned personal trainers that they were, Macfadden and Sandow skillfully orchestrated active participation, leading by example.

For both Sandow and Macfadden, editing and publishing constituted an important part of a larger entrepreneurial vision. Most obviously, owning a magazine helped the publishers sell their other products. *Sandow's Magazine* advertised the strongman's Institute for Physical Culture, his live performances, his photographs and books, and various "appliances" he promised would help readers obtain strength and beauty, such as "Sandow's Patented Spring-grip Dumbbells." From the start, Macfadden's *Physical Culture* promoted the editor's exerciser, lectures, and photograph sets, quickly expanding thereafter to include an ever-growing array of products and business ventures. Before long, there was a high-fiber breakfast cereal, penny restaurants that served affordable vegetarian food, and a health home offering to cure patients of bodily ailments through natural healing methods. Meanwhile, Macfadden continued to create new books and periodicals. Words, when he wrote them himself, were free of charge and seemingly available to him in an infinite (if rather repetitive) supply. Though *Physical Culture* remained the flagship title of his publishing house, Macfadden soon spun the magazine off into other magazines, including the first health and fitness periodical marketed to women, known for most of its run as *Beauty and Health,* and a separate juvenile title called *Physique Culture for Boys and Girls.* For a short time beginning in 1903, the Physical Culture Publishing Company even put out a political weekly called *The Cry for Justice* (soon retitled *Fair Play*), which advocated for economic justice and progressive social and labor reforms until it folded eighteen months later due to Macfadden's lack of devotion to its causes. While the editor's advocacy of health and fitness brought him into association with a wide range of reformers, his main commitments remained promoting physical culture, his company, and himself.

Importantly, Macfadden also printed separate British editions of some of his magazines, making the Physical Culture Publishing Company transnational at its start. Though he chose New York for his headquarters in 1899, he also established an office back in London, where he had first entered the publishing field. This office printed and distributed *Physical Development* (1899), the British edition of *Physical Culture* whose modified title reflected the precedence of Sandow's magazine there. The images and articles in the different versions of Macfadden's magazines were mostly the same, but each contained locally specific editorials, advertisements, and correspondence, features made possible by having the London office. This outpost of the Physical Culture Publishing Company business published local editions of its magazines for women and children, as well as the company's growing collection of books.

Beginning with a bound copy of *The Athlete's Conquest,* a polished version of the fictional melodrama Macfadden had penned years earlier, the Physical Culture Publishing Company churned out books written by its founder at a breathtaking pace. *Hair Culture* (1899), *Physical Training* (1900), *Fasting, Hydropathy, and Exercise* (1900), *Virile Powers of Superb Manhood* (1900), *Power and Beauty of Superb Womanhood* (1901), and *Strength from Eating* (1901) appeared one after another. When this outpouring of prose allegedly rendered the author nearly blind, he set about curing himself through ocular exercises, which were duly described in *Strong Eyes* (1902). Meanwhile, around this time (the details are fuzzy here) Macfadden wedded a fellow exercise machine demonstrator named Tillie, only to have the marriage annulled soon after. Another marriage followed in 1903 to a Canadian nurse named Marguerite, who gave birth to a daughter named Byrne. Within a few years, this coupling also turned sour, and Marguerite returned to Canada with the child. Concurrently, it seems, Macfadden was also carrying on a relationship with his secretary, Susie Wood. During this time, Wood gave birth to a daughter named Helen. Later, Macfadden would erase these two marriages, as well as the nature of his association with Wood, from his public biography; at the time, however, he drew on these romantic experiences to write, sans irony, *Marriage: A Lifelong Honeymoon* (1904). Detecting his public's apparent thirst for information on anything that might be related to sex, Macfadden also published *Building of Vital Power* (1904), *Health, Beauty and Sexuality* (1904), and *A Strenuous Lover* (1904). Sex sold, and it also happened to be good exercise.

The dozen-plus books the publisher wrote during his first decade in publishing culminated in *Macfadden's Encyclopedia of Physical Culture* (1911), a mammoth five-volume reference work coauthored with anti-aging guru Sanford Bennett and various other "specialists in the application of natural methods of healing." This sheer volume of output speaks not only to Macfadden's obsessive productivity but also to the extent of the demand for understandable instruction and advice on health, fitness, and intimate affairs. With all these books and magazines, and with a presence in both New York and London, the Physical Culture Publishing Company rapidly became a leading purveyor of English-language health and fitness media, while its founder became well known in physical culture, bodybuilding, and reform circles.

International Mobility and Imperial Circulation

Perhaps because their own experiences had been so profoundly shaped by foreign influences, travel, and migrations, Sandow and Macfadden looked through and beyond national borders in envisioning the markets they might reach. With the linguistic "medium of English" and the expansive geographies of British and American empire working to their advantage, they targeted increasingly international audiences.[22] Once again, it was Sandow who led the way—but not for long.

Now a publisher and proprietor of a chain of fitness institutes with hundreds of performances under his belt, Sandow resumed international touring with a visit to North America in 1901–1902. Soon after, he announced an Antipodean tour and, with much accompanying fanfare in his magazine, traveled with an expansive troupe of entertainers to the Pacific by way of Italy and the Suez Canal. First arriving in Perth, Sandow performed for enthusiastic crowds in cities and rustic gold-towns across

Australia. Next, this act was repeated throughout New Zealand in what locals dubbed "Sandow Season."[23] Heading westward, back to the United States, he opened Sandow's College of Physical Culture and established an American edition of *Sandow's Magazine* in Boston in 1903. This periodical never gained a firm footing, however, perhaps because Macfadden was busy saturating the market with his own output. It probably did not help that *Sandow's* promoted itself as "the American edition of the beautiful and chaste English publication," a description that likely sounded stuck-up and even boring to consumers conditioned to Macfadden's more libertine tone. In any case, Sandow cut his losses and headed back to Europe in 1904 to prepare for his most extensive world tour of all.

Over the course of the next eighteen months, Sandow made appearances in South Africa, China, Japan, Dutch Java, Burma, and India, meeting loyal readers and inspiring new fans everywhere he went. During the Asian portion of his tour, he enjoyed the greatest success in India. On the subcontinent, he traveled with an enormous tent designed to shelter thousands of spectators that was nevertheless often unable to contain the crowds who turned out to see him. The strongman's fans in India included British colonists, soldiers, and administrators, who recognized the usefulness of physical strength in holding on to their imperial power, as well as locals who possessed their own long-standing physical culture traditions, such as club-swinging, wrestling, and yoga. Thereafter, *Sandow's Magazine* proudly published photos and letters sent to it from South Asian fans. Many Indian bodybuilders who became health and fitness entrepreneurs themselves remembered Sandow's tour as "a defining moment" in the physical culture history of modern India.[24]

Through his world touring, Sandow hitched his business empire to the wider physical geography of the British empire and the settler colonial Anglophone World. Moving his body and publications through his adopted country's imperial and neo-imperial territories, he helped lay the groundwork for the increased globalization of English-language print media focused on health reform, fitness, beauty, and physical culture. In doing so, he forged new audiences, networks, and markets that visibly diversified his English-language physical culture publications. In coming years, these developments would directly benefit Macfadden, helping to widen the reach of his Physical Culture Publishing Company.

As Sandow dazzled global audiences, Macfadden was working on expanding his own fame and growing business. To promote his stable of fitness-related publications, he embarked on lecture tours up and down the East Coast and the Midwest, occasionally crossing into Canada. Performing with a posse of attractive physique models, he impressed audiences with displays of "well rounded muscles," "graceful posing" and "feats of strength," afterward lecturing on health issues in a style "more in the nature of a heart to heart talk, with no attempt at oratory."[25] Soon, he was also offering audiences the opportunity to receive training and diplomas by mail from a new business he called the Physical Culture Institute.

While touring suited his itinerant nature, Macfadden also dreamed of bringing acolytes together in one place, which he envisioned as a communal utopia where health and fitness would be the highest laws of the land. To make this dream a reality, he acquired a "salubrious" 1,900-acre plot of land in the New Jersey pine barrens to create what he called the Physical Culture City, an intentional community dedicated to freedom from "prudishness, corsets, muscular inactivity, gluttony, drugs, alcohol, and tobacco."[26] Built by Macfadden and a group of like-minded fans, which included not only Americans but also members from Canada, Cuba, and South America, it boasted amenities such as an artificial lake, an athletic field, a cafeteria, cabanas for (nude) sunbathing, and a health home for treating patients. There were also hydropowered printing facilities for the Physical Culture Publishing Company. Like most utopias, it was not long before this experiment was beset by problems, however, including voracious mosquitoes, internecine squabbles, prying journalists, indignant neighbors, and financial woes. Within a couple of years, the Physical Culture City was deserted, and the headquarters of the Physical Culture Publishing Company returned to New York.

Throughout all this activity in North America, Macfadden continued to mind the British side of his business. Between 1902 and 1905, the editor claimed a US circulation for *Physical Culture* of 160,000 plus another 70,000 for his London edition, which indicates the transatlantic distribution of his media products.[27] Braving seasickness, Macfadden traveled to England in 1902 and again in 1905 to foster growth there. During these trips, he toured the British Isles again, strategically tapping into and building on preexisting physical culture circuits to gain new readers for his publications. Students at the University of Cambridge for instance, received free copies of *Physical Development*, leading Oxford's campus magazine to poke fun at its rival school's new "MacFaddists."[28] Such investments likely paid off for the publisher by allowing him to attract well-heeled young men who were already interested in sports and athletics (and no doubt, sex) and therefore represented a potentially lucrative future readership.

Paralleling these travels, Macfadden cultivated a transnational network of reform-minded consumers by establishing Physical Culture Societies in Britain, Canada, and the United States. By the midpoint of the first decade of the century, *Physical Development* provided the names and addresses of societies located in nearly twenty cities throughout Great Britain, while *Physical Culture* listed dozens more in North America. These societies organized exercise-related meetups and festivities. For instance, at the First Annual Banquet of the Brooklyn Physical Culture Society, held at the Bedford Mansion and attended by Macfadden himself, members listened to a series of nonalcoholic toasts on topics including "Physical Training, A Science" and "The Joy of Living" before digging into a vegetarian meal followed by music and dancing.[29] Physical Culture Societies also helped members exchange ideas and literature with each other through the mail. Through facilitating such interactions, the Physical Culture Publishing Company helped internationalize physical culture while spreading its products and the Macfadden brand.

Another way Macfadden appealed to a geographically dispersed readership while encouraging the idea of a transnational physical culture community connected through his media was by organizing physical culture competitions. In 1901, Sandow held what many historians consider to be the first major public bodybuilding competition, for men, at London's Royal Albert Hall. Soon after, Macfadden organized his own high-profile event for men *and women.* Advertised heavily in his magazines, the contest offered $1,000 in prizes. To enter, readers, following the instructions in *Physical Culture* or *Physical Development,* sent in photos with their bodily measurements. Selected finalists were then invited to appear in person for the last round of judging in front of a public audience. Though originally planned to take place in London, the big event ended up being held at Madison Square Garden in December 1903, the first competition of its kind in the United States.[30] In its own coverage of this event, the Physical Culture Publishing Company portrayed it as an international competition. Illustrating this point, Macfadden's magazines presented readers with an impressive photographic montage of "England's Representatives in the Madison Square Garden Exhibition" and "Likely Competitors from New Zealand for the $1000 Prize."[31] A second and even more widely publicized competition designed in the same mold two years later drew a similar panoply of contestants and great public interest.

As Macfadden worked to establish his publishing company and to build a personal brand of fitness culture in the United States and Britain, he benefited enormously from Sandow's contemporaneous popularization of physical culture during his world tours. For a while, these tours had proved lucrative for the professional strongman; however, constant travel, along with the march of time, took its toll. When Sandow arrived back in his adopted homeland at the end of his world tour, disembarking to the tune of "See, the Conquering Hero Comes," he put his hectic travel schedule

Fig.2.2 The Physical Culture Publishing Company's early magazines for sale on an urban street corner, c. 1903. Terry and Jan Todd Collection/H.J. Lutcher Stark Center for Physical Culture and Sport

aside for good. Then, in June 1907, *Sandow's Magazine* announced its final issue.[32] After a decade of circulating his own words and body in print, the strongman decided to move on to other activities. Until his death in 1925, the Great Sandow would remain a busy physical culture entrepreneur, but not by publishing magazines.

Macfadden did not mention the closing of *Sandow's Magazine* in 1907 in his own periodicals; yet as a businessman, he probably felt excited at the demise of his main competition. His own transatlantic business connections, combined with the legwork Sandow had performed in building up a globe-spanning audience, left Macfadden ideally positioned to fill the strongman's worn-out gladiator sandals. Going forward, the Physical Culture Publishing Company's media, particularly its British editions, would increasingly travel through the imperial and neocolonial networks on which Sandow had so shrewdly capitalized.

This shift became evident within the pages of Macfadden's magazines. After Sandow's magazine folded, a telling letter from H. R. Hyatt of New Zealand, a former Sandow correspondent, reported that he was "pleased to see the increased circulation of *Physical Culture* in New Zealand," an observation mirrored by another reader from Invercargill who was "aware of a great number of people" in New Zealand now subscribing to *Physical Culture*. A letter from Herbert Barringer, a bodybuilder and physical culture instructor in Adelaide, demonstrates the relationship between Sandow and Macfadden's products in Australia: "Sandow aroused my desire to be strong," Barringer wrote, and seeking out other "prominent physical culturalists both at home and abroad" led him to Macfadden, who perhaps had piqued his curiosity by penning an "open letter" to Sandow that appeared in Barringer's local newspaper in 1902.[33] In this newspaper missive, the "noted American physical culturalist" had remarked, "I yield to no one in my admiration of Mr. Sandow and his system of physical culture for the body, but I don't think he goes far enough."[34] While piggybacking on the strongman's vast audience, Macfadden had been simultaneously crafting an independent identity rooted in a more radically immersive approach to physical culture that sought to overturn many of the Victorian norms that Sandow and his magazine had embraced. Over time, "images of Sandow's body became less common, only to be replaced with photographs of his American equivalent, Bernarr Macfadden."[35]

Further correspondence from the Pacific emphasizes that those who discovered Macfadden's publications in the early years of the twentieth century often helped to spark others' interest in them. A "New Zealand Metaphysician" informed the editor that he "receive[d] both [the] English and American magazines," which he never failed to lend out "to patients and others interested in the cause of health." Writing from Melbourne in 1907, Dr. C. W. Healy, a physical culture lecturer, noted that he "emphasized the value of [Macfadden's] interesting magazine to [his] pupils," while requesting the inclusion of more pictures of Australian athletes in the magazines. Elsa Schmidt, an articulate "physical culture girl" from Victoria, told Macfadden that she had "read several of [his] books, and have lent them and your magazines to my friends," and thus "succeeded in making them interested in physical culture" too. Andrew E. P. Summerbell, from Sydney, even traveled to the United States to study Macfadden's methods, which he may have been teaching to local students when he wrote to the publisher.[36]

While particularly mobile or enthusiastic fans, such as those mentioned above, served as important individual brokers for Macfadden's publications, distribution companies and larger local outlets also played an essential role. Within five years of their founding, Macfadden's *Physical Culture, Physical Development*, and *Women's Physical Development* listed, in addition to American and British headquarters, the names of various official colonial agents, which included companies located in Melbourne, Sydney, Adelaide, Brisbane, and Cape Town. Newspaper ads from New Zealand and Australia from the early years of the century indicate the parts that international booksellers and importers played in creating and satisfying demands for Macfadden-brand products. As early as 1902, a sporting goods dealer in Tasmania invited consumers to "View Our Splendid Show of Macfadden and Sandow Exercisers," as though the display of goods was itself a form of entertainment. To sweeten the deal, the company offered a free home subscription to *Physical Culture* to anyone who purchased an apparatus. Already in 1904, Cole's Book Arcade in Melbourne had eight different books by Bernarr Macfadden in stock. In New Zealand, H. I. Jones and Sons in Wanganui, one of the country's oldest bookshops, took out newspaper ads solely to advertise its collection of works by Macfadden and the availability of subscriptions to both *Physical Culture* and *Physical Development*. Patrons who wished to have their books or magazines mailed to them needed only to enclose an extra shilling for postage.[37] That Macfadden-brand products held appeal not just with bodybuilders but among a larger body-conscious public is suggested by a 1909 ad created by Albert and Sons, of Perth, Australia. In bold letters, the company announced that "FRESH SUPPLIES" had arrived of "Bernarr Macfadden's Latest Books—The BEST BOOKS on HEALTH and SEX ever Written."[38]

Less evidence is available about the Physical Culture Publishing Company's distribution in India and South Africa before the First World War, yet it appears that these other major stops on Sandow's itinerary also created channels for the circulation of Macfadden's media. As early as 1902, the Physical Culture Publishing Company listed a "branch office" (probably a local news seller) in Cape Town. In his memoirs, Macfadden delighted in revealing that an "admirer in South Africa" became so enamored with one of his pseudonymous female personas that the admirer sent "her" an ivory paper knife and framed portrait, requesting a photograph in return.[39] The physical culturalist Stanley Lief, who would later come to work for Macfadden in the 1910s, offers further evidence of the company's reach in this area. Born in Latvia around 1890, Lief suffered a childhood illness that convinced his parents to seek a better climate for their son in South Africa, where he encountered *Physical Culture* in his teens, likely in his father's trading store.[40] The young man was so inspired by Macfadden's publication that he traveled to America to attend Macfadden's training institute, thereafter going on to become a world-renowned pioneer of neuromuscular therapy, cofounder the British College of Naturopathy, and publisher of a monthly magazine called *Health for All*. Another well-known South African who encountered Macfadden's publications in the early twentieth century was the politician and diplomat Tommy Boydell, who became an "Honors Diploma Graduate" by mail of the Macfadden Institute, and later wrote that he had exchanged considerable correspondence with the American publisher while practicing as a health specialist in Cape Town in his early career.[41]

By the end of the first decade of the century, the Physical Culture Publishing Company had acquired an agent in Bombay as well. Historians of physical culture have noted the widespread interest in various physical culture movements in India in the late nineteenth and early twentieth centuries, and studies of Indian clubs, yoga, and vegetarianism have demonstrated that India's entry into the world of physical culture was a two-way phenomenon.[42] At the same time that South Asian physical culture practices gained popularity elsewhere, as evidenced in the Indian club phenomenon, South Asian audiences with available means became avid consumers of Western media on health reform and bodybuilding. As *Physical Culture* was publishing articles like "The Yogis of India" (1903) and "The Strong Men of India" (1908), issues of Macfadden's magazines made their way to the subcontinent. In 1911, a reader from Bombay urged Macfadden to take better advantage of "a good economic opportunity" and send students to lecture or open businesses in cities in India, where his expertise would be recognized and appreciated.[43] Macfadden did not follow through on this advice, but his media continued to attract Indian subscribers, as well as other readers dispersed throughout the geographical spread of Sandow's tours.

Meanwhile, widening spheres of American power, forged by both state and nonstate actors, also helped to shape the reach of Macfadden's mass-market magazines. The founding of the Physical Culture Publishing Company coincided with the growth of overseas US political and military power, as well as the continued expansion of America's moral and market empires. Macfadden's earliest media flowed through these formal and informal channels in ad hoc ways that nevertheless reflected and built upon larger processes of globalization that caused many contemporary commentators to envision an impending "Americanization of the World." The War of 1898; the planning and building of the Panama Canal; an energized American missionary movement; economic and military interventions in the Caribbean, Latin America, and Asia; and the ascendency of American manufacturing and financial corporations provided important contexts for the company's development and growth in these early years. As the correspondence published in its magazines attests, the Physical Culture Publishing Company's media was transported beyond its domestic markets by English-speaking intermediaries such as soldiers, missionaries, teachers, merchants, and laborers, who acted as conduits for the flow of American culture, expertise, and consumer goods abroad.[44]

The same year that Macfadden entered the publishing business, the United States incited the War of 1898. While the first front in Cuba was advertised to the American public as a fight to liberate Cubans from Spanish oppression, Americans quickly opened a second front in the Philippines, while President McKinley annexed the strategically located Hawaiian Islands against opposition from Hawaiian leaders. Within just ten weeks, the "splendid little war" with Spain concluded, but enormous political questions loomed. At the subsequent Treaty of Paris, the United States acquired broad powers over Cuba, acquired the territories of Guam and Puerto Rico, and purchased the Philippine Islands from Spain for $20 million. While Americans hotly debated this overseas imperial turn, and other countries looked on with anxiety, Filipino independence fighters headed by Emilio Aguinaldo struggled to achieve independence. The resulting Philippine-American War, officially fought until 1902 but really lasting much longer, and its colonial aftermaths brought around 125,000 US soldiers as well as bureaucrats, administrators, teachers, and other Americans to the archipelago.[45]

Against this geopolitical backdrop, some of the Physical Culture Publishing Company's earliest correspondence came from the Caribbean and the Pacific where American forces were stationed. In 1905, a US soldier who had been living in the islands for the last six years sent Macfadden a letter about the popularity of physical culture among his fellow soldiers. Another described having been "run down" by his tour in the Philippines and restored to health only after following Macfadden's advice. This reader proclaimed that he bought extra copies of the magazine to share with friends. Similarly, a veteran named R. A. Holman recalled in *Tomorrow* magazine, "[s]o sick and emaciated was I after a long siege of campaigning in the Phillipines [*sic*] . . . that no hopes were entertained of my ever again gaining health." According to Holman, it was the "Editor Patriot" Macfadden whose teachings had restored him to health.[46] To cater to this new imperial market, the Physical Culture Publishing Company established a distributor in Manila for its books and magazines.

In addition to soldiers, American missionaries and health reformers (who were sometimes one and the same), fanned out through the globe in this period. The religious zeal Macfadden directed toward promoting physical culture was characteristic of the evangelical ethos of US progressivism, whose advocates sought to "extend the American moral reach" and "stamp their own imprint" on "the nation's global role" through efforts to reform foreign bodies and souls.[47] Macfadden's media, which was compatible with ideologies of muscular Christianity and programs that aimed to spread the muscular Christian gospel, appealed to Americans associated with missionizing institutions like the YMCA and the Women's Christian Temperance Union.[48] Such groups provided infrastructure for networks of transnational readership, which benefited Macfadden's company and helped to sanction and promote many of the editor's various campaigns. For instance, when his publications were criticized as lewd, Macfadden defended himself by referencing the hundreds of letters of support sent to him by "YMCA secretaries and ministers."[49] The internationalized YMCA, an organization that originated in London but was popularized and expanded by American reformers in the early twentieth century, continued to provide an important channel through which Macfadden's media reached foreign shores.[50]

Macfadden's unceasing ambitions to enlarge his company placed him in stride with traders and businessmen large and small, many of whom aggressively chased new markets that could absorb America's growing flows of consumer products and finance capital. As the publisher worked to build up his company in the United States and Britain, individual merchants and laborers, alongside local print culture importers and distribution agents, propelled the international mobility of his media. William Collins, master of the schooner *Evadne,* wrote Macfadden from the Canary Islands in 1905, "While I hate to part with [my copies of *Physical Culture*], I have given away the entire year of 1905 and find a great number of people becoming interested in the movement for a cleaner and better life." Other traveling merchants and laborers who corresponded with the Physical Culture Publishing Company similarly described passing out back issues on their journeys. Writing in 1910 from the Canal Zone, where the US Isthmian Canal Commission employed tens of thousands of migrant laborers on the engineering marvel of the century, Daniel E. Henriquez wrote that he had been a fan of Macfadden since "long before [he] left his home for the Isthmus of Panama" three years earlier.[51] Perhaps due to acolytes like Henriquez, the Physical Culture Publishing Company acquired a distribution agent around this time in the Canal Zone, the area of Panama that the United States would hold as its territory for decades.

As these letters to Macfadden sent from readers outside America and Britain attest, many of the company's first international circulations were ad hoc, informal, and transitory, made manifest in the historical record only by the regularity with which far-flung audiences recorded their experiences or had their correspondence published. But this does not mean that they were random or inconsequential. America's interconnected military, moral, and market empires provided, along with British colonial and neocolonial channels, important paths of media globalization in the early twentieth century. These paths would become more regularly and densely trafficked by Macfadden's media and other forms of American mass culture in the years to come.

• • •

Through frequent travel, and occasional trips abroad, Macfadden was successful in growing his company on both sides of the Atlantic from his home base in New York. However, with its increasing circulations and high-profile physique contests, the Physical Culture Publishing Company and its founder predictably entered the crosshairs of American censors. In particular, they attracted the sustained attention of the US postal inspector Anthony Comstock, who was also head of the New York Society for the Suppression of Vice.

Wielding enormous authority to police the boundaries of public culture and communications in New York, and thereby the nation, Comstock and his zealous associates monitored newsstands, booksellers, and the mail, looking for works that violated the 1873 Act for the "Suppression of Trade in, and Circulation of, Obscene Literature and Articles of Immoral Use," more commonly known after its author as the Comstock Act.[52] Of particular concern was pornography—or really, anything potentially erotic—as well as materials communicating information about sex or birth control. When publicity for the second Madison Square Garden Competition featuring images of scantily clad women appeared in 1905, Comstock raided the Physical Culture Publishing Company's offices and arrested Macfadden. The editor posted bail, and the show went on, with crowds swelling to over 20,000 people, thanks, no doubt, to the publicity generated by its organizer's arrest. This further propelled Comstock on a mission to take down the upstart publisher.

In 1907, Macfadden was arrested again for violating the Comstock Act. His crime this time was the distribution of "Growing to Manhood in a Civilized(?) Society," a didactic *Physical Culture* serial about the dangers of venereal disease that blamed American prudery for the ignorance that led to the spread of sexually transmitted infections. Macfadden immediately took to his soapbox to express outrage and indignation at Comstock, who he called the "King of Prudes." But despite his protestations, and an impassioned letter-writing campaign to the White House organized among his fans, he was fined $2,000 and sentenced to twenty-four months of hard labor.[53]

The editor appealed the court's decision, but as the legal process crept forward, he decided it might be best to skip town. This time, he headed west. Turning his attention to the health home business, he leased a sanatorium in Battle Creek, Michigan, right near John Harvey Kellogg's more prestigious facility. The most famous patient at the Macfadden Sanatorium here was Upton Sinclair, the socialist muckraker and author of *The Jungle,* who paid for his treatments by writing articles for *Physical Culture.*[54] Next, the publisher relocated to Chicago, where he opened the Bernarr Macfadden Healthatorium and Physical Culture Training School, a grand five-story building featuring modern amenities like a sixty-foot swimming pool. Students and patients alike practiced drugless healing, experimented with vegetarian diets and fasting, and turned out on Tuesday nights to hear Macfadden lecture. Those who could not make it in person could keep up by reading his magazine editorials on topics like "White Bread Starvation Food" and "The Vaccination Scourge."

The AMA, headquartered in Chicago, was horrified to find Macfadden's Healthatorium in its own backyard. Launching a campaign against "quackery," the society warned the public against the editor's unscientific opposition to pharmaceuticals, vaccinations, and doctor-assisted childbirth, opinions all expressed in his writings.[55] Macfadden gleefully converted these attacks into further promotional fodder for his own natural health campaigns, but the AMA's effort to undermine his credibility were exhausting. Yet another stressor emerged when his now-estranged second wife (the Canadian nurse) filed for divorce. These legal, financial, and personal troubles were only partially alleviated when William Howard Taft, the famously large US president, announced that he had decided to commute the prison sentence of America's most famous physical culturalist.

Macfadden was no longer facing time in jail, yet the stress, financial penalties, and legal fees—along with the AMA's campaign and the divorce—had taken their toll. Moreover, Comstock was not yet finished with the Physical Culture Publishing Company, whose publications continued to defy elements of the Comstock Act. In 1912, Macfadden was taken briefly into custody once more, and his books were banned from the mail. Recognizing the signs of impending disaster, the publisher quietly transferred his assets to a few loyal associates, including his friend Charles H. Desgray, and announced to American readers that he would be taking a hiatus from the publishing business to attend to other physical culture affairs. Then, in late 1912, he inconspicuously crossed the northern US border into Canada and boarded a ship bound for England. Crossing the Atlantic yet again, Macfadden was brimming with plans waiting to be put into action as soon as he set foot on the familiar foreign shore.

CHAPTER THREE

Circulating Physiques in an Age of Imperialism and Migration

Upon arriving in England in late 1912, Macfadden announced a new physical fitness competition. This time, he was looking for Great Britain's Perfect Woman. Ladies from throughout the British Isles were invited to apply by sending in their physical measurements and photographs of themselves stripped down to exercise tights. Hundreds of *Physical Development* and *Beauty and Health* readers responded, mailing their materials to the editor's office, hoping to win the £100 prize and whatever fame went along with the cash. After reviewing the applications, Macfadden brought twenty-five finalists to London for inspection by himself and a panel of colleagues. Finally, a winner was selected: nineteen-year-old Mary Williamson of Halifax, West Yorkshire was Great Britain's Perfect Woman. An accomplished swimmer, the buxom Williamson won over the judges with her 38-25-39" figure, showed off to perfection in a brief, bare-legged swimsuit.

Williamson's life changed overnight. Leaving behind her Baptist family and job at a carpet mill, she joined Macfadden and a chaperone for a four-month-long publicity tour through the British Isles. Appearing on stage as "The World's Most Perfectly Developed Man and Woman," the duo posed as Grecian statues and performed vigorous exercise routines together. After each show, Macfadden would lecture on health and peddle books, magazines, and postcards. Local newspapers delighted in printing Williamson's story and photo, as she "had become a sort of Cinderella legend of human interest."[1] Her postcards sold briskly and fan mail from both sides of the Atlantic stacked up, including a marriage proposal on official stationery from a bachelor US congressman. Noting the ingenue's growing popularity, Macfadden cut to the chase. Within a few weeks of the start of the tour, Mary Williamson had become Mrs. Bernarr Macfadden.

The Perfect Couple's nuptials, followed in less than a year by the birth of a daughter named Byrnece, symbolized the consummation of an intimate Anglo-American alliance that was a central theme in Macfadden's publications and would shape the future growth of his business. Since its inception, the Physical Culture Publishing Company had primarily hailed an "imagined community" of geographically dispersed readers presumed to share an Anglo-Saxon heritage and identity.[2] In publications, this community was conceptualized in racial terms as inherently superior to other peoples, yet also under threat by forces of demographic flux, emerging geopolitical rivalries, anticolonial movements, and the supposed fatigue of living on the cutting edge of modernity. Declaring with pride in *Physical Development* in 1913 that "[m]y life has been devoted to building-up the English-speaking race," Macfadden underscored the linkages between his business and this powerful racial formation, which would be further reinforced through his coupling with Mary.[3]

As Macfadden's own words and actions reveal, his publishing empire channeled ascendant discourses of Anglo-Saxon supremacy and imperilment rooted in gendered and racialized constructions of bodily difference, furthering their development while simultaneously benefiting from the transnational purchase they found. Via textual and visual formulas, the Physical Culture Publishing Company linked outward bodily appearance, physical health and ability, and inner racial value in ways that idealized heterosexual white bodies from the Anglophone World. Its media brokered representations of vitalized Anglo-Saxonhood that framed muscular, light-skinned physiques—particularly those in procreative heterosexual unions—as the apotheosis of civilizational advancement and suitability for power. Indeed, correspondence to Macfadden and his magazines provides insight into how readers wedded not only the physical culture movement but also specific media from the Physical Culture Publishing Company to white supremacist, imperialist, and eugenic ideologies and projects, which in turn helped propel the publishing house's growth.

In reaching out to and connecting consumers across spaces of British and US empires however, the Physical Culture Publishing Company would also make visible points of difference, debate, and resistance to dominant norms and narratives that existed within—and were sometimes mobilized by—its transnational media and the forces of globalization that expanded its reach. Closely reading the assemblages of content that came together in Macfadden's physical culture publications, which might be described as "transnational participatory pastiche," provides a rare window onto wider formations of embodied subjectivity formed in dialog with this media during an era of imperialism and migration. Though founded on the principle of revitalizing whiteness, Macfadden's publishing empire would in practice produce a proliferation of imagined communities, some of which would use physical culture and its associated media to destabilize racialized notions of fitness and refashion the mass-mediated iconography and geographies of health, ability, beauty, and modernity.

Physical Culture and the Global Color Line

At the turn of the century, the African American intellectual W. E. B. Du Bois famously opined that "the problem of the Twentieth Century" would be "the problem of the color-line."[4] Born the same year as Macfadden, Du Bois had witnessed the intensification of segregation within the United States and beyond. Throughout the world, taxonomies of human difference constructed by elites, which were often transmitted by and reinforced through media circulations, structured landscapes of gross inequality that oppressed people of color. As Du Bois also observed, the problem of the color line went hand in hand with the institutionalization of a "new religion of whiteness."[5] This emergent racial formation, as he saw it, reflected shared geographic origins and culture, yet it also represented global elites' defensive longings for greater power in response to competing demands for equality levied by restless underclasses of color.

The global color line and the religion of whiteness that sustained it were shaped and maintained in dialog with the physical culture movement and its globalizing media.[6] W. E. B. Du Bois understood this when, traveling to France for the 1900 Paris Exposition, he brought along photographs of African American athletes and exercisers to put on display for the world to see.[7] He also understood this as editor of *The Crisis*, the official organ of the National Association for the Advancement of Colored People, where he regularly spotlighted Black physical culturalists.[8] In contrast, Macfadden's books and magazines, like other forms of popular culture originating in the United States, participated in examining, analyzing, and displaying (or not displaying) human bodies in ways that shored up ideologies of racial difference and hierarchical taxonomies of the world's people. In particular, his company's periodicals circulated textual and visual content that promoted evolutionary theories, millenarian rhetoric, and gender discourses that supported the construct of the color line and bolstered transnational formations of white supremacy that strengthened patriarchal systems of racism and empire.

While the topics it covered were varied in scope, much of the Physical Culture Publishing Company's media hailed readers by speaking to gendered concerns about, and utopian hopes for, the white body and white bodies politic—what the scholars Marilyn Lake and Henry Reynolds refer to as self-styled "white men's countries."[9] When Macfadden first branched out into publishing, the target market for his ideas and products was middle-class men in the United States and Great Britain, who possessed disposable income and had already exhibited an enthusiasm for physical culture and periodical reading in general.[10] His publications skillfully fanned anxieties about modern manhood while framing his own products as the key to regaining and expanding manly power. For instance, *The Virile Powers of Superb Manhood: How Developed, How Lost, How Regained* (1900), one of his first books, focused on curing neurasthenia, a disease that supposedly afflicted middle-class men with "lack of nerve force" and even impotence, allegedly evidenced in the middle class's declining birth rate. Arguing that "the great importance of strong sexual powers cannot be too strongly emphasized," *Virile Powers* offered readers a system of exercises, habits, and behaviors that would produce lifelong potency in and out of the bedroom.[11] Natural foods, circulation-boosting calisthenics, the avoidance of masturbation and prostitutes, and frequent sexual intercourse within marriage were its prescriptions. This discussion was echoed in the author's magazine column "My Confidential Letters to Men" and other works.

In promoting his physical culture media through promises of rejuvenated white masculinity, Macfadden seamed together male power and racial dominance, engaging what the scholar Gail Bederman has called the "discourse of civilization."[12] As *Virile Powers* told readers, "You cannot build a house without a foundation to rest upon, and virile manhood is the foundation upon which must rest all the results that accrue from . . . civilized life."[13] At the turn of the century, the concept of civilization was often used as shorthand to signify the highest stage of evolutionary progress, which Macfadden and many of his contemporaries assumed should be led by white men and particularly Anglo-Saxons. Macfadden's print media reflected and helped shape this gendered discourse of civilization by presenting the upward evolution of the race—and thus civilization itself—as dependent on radical improvements to the health and fitness of its men.[14] Conveniently, this rhetorical commitment to advancing civilization provided a veneer of respectability to the company's hastily produced, cheaply bound publications full of near-nude figures, which moralists accused of catering to society's "baser" elements. It also provided a useful form of transnational address, for, at a time when many magazines directed themselves to a national readership, Macfadden's frequent appeals to civilization allowed him to hail a more geographically dispersed audience. Those who saw themselves as representing advanced civilization, especially white men who imagined that human progress was closely yoked to their own achievements, were encouraged to see themselves as part of a physical culture fraternity connected by the publishing company and the imperial and settler colonial networks that propelled its circulations.

Linking physical culture to a racial and gendered ethos of progress, *Virile Powers* foreshadowed what would become an enduring theme of Macfadden's fitness publications—the idea that fitness for power was an ongoing competition between peoples whose bodies—including their abilities to reproduce as well as fight—would determine their failure or success. Macfadden's print media amplified the twinned narratives of masculine and civilizational decline by stoking fears of international and interracial rivalries and framing them as physical culture concerns. For example, the toll exacted on Anglo-Saxon soldiers in the Philippine-American War and in the South African Boer War was discussed with alarm in *Physical Culture* and *Physical Development*. As the article "The Strong Men of the Transvaal" told readers, each Boer "has the strength of two men reared under conditions that prevail in our civilization." Similarly, in the wake of the Russo-Japanese War, numerous articles referenced Japan's threat to white power in the Pacific. When discussions of a possible US-Japanese war filled the newspapers in Great Britain during his 1907 tour, Macfadden warned, "The Japanese Will Whip Us" because of their better physical culture preparation.[15]

Threats to white manhood and thus civilization were also presented as lurking closer to home. In his early years as editor, Macfadden participated in a nativist discourse, pronounced in the United States and British Commonwealth nations, that framed both domestic racial minorities and "new immigrants" as inferior.[16] In 1907, as migration to the United States reached new heights, Macfadden lamented that "the human material that we have had to absorb from the various foreign nations for the last generation, has often been of a low order."[17] African Americans—particularly those seen as transgressing or challenging the color line—also came under scrutiny, as the 1905 series "Penalty of Marriage Between Caucasian and Negro" attests through its anxious portrayal of mixed-race children. Such content made explicit the racial politics of sentiments like "Physical Culture Our Only Hope for Regeneration," a cry whose "our" assumed and encoded whiteness.[18]

To counter challenges posed by overcivilization, geopolitics, and population mixing, Macfadden joined other reformers seeking to reconnect modern Anglo-Saxon men with their past, when members of the race had supposedly possessed a degree of physical strength and endurance that had since been lost or abandoned along the path to advanced civilization. US president Theodore Roosevelt, who appeared on the covers of *Physical Culture* and *Physical Development* in 1904, referred to these qualities as "barbarian virtues," reflecting Darwinian theories that assigned certain non-white populations to an evolutionary if not chronological past tense. "Unless we keep the barbarian virtues, gaining the civilized ones will be of little avail," he once wrote, advocating for the "strenuous life" at home as well as a muscular foreign policy abroad.[19] Macfadden could not have agreed more with the Hero of San Juan Hill. Denouncing the "monstrous evil" of luxury and excess that had "made man himself . . . his own worst enemy," he presented his media as a cure for the virility-sapping forces of overcivilization that worried men like Roosevelt.[20]

At a time when displays of exotic, foreign, and supposedly premodern people were common elements of mainstream print and entertainment culture, Macfadden's magazines constantly spotlighted bodies from foreign cultures, which were depicted as possessing the "barbarian virtues" white men needed to acquire through contact and conquest. The alleged "Remarkable Powers of Endurance of Primitive People," as one article put it, were discussed in issue after issue.[21] Following examples set by *National Geographic* and other publications, *Physical Culture* printed a host of "armchair traveler" articles depicting foreign peoples and ways of life.[22] This popular genre, suffused with the language of ethnography and physical anthropology, meshed easily with the discourse of civilization that permeated Macfadden's media, and amplified it. Conveniently, these travelogue-type essays were cheap to acquire and easily tweaked to promote physical culture themes. *Physical Culture* features including "Our Indians in the West," "The Aborigines of Australia," "Samoa, the Isles of Eternal Summer," "Hawaiians of Yesterday and Today," and "Nudity and Morality Among East African Tribes," all describe societies whose members possessed the premodern virtues of strength, virility, and closeness to nature that Macfadden admired and advised his readers to obtain.

And speaking of possession, it was no coincidence that many of the travelogue-style physical culture articles that filled Macfadden's magazines featured foreign peoples and places that had encountered US and British colonial ventures or been incorporated into their continental and overseas empires. The turn-of-the-century boom in ethnography, travel writing, and other documentary styles was spurred by impulses to introduce and analyze people entangled, often through acts of resistance, in imperial projects.[23] Such writings (and accompanying images) tended to imply that some foreign societies lacked the racial capacity for modern sovereignty, especially nationhood, with the genres of travel writing and ethnography feeding "directly back into the loop of political discussions whose highest stakes included the formation of state policies for managing foreign peoples and populations."[24] The Physical Culture Publishing Company's ethnographic articles soothingly portrayed the appropriation of foreign and non-white physical culture habits and ideas, and the expropriation of related resources, as compatible with the racialized discourse of civilization that undergirded imperialism, settler colonialism, and conquests of foreign peoples and markets.

"The Igorrotes, a Hardy, Vigorous People" provides an apt example. In this 1910 feature, *Physical Culture* spotlighted the physical qualities of an Indigenous Filipino "tribe" that had been maligned in US media during the Philippine-American War as primitive, savage, and ugly.[25] Here, as Macfadden puts it in the article's preface, "There are not a few races of half-savage people that have habits and characteristics that should be of interest to all who are striving for physical excellence." The Igorrotes [sic] are lauded as the "most splendid specimens of physical development" on the islands because, as the author explains, their crude understanding of agriculture forces them to perform constant physical labor in order to survive. The Indigenous peoples of America's hard-won Pacific empire were helping to model barbarian virtues; simultaneously, US tutelage was providing them the opportunity to "some day become a peaceful, industrious, progressive, useful people."[26]

Contributions submitted to Macfadden's magazines from writers and correspondents demonstrate that individual readers wedded the Physical Culture Publishing Company's media to exclusionary transnational racial imaginaries organized around embodied ideals of revitalized white manhood, which then helped attract more readers to its magazines. During the Philippine-American and Boer Wars, American and British Commonwealth soldiers stationed abroad described how Macfadden's publications had contributed to their missions of conquest. Alfred W. Milor, writing in 1902, bragged that thanks to the "hard training" outlined by Macfadden, he had gone from being "all run down" to becoming the champion weightlifter of the First Battalion of the Fourteenth Infantry.[27] Macfadden's brand of physical culture, according to such letters, not only followed but actually enabled the expansion of America's overseas empire by swelling the muscles and the race pride of soldiers. British Commonwealth readers voiced similar stories during the Anglo-Boer War, an imperial conflict often interpreted at the time as a test of Anglo-Saxon vigor. For example, one correspondent from Liverpool described how his brother, initially rejected as unfit for military service, added over an inch of muscle thanks to Macfadden's magazines, making both brothers fit to fight together in South Africa alongside fellow "sons of empire."[28] A brutal testimony on this theme came from the Australian R. Clifford, who told the editor, "I have been a reader of your paper for some time and have gained much useful information from it. I carry it with me on the track in our skirmishes and battles with the native blacks."[29] Clifford's letter explicitly placed Macfadden's publication at the scene of a campaign of domination and attempted extermination of Indigenous peoples that was essential to the production of White Australia.[30] The participatory format of Macfadden's magazines encouraged and disseminated representations of a global Anglo-Saxon brotherhood united by both the modern, mass-mediated physical culture movement, which provided resources for military exploits into foreign lands, and militarized violence against non-Anglo-Saxon bodies and nations.

While many of his contemporaries remained fixated on regenerating white masculinity, Macfadden quickly emerged as a pioneering "reformer of feminine form" dedicated to improving white womanhood as well.[31] The founding of the Physical Culture Publishing Company corresponded with the rise of the New Woman, a transnational figure who claimed greater personal, economic, and political autonomy for some members of her sex.[32] From day one, Macfadden worked hard to cultivate a female readership, recognizing the New Woman's formidable purchasing power and growing interest in health culture and social reform. In addition to inaugurating American and British editions of the magazine *Health and Beauty* and writing books such as *Power and Beauty of Superb Womanhood* (1901); *Health, Beauty, and Sexuality* (1904); and *A Perfect Beauty* (1904), he peppered *Physical Culture* and *Physical Development* with features by and for women health enthusiasts.

Influenced by the writings of nineteenth-century domestic reformers like Catherine Beecher as well as some contemporary feminist thinkers, Macfadden presented himself and his publishing house as radical advocates for the advancement of white women's rights.[33] One of the editor's earliest causes, for example, was dress reform, a movement that had been kicking around for decades in reform circles. The Physical Culture Publishing Company's media in its early years advocated loose Grecian-style gowns, sensible sportswear, and a greater tolerance for bare limbs. Indeed, along with refined flour, vaccines, censors, and the AMA, the corset was one of Macfadden's greatest enemies. In addition to publishing pamphlets such as *The Corset Curse: Enslaves Women, Destroys Sex, Crushes Soul, Deforms*

Body (1904), the Physical Culture Publishing Company made it a point to print pictures of women with natural waists and refused to accept corset advertising, even though it would have brought in much-needed capital. Cosmetics, high-heeled shoes, too-long skirts, and other circulation-restricting apparel were similarly scorned, as they too represented a "Menace to the Future of the Race."[34] Once appropriately attired (or unattired, as was often the case), girls and women could, Macfadden's media argued, excel in sports and commit to serious exercise and weight-training regimes. The muscular yet unmistakably feminine forms of *Health and Beauty*'s cover models, which included well-known theater stars and sportswomen, showed that physical culture enhanced rather than degraded white womanly charms.[35]

Just as women played central roles in the projects of imperialism and racial conquest that spurred interest in physical culture, they were portrayed in Macfadden's media as partners in "building-up the English-speaking race."[36] Regenerating white civilization, Macfadden contended, required superb womanhood, but white women had strayed even farther than men had from the physical culture path. "There is not a society woman but would give a thousand dollars to be able to walk across a ball-room floor with the willowy ease" of a Native American, one article proclaimed.[37] Another lamented that "when stripped of her furbelows and fancy frills," the "average woman of today has nothing to boast of."[38] According to Macfadden, the "Unshapely Anglo-Saxon Leg" gave modern ladies little to stand on in international and cross-racial comparisons; however, the Physical Culture Publishing Company promised immanent reformation, coaching women on how to repair their overcivilized bodies by selectively appropriating and adopting the behaviors and customs of preindustrial peoples, past and present, in order to become fitter mates and better "race mothers."[39]

In light of the ignorance and misinformation that prevailed about women's bodies, Macfadden also maintained that female readers needed better information about the facts of life, especially regarding sexuality, mate selection, pregnancy, and child-rearing. The Physical Culture Publishing Company used a lot of ink discussing what constituted healthy heterosexual desires and couplings, as Macfadden believed removing taboos around the subjects of intimacy and reproduction was essential to avoiding the perils of divorce, infant mortality, and weak offspring who were unequipped to assume their rightful places at the head of civilization. Macfadden framed virile manhood and superb womanhood as complementary ideals that would achieve their greatest expression in physical culture marriages that channeled mutual sexual attraction into the production of expansive physical culture families. And here, he intended to lead by example with Mary, whom he had married with the intention of producing the world's most perfect physical culture family.

Racial Fitness and Eugenic Aesthetics

Macfadden's familial turn, as well as the enormous amount of attention paid to the subjects of marriage and reproduction in the Physical Culture Publishing Company's media, reflected engagement with a coalescing transnational eugenics movement that sought to apply new understandings of genetics to engineer more superior human populations. Eugenics helped to catalyze the growth of physical culture media and its wide circulations, while physical culture media helped influence the popularization of eugenics.

International in scope, networks of eugenicists were seeking to understand the relationship between biology and identity and to put the knowledge they acquired about evolution and heredity to use. The push for more scientific breeding gave rise to contentious scientific, ethical, and political debates, which not surprisingly filtered into popular discourse. Drawing on anthropology and anthropometry, as well as agriculture and animal husbandry, the eugenicists who dominated the Anglo-American branch of the movement argued that Anglo-Saxon blood or "germ plasm" produced superior people and societies. Since inferior human "stock" was seen at an immutable cellular level, and thus could only taint the race and drag down civilization, they argued that it was imperative to figure out whose bodies were eugenically fit and which biological traits threatened the integrity of the race.[40] The concept of "racial fitness" provided a natural rhetorical bridge between eugenics and physical culture, shaping the discursive terrain in which physical culture media was produced and received.[41] In turn, Macfadden's publications eagerly adopted and disseminated some of the scientific language and programmatic concerns of the eugenics movement.

The Physical Culture Publishing Company devoted considerable space to discussions of what constituted the eugenic body and how a eugenic society might be achieved through physical culture and its media. This was, in some respects, a tricky business, as theories of strict biological determinism that were prominent in the Anglo-American movement could directly undermine the messages of bodily improvement and transformation that were at the heart of the Physical Culture Publishing Company's products. Rather than simply accepting or rejecting eugenics, Macfadden's periodicals came to play an important role in shaping a nascent realm of "popular eugenics," as they provided a mass-market outlet where prominent thinkers discussed eugenic ideologies and policies in terms meant to engage lay readers.[42] Generally, the company's publications advocated that racially fit individuals should be encouraged to reproduce while "the unfit" should be discouraged from propagating. Macfadden asserted, "The whole previous life of the individual is or should be more or less preparation for parenthood"; but he also agreed with many of his peers that parenthood should be pursued only by the physically and mentally qualified, reflecting a larger concern with the potential taint of disability.[43] Eugenics and the racialized discourse of civilization often meshed easily within the physical culture genre's portrayals of desirable procreators. For example, articles such as "Women Athletes as Saviors of the Race" and "Can We Breed Better Men?" promoted a pronatalist strain of white supremacy.

At the same time, Macfadden's publications provided a platform for the birth control pioneer Margaret Sanger, who worked hard not only to empower women but also to stem the birthrate among the urban poor and developing nations.[44] Macfadden admired and supported Sanger, who advertised her own publications in his media and contributed feature articles to *Physical Culture*. Sanger's friend, the renowned British sexologist Havelock Ellis, vice president of the Eugenics Education Society, chimed in with similar thoughts on birth control and sexual health. The author Charlotte Perkins Gilman also used *Physical Culture* to espouse ideals of "eugenic feminism." In her *Physical Culture* series on male-female relations, including "What May We Expect of Eugenics?", Gilman argued that an expanded intellectual and economic place for women in the public sphere, and better attention to mate selection, were essential to the advancement of the (white) race.[45] Carl Easton Williams, who served as interim editor for *Physical Culture* when Macfadden was living in England, kept debates over eugenic policies in the spotlight with his own frequent articles on the subject. Those who wrote about eugenics for the company possessed varying political agendas and visions, yet they tended to share an ideological commitment to white supremacy, racial progress, and the important role that able-bodied women could play in attaining these ideals. Eugenics, they argued, provided a modern solution to the looming specter of racial decay that threatened the advancement of the Anglophone World. While enthusiastic procreating among healthy Anglo-Saxons and birth control for others would ideally be voluntary, a certain amount of coercion was presented as appropriate to achieve these goals. For example, Williams's 1913 article "What Shall We Do with the Unfit?" presented the case for compulsory sterilization programs, which had recently been legalized in the United States.[46]

Correspondingly, Macfadden centered eugenic physical culture ideals in his personal life with Mary. At the outset of their marriage, he had his young bride sign a written contract declaring her eagerness for maternity and promising to shun medical and pharmaceutical interventions in childbirth that he deemed to violate physical culture principles. Initially, Mary was excited at the prospect of incubating the world's first 100 percent physical culture babies. After Byrnece was born, a cheery publicity photo was distributed through her husband's magazines introducing readers to the new Anglo-American Macfadden family. To supplement the photo montages of white physical culture mothers and babies that continuously appeared in his magazines, Macfadden now had his own exemplary wife and daughter to display.

In addition to providing a platform through which some of the era's most prominent eugenicists could address a transnational audience, the Physical Culture Publishing Company played an important role in brokering a eugenic aesthetic that emphasized how the body's outer appearance might evidence inner essence. Racial fitness, as portrayed by the company's media, was a quality that expressed itself on bodily surfaces, which constituted, according to its logic, the most reliable index of superior health and wellness. Thus, it is significant that in advocating virile manhood and superb womanhood, Macfadden's periodicals developed and circulated racially differentiated representational formulas that visualized modern fitness as the domain of white-appearing bodies. The photographs and illustrations of strong bodies that filled these magazines exhibited marked contrasts in dress, style, and mise-en-scène, with certain visual elements tending to correspond with the geographic origin or racial appearance of subjects being pictured. Through juxtaposing different visual styles and tropes of representation, Macfadden's media encouraged readers to note the distinction between bodies and *physiques*; unlike bodies, which everyone had, physiques were shaped in conversation with modern eugenic principles and physical culture media. In this way, the Physical Culture Publishing Company's image-laden periodicals circulated a visual vocabulary that supported scientific and ideological constructions of racial difference and hierarchies of ability that powered imperial iconographies and structures, including the eugenics movement.[47]

As Macfadden's media extolled barbarian virtues, it recapitulated established anthropological tropes in depicting non-white people, often picturing their bodies as vestiges of the preindustrial past. The ubiquitous travelogues characterized foreign figures and societies as suspended in a state of evolutionary stasis, with retarded intellectual development and deficient political and social institutions. The stock photographs accompanying these articles

were usually static mid-shots. They presented their subjects in "natural" surroundings, unaware of the camera, or at least appearing ignorant about how
to engage with it to produce a confident self-image. For example, the afore-
mentioned "The Igorrotes, a Hardy, Vigorous People" was accompanied by
images captured at the 1904 St. Louis Fair's forty-seven acre "Philippine Reservation."[48] In the opening photograph, several so-called "warriors" cluster
around a fire; an uncovered buttock, rather than a face, points toward the
camera. Behind them, fair attendees stare over a fence at the overexposed
bodies of America's colonial wards. In this image, taken at an imperial exhibit designed to represent Filipino peoples as simultaneously primitive, con-
quered, and tractable, the color line separating white and non-white is
strikingly obvious. In *Physical Culture*'s articles, as in other realms of popular culture, non-white bodies appear to have little control over their own
image; instead, they are represented from the perspective of the white gaze as
relics from the past, useful for illustration, but not to be understood as sovereign inhabitants of a parallel and interconnected modernity.

The Physical Culture Publishing Company's depictions of white physiques, in contrast, underscored the alleged evolutionary distance between
primitive bodies and modern physiques. While Macfadden singled out
some poorly developed figures as evidence of racial degeneration, his magazines simultaneously provided a forum through which ideals of Anglo-
Saxon physical supremacy were being fashioned and circulated. In its
periodicals, the Physical Culture Publishing Company helped codify an
influential aesthetic that might best be described as spectacularly visible
cosmopolitan primitivism.[49] Light-skinned figures embodied this style by
combining strategically appropriated barbarian virtues with skilled
presentations of themselves mastering modern techniques of bodily self-
fashioning and appearing. In the early years of the century, the participants
in Macfadden's physique contests illustrated this style with their simple
costumes, bare limbs, and use of props like gladiator sandals, buckskin,
and animal pelts. By the early 1910s, this aesthetic tended to juxtapose ar-
tifacts associated with premodernity with exuberant poses that referenced
the aesthetic conventions of modern dance; films; advertisements; and, of
course, fitness media itself. This included gazing confidently and knowingly at the viewer and exhibiting the body and face in a way that showed
off to maximum advantage the qualities Macfadden associated with virile
manhood, superb womanhood, and eugenic fitness. While other peoples
were forced by racial limitations to live in a state close to nature, and thus
developed muscles and endurance through necessity, the white figures
that adorned *Physical Culture* were presented as masterful practitioners
of modern bodybuilding and self-fashioning who knowingly maximized

their bodily potential through appropriation, expropriation, and mass mediation.

The association between the modern cosmopolitan primitive ideal and white racial identity was reinforced by the participatory dynamic that Macfadden's media cultivated, as well as through less visible editorial policies that determined whose participation in the modern, mass-mediated world of physical culture could be made visibly apparent. For example, although Macfadden declared his health and fitness contests open to subscribers worldwide, the photo collages he published of posing and flexing contenders from throughout the Anglophone World featured almost no recognizably dark-skinned readers during the first two decades of the century. As the bodies of white contenders of various national backgrounds were displayed prominently, others were excluded from such visualizations of superior fitness. Because Macfadden's publishing company left behind no official archive, it is impossible to ascertain whether specific editorial policies, a lack of non-white applicants, or a combination of both these factors determined the composition of its contest collages. Yet the almost total invisibility of African American bodies in *Physical Culture* at a time when Black Americans represented some of the world's most accomplished athletes indicates that the company enacted implicit or explicit editorial policies enforcing the exclusion of certain bodies from its main content.

Rare discussions of African American physical culturalists, who as both people of color and accomplished US citizens had the potential to confound the racialized discourse of civilization promoted in Macfadden's early media, were exceptions that proved the rule. In 1910, for instance, *Physical Culture* included two articles that examined African American bodies. In "Keeping Tuskegee Students in Physical Repair," Booker T. Washington, the well-known African American educator and political leader, lauds the athletic programs at his Tuskegee Normal and Industrial Institute in Alabama. Washington's focus on vocational education and his strategic accommodation of Jim Crow segregation had, by this point, attracted considerable criticism from many progressive Black intellectuals, most notably Du Bois. While his article presents portraits of several strong, attractive, and talented Black athletes to *Physical Culture* readers, it also stresses that these Tuskegee students participated in "many kinds of harmless sports and exercise," while the more vigorous men's outdoor sports were organized under the direction of the YMCA.[50] The circumscribed portrayal of Tuskegee athletes as "harmless" and tractable must be understood not only in the context of Washington's political and educational philosophy but also in light of the attention Black male athletes were garnering at this time.

Four months after Washington's article appeared, *Physical Culture* covered the upcoming prizefight between the African American world heavyweight champion Jack Johnson and Jim "The Great White Hope" Jeffries, an event that transfixed physical culturalists. In "A Great Battle and Its Lessons," the magazine participated, along with many other media outlets throughout the world, in framing the Johnson-Jeffries fight "as a contest to see which race had produced the most powerful, virile man."[51] According to this article, Johnson, though "really a wonderful boxer," is "hot-headed," less disciplined, and more unevenly developed than his white opponent, an argument that tapped into racist tropes of African American lack of control, hypersexuality, and evolutionary inferiority.[52] This article also took specific aim at the confident and modern public persona Johnson famously projected. While Jeffries's method of getting back into shape on a farm is celebrated as a savvy return to nature, Johnson is criticized for his enjoyment of urban living, stimulating cafés, and reckless motoring in an expensive automobile. The article suggests that while Jeffries combined the vitality of barbarian virtues with the great intelligence and "stability of character" inherent in the white race, Johnson possessed the outer accoutrements of modern physical culture but not the advanced inner development of his opponent. Black bodies, though feted in supposedly "primitive" forms, were rendered incompatible with modern fitness as it was described and aestheticized in Macfadden's magazines. When Johnson easily bested Jeffries a few weeks later, the prizefighter's win was greeted by mob violence, while angry voices proclaimed the match a wake-up call to white men everywhere.[53] This reaction resonated with the messages Macfadden had circulated for over a decade, and would continue to circulate, regarding the precarious state of white power and physical culture's capacity to strengthen its hold within and across national borders.

Transnational Participatory Pastiche

In cultivating a transnational readership organized around ideals and aesthetics of revitalized whiteness, the Physical Culture Publishing Company's media reflected and reinforced hierarchies constructed by settler colonialism, imperialism, the Anglo-American eugenics movement, and formations of anti-Blackness and segregation. Yet even as certain bodies were erased or relegated to the margins of the world mapped in *Physical Culture,* the participatory nature of Macfadden's media and its enmeshments in transnational networks simultaneously resulted in a complex text. Its pages opened avenues of interpretation and expression through which the connections between civilization, race, and fitness could be challenged, disaggregated, and reconfigured.

As we have seen, the Physical Culture Publishing Company championed making passive habits active ones, and this extended to the types of reading practices it encouraged. Inviting its audiences not only to read its texts but also to replicate exercises and diets, read and write correspondence, enter contests, submit articles and photos, and respond to its advertisements, the company's publications promoted a form of active engagement that shaped the contents of its media and its possible meanings. *Physical Culture*'s reliance on multiple authors and consumer-generated textual and visual content produced crowded, dynamic collages of words and images—an aesthetic of assemblage, juxtaposition, and contrast that might be termed *participatory pastiche*.[54] As theorists of modern media have argued, audiences make sense out of disjunctive cultural texts by endowing "disruptive sequence[s] . . . with synthetic meaning" in ways that reflect their own experiences, desires, and sensibilities.[55] The Physical Culture Publishing Company magazines' aesthetic of participatory pastiche, combined with their transnational content and circulations, were qualities that could amplify one another. As their circulations widened and new contributors, correspondents, and promoters joined the fray, these magazines became increasingly multivocal. Thus, even while Macfadden professed his commitment to revitalizing the "English-speaking race," his media provided a stage for other messages to cohere and circulate, including those that unmoored this shorthand for Anglo-Saxon identity from its original racial and ethnic referents and retooled it for different purposes.

The dynamics of participatory pastiche created opportunities for producing oppositional self-representations, subversive readings, and radical claims to inclusion. While the company's fitness publications granted foreign and non-white bodies heightened visibility in ways that served to support racialized evolutionary frameworks, subjects nevertheless called attention to their own parallel or linked modernity within even such circumscribed representational spaces.[56] The frontispiece of the September 1907 issue of *Physical Culture*, "A Group of Splendidly Developed Natives of the Fiji Islands," provides one useful illustration of how the explicitly transnational participatory pastiche of Macfadden's publications, combined with the wide circulations achieved by physical culture media, encouraged such patterns from early on in the company's history.

The photograph, which readers saw as soon as they opened the issue, shows fifteen muscular men from Fiji, stripped to the waist. At the center of the group sits a light-skinned man wearing a suit and eyeglasses (or "eye crutches," as Macfadden disdainfully called them). He is flanked by two similarly complexioned, shirtless companions. The formally attired man is the correspondent from New Zealand, F. A. Hornibrook, provider of this photograph and a corresponding article, "The Fijians and Physical Culture," which appeared later in the issue. Hornibrook's piece, in which a Euro-Australian authority examines culturally foreign bodies on display, typifies ethnographic features *Physical Culture* printed in its contrasting of "modern" versus "native" civilizations and its framing of strong, indigenous bodies as "natural" manifestations of primitive culture. Furthermore, the author asserts that when these men from Fiji had attended the recent New Zealand International Exhibition (as part of an exhibit), they were awed by "white physical culturalists" like himself, "particularly their exercising equipment."[57] Viewers of "Splendidly Developed Natives" might have taken away a message that undermined rather than supported Hornibrook's text, however. The Fiji Islanders, standing with flexed biceps, sitting with crossed arms, and turned in profile to highlight their chest expansion, are clearly and effectively working to show off their bulging muscles to best advantage. Theirs are not bodies honed by a "natural" lifestyle; instead, they are clearly sculpted *physiques* being self-consciously displayed for the camera in keeping with bodybuilding photography's best practices. This message was absorbed even by *Physical Culture*'s own caption writer (likely Macfadden himself), who, despite Hornibrook's identity as a leading white fitness authority, instructed readers to "Note the Contrast with White Men in Center of Photo."

Features intended by their authors to advance narratives of Anglo-Saxons' superior expertise about the world of human bodies, could, inadvertently, circulate evidence of their supposedly primitive subjects' knowledge about—and superlative embodiment of—modern fitness. Even within a media terrain defined by enormous differentials in power and access to self-representation, without saying a word, photographed subjects could portray themselves as active and sovereign participants in modern forms of self-fashioning mediated by transnational print and entertainment cultures through dress, comportment, expression, and musculature. In addition to being seen in features like "Splendidly Developed Natives," this also characterized the ways non-white athletes such as Jack Johnson and the Native American Jim Thorpe (Sac and Fox) posed for cameras and otherwise engaged mass media that steadfastly refused to include proportionate representations of strong Black or Indigenous bodies. No matter what the Physical Culture Publishing Company's articles *said* about racial fitness or eugenic worth, collections of images communicated their own messages within a medium that became increasingly visual and more widely dispersed with every passing year.

Fig.3.1 "A Group of Splendidly Developed Natives of the Fiji Islands," the featured photograph in the September 1907 issue of *Physical Culture*. Terry and Jan Todd Collection/H.J. Lutcher Stark Center for Physical Culture and Sport

Indeed, Macfadden's magazines fueled this process by circulating illustrated instructional guides that helped readers learn to "work" the camera with the skill of a physique model. Amateur portrait seekers were given specific and simple advice in articles like "Hints on Posing the Physique Beautiful," which explains, "Outdoors is the best place to photograph a muscular pose . . . Try to *look* the pose, submerge self and every distracting thought," and "It is always best to pose on a pedestal . . . this lends a statuesque appearance, unobtainable by other means. A pedestal can be improvised at little or no expense."[58] Readers from many backgrounds avidly followed such approachable advice, increasing the possibility that the limited spaces of representation afforded by Macfadden's media to foreign and non-white or otherwise marginalized bodies could be used to visually disrupt associations between whiteness and fitness and foster alternative identifications. This becomes especially apparent in the correspondence sections of *Physical Culture,* which attracted and more frequently printed letters and photographs from non-white readers. Employing the magazine's own advice about displaying their bodies to maximum advantage, non-white colonial subjects and foreign readers from occupied territories regularly demanded attention and admiration within this space, as did visibly "ethnic" immigrant ones.

Macfadden witnessed firsthand the enormous magnitude of immigration to the United States in the decades surrounding the turn of the century, which was highly visible in the Midwest and in New York City. Perhaps resulting from his awareness of this potential audience, his publications spoke to immigrant audiences in a way that middlebrow journals and advice literature did not. Like dime novels, the urban penny press, and early motion pictures, Macfadden's magazines were inexpensive and democratic in tone. Chockablock with pictures and articles composed within the limits of their publisher's own highly circumscribed vocabulary, they were accessible to readers possessing limited English. Furthermore, because the physical culture movement that drove Macfadden's publishing company had deep roots in Europe, as we saw in Chapter 1, aspects of the company's media would have been immediately familiar to many of the new immigrants who perused American newsstands around the turn of the century. *Physical Culture* articles like "The Wonderful Vitality of the Jewish Race" (1903), "The German American Turner Movement" (1906), "Greek Ideals and Physical Culture" (1907), "Athletics Among the Latin Races" (1910), and "The Balkan Soldier's Physique" (1913) featured images of people and places directly linked to major immigrant diasporas with long-standing physical culture traditions of their own. While Macfadden complained about the "quality" of America's "new immigrants," his publishing company increasingly came to rely on their patronage and projected different messages about immigrant and diasporic bodies in its periodicals. Pushed out of their homelands by economic necessity, political instability, and religious persecution—and pulled to countries like the United States (and Australia, New Zealand, and Canada) by industrial and agricultural labor opportunities—workers and families from Europe (and to a lesser extent from other parts of the Western hemisphere) provided a growing audience for American mass-market print media and other forms of entertainment culture.

Letters sent from one Hungarian family to *Physical Culture* illustrate how European fitness trends shaped the market for US physical culture media within the larger context of migration streams that often flowed in multiple directions. In 1910, a young man named Aurel Erdos, who was currently living in Monson, Hungary, wrote Macfadden to inquire about a physical culture colony that some readers were planning to start in the territory of New Mexico. As Aurel explained, he and his sister considered themselves indebted to Macfadden's diet advice, which offered a "tremendous advantage" to those in "difficult physical or financial circumstances."[59] This letter painted a picture of a young man, perhaps in difficult financial circumstances himself, looking to improve his prospects by possibly relocating to the healthful American West he saw promoted in *Physical Culture* and presumably other media. How this Hungarian had gotten his hands on Macfadden's magazine in the first place was illuminated the following year by Corrine Erdos, Aurel's younger sister and herself a fitness enthusiast, who wrote: "I was twelve years old when we learned in school about 'mens sana in corpore sano,' and this was the first powerful incentive that led me to resolve that I wanted to live in the most healthful way possible ... [Then] two years ago, my brother, Aurel, came back from the United States of America. He brought several copies of your magazine along." As a result, Corrine's "interest in physical culture teachings grew so high that [she] resolved to study English," which allowed her to pursue Macfadden's recommendations about vegetarianism, fasting, and raw foods.[60] A full-figure photograph of Corrine in an abbreviated bathing costume and a snapshot of Aurel flexing his arm muscles showed off the results they had achieved.

This published correspondence from the Erdos siblings suggests how immigrants from central Europe, such as the 2.1 million people who moved to the United States from Austria and Hungary between 1901 and 1910, may have constituted a ready audience for Macfadden's media because they arrived on US shores already familiar with physical culture themes and programs. Furthermore, such letters provide insight into how Macfadden's company, almost from its inception, reached international readers in many places around the world. It seems that Aurel, like at least a quarter of Hungarian immigrants who arrived in the United States during this decade, sojourned only temporarily.[61] Historians have estimated that as many as one-third or more of the "second wave" of American immigrants actually returned to their homelands, a trend that was particularly pronounced for non-Jewish male laborers.[62] While scholars have only begun to analyze the importance of these two-way migrations to the dispersion of US-produced mass culture, it is essential to note that Aurel was not alone in his personal exportation of Macfadden's magazines. Other correspondents who wrote to Macfadden around the same time, including the swimmer Guy de Villepion (a Frenchman living in Guatemala) and Dr. Theodor Gatti (an Italian), also noted that they first came across *Physical Culture* in the United States in the early years of the century through travel or temporary migration. A letter by the Swedish immigrant Hjalmar Hammersen reminds us that for many people seeking a better life during this era, migrations, and thus personal exportations of Macfadden's media, could be multiple. Hammersen, who likely would have already been familiar with Swedish forms of physical culture, came across Macfadden's publications when he moved to the United States in 1910, but by the time he wrote to *Physical Culture,* he had relocated to Santiago, Chile, having packed his favorite reading material for the journey.

Correspondence from a twenty-year-old Mexican man named J. V. Prada further elucidates the centrality of transnational networks of encounter, consumption, and engagement to the production of the Physical Culture Publishing Company's participatory pastiche and its multivocality. Writing in 1911 from Celaya, a town one hundred miles north of Mexico City, Prada expressed his "sincerest gratitude" for the editor's bodybuilding advice as well as his "high moral principles," which Prada had "accepted as [his] own standard." Though merely "one hundred and twenty pounds stripped," Prada had come to possess the proportions and abilities of a much larger bodybuilder, a claim supported by an impressive photograph showing off his well-developed torso and arm muscles.[63] When Physical Culture published this photo, it is possible some readers recognized its subject, as Prada had written before. Back in 1908, the teenager had introduced himself as a fan and described a transformative encounter with Macfadden's media while attending school in Indiana.[64] A corroborative historical record sheds more light on how this Mexican youth became a participant in Macfadden's growing media empire. The son of the mayor of Celaya, Prada attended high school at Notre Dame, an institution known for its physical education program.[65] Prada's journey from central Mexico to Indiana speaks to the efforts that Notre Dame made, as part of a larger missionizing platform, to attract foreign Catholic students to its primary and secondary education programs. Taking a cue from the circus, the university's vice president, Father Zahm, personally chartered a Pullman railcar and traveled around Mexico promoting the benefits of Notre Dame and distributing colorful Spanish-language maps and pamphlets.[66] His was the first international special to travel to Mexico City over the newly completed Central Railway of Mexico, and he returned "bearing a colony of young Mexicans who were coming to matriculate."[67] Ten years old in 1901, Prada was among several students from well-off families who made this trip. When he graduated with a commercial diploma from Notre Dame's high school in 1907, Prada had attained a remarkable body, purportedly with the help of Macfadden Publications (but also presumably through the gymnastics course that school records show he took in school). He then joined up with the gymnast Ottley Coulter (who would later become a historian of bodybuilding) to form a touring circus act called "Marvelous Strength Feats"—the photograph that Prada submitted to *Physical Culture* in 1911 was the publicity photograph that he used to advertise his show. As Prada toured, he carried Macfadden's publications with him on his travels. Upon returning to Mexico, he set up a small gymnasium and translated a few of what he judged to be Macfadden's most important articles into Spanish for his acquaintances: "Oh! would that we had a magazine like PHYSICAL CULTURE in our own language," Prada professed, "It would be a boon to this nation."[68]

As the examples of Prada, the Erdos siblings, and other correspondents makes clear, the massive, multidirectional migrations to and from the United States (and America's empire) that characterized early twentieth-century globalization played an important role in propelling the popularity and mobility of Macfadden's early books and magazines among diverse readers living within and beyond the borders of the United States. The correspondence these readers contributed illustrates how they used the participatory dynamic of Macfadden's media to articulate definitions of modern fitness that could undermine the racial politics of the aesthetic of vitalized Anglo-Saxonhood that dominated early twentieth-century health and fitness print culture. Laying claim to advanced health knowledge and superlative bodies in their letters and photographs, they positioned themselves as assets to any modern eugenic nation, helping to structure imagined communities around shared physical culture sensibilities that cut across racial and ethnic as well as geographic and geopolitical lines.

Physical Culture's correspondence forums also provided a way for foreign readers to assert more nationalist and sometimes even explicitly anti-colonial forms of belonging in the world of physical culture that Macfadden's company mediated. American, British, and British Commonwealth consumers, particularly those involved in economic, political, and cultural empire-building projects, brought Macfadden's media abroad, but publications that started out in their hands did not remain there. By the 1910s, locals in India, Japan, the Philippines, and the Caribbean who knew English inserted themselves into the transnational participatory pastiche of Macfadden's periodicals through their correspondence columns. Sometimes this took the form of advice letters, such as the one in which a Jamaican reader described a natural remedy for seasickness, the malady that afflicted Macfadden so badly on his transatlantic journeys. Significantly, this writer drew attention to his or her status as a savvy non-white physical culturalist through signing off as "A COLORED READER."[69] Meanwhile, foreign readers with access to cameras submitted abundant images of themselves, often showing off and explaining their own exercise routines or athletic feats. A Japanese entrepreneur named Masanobu Sugimoto, for instance, wrote in to demonstrate the merits of a machine he had invented for strengthening the abdomen, and the photos he provided of himself using the machine gave credence to these claims when they were printed around his letter. Other Japanese correspondents demonstrated martial arts techniques, contributing to the growing international popularity of jujitsu in particular.[70] While an Orientalist "yellow peril" discourse was proliferating through the Anglophone World, these East Asian correspondents portrayed themselves as fellow participants, with much to share, in a modern fitness culture devoted to honing the human body through both technology and technique. A similar tone characterized letters from Latin America, with one correspondent sending a picture of Guatemalan president Manuel Estrada Cabrera's new physical culture institute, couching it as evidence of an evolving "pan-American fraternity" facilitated by shared health and fitness values.

As *Physical Culture* gave visibility to long-standing indigenous traditions of body cultivation in South Asia, local readers emphasized their claims to them. This was particularly true in the case of correspondents from India, whose own physical culture traditions—including vegetarianism—had had a demonstrable impact on Macfadden and his publications. For example, in 1914, Jamshedji Kanga, the eighteen-year-old captain of the Navsari Walking Club, sent Macfadden a bodybuilding self-portrait "showing the results [he] gained through physical culture" as well as a group portrait of his club. Eager to correspond with foreign readers, Kanga was soon able to "very thankfully acknowledg[e]" fellow readers in the United States and Canada who had heeded his call.[71] Through his access to international mail, Kanga emphasized his knowledge about Western physical culture, which he hoped would soon be practiced "on a much larger scale than at present" in India and the Far East, while also foregrounding the efficacy of his own local traditions. Another Indian correspondent, G. Y. Manikrao, was quick to stress, "We have our Indian system of exercise, but it is not incompatible with Western scientific notions of that art. We much appreciate the work your PHYSICAL CULTURE is doing in America and other directions in which it is circulated."[72] Emphasizing the rigor of Indian physical culture as well as the artistry of local bodybuilders (including himself), and painting America, too, as missionary field that needed to be converted to health, Manikrao subverted the language of uplift and East-West incompatibility so often used to justify cultural and political hegemony in this era.

In participatory forums, correspondents could undercut the logics of racism and colonialism by demonstrating not just physical culture comradeship but also superlative discipline, development, and self-mastery. These were politicized qualities when read alongside justifications of conquest and oppression—common enough in Macfadden's own magazines—that characterized non-white men as effeminate, undeveloped, dysgenic, and disabled. Consumer-generated representations of masculine power that highlighted local knowledge and indigenous physiques gave textual visibility to foreign bodybuilding and sporting subcultures that developed within and against colonial structures. In places such as India, these subcultures could be linked not only to international community but also to specific formations of "muscular nationalism" tied to oppositional political movements.[73] Physical culture media became part of the "transnational grid" unto which nationalist subjectivities, including explicitly anticolonial ones, were built and expressed in the twentieth century.[74] And Macfadden's magazines constituted an important part of this transnational grid, as they not only disseminated fitness knowledge but also provided a stage on which subversive embodied identities and political imaginaries achieved visibility and circulation within globalizing popular print culture.

• • •

While the Physical Culture Publishing Company's media products—and many readers—were achieving widening circulations, Macfadden was plotting about how to make a bigger name for himself in Europe. To this end, after completing the Scottish leg of their British Isles tour, The World's Most Perfectly Developed Man and Woman established a health home in the seaside resort of Brighton. The enterprise took off quickly. Over fifty patients came seeking variety of "nature cures" for their ailments, including the vegetarian playwright George Bernard Shaw and frequent *Physical Culture* contributor Upton Sinclair, who paid for room and board with his pen.[75] Macfadden dispensed health advice and began dictating a memoir about his physical culture awakening and subsequent triumphs. In addition to taking care of their new baby, Mary helped run the home. Soon, an American girl named Helen came to live with them as well. Introduced as an orphan whom Macfadden had benevolently promised to raise, the quiet redhead was really (as Mary must have suspected immediately) his biological daughter from an earlier affair with his secretary Susie Wood.

On clear days, visitors to the Brighton health home could look across the water and make out the French coastline. But the view was marred for Macfadden by France's preponderance of "wine-drinking eccentrics hellbent on race suicide"—a white citizenry that remained as unrepentantly ignorant of his teachings as he was of France's own physical culture trends.[76] Mary was thus understandably surprised when her husband announced in early 1914 that their family would be decamping to Paris. The City of Lights, though packed with "unrestrained gluttons who started the day with a bottle of champagne for breakfast," was to be their headquarters while he attempted to win over the Gallic masses.[77] Quickly thereafter,

the Macfaddens moved into a rented apartment in Paris and began planning a tour of the country.

As it turned out, the Parisians were pretty blasé about "Bernarr Le
Grand, Le Napoleon de la Force Humaine," who spoke almost no French,
railed against wine and spirits, and espoused what likely seemed to them
to be completely insane ideas about what constituted good food. Furthermore, the whole strongman act might have felt too reminiscent of German
military culture at a time when tensions were rising between the nations.
The publisher had made little headway with his act when Archduke Ferdi-
nand and his wife were assassinated in Sarajevo. As war clouds gathered
over the Continent, the Physical Culture Family hightailed it back across
the channel. The most sensible thing to do, Macfadden then decided, was
to return to the United States. After transferring his health home into the
hands of Stanley Lief, the promising naturopath from South Africa who
had come to work with him, he booked passage for four to New York.

In October 1914, the Macfaddens boarded the *Lusitania*. What was a
tense, nerve-racking journey for all passengers was an especially night-
marish one for Mary. Pregnant again and constantly sick, Great Britain's
Most Perfectly Developed Woman was confined by her husband to their
cabin, where she ruminated anxiously on submarines, icebergs, and war.
Her fears were not misplaced. Only two years had passed since the *Titanic*
disaster, and the *Lusitania* would be torpedoed the following spring,
causing the deaths of nearly 1,200 passengers and crew. Macfadden responded to his wife's distress by ordering her on a transatlantic fast.
Fasting, he believed, cured most ailments—plus, he saw an opportunity to
test a theory he had heard about calorie restriction in pregnant women
being correlated with male offspring. Unfortunately for Mary, the crossing
would take several days longer than usual due to U-boat aversion maneu-
vers. During this time, she began learning, from experience, how the lib-
eration from ill-health and sexual ignorance her husband and his media
promised women could go hand in hand with patriarchal control and co-
ercive forms of maternity.

While Mary was languishing ill and hungry in their cabin, and fellow
passengers were conversing in hushed tones about submarines and the de-
terioration of international order, Macfadden got to work penning a grandiose homecoming announcement for himself. "The return of Bernarr
Macfadden to America signalizes the extraordinary progress of the world
physical culture movement since he has been abroad. We are living in a
truly remarkable age. Things are happening! This is indicated not only by
the gigantic struggle seen in the European war, but in many phases of
human endeavor. Revolution is in the air!" he wrote. Covering five pages

when it was subsequently printed in his flagship magazine, this missive outlined the publisher's optimistic aspirations for growth. From the United States, Macfadden would, he predicted, lead the impending and inevitable global physical culture revolution. With a supportive, fertile young wife by his side, he had no intention of letting the war and the hasty relocation it necessitated get in the way of his dreams of expansion. His publications and business ventures were mobile and transplantable, for, as he assured his readers, "The value of strength . . . represents a capital that is stable and fundamental." In sum, Macfadden's "faith in physical culture as a world movement" was "greater than ever!"[78]

With its revolutionary rhetoric and claims to global renown, Macfadden's bombastic homecoming announcement was over-the-top and perhaps even delusional. But it did capture an essential truth: notwithstanding "Bernarr Le Grand's" recent flop, physical culture truly had become a world movement, due in large part to the influence of print media like Macfadden's books and magazines. As one of the world's first popular fitness periodicals and the most prominent and successful English-language publication of its kind, *Physical Culture* played a central role in shaping the trajectory of modern physical culture as a transnational cultural form with global reach. Over the previous decade and a half, it had assembled and circulated among and between different communities of reformers, acolytes, and consumers, a set of healthy living ideals and practices, including representational formulas and conventions regarding the judgment and display of human physiques. But while the value of strength—and the appearance of strength—had indeed proven fundamental to modern understandings of health, beauty, and progress on a global scale, neither physical culture nor Macfadden's media was reducible to any stable or universal meaning.

Designed to appeal to middle-class audiences and spread through various local, imperial, and neo-imperial circuits, Macfadden's books and magazines helped enmesh physical culture in efforts to define, strengthen, and protect Anglo-Saxon civilization and attendant notions of settler-colonialism, imperial rule, and white supremacy. They did this by promoting evolutionary theories, millenarian rhetoric, and gendered and racialized aesthetics that bolstered transnational formations of white supremacy. They also fostered linkages between physical culture and other Progressive Era movements, such as eugenics, that aimed to limn racialized hierarchies rooted in physical and cultural differences and conquer, rule over, and erase non-white bodies. World progress, as Macfadden and many of his writers contended, was embodied in the spectacularly visible physiques of white cosmopolitan primitives, whose strength, beauty, and inherited evolutionary superiority mandated that they reproduce themselves and their civilization across the globe. Barnstorming lecture tours and the spread of proscriptive print culture was one way in which this could be accomplished, but other more violent and destructive systems were in place as well. *Physical Culture* and Macfadden's other publications did not only circulate through imperialism and whiteness—they also served the causes of empire and white supremacy.

Yet while Macfadden worked toward "building up the white race," his media and the reforms, practices, and modes of engagement that it championed simultaneously fostered alternative and oppositional imaginaries. *Physical Culture* in particular encouraged modes of active readership and provided avenues through which individuals could accrue and publicly perform fitness in ways that challenged racist representational tropes and underlying narratives about civilization, modernity, and progress. The magazine's reliance on reader contributions resulted in assemblages of words, images, and ideas that were not only transnational but also multivocal. Now, however, the Physical Culture Publishing Company's formulas would need to be updated to respond to a period of unleashed nationalisms and world war.

CHAPTER FOUR

Building Up the Nation during the First World War

THE *LUSITANIA* CARRIED THE PHYSICAL Culture Family safely across the Atlantic, reaching New York on the last day of October 1914. Pregnant and starving from an imposed fast, Mary admired how well-fed Lady Liberty looked as the statue welcomed them ashore. At Ellis Island, steerage-level passengers faced rounds of scrutiny by border agents, but the World's Most Perfectly Developed Couple and the two children disembarked and clear customs without hassle. The family piled into a taxi, and they were off. Speeding and swerving through New York traffic, Mary felt overwhelmed by the fast-paced "whirlpool of humanity" that thronged the city's busy streets, sensing that "nature, which took its own time for everything, was being shoved and whiplashed over here."[1] This feeling would not go away for a long time.

Macfadden had promised his young wife that a new world of opportunity awaited them in America, and he was eager to get back to business. Their first destination was the home of his friend and associate Charles H. Desgray. Before fleeing to England, the publisher had signed over most of his holdings to Desgray, who then took over the day-to-day operations of the Physical Culture Publishing Company. Desgray was therefore shocked to learn now that not he, but Mary, would be Macfadden's business partner going forward.[2] With this unpleasantness taken care of, the family moved into a drafty cottage in Far Rockaway, Long Island, rented cheaply for the off season. From here, husband and wife commuted into

Manhattan, to the Physical Culture Publishing Company's office in the Flatiron Building.

In Macfadden's absence, the company had been losing money, and *Physical Culture* was in debt to its printer. Still, readers remained enthusiastic, and letters and manuscripts continued to flow in from professional writers, reformers, and fans. While waiting to give birth, Mary worked alongside a disgruntled Desgray and *Physical Culture*'s current editor, Carl Easton Williams, to triage submissions to the magazine. Meanwhile, Macfadden started writing new books and articles and plotting their next moves. When plummeting winter temperatures froze their cottage, he proposed a trip to Chicago to check up on his International Healthatorium and College of Physcultopathy, which was managed by Macfadden's secretary (and former paramour) Susie Wood and her husband. Mary was anxious to finally meet Macfadden's indispensable "right arm," and Wood was equally curious about her. To everyone's great relief, the women got along nicely—even when Wood insisted the couple would surely be more comfortable sleeping in separate beds.³

After returning to New York, the family moved into another rental property, this time a rambling Long Island mansion with room for boarders and a long driveway. Finally, after years of resisting the automobile, Macfadden bought a (very) used 1903 Palmer-Singer that was basically a "cross between a prehistoric hearse and an early Barnum circus wagon."⁴ He was a terrible driver, but the car proved handy when it came time to fetch a midwife. Mary's second delivery was a lengthy, traumatic ordeal. Suffering an excruciating hernia, she begged her husband to call a doctor, but he refused, insisting that medical interference had no place in a true physical culture birth. Eventually, a healthy baby girl arrived, who received the "B" name of Beulah. Within just a few months, Mary was pregnant again.

With his family growing quickly as planned, Macfadden fished around wildly for ways to make more money. He expanded his penny restaurant business, turned the family's rented mansion into a boarding house for health seekers, and tried to patent several inventions of his own creation, including an indoor air-cooling system, a crowd-distributing double-decker subway car, and the Peniscope, a glass tube-and-pump device that promised to engorge the male sex organ. Meanwhile, perhaps worried about his own physique aging, Macfadden kept himself and his family on a stringent exercise routine. During a world war was no time to let anyone go soft.

The Great War would pose numerous challenges for Macfadden and his publishing company. Amid British mobilization and war-related disruptions of transoceanic communications and commerce, the London-produced version of Macfadden's flagship magazine, *Physical Development,* ceased publication. Going forward, the publisher would need to focus on his US circulations, and if he got in trouble with Comstock again, it would be harder to flee. Moreover, the potentially harmonious relationship between war and physical culture was being counteracted by mass movements of Americans who wanted peace, or at least for the United States to stay out of other countries' conflicts. Yet despite these setbacks and complications, there were also promising new opportunities in the air. Due in part to the publisher's past decade and a half of efforts, physical culture values and pastimes were growing in popularity, with more Americans than ever playing sports, monitoring their weight, and exercising for health and leisure. The lurking threat of war was unlikely to reverse such trends, as health and strength were tied to issues of national security and military might. From another angle, it was also the case that the Physical Culture Family's hasty exodus from Europe had brought them to the center of the English-language publishing world at a propitious moment. Migration, urbanization, and economic and cultural changes of various kinds were producing a more expansive potential audience for American print media and consumer culture.

For the last few years, Macfadden had been chasing wider renown among foreign audiences. Now, back in his home country and aided by the labor of a young wife, he had the chance to draft new readers and improve his company's profile and finances. But first, the Physical Culture Publishing Company would need to navigate the complex politics of neutrality, stay on the right side of censors, and survive the war. Without abandoning a commitment to transnational movements dedicated to "building up the white race," the Physical Culture Publishing Company's wartime circulations would mediate a flexible conception of national fitness that cohered around embodied experiences of improvement and mobility that were widely shared but unequally accessible, mirroring broader trends in discourses of American identity, citizenship, and consumer culture during the First World War.

Navigating Neutrality and Promoting Preparedness

Working at the Physical Culture Publishing Company during the second half of the 1910s proved to be a similar experience to Mary's first New York cab ride: things were always busy and moving fast, yet it was never clear to those inside where they were heading. As Macfadden pursued new ventures and audiences for his products, it remained unknown whether his manic entrepreneurial pursuits would keep the business afloat or sink it entirely. Mary, watching her husband flit from one money-making scheme to another, increasingly feared the latter. Child-rearing, back-to-back pregnancies, and worrying about friends and family back home compounded her stress.

Initially, Macfadden expected the eruption of the Great War to benefit his business by highlighting physical culture's value to national defense. However, the historical associations between physical culture, foreign armies, martial nationalism, and various immigrant subcultures would complicate matters for the Physical Culture Publishing Company. At this point, many Americans did not imagine that the United States should or would become a combatant in a foreign conflict. Additionally, the war seemed an anathema to ideas about universal cooperation and progress that had thrived during the Progressive Era, with the mechanized violence being unleashed on modern battlefields striking horrified viewers as the antithesis of healthy, civilized behavior. Many Americans began denouncing not only the current conflagration but also militarism more broadly, throwing themselves into peace activism.[5]

Concurrently, a popular antiwar movement was emerging. Spanning the political spectrum, this movement drew support from elite circles as well as from labor unions, women's groups, churches and synagogues, and innumerable civic organizations. Though certainly harboring many who wanted to stay out of Europe's problems, this movement appealed for moral, economic, and political reasons that cannot be simply summed up as "isolationism." Often, participants couched their position in internationalist language, citing concern for women's rights, faith in global diplomacy, and eugenic goals. Others underscored the importance of working-class solidarity against a capitalist war machine intent to convert dead bodies into industrial profit. The diasporic attachments of some of the country's most sizable immigrant groups—including German Americans, Irish Americans, and Jews who had fled the Russian Empire—further swelled the ranks of peace and neutrality advocates.[6]

Reflecting popular sentiment, President Woodrow Wilson was promising to maintain US neutrality. But even neutrality was controversial. Some Americans, seeing antimilitarism as naive and even dangerous, began advocating for "preparedness" instead. In practice, this meant advocating for economic and military mobilization, stricter Americanization campaigns for immigrants, and the pursuit of an "Atlanticist" foreign policy that would strengthen ties between the United States and the Triple Entente. Preparedness did not contradict neutrality, per se, yet champions and critics alike predicted it would bring the United States closer to entering the war to help Great Britain. American loans, supplies, and humanitarian efforts

certainly started to flow overwhelmingly in this direction. While some accused the United States of violating the spirit of neutrality, preparedness
supporters underlined the necessity of unrestricted trade and self-defense.
Americans were, in short, deeply divided. Antiwar factions were protesting
that militarism perverted democracy, alienated immigrants and workers,
enriched greedy bankers and manufacturers, and undermined America's
claims to moral superiority; advocates of preparedness, in response, portrayed antiwar groups as overrun by women, weaklings, and disloyal foreign sympathizers.[7]

Personally, Macfadden harbored little compunction about armed engagement. Like many of his generation born after the Civil War, he tended
to romanticize military life. Plus, he had long wanted the United States to
import other countries' marital traditions, which a preparedness movement could help bring about. Yet, the company's current and potential
readers were too politically, socially, and economically diverse to be in
alignment on the war, so appearing too hawkish could hurt the company's
prospects. Fortunately, the unabashedly pluralistic reform agenda of its
earlier print circulations, along with the participatory dynamic and aesthetic of pastiche it had cultivated, proved useful for helping the company
mediate between antiwar politics, international pacifist visions, and
surging nationalist and nativist sentiments.[8] While the United States remained officially neutral, then, the Physical Culture Publishing Company
would avoid directly engaging with hot-button questions such as whether
the United States should enter the conflict, broker peace, or engage more
actively in international governance. Instead, its publications would focus
on portraying physical culture as an immersive, accessible, and forward-
looking modern lifestyle that transcended the short-term vicissitudes of
contemporary geopolitics. Audiences would be encouraged to look inward
and focus their energies on reforming and optimizing their own bodies;
and perhaps after succeeding in the personal arena they would find themselves able to exert more control over public ones.

In its mid-1910s media, the Physical Culture Publishing Company centered themes of individual growth and transformation expressed through
personal narratives. Building on the correspondence and advertising patterns established in its earlier media, it highlighted first-person testimonials that emphasized themes of triumph over adversity through
self-improvement. Macfadden set the tone in "My Life Story," a serialized
autobiography that ran in *Physical Culture* in 1914–1915. Beginning with
the assertion that "[n]o namby-pamby silver-spoon experience has been
mine," he described his tumultuous childhood and eventful career, de-
tailing how he had overcome seemingly insurmountable setbacks through

physical culture methods.[9] In this celebratory account, the author presented himself like the heroes of the Horatio Alger dime novels popular in his youth. But while Alger's protagonists succeeded by clinging to respectable middlebrow values such as thrift and humility, Macfadden stressed the importance of breaking with tradition and crafting an individualistic identity based on self-directed experimentation.

"My Life Story" was notable for what it did not say as well. Macfadden chose not to acknowledge Mary's help, nevertheless the existence of his two previous wives. He also glossed over the enormous influence that German American gymnasts and the Prussian-born strongman Eugen Sandow exerted on his own personal development and the development of his business. As late as January 1914, articles such as "The Turnverein and Its Work" were celebrating the specific influence of German culture on the health of American citizens, but for obvious reasons such content soon stopped. With its deep roots in Central European military traditions and immigrant communities, physical culture needed to be rebranded as a more purely American pastime. This mandate meshed easily with Macfadden's tendencies toward self-aggrandizement and credit-hogging. Going forward, the publisher would downplay the role of immigrants in his adolescent training in St. Louis and neglect Sandow, even though the strongman had been a British citizen since 1906. Overlooking the impact of these "foreign" influences enabled Macfadden to simultaneously avoid associating his publishing house with Germanic cultural forms while furthering narratives of his own exceptionality.

Readers responded to "My Life Story" by flooding *Physical Culture* with their own detailed, autobiographical, and naval-gazing (sometimes literally) health-building stories. The magazine's editors, which included John Brennan and John Brisbane Walker before Macfadden retook the reins in 1916, encouraged this behavior by soliciting contributions on endless variations of "How Physical Culture Brought Me Success." Despite the international situation, the topic of the current war surfaced only occasionally in the content they printed. Instead, apolitical narratives of personal growth predominated, with illnesses, particularly those exacerbated by modern work and professional medicine, serving as the main antagonists to health and well-being. When war was mentioned, it was usually metaphorically, as in *Physical Culture*'s encouragements for readers to fight a war against weakness, prudery, and other social ills.

Meanwhile, *Physical Culture* assured readers that they could conquer any barrier to success by optimizing their own physiques and bodily systems. This emphasis on self-mastery was part of a more general shift in which Macfadden's publications adopted an overtly therapeutic tone in the mid-1910s. As historians have explained, therapeutic discourse centered on individual fulfillment became a defining feature of America's new consumer culture around this time. The Physical Culture Publishing Company played an active role in this process. In addition to emphasizing the capacity of physical culture to improve one's physique and bodily functions, its media touted the possibility for readers to achieve a more holistic state of "self-actualization" built on mind-body harmony. Much of the company's published content smacked of new trends in popular psychology, in which deep-seated religious conceptualizations of spiritual transcendence mixed with modern, secular notions of self-care and definitions of success formulated by an emergent class of advertising professionals.[10]

Indeed, Macfadden showed great facility in generating this lingo and adapting it toward his own purposes. In his 1915 book *Vitality Supreme,* which promised readers to "make your body splendid, your mind supreme," he explained that adhering "to the principles laid down herein" would not only bring "splendid achievements" in health and business but also "help each human entity to become a live personality . . . [and] live fully, joyously." Chapters on posture, digestive health, breathing, outdoor living, and diet detoxification vowed to take audiences from the pale shadows of a life half lived to a new state "full of vim and energy," in which anything could be accomplished. Martial references sprinkled throughout this book mostly served as generic blandishments. Who wouldn't want to "heed the war-cry . . . for efficiency" and become "a positive dominating force in the world?" Often, the prose veered into the territory of the brazenly libidinal: "You, too," every reader was assured, "can feel these throbbing vital forces stirring your every nerve, thrilling your very soul."[11]

Magnifying its focus on more intimate arenas of health and fitness culture, the Physical Culture Publishing Company continued to pay close attention to the subjects of romance, conjugal relations, and family formation. In the past, Macfadden had gotten into a lot of trouble discussing intimate relations, but social mores were changing. The second decade of the twentieth century witnessed growing popular demand among both men and women for information and advice on romantic relationships and the body's sexual functions. Having always considered frank discussion of sex and reproduction a necessary cornerstone of physical culture, Macfadden remained committed to supplying the sexual knowledge industry and influencing public attitudes about interpersonal relationships and family formation. Producing new writings and republishing old ones, now illustrated with photographs of his own growing family, he advised physical culturalists to approach love and marriage with the same studious devotion they applied to weight lifting; likewise, those seeking romantic fulfillment were

encouraged to acquaint themselves with physical culture media. Meanwhile, the illustrated covers of his flagship magazine, which had long dab-
bled in nudity, now often oozed erotic vitality. Buxom young women in
leotards, sensual dancers and athletes, and dynamic nude statuary beck-
oned to curious readers, hinting that paths to new heights of romantic and
sexual satisfaction lay ahead. Such exhortations were pitched to a presumed
heterosexual audience; yet the abundance of images of homosocial couplings
could be read subversively as promising the fulfillment of queerer personal
pleasures as well. For example, the January 1915 cover of Physical Culture
depicts a pair of smooth, nearly naked wrestlers locked in ecstatic embrace
in the foreground, with a background featuring Classical iconography
that for some readers would have evoked associations with same-sex love
in ancient Greece.[12] In any case, when Anthony Comstock died in 1915—
with the New York Times' snarky, front-page obituary attributing the
cause of death to "overwork and overexcitement"—Macfadden was probably ecstatic.[13] Other vice crusaders would continue to look for and pros-
ecute obscenity, but intimate affairs could be discussed and depicted with a
freer hand with the "King of Prudes" out of the way.

The immersive physical culture lifestyle promoted in this mid-1910s
media, which centered themes of romance, self-transformation, and personal fulfillment, wooed audiences with a softer, less dogmatic formula of
health reform than some of Macfadden's publications had championed in
the past. This did not mean, however, that the company's publications lost
their zealous commitment to reform. Instead, they emphasized the message that even the most intimate and personal realms of health and fitness
could have wider social, political, and civilizational stakes. Linking the
personal and intimate aspects of physical culture to issues of public health
and national security in an unpredictable world was a common theme in
Physical Culture, where travelogue-style articles like "Drink and Diet in
the European War" reminded readers that even the most quotidian ways
in which citizens treated their bodies could become matters of life and
death. Relatedly, eugenics, a topic that bridged the personal and political,
remained a common theme in this magazine and the company's other publications, which depicted baby-making in an era of war-related population
loss as an urgent social prerogative and personally fulfilling mission for
appropriate couples. To this point, in October 1916, the Macfaddens welcomed their third offspring into the world, with Mary once again forced to
labor without the aid of a doctor or anesthesia. Initially disappointed at
the appearance of another girl, Macfadden's mood lifted when his daughter
weighed in at a whopping thirteen pounds, earning the name Braunda (a
toned-down version of "Brawnda"). Mary's body tore and hemorrhaged a

Fig.4.1 A pair of wrestlers intimately intertwine on the cover of the January 1915 issue of *Physical Culture*. Terry and Jan Todd Collection/H.J. Lutcher Stark Center for Physical Culture and Sport

terrifying amount of blood delivering such an enormous baby, but this information was not shared publicly with readers, who only saw what Macfadden shared with them.

Eugenic themes in the company's media and Bernarr and Mary's growing Physical Culture Family increasingly resonated with the contemporary preparedness movement's emphasis on the desirability and productiveness of Anglo-American solidarity. The Great War induced a rising tide of sympathy for the fighting British, who were often conceptualized by US elites as imperiled racial brethren.[14] Macfadden, who had previously spoken of Germany's threat to both "English and English-stock in the US," continued to show concern about the war's endangerment to Anglo-American civilization, which strengthened his impulses to link together physical culture and relatively nonpartisan formulations of preparedness. This goal motivated the publisher in 1915 to branch out into the world of moving pictures, which had only recently become a popular storytelling medium. Teaming up with the Universal Film Company, he produced *Building the Health of the Nation,* a series of one-reel instructional films teaching viewers how to exercise. Played by Universal's chain of theaters, *Building the Health of the Nation* stressed the importance of individuals pursuing physical culture not only for purposes of self-improvement but also for the betterment of public health and national security. As advertisements for the series explained diplomatically, Macfadden's films would prepare Americans to fight in the "battle of life," which of course might also happen to prove useful in other kinds of battles that might lay ahead.

The inclusion of preparedness discourse within the Physical Culture Publishing Company's media intensified as US relations with Germany deteriorated. In March 1916, Macfadden took to the pages of his flagship magazine to propose a National Defense League, imagined as an interlinked series of voluntary physical training corps headed by his most advanced followers. Proclaiming, "I BELIEVE IN WAR—when necessary to avoid dishonor, slavery, ruin, or death," he now channeled disillusionment with neutrality while covering his bases through linguistic vagaries. "Call it what you may, physical culture, physical training, or military training, but let this great man-building influence be introduced without delay into our national life," he entreated. Completely unsolicited, he volunteered to help Washington implement a national physical education and military training program that would whip Americans into shape. Frustratingly, no official appointments proved forthcoming from the federal government, although several members of Congress did write to express approval. The idea that polarized Americans could be molded into a more disciplined, coherent, and healthy whole through shared training and rituals was a compelling one, especially as US entry into the war came to seem more likely.

Military Training and 100% Americanism

Having secured reelection on the laurels that he "kept us out of war," Woodrow Wilson used his second presidential term to call on combatants to accept a "peace without victory."[15] But after the Zimmermann Telegram, tensions escalated rapidly, and on April 6, 1917, the United States declared war on the German Empire. Wilson acted quickly to mobilize the country, using all the resources at his disposal and creating more. To staff the armed forces, Congress enacted the Selective Service Act of 1917, which set up a network of draft boards and military training camps. More creative measures were deemed necessary to adequately marshal public support. To this end, Wilson founded the Committee on Public Information (CPI), a government agency tasked with mobilizing public opinion. Under the leadership of a former journalist named George Creel, the CPI organized propaganda campaigns designed to unite citizens at home around a common national identity while communicating to the world US war aims and "the justice of America's cause."[16]

In its attempts to muster military might and public support, the Wilson administration had to contend not only with the after-effects of the peace movement but also with social fissures and political animosities wrought by over a generation of demographic change that had transformed the nation. A flashpoint for public debate, and thus a primary focus of the government's propaganda efforts, was the role of "new immigrants" in the body politic. To perform its job of uniting the country, the CPI attempted to broadcast a portrait of national identity emphasizing qualities, values, and goals Americans shared. Through a range of measures that expanded the government's power over public discourse, it endorsed an ideal of patriotic pluralism that was encapsulated in the slogan "100% Americanism."

Built on understandings of domestic diversity as an urgent social and political problem that could be addressed through a mix of educational, cultural, and political interventions, 100% Americanism was, on the surface, an inclusive ethos. It accepted and even celebrated cultural differences—so long as these differences remained subsumed under an overarching loyalty to the dominant policies and norms of the United States, as defined by those currently in power.[17] Via a range of media platforms, the CPI sought to compel Americans' allegiance to the state and its professed ideals. This included working with immigrant community leaders to organize fundraising drives and pro-war speeches at public gatherings as well as plastering the country with posters. A subset of propaganda vilified the enemy as blood-thirsty "Huns," employing imagery long associated with Orientalist and anti-Black cultural tropes; other messaging focused on depicting a multiethnic population joined by bravery; democratic values; and not least of all, radiant youth, health, and beauty.[18] Private industry—particularly media producers—were encouraged to aid the CPI in spreading government messaging, and the Physical Culture Publishing Company fell into step while pursuing its own goals. For the duration of the war, Macfadden, having resumed editing *Physical Culture* in late 1916, enhanced the patriotism of his media while using the occasion of wartime emergency to promote his business. Contending that physical culture could no longer be dismissed as simply the domain of athletes, reformers, and "health cranks," he sought to appeal to a wider public that wartime discourse was increasingly bringing into focus as a multiethnic domestic market.

Having long stressed the linkages between the personal and public aspects of the bodily health and fitness, the Physical Culture Publishing Company used the war to add immediacy to questions about what a strong and healthy US body politic should look like and how it could be produced. Predictably, in answering such questions, Macfadden doubled down on his preparedness platform and demands for universal physical training and education, asserting that the principles espoused in his publications would build up the military and exert a "great cementing force" on the general population.[19] The institution the 1917 Conscription Act provided fodder for this argument, as draft officials claimed to find a large proportion of Americans physically, mentally, or emotionally unequipped for military service, findings some blamed on immigrants and minorities who were accused of undermining both American war efforts and the nation's overall fitness.[20] Macfadden turned the fallout of the Conscription Act into an "I-told-you-so" moment that vindicated messages he had long been circulating about civilizational decline, whatever its cause. If the United States wanted to win the war, then Americans needed to shape up before they shipped out, and this would require a transformative national effort aimed at reforming the bodies of men, women, and children en masse.

Across a variety of features, *Physical Culture* advocated a mass movement of mass movement while casting large-scale bodybuilding and physical education programs, which had long been associated with foreign governments, immigrant subcultures, and international movements, as 100% American. Alongside the publisher's own articles, a parade of reformers, politicians, and bureaucrats expounded on the ties between physical culture and democratic pluralism. For example, William J. Lee, the director of athletics of New York City's Park Playgrounds, argued, "Universal military service and the development of our NATIONAL ARMY will do more to democratize this nation (which is composed of a mixed mass of the world's population) than any act since the adoption of the Constitution."[21] Writing on "How Can We Have Universal Military Training," Raymond Fosdick, a commissioner working for the secretary of war, testified that army training camps taught "the lessons of teamwork."[22] In both articles, these authors implied that physical culture would help ease regional and racial domestic tensions through disciplining and assimilating minority groups into more nation-facing collectives. Accompanying pictures communicated this message visually. For instance, wartime issues of *Physical Culture* featured photographs taken at public schools, parks, and settlement houses depicting children of immigrants participating in supervised recreational activities that were characterized as building bodies and patriotism in tandem. In Lee's article, an assembly of city kids, dressed all in white, performs a calisthenics routine holding both wooden rifles and American flags. Images of military training, provided to media outlets like Macfadden's by the CPI, depicted similar scenes. In the lead image of Fosdick's piece, a racially diverse group of soldiers march in formation. Such images imbued military training camps, and soldiering more generally, with the potential to instill unity and cooperation among citizens from different backgrounds.[23]

Even as it extolled the possibilities of physical fitness pluralism, however, Macfadden's media also brought into focus tensions that structured assimilatory models of national identity, particularly as they concerned how actual human bodies fit into the body politic as it was being conceptualized and represented in mainstream discourse. This can be seen in the continued discomfort expressed by some correspondents regarding what they saw as the dysgenic effects of wartime mobilization. One irate correspondent from Oregon, for instance, challenged Macfadden's ignoring of "the completely anti-eugenic selective effects of modern war," emphasizing that when "[t]he fit are selected for slaughter and the unfit for survival," nothing but "racial decay" could result. Deriding the editor's enthusiasm for national military training, this author recommended sending only "slum dwellers" to Europe, because they "are best adapted by training and past experience for life in the trenches."[24] Clearly, wartime visions of disciplining and assimilating bodies were shadowed by a eugenics-inflected discourse of ethnic nationalism that promoted various forms of segregation, exclusion, and even what some theorists today might call necropolitics— that is, social and political policies that unevenly distribute death onto specific populations.[25] For the most part, however, the Physical Culture

Publishing Company's media characterized militarized physical training and military service as promising to realize the CPI's salubrious vision of "the people of the United States" being "weld[ed] into one white-hot mass" of loyal citizens through processes of voluntary subordination to externally imposed order, which was often communicated through textual and visual representations of uniform-clad bodies being choreographed or arranged by rank in orderly formations.[26]

As the US government promoted inclusion through Americanization for some minority groups during the war, it also brought increased state power to bear on sustaining and enforcing certain political and social hierarchies and methods of exclusion. Quickly, the government cracked down hard on remaining antiwar and peace activists, with Congress passing strict sedition and espionage laws that criminalized dissent, imprisoned protestors, and deported foreign-born radicals.[27] Immigrants, including US citizens, bore the brunt of surveillance and suspicion, showing the limits of wartime multiculturalism. Even though many Americans had long nurtured multiple national affiliations and civic identities, pressures to embody a narrowly defined version of loyalty mounted. As Wilson would eventually put it, "Any man who carries a hyphen about with him carries a dagger that he is ready to plunge into the vitals of this Republic."[28] In this context, a revitalized nativist movement, mobilized by eugenics-related science and publications, saw the war as an opportunity to purge the national population of undesirable elements. Even as the economy and military relied on the labor of migrant bodies—for instance, nearly 40 percent of soldiers were foreign-born or the children of immigrants—powerful voices worked to reverse recent demographic transformations through enacting greater restrictions on immigration.[29] With popular support, Congress denied entry to poor migrants, anarchists, and those deemed mentally or physically disabled; expanded previous policies of Asian exclusion; and laid the foundation for a dramatically revised immigration regime that would be pegged to national (and therefore, to what many perceived as racial) origins. Meanwhile, Wilson enforced racial segregation in Washington and in the US Armed Forces, reversing African Americans' hard-fought civil rights gains. The United States proclaimed to be making the world "safe for democracy," but in the process, it was clear that many people could and would be rendered second-class citizens within the nation and its territories or excluded from democracy and its supposed protections entirely.[30]

Against this backdrop, the Physical Culture Publishing Company bowdlerized connections with some radical socialists and foreign and diasporic groups that had previously exerted a powerful influence in shaping its media. It also continued denying visibility to Black physiques, even as African American leaders were adapting the discourse of 100% Americanism to claim rights and recognition for Black soldiers. Furthermore, alongside its depictions of proto-American bodies being molded from above into worthy soldier-citizens, Macfadden's wartime media constructed representations of white, native-born Americans who came into possession of superior inborn qualities through militarized physical culture. In other words, the theme of revitalized white masculinity that had always been present in the company's publications took a distinctively ethno-nationalist slant during the war.

The August 1918 *Physical Culture* cover story "The Regeneration of a Coward" illustrates this trend. The winning entry in a contest that asked readers to describe "How Health and Energy Brought Me Success," this story follows a scrawny, pampered white man who is unwillingly drafted into the army. When he first arrives at boot camp, the protagonist is shocked to find that "I, who had had great hopes for myself, was nothing more, or less, than John Pochinski, the Pole by my side, or Tony Garros, from the city's little Italy." Seeing that "We three, and all the others, were on level footing," troubles the narrator deeply because, "[i]n civil life they were my inferiors, mentally, and my mind rioted in understanding." Rather than provoking egalitarian feelings, camp causes the narrator to realize just how far he has sunk below his true potential. The remainder of the story details his pursuit of superiority through a disciplined training routine. Soon, the narrator is promoted to the rank of corporal, which puts him in charge of his Polish and Italian bunkmates. In the conclusion, it is revealed that the narrator is now a strapping lieutenant fighting on the front in France, while "John Pochinski and Tony Garros are still privates."[31]

In this and other features, the Physical Culture Publishing Company justified its militarism by emphasizing the army's ability to create a landscape of patriotic physical culture pluralism through universal conscription while still maintaining political and social order through systems of internal segregation and gradations of ranking. Such content displayed a continuing eugenic commitment to "building up the English-speaking race" while simultaneously channeling assimilatory discourses of Americanization that did not contradict this commitment. An October 1918 editorial from Macfadden celebrating how fitness education and military training had brought so many citizens "into their true physical inheritance" further illustrates this dynamic, revealing the extent to which the biological and hereditation language of eugenics was made compatible in his company's media with an ethos of identic mobility that portrayed individual American bodies—and the US body politic itself—as exceptionally capable of improvement and transformation. Looking forward to peace-time, the editor celebrated a future where "every American" would have the opportunity to realize "the strength, endurance, and efficiency of body and mind" that "is their birthright."[32]

A Multiethnic Market of Consumers in Flux

Frictions between eugenics-inflected ethno-nationalist discourse and prom-ises of mobility and inclusion for all Americans would not be resolved within *Physical Culture*—nor in any other arena of politics or culture—during the war. Yet Macfadden's media, without abandoning conceptual-izations of the United States as a normatively white body politic threatened from within and without by racialized perils, did increasingly address itself to a multiethnic society in which conceptualizations of race, ethnicity, iden-tity, and Americanness were undergoing flux.

During the Great War, many "new immigrant" groups attained legal, financial, social, and cultural benefits that had historically been associated with whiteness. This shift was influenced by Americanization programs and CPI propaganda that responded to contemporary political impera-tives. It was also shaped from below by first- and second-generation im-migrants' own bids for respect, which influenced the terms on which they supported the war and participated in military service.[33] Macfadden's wartime media and its emphasis on physical training offered resources for new immigrants to stake claims of belonging to the body politic. However, to portray engagement with his physical media as a means through which "ethnic" Americans "became white" would be too simplistic if we inter-pret this to mean assimilation to Anglo-American norms and values. Phys-ical culture in the United States had been seeded by many immigrant groups, and new immigrants, now often from southern and eastern Eu-rope, constituted an increasingly important demographic of physical cul-ture enthusiasts and potential consumers during the 1910s who brought their own perspectives and desires to Macfadden's publications.

In his study of British physical culture, Michael Anton Budd argues that early twentieth-century health and fitness magazines often "substantiat[ed] the idea of diversity while at the same time perpetuating the idea of the ideal reader" who was Anglo-Saxon and middle class.[34] This insight con-textualizes much of *Physical Culture*'s WWI-era content, including not only features discussed above but also its long-running advertisements for hair-removal systems, courses to "Learn Correct English," and devices to reshape the nose, which promised to make over qualities associated at the time with foreign "otherness."[35] The magazine's contributions to a "normalizing discourse" that was, as we have seen, a major thread of American political culture and US propaganda messaging extended to its ads.[36] Yet it was also the case that *Physical Culture* became a platform for the hailing of ethnically diverse readers through content that validated their great inner potential and unique contributions. Already a feature of interactive correspondence columns, this pattern also manifested in and through advertising, editorial content, and contests.

Regarding advertising, Macfadden's wartime-era media attracted clients whose customers were already, or were expected to be, from immigrant backgrounds. One regular client, for instance, was Dr. Page, whose Page System, a natural program for treating disease, was regularly promoted in *Physical Culture*. Dr. Page's ads begin with the headline proclamation "RICH GIRL DYING: POOR BOY CURED. WHY?" and then go on to contrast the fate of an "heiress of millions" who lies "dying in hospital" to "Felix Sagarino, 18," a sick young man near Boston, who saw Dr. Page's ad in *Physical Culture* and "begged his father to consult" him. "Had the Sagarinos been rich they might not have seen this magazine, nor have known about me and my world, and this Italian lad would have died before he was 19," Page emphasizes. This depiction of an "Italian lad"—and one who census records suggest was a real person, S. Felix Sagarino of Revere, Massachusetts, born in Connecticut in 1894 to parents from Italy—shows who this advertiser saw as his own and Macfadden's customers, as well as how such customers might most effectively be addressed. Page and other advertisers who bought space in Macfadden's wartime-era publications pitched their products in similar ways; that is, they addressed their customers as working-class Americans, likely to be from immigrant backgrounds, who not only did not desire subservient assimilation to elite or middlebrow Anglo-American norms but also sometimes distinguished themselves in opposition to them.

The subject of how non-elites, including immigrants, interacted with mass media and consumer culture has been researched extensively by historians, who have traced the ways that popular audiences developed reading and consuming preferences and practices that allowed them to affirm their dignity as laborers and worthiness as members of the body politic.[37] It is thus worth emphasizing the extent to which Macfadden and his media validated consumption norms associated with working-class immigrant communities pathologized in other quarters. For instance, in addition to promoting natural methods of healing that eschewed elite doctors, *Physical Culture* continued to celebrate the importance of diets that were heavy on fresh fruits and vegetables rather than canned and processed foods hailed by elites as more modern. Similarly, Macfadden embraced film, a media format then primarily associated with the urban working class: "To you—the masses—the men and women from all walks of life . . . this series of health building exercises is dedicated," he had professed in *Building the Health of the Nation*. The editor also took a public stand against the push for countrywide Prohibition, a movement fueled in part by nativist politics, despite his personal disapproval of alcohol. In all these respects, the health and fitness media and consumer culture promoted through Macfadden and the Physical Culture Publishing Company meshed with cultural practices and preferences common among diverse immigrant groups who together represented an increasingly important market for US media and consumer products.

For foreign-born and immigrant-affiliated American men in particular during this period, physical culture and its media were useful for doing more than merely asserting one's fitness under the guise of an assimilatory 100% Americanism. For instance, throughout this period, first- and second-generation soldiers linked feats of physical strength and bravery they performed to domestic and homeland political agendas.[38] Manual laborers, a common job category for new immigrants, could wed musculature they acquired on the job with physical culture methods of shaping and display to challenge stereotypes that cast them as unfit or brawn without brains. And in the massive labor uprisings that bookended the war years, the hard bodies of male workers conveyed personal and professional pride, resistance to exploitation, and claims to wages and benefits that would allow male heads of household to support dependent families.[39] Across many different situations, then, physical training, bodybuilding, and individual and group performances of muscularity and fitness served specific functions for immigrants and immigrant-heavy working-class communities whose engagements with physical culture and Macfadden's media should be understood in this broader context.[40]

On this point, it is useful to consider an especially consequential relationship that first developed in the 1910s between Macfadden's media and one specific Italian American fitness enthusiast. Angelo Siciliano was born in 1892 in the Calabrian town of Bisignano in southern Italy and immigrated to the United States with his unmarried mother. Like many from their region, the family settled in multiethnic Brooklyn, where Angelino, as he was then known, spent his boyhood working in a handbag factory and frequenting the Italian Settlement School. Siciliano began bodybuilding in this milieu, which was not unusual, for as scholars have emphasized, *far bella figura*—making and presenting a good figure—was an important value in Italian public culture that traveled with migrants throughout the Italian diaspora, and Italians in America often invested considerable effort and resources into shaping their bodily self-presentations.[41] With the physique he developed, Siciliano was able to book gigs modeling exercise equipment and performing in a strongman show on Coney Island. That he engaged with Macfadden-brand fitness media while doing so is suggested by the appearance of his photograph on the cover of *Physical Development* in its final year of publication. Then, when Macfadden held a contest after the war in Madison Square Garden to discover "The World's Most Handsome Man," Siciliano triumphed over thousands of competitors, winning a $1,000 prize and a lush photo spread in *Physical Culture*.[42] The next year, after starring in a Macfadden-produced film called *The Road to Health,* Siciliano began promoting his own soon-to-be world-famous bodybuilding course in the Physical Culture Publishing Company's magazines under a new name: Charles Atlas. And Atlas, of course, would subsequently go on to become one of the most famous and successful bodybuilding entrepreneurs of all time.

Angelo Siciliano's makeover into Charles Atlas can and has been interpreted in different ways. On one hand, this transformation can appear to feature an immigrant from southern Europe casting off his ethnic identity, symbolized most obviously by his name, and remaking himself into a whiter American. On the other hand, as the scholar Dominique Padurano has shown, Siciliano-Atlas used his immigrant origin story and Mediterranean looks to "cultivat[e] an explicit connection to the Greco-Roman world" in a way that maintained Italian-Americanness as central to his persona and personal brand, which grew in large part through his ability to connect with an economically and racially diverse array of American and international consumers.[43] In doing so, he disaggregated contemporary associations between southern European immigrants and unfitness, framing the ideal American body as a recognizably Italian one, which was then turned into a universal ideal through his global success. Notably, as his persona was coming together in part through the pages of *Physical Culture,* Siciliano channeled Macfadden's ethos, asserting, "Out of the thousands of weaklings in the world there is probably a very small percentage that cannot, with no great effort, build themselves up in to splendid manhood and yes, womanhood too."[44] Subsequently, the defining feature of Atlas's bodybuilding system (which was originally marketed to men and women), was the eschewal of costly external apparatuses in favor of isotonic exercises that worked different muscle groups in "dynamic tension" against each other. The idea that radical improvements and transformations could be produced from within bodies whose potential had not before been adequately appreciated or tapped was an ethos that connected the Physical Culture Publishing Company's 1910s media and Charles Altas's soon-to-be world-renowned system that would long continue to be a staple advertiser in Macfadden's publications.[45]

To a degree much less visible in the Physical Culture Publishing Company's publications, Black Americans were also active participants in health and fitness culture during the 1910s. African American reformers during the Progressive Era promoted healthy living and physical education programs in churches, schools, and settlement houses. Meanwhile physical culture clubs that had been established in urban Black communities provided gymnasium facilities and organized athletic competitions for men, women, and children.[46] Although never an advocate for civil rights or racial equality, Macfadden responded to African Americans' interest in fitness at a time when many entrepreneurs ignored Black consumers. In turn, the Black press reported on the publisher's personal appearances and reviewed Macfadden's books and magazines, with Baltimore's *Afro-American* deeming *Physical Culture* "a publication that is always worth while."[47]

Fleeing racial terrorism and limited opportunities for advancement available to them in the rural South, African Americans moved north and west in great numbers in the 1910s, ushering in the first phase of the Great Migration. As more migrants settled in cities such as New York, Chicago, Philadelphia, and Detroit, some of which were also home to diasporic Caribbean populations, a "New Negro" ideal took shape that emphasized race pride and the strength and beauty of Black bodies. This ideal was developed and circulated through print culture, and it was also influenced by the arenas of sports and athletics. In a country where Black workers, male and female, were often relegated to the lowest-paying forms of menial labor, sports and athletics allowed talented men especially to express "dignity, distinction, and even defiance of black bodily servitude."[48]

When war came, military training and soldiering promised similar benefits, at least in theory. Demonstrating skill and bravery, African American soldiers put their bodies on the line for the nation and in return demanded civil and economic rights, legal protections, and public respect.[49] What they often got, however, was continued segregation, disenfranchisement, labor exploitation, and white supremacist violence targeting veterans while Congress refused to pass federal anti-lynching legislation. Meanwhile, the wider Black world continued to suffer the depredations of US and US-supported colonialism. Against the backdrop of these unfolding events, what was then sometimes called the "New Negro Manhood Movement" promoted an ethos of martial masculinity in the late 1910s and early 1920s. In Black periodicals, bodily displays of muscularity, upright posture, and physical self-confidence were linked with commitments to self-defense, community protection, civil rights activism, and anti-imperial politics.[50]

The Physical Culture Publishing Company and its advertisers did not reach out to Black physical culturalists in the ways they did to first- and second-generation immigrant Euro-Americans. Instead, the company's media participated in a broader trend of excluding Black bodies and communities of consumption from the political, cultural, and economic world depicted in its pages. Considering Macfadden's previous attempts to reach African American audiences interested in health and fitness, it seems likely that an intentional choice was made to observe an unstated "color line" within the company's media. This does not mean that Macfadden's publications did not attract Black readers (though it is entirely possible that some avoided them for this reason, as consumer boycotts were already a common political tactic). But it does indicate that such non-white readers had to engage with the Physical Culture Publishing Company's participatory media on especially circumscribed terms. Black physical culture enthusiasts who linked their health and fitness practices to Black nationalist, Pan-Africanist, or anti-white supremacist politics could not articulate such linkages in *Physical Culture*. Nor could they count on this magazine to assert their membership in the national imaginary of fit American bodies it was constructing and circulating. Relatedly, in contrast to some other previously marginalized groups, Black audiences did not become visible in Macfadden's publications during the 1910s as an American or transnational market whose ideas, tastes, politics, and preferences were worthy of attention and accommodation.

Still, a few individual readers' experiences with Macfadden's participatory publications become visible if one looks beyond the printed pages of *Physical Culture*. The scholar Jacqueline Stewart conceptualizes Black viewing practices through *reconstructive spectatorship*, "a formulation that seeks to account for the range of ways in which Black viewers attempted to reconstitute and assert themselves in relation to . . . racist social and textual operations."[51] Although Macfadden's texts themselves offer few clues into the ways Black consumers interacted with physical culture media in this era, other sources provide materials for constructing glimpses of this history; this is especially the case because the First World War and the Great Migration ushered in not only a New Negro Manhood movement but also the Harlem Renaissance, a period of artistic fluorescence marked by probing reexaminations of the bodily politics of race and an emphasis on crafting new representations and celebrations of African American bodies and Blackness.[52]

One window onto African American interactions with Macfadden's 1910s media comes from the archives of Jean Toomer, the Harlem Renaissance poet and writer. Born in 1894 to a biracial family, Toomer moved between Black and white neighborhoods and schools during his youth, developing a keen understanding of the politics of bodily difference and the instabilities of racial categories. When the adolescent Toomer began experiencing "an avalanche of sex indulgences" (masturbation), as well as general ill health that he perceived to be the result of his sexual transgressions, he turned to the physical culture movement for support. As he would later recall, "I saw myself falling to pieces. Some strength of my nature arose to fight . . . I began searching to find a way of building myself up. I hit upon a physical means . . . I went in for physical training." In this pursuit, Macfadden's publications provided a guide. Toomer acquired his five-volume *Encyclopedia of Physical Culture* and "read each page of each book," following Macfadden's health advice and "arguing his ideas with everyone."[53] He read *Physical Culture*, "from cover to cover, articles, sermons, editorials, exercises, letters to the editor, advertisements and all." As he would later describe the importance of this publication, "At once I became a neophyte on the threshold of a new world, with the well-thumbed pages of this magazine as my card of entrance . . . For here were no mere gestures and flappings of the parts of your body; here was an attitude, a doctrine of health and life that ranged from farting to philosophy, a way of life with an ascetic tone which appealed to me, a discipline which promised its followers not only a healthy mind in a healthy body but a strong brilliant mind in the body of a Hercules or an Apollo—you could take your choice."[54]

Responding to ads in *Physical Culture,* Toomer sent in for correspondence courses, health food, a lung-capacity builder, and a set of barbells. And each week, he recorded growing physical dimensions. In a scrapbook, Toomer pasted cutout images from the Physical Culture Publishing Company's media, including several of Macfadden flexing.[55] A few years later, when Toomer failed out of the University of Wisconsin and found himself searching for a new path in life, he saw an ad for Macfadden's Training College in Chicago and applied. A shirtless photograph taken during his time in Chicago highlights his muscular arms and torso and proud, steady gaze.[56] Just a few years later, Toomer would begin his career as a writer, going on to become a luminary of the Harlem Renaissance whose literary productions would engage deeply with themes of bodily identity, visibility, and transformation.

The Physical Culture Publishing Company's availability and appeal to Black readers in the late 1910s is also illustrated by the example of Richmond Barthé. Born into a Creole family in Bay St. Louis, Mississippi, in 1901, Barthé was an artistic youth, but his access to resources was highly circumscribed in the Jim Crow South, with the public library in his community barring Black patrons. Nevertheless, as a boy Barthé studied, drew, and painted the human figure by obtaining copies of *Physical Culture*.[57] A survivor of typhoid fever, which struck him at age fourteen, it is possible that he also found the magazine's health advice as useful as its pictures. According to a biographer, "Barthé, with his slight build and effeminate manner, was as heartened by Macfadden's revolutionary philosophy as he was excited by the figure studies in his magazine," even though "Barthé never saw Black people pictured there or anywhere else."[58] In the 1920s, after a period of artistic training, Barthé would become a painter and sculptor known for his dynamic renderings of muscular and elegant Black physiques.

Toomer's and Barthé's engagements with Macfadden's media, which entered the historical record because of their ensuing fame, provide insights into how racially marginalized domestic audiences interacted with Macfadden's fitness publications, allowing us to reconstruct not only the connections between fitness culture and the New Negro movement's emphasis on strong Black bodies but also the ways that specific individuals may have been able to connect physical culture media and consumer culture to diverse personal, artistic, and intellectual projects that were in formation at this time. Both Toomer's and Barthé's literary and artistic oeuvres emphasized themes of embodiment, identity, representation, while articulating complex ideas about race and sexuality in relationship to Blackness and Americanness.

Toomer, as literary critics have discussed, would exhibit a lasting preoccupation with the relationship between the physical body and identity in both his personal life and his creative works. Though he described himself as "Scotch, Welsh, German, English, French, Dutch, Spanish, with some dark blood," he was classified by the US census and white American society more generally as Black. Since the days of slavery, this classificatory system had served as a mechanism for maintaining white supremacy, with the rise of eugenics further codifying "dark blood" as a source of social taint. Toomer, however, confounded biological constructions of racial difference and sought to articulate a more fluid conception of identity that transcended racial binaries and centered human capacities for fluidity and change.[59] Scholar Mark Whalen has posited that *Physical Culture*'s examples of how individuals could master their bodies and appearance may have had a profound effect on Toomer's artistic output and sense of self. Bodybuilding could offer an empowering and liberating ethos of self-control, particularly "when appropriated by racial groups whose bodies [and to this I would add understandings of identity] have been overdetermined by white racist discourse." While *Physical Culture*'s representational conventions participated in the "overdetermination" of racial and ethnic boundaries, the magazine's contents also presented the opportunity for individual readers such as Toomer to "engage[e] with mass cultural discourse as a way of disturbing normative practices of racialization" in the United States.[60]

Barthé, meanwhile, would craft sought-after sculptures of African diaspora and Black figures whose bodies were so noticeably absent from the era's visual culture. His graceful boxers, dancers, and historical figures mix "Eurocentric and Afrocentric visual and cultural tropes" in ways that underscore their common humanity, spirituality, and sensuality.[61] To some, Barthé's figural work radiates a homoerotic sensibility that was also discernible within physical culture media. Barthé, who had intimate relationships with other male artists now considered to have been queer, proved adept at capturing the sexual desires, tensions, and possibilities that could be encoded within depictions of unclothed bodies. In simultaneously conveying both "public strategies of racial uplift and internal expressions of homoeros" his art illustrates the kinds of oppositional and subversive identifications and messages that Macfadden's publications could engender among marginalized readers, who could subversively use visual, textual, and consumer resources this media circulated to craft embodied identities and representations of modern Blackness and Americanness that centered African American histories, experiences, desires, and subjectivities, including queer ones.[62]

In summary, the participatory dynamic and multivocal quality that the Physical Culture Publishing Company acquired in the early years of the twentieth century helped it weather and respond to a range of political, social, and economic transformations that arose during the Great War. Initially, the company's focus on intimate bodily affairs and solicitation of personal narratives allowed it to turn inward, away from divisive political terrain, toward subjects such as personal growth, romance, and reproduction. Increasing coverage of eugenics provided a conduit for social reform impulses, helping to maintain the connection between Macfadden's publications and a transnational social hygiene movement dedicated to white racial uplift while also offering connections to the "preparedness" movement. When the political climate shifted after the United States entered the war, Macfadden effectively yoked his periodicals to an ethos of "100% Americanism" promoted by the CPI, emphasizing how physical culture might not only rejuvenate individual bodies but also heal the fractured body politic to reveal new national potential.

Because of its ability to simultaneously mediate internationalist visions of transatlantic progressivism, surging nationalist sentiments, and a range of inclusionary and exclusionary plans for promoting greater political discipline and social cohesion in America, the Physical Culture Publishing Company weathered the war and came out the other side more attuned to opportunities for expansion and profit offered by a domestic readership. Particularly important was the growing purchasing power of middle-class women as well as America's ethnically diverse, mobile, and urbanizing population of working-class citizens and consumers. Regarding female readers, Macfadden's contemporary publications promoted expanded access to political rights and sexual knowledge for some women while at the same time reinforcing a prevailing gender system that prioritized male authority and women's reproductive capacities—a dynamic that was nowhere more apparent than in Macfadden's own marriage. Meanwhile, "new immigrants" as a group achieved more visibility within the company's periodicals, which increasingly, albeit unevenly, recognized them as a distinct and desirable market. Black audiences, in contrast, faced continuing exclusion, despite African Americans' contributions to the war and avid participation in physical culture, leaving them to fashion repertoires of health- and self-building that drew from Macfadden's publications but whose results would manifest in other arenas of politics and culture.

• • •

In August 1918, Macfadden reached an important milestone: his fiftieth birthday. Believing his semicentennial to be an opportune moment to codify his legacy, the publisher placed a feature story in his flagship magazine that described his many accomplishments, wide influence, and enduring potency. On this latter point, he was able to cite the continued growth of the Physical Culture Family. In rapid succession, Mary had given birth to four children: Byrnece, Beulah, Braunda, and Beverly (born in 1918), all without the aid of a doctor. Macfadden swelled with pride at this abundance of offspring who carried on his initials. That BM was the common initialism for "bowel movement" did not embarrass him a whit, as regular occurrences of those too, as *Physical Culture* often reminded readers, indicated superior health and efficiency.

To those who looked closely, however, Macfadden was showing signs of wear. His celebrated physique, though still powerful, had started to take on a tauter, sinewy quality. His unruly mop of hair remained lush, but it was now gray. And when no one was paying attention, the author of *Strong Eyes,* who dismissed eyeglasses as "eye crutches," furtively donned spectacles to decipher small print. Of growing concern to Macfadden, there was also his lack of a male heir, which was especially troubling because Mary was getting tired of trying for a son.

There were also financial concerns with Macfadden's business, for the Physical Culture Publishing Company had become overextended. Perhaps unsurprisingly, the ability to do so many things at once while being many different things to different people—the very feature that helped sustain the company during the war—had exacted a toll in terms of coherence. As it switched between multiple editors and broadened its range of topics and target audience, *Physical Culture* had come to appear almost randomly strung together at times, an effect magnified by inconsistencies in the tone and quality of its articles. The lack of a clear overarching sense of purpose and direction, combined with its shifting concept of audience, limited its ability to attract more lucrative advertisers, which made it hard to keep the bills paid. It did not help matters when Macfadden decided to embark on another foray into the moviemaking business, which resulted in *Zongar* (1918), a five-reel feature film about the heroics of a high-society man turned adventurer-strongman. With a plot that was somehow even skimpier than the leopard-skin strongman costume donned by its titular character, *Zongar* was a bust at the theater. Mary, wondering if her husband was becoming unmoored from economic reality, started feeling like they were adrift on a "rudderless" journey.[63]

But then something very important happened that would change everything. Inspired by the constant flow of personal testimonies, letters, and detailed requests for advice that readers kept sending to *Physical Culture*, either Bernarr or Mary—the two would later contest this part, so perhaps it is best to just say Bernarr and Mary—were struck by inspiration. What if they took some of these submissions and made an entirely new magazine devoted to the telling of personal stories as written by actual readers? In other words, what if their publishing house *leaned in* to the unpredictable cacophony that had come to characterize its media and amplified it *even more*? Giddy with excitement about this idea but knowing they would need some cash to get it off the ground, the Macfaddens dressed up in their nicest outfits and headed to the bank to pitch a new magazine called *True Story*. Finally, the revolution Macfadden had forecasted back at the start of the war was about to arrive.

CHAPTER FIVE

The Sensational Rise of Macfadden Publications Inc.

T HE IDEA FOR *TRUE STORY* was exciting enough to attract a whopping million-dollar loan. With this infusion of cash, the Macfaddens got to work on their new magazine, which would publish stories written by regular people instead of only professional writers. After years of moving nomadically between furnished rentals, the family finally settled down in a house of their own. Mary, it was decided, could take time off from childbearing while her husband conducted research about how to ensure their next child would be a boy. For now, they would focus on birthing *True Story* and expanding the publishing company.

History provided a dramatic backdrop for these events. The year 1919 was tumultuous in many places around the world. The Great War was over, but many of its travails were not. A deadly influenza pandemic that had begun during the conflict continued spreading, infecting one-third of the planet's population and adding tens of millions of deaths to the forty million killed during the war. The complex peace negotiations unfolding in Paris, meanwhile, took place amid anti-imperial protests and revolutionary movements that erupted around the globe. Promising to spearhead a "new world order," Woodrow Wilson proposed a League of Nations to help manage international affairs, but Congress rejected his plan, leaving the League to operate without the United States.

At home, Americans were debating their country's future as protest movements and conflicts that had been simmering on the back burner during the war now boiled over. Following decades of activism, the passage of the Nineteenth Amendment, which Macfadden had supported, granted many women the right to vote. Yet African American citizens of both sexes continued to face disenfranchisement, segregation, and racial terrorism, which they fought through political movements and everyday acts of resistance, including migration. The end of wartime production led to concerns about jobs and the economy, resulting in massive labor strikes and government crackdowns on political activists. Union leaders, socialists, leftist revolutionaries, and conservative voices promoting capitalism and a "return to normalcy," as the Republican Warren Harding's campaign motto phrased it, would vie for attention in the coming months and years.[1]

Culturally, 1919 was characterized by widespread feelings of disillusionment and "lost innocence."[2] Dreams that such a costly war would at least lead to lasting structures of international cooperation, self-determination for colonized peoples, expanded civil rights, and the fulfillment of progressive goals died hard, as reflected in many works of art and literature from this period. Still, a tenor of optimism was discernible, as Americans had been spared much of the deprivation and damages that afflicted other countries. In fact, the United States emerged from the war in a position of unprecedented economic strength. Uncertainty remained, but a new world order of American prosperity and opportunity seemed possible. For instance, those who had been watching the mushrooming popularity of film in the last few years took note of the profits to be made in catering to the interests of non-elite audiences with disposable income at home and global markets abroad.[3]

This was the landscape in which *True Story* took shape, and Macfadden proved remarkably attuned to it. Non-elite and marginalized peoples were clamoring "from below" for fairer representation and greater public voice across myriad arenas. Women, laborers, city-dwellers, young adults, and Americans from immigrant backgrounds were wielding increasing power as citizens and consumers in the United States, casting influential "votes" in the marketplace as well as the ballot box.[4] And as mass consumption became a primary driver of national growth, "the masses," whoever that was, mattered in new ways—not just economically and politically but also culturally. These trends were reflected in *True Story*'s formula and in the distinctive editorial method that Macfadden developed for his company's new periodical. In addition to being a novel literary *product,* the magazine would be represented as an innovative and accessible *platform* through which those who were willing to narrate their own stories could shape the tenor and politics of modern mass culture.

True Story's debut would mark a decisive turning point for Macfadden's publishing house. Earlier in the century, the company had centered the anxieties and desires of middle-class consumers while fostering participatory modes of content creation and consumption that imbued its publications with international appeal. During the war, the Physical Culture Publishing Company had catered more prominently to a fragmented domestic readership, combining appeals to readers as individuals with appeals to the national body politic, whose ethnic diversity represented an unresolved source of tension. Now, the company set its sights on potential readers whose experiences and preferences tended to be ignored by other periodical publishers. Through *True Story* and other methods, it placed non-elites—especially young women and the urban working class, ethnically diverse groups containing many first- and second-generation immigrants—at the center of its business model. The result was a period of dizzying growth that would propel Macfadden and his publishing house to unimagined success during the 1920s.

Truth Is Stranger Than Fiction

To understand the impact of *True Story,* it is important to have a sense of the periodical landscape. Over the previous few decades, two trends had shaped the architecture of this landscape. On the one hand, there was a trend toward market segmentation, as publishers created specialized products for specific groups of readers that they defined in opposition to other readers. On the other hand, there was a rise in "general interest" periodicals that associated themselves with, and helped to construct, middlebrow taste and a national market. These seemingly countervailing developments worked together to determine what magazines were available to readers as well as which segments of the population did—and did not—participate in magazine consumption.

A prominent sector of the magazine publishing landscape consisted of specialist titles designed to inform and create conversation between educated readers. This category of magazine catered to men from elite or professional backgrounds who were interested in the writings and opinions of others like themselves and able to pay substantial yearly subscription fees. Some of the Physical Culture Publishing Company's readers would have subscribed to these kinds of periodicals, but probably not many. With his limited education and attention span, Macfadden was likely in the latter group, though this did not mean he did not see himself as the intellectual equal (or better) of those who consumed titles such as *New Republic* and the *North American Review.*

Next, and more numerous in number and audience, were the "general magazines." Since the "magazine revolution" of the 1890s, when the growing availability of advertising revenue allowed magazine publishers to slash subscription prices, a vibrant middlebrow periodical culture had flourished across the Anglophone World.[5] American titles like the *Saturday Evening Post* and the *Ladies' Home Journal* offered an agreeable mix of journalism, fiction and poetry, cultural commentary, and illustrations—all for the low price of five to fifteen cents. This combination of quality content and affordability was possible because these general magazines had grown symbiotically alongside a maturing advertising industry. Revenue from ads made it possible for them to employ professional writers and editors, maintain high production values, and develop interesting content tailored toward those with recognized cultural capital and purchasing power, including women homemakers.[6] Macfadden had modeled some aspects of his physical culture media on middlebrow magazines, and over the years, authors who usually wrote for these periodicals lent their pens to the Physical Culture Publishing Company, often out of personal interest in the reform causes it championed. But Macfadden's physical culture magazines had never been mainstream or attractive to national advertisers.

Alongside this tapestry of middlebrow print culture, the magazine revolution had also produced an undercurrent of alternative periodicals that identified themselves in opposition to mainstream consumer society and politics. During the 1910s, a fluorescence of new journals and "little magazines" self-consciously bucked bourgeois political, literary, and aesthetic norms. While these publications tended to circulate among cultural elites, some hailed racially and economically diverse readerships whose interests cohered around specific movements or causes—for instance, feminism, civil rights, or modern art.[7] The Physical Culture Publishing Company had been fertilized by these kinds of publications, sharing readers and writers attracted to unconventional ideas and radical political causes. But Macfadden craved greater commercial success.

In addition to highbrow periodicals, middlebrow general magazines, and alternative journals, a more explicitly commercial genre had emerged to cater to and profit from non-elite and working-class readers—the pulps.[8] Descended from dime novels and penny papers, pulp magazines appeared first around the turn of the century and then "divided, amoeba-like" across the United States.[9] Mass-produced as cheaply as possible, pulps were seven by ten inches in size and printed on acidic, low-grade paper stock with rough-cut edges. Their exaggerated cover illustrations promised excitement and pleasure, often within clearly delineated genres and subgenres aimed at juvenile consumers and working-class men. While pulps usually carried a few pages of ads for cheap products, they did not attract the kinds of advertising clients whose campaigns could subsidize higher production values. Having to keep production costs low while attracting readers at the newsstand in an increasingly crowded marketplace was a recipe for maximal sensationalism. Appalled by this sensationalism, educators and moralists regularly bemoaned that publications like *Snappy Stories, Saucy Stories* and *Western Story Magazine,* were flooding the market with reams of disposable fiction—some of it violent and sexually explicit—that cost less than a loaf of bread. It did not help that pulp publishers were frequently first- or second-generation Americans with ties to radical political movements or underground industries, including pornography and bootlegging.[10] Macfadden, of course, knew that many of his readers enjoyed pulp fiction, and *Physical Culture* had employed pulp writers. The most prolific of these was John R. Coryell, who created the immensely popular Nick Carter detective series and penned popular romance under the name Bertha M. Clay in addition to working for the Physical Culture Publishing Company. With *True Story,* the publisher wanted to keep costs low and attract a mass readership like the pulps did, but with his own Macfadden twist.

Within this increasingly crowded magazine landscape, consumers and advertisers could usually tell just by looking at a title which kind of publication it was. Legibility, particularly regarding the class and gender of the target reader, was a defining feature of periodical culture, central to the industry's publishing and marketing strategies. With *True Story,* however, Macfadden created a magazine that did not slot into any preconceived category or genre. The magazine's unusualness would be apparent from its inaugural issue, which hit newsstands in the spring of 1919. On its cover, a colorful yet clumsily rendered man and woman were pictured facing off in profile, accompanied by the headline: "And their love turned to hatred." This cover, with its scowling couple, set the magazine apart visually from that month's middlebrow fare. At the same time, the representational scene it depicted lacked the fantastical and exaggerated visual elements associated with pulps. It also failed to communicate clearly the gender of the intended reader: *love* might have suggested romance prose for women, yet the word *hate* immediately troubled this association. The incongruousness of this new magazine in terms of genre—was it journalism? literature?—was underscored by a brilliant catchphrase: "Truth is Stranger than Fiction."

In format, *True Story* looked most like a pulp at first, but after a few issues, Macfadden adopted an "in-between" format, using paper that was larger and smoother than pulpwood stock yet not as nice as the paper used by "class" magazines. Its price was also unconventional. First sold for twenty cents (and later, twenty-five), Macfadden's new title cost considerably more than not only pulps but also general magazines, even as it blatantly eschewed literary refinement and big-name writers. It was a magazine that looked cheap, but not that cheap, and was priced similarly to a movie ticket. Perhaps because of his experience with *Physical Culture,* which had drawn on various aspects of middlebrow, working-class, and specialist print cultures over the course of its own idiosyncratic trajectory, Macfadden felt unconstrained by industry norms.

Making *True Story* so distinct from previously delineated periodical formats and markets was a gamble. It meant that readers and potential advertisers would not immediately recognize for whom the magazine was designed. But this gamble paid off. Curious about the new publication, and why the couple's love turned to hatred, "[s]warms of people put their double dimes down on the newsstands" to get a copy of its first issue, which sold 60,000 copies. As Mary remembered with pride, *True Story,* though its advertising columns "were freakish," nevertheless "astounded the publishing world" with its strong debut.[11] After two decades in the publishing business, Macfadden finally had a hit on his hands.

The Macfadden Method Upends an Industry

In his 1921 inaugural address, President Warren Harding painted a sanguine portrait of Americans' economic future. As "[p]eoples are turning from destruction to production," he declared, the "forward course of the business cycle is unmistakable."[12] Hearing that the nation's new leader suffered from heart trouble, Macfadden sent him copies of *Physical Culture,* receiving back a note of appreciation and an assurance that the president was performing his recommended exercises. Then, just like Harding had promised, a period of dramatic expansion ensued that transformed Macfadden's publishing house. Riding a wave of success financed by the popularity of *True Story,* the publisher moved his company into a bigger space on West Fortieth Street. Here, Macfadden; his longtime business manager, Orr J. Elder; Mary; and *True Story*'s first editor, John Brennan (who had previously helmed *Physical Culture*) threw themselves into the new magazine, sourcing novel streams of content and developing an innovative editorial method and ethos of experimentation that would set the company apart from other publishers.

Doubling down on the formula of reader participation he had employed in earlier media, Macfadden dedicated most of the space in *True Story* to "confessions" authored by anonymous narrators. Starting with the first issue, the magazine directly solicited readers for articles and correspondence that dealt with the trials, tribulations, adventures, and romances of everyday people. "*True Story* is a magazine you may get something out of, not merely by *reading* but by *writing*," audiences were repeatedly informed. Arguing that *everyone* contained at least one "great story," the editor persistently wanted to know: "What's your story, and where is it?" To stimulate interest and compensate its writers outside the marketplace standards of wages or payment-per-word, *True Story* offered "prizes." Readers were enticed, even beseeched, to enter upcoming competitions that paid sizable sums for autobiographical tales of romance, adventure, business, and drama drawn from life. A typical contest in the early years of the decade, for instance, awarded $5,000, with the grand-prize winner getting a check for $1,000. "Never before did men and women who are not professional writers have such a glorious opportunity to turn their life experiences into handsome sums of money," the magazine professed.[13]

On top of encouraging readers to provide its main content steams, Macfadden's publishing house subverted traditional editorial methods as well. To create realistic features that would set *True Story* apart, the company developed what became known as the Macfadden Method, an editorial process that eschewed magazine professionals in favor of the insights of regular people whenever possible. Brennan was reportedly told that as editor of the magazine, he should "have nothing to do with the selection of the stories" because "any trained editor . . . would spoil [the] plan."[14] Instead, a special Reading Department was created to perform this task. This Reading Department, which was where Mary worked, was primarily composed of stenographers, employees' wives, and others without previous industry experience. It received and vetted all manuscripts sent to the company, passing forward only those its members found compelling and believably amateur. As Mary remembered, if the department suspected that a good story sounded too "high-brow," then her husband "asked the office elevator operator to read it."[15] This system enshrined a topsy-turvy atmosphere at the company's offices that attracted widespread fascination and disbelief within the industry. At one point, a parody "confession" would work its way around the company's office titled "How I Was Demoted to Editor of *True Story* and Worked My Way Up to Elevator Man Again."[16]

Macfadden, with the help of Brennan, developed a distinctive visual style for *True Story* as well. "If the pen is mightier than the sword," the publisher asked, "what of the camera?"[17] Adopting the rotogravure printing method used at the time primarily for weekend newspaper supplements, the company filled *True Story* with posed photographic tableaux featuring models enacting scenes from its stories.[18] Captioned by enticing snippets of dialog, such as "I saw two lovers billing and cooing . . . the sight almost maddened me," these illustrations, which looked like film stills, turned out to be "precisely the right thing needed to give an atmosphere of reality to the ordinarily lifeless printed page."[19] To make them, Macfadden built a photography studio, and within a few years, this studio was providing work for scores of amateur models and would-be actors every week, some of whom would go on to Hollywood.

Having established a winning formula for *True Story,* Macfadden aspired to create more illustrated magazines. To help him, in 1921 he hired a sharp twenty-eight-year-old Broadway trade journal editor, writer, and semiprofessional magician named Charles Fulton Oursler to serve as supervising editor of the company. This was the beginning of a long and fruitful relationship. In addition to possessing "an eye and a natural instinct for popular and salable magazine material," Fulton Oursler, as he was thereafter known, got along famously with his boss. Mary, who was less fond of this new associate, would describe him as her husband's Cardinal Richelieu, a reference to King Louis XIII's ambitious political adviser.[20] Constantly bouncing ideas off one another, the two men took an experimental, maximalist approach to creating new magazines. Whatever they thought sounded like a good idea, they would try and then see how the public responded. To reflect the company's widening mandate, the Physical Culture Publishing Company received a new name: Macfadden Publications.

A fast and furious flood of new publications ensued. In 1921, the company introduced *Movie Weekly,* its version of a motion picture fan magazine. A genre that had been growing in popularity since J. Stewart Blackton, a British immigrant to America and one of the leading producers and distributors of early motion pictures, founded *Motion Picture Story Magazine* in 1911, film fan magazines helped filmmakers promote their products, attract new talent, and manage public discourse about the movies.[21] Marketed as a reader- rather than industry-driven product, *Movie Weekly* presented a mix of interviews, articles, and correspondence columns. It also offered behind-the-scenes looks at the personal lives of movie stars and other aspects of Hollywood that were narrated from a first-person perspective. "*Movie Weekly* is the most intimate link between folk behind the screen and those they entertain and amuse—a magazine just made to order for the TRUE STORY reader," its ads proclaimed.[22]

A stranger magazine, *Brain Power,* appeared the same year. Promising inspirational advice about how to gain smarts and success, this monthly featured profiles of interesting businessmen, politicians, and other celebrities, from Henry Ford to Lillian Gish, as well as biographical narratives from regular people describing ways they had improved themselves mentally and financially. Perhaps because customers proved reticent to carry around a magazine whose title might imply they lacked intellectual strength,

Brain Power was renamed *National Pictorial Monthly*. Another improvement-themed publication that appeared at this time was *Beautiful Womanhood* (1922), which combined true and fictional stories with health and beauty advice aimed at female readers.

With *Midnight* (1922), Macfadden and Oursler created a ten-cent competitor to the horror and crime titles that were being put out by down-market pulp publishers. Combining fiction with confession, it titillated readers with offerings like "Baring the Truth of New York's Underworld," "Did the Parson Love the Naughtiest Girl," and "Do Women Make the Best Bootleggers?" Predictably, considering Macfadden's track record, *Midnight* was a magnet for the attention of the New York Society for the Suppression of Vice, which led to its folding. Correcting too far the other way, Macfadden also purchased *Metropolitan* (1923), a failing literary magazine formerly edited by Theodore Roosevelt that was known for printing political commentary and fiction from esteemed authors such as Theodore Dreiser. Despite Oursler's best efforts to turn the magazine around, no one was interested in Macfadden Publications' attempts at being literary.

Finding themselves unable to compete with New York's racier domain of fly-by-night pulp publishers or in the more rarefied domain of highbrow fiction, Macfadden and Oursler turned their focus to innovating within and around the true story genre. In this endeavor, they faced emerging competition, for *True Story*'s success incited a boom in confession magazines. The earliest competing titles came from pulp publishers, who were attracted to the confession style's promise of profit and the ease with which it could be replicated. *True Story*'s most formidable imitator was *True Confessions* (1922), published by Fawcett Publications, a company founded in 1919 by "Captain Billy" Fawcett, a former editor at the US Army's weekly *Stars and Stripes*. Another was the biweekly *I Confess*, which was the brainchild of George T. Delacorte, former president of the pulp magazine distributor Snappy Stories Sales Company. When Delacorte founded Dell Publications in 1922, *I Confess*, "A Magazine of Personal Experiences," was its very first title. While most pulp magazines tended to come and go, these true story pulps would remain strong sellers for many years.

No one capitalized on the promise of the confession genre as prolifically as Macfadden himself, however. In 1923, when *True Story*'s monthly circulation had already exceeded one million copies, his company released a love-centered spin-off called *True Romances*, whose first issue, to Oursler and Macfadden's great delight, sold out on newsstands. Its popularity spurred the creation of similar publications, including the fiction-heavy *Love and Romances* (1923) and *Dream World* (1924), which offered readers an escape into "soft, hazy dramas." While *True Story* hailed a mixed-sex audience at

Fig.5.1 Covers of various Macfadden-brand magazines, 1920–1930. Reproduced from the author's personal collection

the time, these titles were pitched specifically to female readers, especially young single women and "ladies of labor" rather than elite and middlebrow married homemakers.[23] This was also the case for *True Experiences* (1924), a sister publication to *True Story* focused on "the ups and downs of girls in business life" as narrated by working women themselves.

Adapting the first-person true story format in a different direction, Macfadden Publications created *True Detective Mysteries* in 1924. A magazine designed with men in mind, *True Detective Mysteries* was inspired by the long-standing popularity of crime and mystery dime novels as well as the newer detective and crime fiction pulps that had recently started appearing on newsstands. In 1920, the writers H. L. Mencken and George Jean Nathan had debuted the pulp *Black Mask*. Offering a grittier alternative to British mystery stories and a more literary style than newspaper reportage, this magazine helped set the tone for the hard-boiled genre of American detective and mystery fiction. *Black Mask* writers such as Dashiell Hammett, a former Pinkerton National Detective Agency operative, developed a captivating form of storytelling characterized by "direct style, minimum of unessential detail, and maximum of action."[24] Taking cues from *Black Mask*, Macfadden's *True Detective Mysteries* started off publishing fictionalized crime stories based on real events. Soon after, it incorporated the true story format that distinguished its other publications by focusing on first-person accounts of contemporary and historic true crime investigations as well as criminal confessions. For instance, one of the earliest issues of *True Detective Mysteries* featured "Who Killed Bob Teal," a Hammett story that had previously been rejected by *Black Mask*. Rather than presenting the story as fiction, as Hammett had originally done, Macfadden's magazine framed "Who Killed Bob Teal" as an event that had really occurred during author's days as a private investigator.[25] In this way, *True Detective Mysteries* (later known as *True Detective*) inaugurated the true crime magazine genre, which would remain a specialty of Macfadden Publications for decades.

While these magazines were appearing, *Physical Culture,* which remained Macfadden's personal pride and joy, became increasingly confessional in tone. For instance, an article that before the war would have been titled "How to Keep Fit" was now likely to explain "How I Keep Fit"; "How to Make Your Marriage Happy" became "How I Made My Marriage Happy."[26] Editorials encouraged readers to understand that fitness and confession magazines were, deep down, cut from the same cloth. As editor Macfadden explained this linkage, "*Physical Culture* started the fight for the truth as it appertains to the physical man and woman. . . . As we expanded the field of activity, we found that the truth was a factor of tremendous value in every phase of life and literature."[27] In just this one issue of *Physical Culture,* articles that approached physical culture themes through the confessional, first-person dynamic associated with the company's true story magazines included "The Romance of an Old Maid," "The Baby They Said I Couldn't Have," and "Revelations of a Doctor." Subsequently, the periodical that had started out blaring "Weakness is a Crime—Don't Be a Criminal" would change its catchphrase to "The Personal Problem Magazine."

Other health and fitness media remained an integral part of Macfadden Publications as well. Alongside *Physical Culture,* the company published *Muscle Builder* (1923), a fifteen-cent magazine devoted to male body-building. The early 1920s also saw the release of several new books by Macfadden, including *Making Old Bodies Young* (1919), *Truth About Tobacco* (1921), *The Miracle of Milk* (1923), *Fasting for Health* (1923), *Constipation: Its Cause, Effects, and Treatment* (1924), and *How to Raise a Strong Baby* (1924). Meanwhile, at the company's headquarters, employees worked stacked in double-decker cubicles to free up space for a gymnasium, where daily calisthenic drills were held for those who lacked the foresight to duck out to the fire escape for a cigarette. The physique models and fitness buffs who paraded periodically through the office provided additional affirmation that this was no run-of-the-mill publishing operation. On the most exciting days, these visiting fitness buffs were movie stars, as the growing importance of exercise and fitness among body-conscious actors and actresses made for a natural bridge between Macfadden Publications and Hollywood.[28] Macfadden struck up an especially productive relationship with the handsome Italian immigrant and Hollywood actor Rudy Valentino. "The Sheik," as he became known after his most famous movie role, appeared as the author of the amply illustrated *How You Can Keep Fit,* released by Macfadden Publications in 1923.

As Macfadden Publications was growing, so was the Physical Culture Family. After helping to launch *True Story,* Mary returned to the task of childbearing with the mission of producing a male heir. This time, the couple decided to synchronize conception with a specific point in the menstrual cycle, a detail Mary was embarrassed to learn her husband shared with his readers. Mary got pregnant quickly, and in late 1921, when she gave birth to another thirteen-pounder, it was a boy. Now, not only did Macfadden finally have a son, named Byron, but he had also, he was convinced, unlocked the secret to sex determination. Mary's happiness with having a son was shadowed, again, by her husband's refusal to allow the administration of any anesthetic at her home birth, even when she needed fifteen stitches. She had still not fully recovered from this trauma eleven months later when Byron got sick and then died suddenly, just a few weeks shy of his first birthday. Protecting his own reputation, Macfadden publicly attributed Byron's demise to overfeeding and excessive "mother love," an emotion, he explained in *Physical Culture*, with "little intelligence associated with it."[29] This betrayal, published for all to see, stunned Mary, who privately blamed her husband's rigid physical culture dogma and eschewal of medical attention for their loss.

Following Byron's death, Macfadden was in a hurry to try again for another son. Mary conceived quickly, but then experienced a devastating

Fig.5.2 The Physical Culture Family on the cover of *Physical Culture* in the magazine's twenty-fifth year. Reproduced from the author's personal collection

second-trimester miscarriage. Another pregnancy ensued, and nine months later, she gave birth to a large male baby named Berwyn. Now doubly convinced he had cracked the code to having boys, Macfadden was overjoyed.[30] His wife, however, was less enthused. Since Byron's death Mary had been struggling with an overwhelming sense of despondency. Constantly exhausted from work, exercise, and childbearing, she felt increasingly cowed by her husband's thirst for celebrity and unrelenting pursuit of growth at home and at work. When he began angling for yet another son, to help "even out" all the girls, she even began experiencing suicidal feelings. Ultimately, however, Mary's pain remained invisible to outsiders. Seeing his wife and children as extensions of himself, Macfadden carefully orchestrated their public image to project an aura of confidence, control, and boundless energy that reflected well on his capabilities not only as a physical cultural patriarch but also the head of America's fastest-growing publishing house.

Truth and Modernity at the Margins of Culture

In 1924, Macfadden Publications was incorporated in the state of New York. The primary shareholders after this restructuring were Macfadden; his business manager, Elder; and a New York businessman named H. H. Miller. Although it had only been five years since the birth of *True Story*, the company was now valued at $10 million.[31]

Macfadden Publications' transformation from a niche health and fitness company into a publishing powerhouse was made possible by its success among Americans who had not previously been regular magazine readers. Macfadden "takes his readers away from no other publisher" but instead "creates a reading public," was how one journalist would later explain it.[32] Yet in reality, Macfadden Publications' new reading public was more like a patchwork of reading publics, made up of those whose economic and social statuses had previously circumscribed their access to consumer power and cultural influence. This included poor and working-class men and women, first- and second-generation immigrants, new migrants to cities, and young adults.

The true story genre, and its attendant device of confession, played a pivotal role in assembling this patchwork and holding it together. From the start, Macfadden's use of truth rhetoric and confessional formats drew on tropes associated with "poor people's personal narratives" that had long facilitated a "subtle play of power at the margins" of American literary culture.[33] Autobiographical narratives of lived experience recounted by nonelites and social outcasts, including slave narratives; sinners' confessions;

and tales of exile, crime, and imprisonment, provided important literary precedents to the true story magazine.[34] Macfadden's publications innovated in the space such literature had carved out for the "unvarnished truth" in popular print culture, but rakishly flipped the hierarchical dynamics that usually typified confessional discourse.[35] Blurring the distinctions between consumers, editors, readers, and writers, *True Story* encouraged audiences to identify with and through its narrators, and to aspire to become them. When the magazine noted that its "life stories touch, in many instances, on topics that are ordinarily avoided in the printed page," it was not necessarily promising the unusual or scandalous; rather, it was implying that the topics covered would resonate with non-elite readers because they had been written from the perspectives of their peers, whose experiences and voices did not typically appear in periodicals.

But did readers really write Macfadden Publications' true stories? Naturally, this question inspired endless debate, largely among those outside the company's readership. According to numerous accounts, the narratives published in its true story magazines originated from a variety of sources. The copious advice that began appearing right away in writers' trade journals on how to sell true stories indicates the extensive participation of self-identified career writers. At least a few newspaper reporters adapted encounters from their beats into convincing testimonies, while others optioned the life stories of noteworthy figures to create confessional as-told-to biographies. Some of the employees with backgrounds in writing at Macfadden Publications admitted to having submitted stories to the company before coming to work there, including Fulton Oursler.

Nevertheless, Macfadden remained insistent that most of his content came from everyday readers who described true events from their own lives, motivated by the company's assurances that "literary excellence will not be a factor" in the judging of their work.[36] Later, he would even have contributors sign affidavits promising that their words were not fraudulent or plagiarized, and that all names had been changed. Meant to protect the company against libel suits, this requirement provided another layer of authenticity to the confession format. An editor who worked for Macfadden Publications in the 1920s, before becoming a competing magazine publisher himself, later confirmed some of Macfadden's claims about *True Story*, explaining: "The readers, contrary to sophisticated opinion, *do* write the stories, the short ones being homespun manuscripts carefully guarded from professional mishandling . . . The serials are written by experts who elaborate the amateur material into needed lengths."[37] One journalist's conversation with a chambermaid at the Gramercy Park Hotel returned similar information: "Oh I wrote up . . . several of my experiences for a true-story magazine. They sent me twenty-five dollars . . . And now all the other girls at the hotel are writing up theirs," the maid reported.[38]

There is no way to determine who wrote specific confessions or how much was factual in Macfadden Publications' magazines. What is evident, however, is that all the company's publications were easy to read. They were written in vernacular English dominated by common words and even popular slang. Sentences were short and mostly limited to the simple present and past tenses. Dialog was abundant yet easy to follow, with the speaker's tone or meaning always explicated in the text. *True Story*'s solicitations implored, "Don't try to be literary!" Such advice, along with the company's editorial "polishing" (or roughing up, as needed), helped to ensure that its products were approachable for consumers who lacked education, English fluency, previous periodical reading habits, or experience writing prose.

Furthermore, the company's methods of content sourcing and its unusual editorial processes resulted in periodicals that routinely positioned as normative certain experiences and subjectivities associated with nonelites, which made the growing media empire attractive to audiences that had not previously been regular magazine consumers. In terms of topical content, for instance, early issues of Macfadden's confession periodicals centered themes such as migration and urbanization, changes in women's roles, and tensions in modern relationships between the sexes and between generations. While these were common cultural preoccupations in this era, Macfadden's confession media was atypically likely to present them from what might now be called the underdog's perspective. This can be seen in its portrayals of modern girls and new immigrants, as well as in its treatments of the intersecting topics of urbanization, modernity, and social mobility.

Perhaps no figure was more iconic in and of the early 1920s than the "modern girl." A national and global phenomenon, modern girls were young women who flocked to cities; pursued wage-earning jobs outside the home; wore makeup and bobbed their hair; and went out dancing, drinking, smoking, dating, and driving.[39] Media coverage of these women, especially so-called flappers, was obsessive in the early to mid-1920s, reflecting anxieties about the patterns of cultural, political, economic, and social change they presented.[40] Macfadden Publications was part of this trend; images of and discussions about modern girls had appeared earlier in Macfadden's physical culture media, and the company's coverage of independent young women only accelerated in the 1920s. In contrast to other outlets, however, its various true story periodicals prioritized depicting the modern girl from her own perspective. As the editors of *True Experiences* expressed, in all capital letters, "IF YOU ARE A MODERN GIRL, WE WANT YOUR STORY!"

By soliciting narratives directly from "the American girl who earns her own living, who is carving out her own destiny," Macfadden's magazines purported to give voice to people who had customarily exerted limited control over the printed representations of their lives. This point is poignantly illustrated by the early *True Story* feature "The Chorus Girl Speaks." Introducing herself, the narrator proclaims, "I am a chorus girl. I am eighteen years old and have been raised in the theater; and my inborn love of it and respect for myself will not let the people outside the theater believe that it is as black as it is painted." While "[c]horus girls are usually referred to as coarse, immoral creatures," this assumption is objectionable. "That may be true of some, just as in any other walk of life, but it is surely not true of all," she declares, adding that she herself "has found more real friends, more human kindness and big-heartedness among [chorus girls] than among any other group of people."[41]

Another story that exemplifies Macfadden Publications' portrayal of the modern girl can be found in a novella serialized in one of the first issues of *Beautiful Womanhood*. "Salome of the Tenements" (1922–1923) tells the story of Sonia Vrunsky, an ambitious "ghetto princess" from the Lower East Side who marries a wealthy Anglo-American philanthropist. This marriage, however, ends up being an obstacle to, rather than the culmination of, Sonia's personal progress. When the relationship between Sonia and her elite husband dissolves, the heroine responds by learning dressmaking skills that allow her to support herself. After becoming a talented and successful fashion designer, she falls in love with a tailor who has also worked his way up in the world. The couple marry and open their own successful Lower East Side boutique catering to the neighborhood's fashionable factory girls.[42]

"Salome" was a novella with an identifiable author rather than an anonymous article-length true story, yet the identity of its writer and the contours of its serialized narrative made it seem like a true story written by a modern girl. As literary critics have noted, its plot was based on the well-known story of Rose Pastor Stokes, a Russian-Jewish immigrant, seamstress, radical socialist activist, and writer who had shocked New York when she married the millionaire J. G. Phelps Stokes in 1905. The story also had much in common with the life of its author, Anzia Yezierska, who had become a minor literary celebrity by the time "Salome" was published.[43] Herself a Jewish immigrant from what is now Poland, Yezierska grew up in the Lower East Side of Manhattan, where she worked in a sweatshop and a laundry before becoming a widely acclaimed professional writer who specialized in

stories about American immigrants and their families. Like the protagonist of her novella, she too got involved in an agonizing romantic relationship with an elite man, the philosopher and Columbia University professor
John Dewey.[44] Using experiences drawn from her own life, which itself
could have been the subject of a Macfadden-brand true story, Yezierska
gave voice to the "misread, the marginalized, [those] who are attempting
to work out a relationship between their birth cultures and mainstream
America," making her a perfect narrator for Macfadden Publications as it
reached out to modern girls, who were themselves often first- or second-
generation Americans.[45]

People who have come to America from somewhere else, usually Europe, appear often in the company's early 1920s periodicals. "Out of the
Melting Pot" (1921), for example, traces the life of Sam, a Jewish immigrant. When Sam arrives, he ensures unfriendly officials at Ellis Island that
he will not allow any member of his family to become a public charge. To
fulfill this promise, he begins by learning English and soon starts a business selling cheap jewelry to factory girls. With his earnings he opens up a
corner newsstand—the kind of newsstand, one imagines, where Macfadden Publications would eventually place its products. This job brings
him into contact with the president of the local bank, who is impressed by
his abilities and offers him a messenger position. "Today," the story concludes, "Sam occupies the president's chair in the bank he first served as
messenger . . . He is a prominent figure in banking circles, his wife a welcome guest in the most exclusive homes. His sister is married to a successful doctor, his brother is a lawyer whose name is known throughout
the state. He has three stalwart sons, of whom he is very proud, and with
good reason."[46] Although Sam's narrative appears hackneyed today (and
was indeed already shopworn in 1921), it neatly illustrates how immigrants and immigration were often portrayed in Macfadden's magazines.
Rather than something to be debated, as was certainly the case in American political culture at the time, immigration to the United States appears
in many true stories as a normal thing that many people did over the
course of their lives—a personal experience, and one typically characterized by initial hardship followed by integration and mobility.

Tales of travel and migration by women and men away from their families to big cities were another set of experiences commonly narrated in the
company's true story media. Urbanization had long raised anxieties about
the city's corrupting influence on politics and traditional social mores, but
Macfadden's narrators often experienced the move to the city as a nonne-
gotiable economic imperative characterized by opportunity and pleasure
as well as peril. With people streaming in all the time—as of the 1920 census,

America was more urban than rural—new things were always happening in cities, and cities were where the future seemed to first take shape. In addition to depicting them as places of work for both men and women, including many recent arrivals from other countries and other parts of the nation, Macfadden's periodicals portrayed cities as the crucible of American modernity, and their occupants as superlatively modern citizens.

In Macfadden's publications, the modern was not an abstract aesthetic or intellectual concept; instead, it was the here and now, the arena in which everyday people navigated dramatic social and economic transformations with an eye toward the future and no time for nostalgia. New information, skills, and a capacity for change and self-transformation were required to succeed in modern life, especially to thrive within complex urban landscapes and the new modes of living and working they engendered. Macfadden Publications' media offered all these things, doing so in a way that valorized the collective wisdom of the people whose stories appeared in its pages: especially modern girls, newcomers to America, urban denizens of the laboring classes, and others who had achieved mobility or personal growth, which was indexed not necessarily by money or status but by the capacity to successfully tell one's story in a distinctively modern way.

This dynamic is illustrated in the *True Story* feature "Suzanne of the Studios: Her Own Story of Her Glimpse Behind the Silver Screen." Before becoming the sophisticated and successful "Suzanne," the narrator is just "Susie," a secretary working in a mill town. Her employer's son charms her away from her stalwart hometown fiancé with promises of taking her to the city and helping her become a movie actress. Once in New York, however, it becomes clear that the employer's son expects sexual favors. Horrified, Susie refuses. Left alone in the city, too embarrassed to return home and still ignorant about how to find a career in the movies, she turns to magazines for help: "I didn't have any idea of how to set about making my first effort, but luckily that came to me in the middle of the first awful night, when I waked up in the clutch of a panic of terror. I don't know how it came, but it did—I must go out in the morning and buy all the magazines I could find that were devoted to moving pictures. In one of them I was sure I would find something to guide me."[47] After making herself "look as pretty as [she] knew how," Susie goes out to an audition, only to be sexually harassed by the casting agent. Luckily, a kindly woman gives her the address of a reputable studio looking for models, where she gains a foothold in the industry and a contract for work in Los Angeles. On the West Coast, however, she faces constant harassment from her director, who eventually kidnaps the actress on set, presumably to rape her.

At this point, her former fiancé, who has entered the movie business to find her, intervenes. By the end of the story, Suzanne is married with a child and has become a fabulously successful Hollywood screenwriter whose breakthrough story was based on her own tumultuous journey from mill-town Susie to "Suzanne of the Studios."

When *True Story* and its sister publications covered the perils of the city, they often discussed urban sophisticates or employers, usually men, who exploited common people, often vulnerable younger women seeking work and romance. Modern mass media, such as films and the movie magazines consulted by Susie, presented visions of what success might look like, but it was the first-person confessional form that allowed for the transmission of experiential information about quotidian perils such as duplicitous men, exploitative contracts, and sexual harassment from employers that one might encounter along the way.[48] By centering the experiences of regular people, and providing conduits for the flow of information and advice between them, Macfadden Publications represented individuals whose perspectives would be marginalized in other media as sources of valuable knowledge and models for living successful modern lives.

Furthermore, continuing a tradition long established in his physical culture publications, Macfadden's true stories contrasted the natural morality of humble narrators with the immorality, foolishness, and unfounded prejudices of elders or alleged social betters. Comparing Suzanne's tale with another from the same year illustrates this point. In "Under Sentence of Marriage" (1920), the narrator goes on a date with a duplicitous man who takes her to the city, where they stay overnight. When the woman finds herself pregnant, she is pressured by the social norms of her town to marry the man, despite her own strong misgivings about his character. At the end of the tale, she explains, "I am a respectable woman, wife of a respectable man. I have four children. We live in a comfortable home, on the middle-line between poverty and riches which is supposed to be so happy and wholesome a state. My neighbors accept me as their equal. No one reproaches me. Yet," she concludes, "I think I am the most miserable sinner alive. . . . How did it all come about? It was all for the sake of respectability."[49] In this and many other true stories, social approval and the outward trappings of middle-class respectability, along with small town environs mired in tradition, are depicted as stifling and even backward. Meanwhile, individuals who follow their own moral compass, even if they initially face obstacles or rejection, find paths forward toward fulfilling futures.

Analyzing dominant tropes, themes, and motifs in Macfadden Publications' early 1920s true story media suggests the institutionalization of an influential feedback loop of sorts that powered the company's connection to non-elite audiences. Through constantly eliciting contributions from readers, and instituting the Macfadden Method of editorial selection, the publishing house opened windows onto popular interests and tastes during an era of accelerating social and cultural change. In response, its periodicals tended to highlight topics, experiences, and subjectivities normally rendered invisible or marginal by cultural gatekeepers, which enticed those whose access to self-representation was circumscribed in other arenas of media and culture to participate in Macfadden's media empire. As Macfadden Publications reached marginalized reading publics, which it was always encouraging to become writing publics, the publishing house developed a few core themes that connected its proliferating array of media products and helped define its emerging brand identity. These included the dignity of working-class individuals, especially working women, and the normativity of experiences associated with working-class lives, such as migration, urbanization, intergenerational tensions, and run-ins with prejudice and exploitation. A corollary to these themes expressed in the company's true stories, and one that resonated with its physical culture offerings, was the message that consuming and contributing to the right mass media could help regular people navigate the challenges of contemporary life while actualizing their most authentic, successful, and empowered modern selves.

Cross-Media Experimentation and "The Largest News Stand Sale in the World"

Amid the mounting popularity of its true story periodicals, Macfadden Publications continued to release new products, cultivating dense intertextual linkages between its circulations and the wider realm of mass-mediated popular entertainment that flourished at the time. This was another way that the company distinguished itself. Instead of attempting to stave off incursions of competing media forms and genres, as some other purveyors of print culture were doing, Macfadden's company took the opposite approach, aligning its print culture with popular activities such as listening to the radio, dancing, and going to the movies. It also branched out into the tabloid newspaper business. Through these endeavors, which overlapped and coincided with its continued production of confession, physical culture, and other experimental magazines, Macfadden Publications solidified its reputation as an innovative, cross-platform media empire.[50]

Macfadden's interest in radio was enthusiastic and prescient. Although not a new technology, radio did not become a mass medium until the advent of commercial radio broadcasting after the First World War. As radio sets dropped in price and commercial broadcasting took off in the early 1920s, Macfadden staked out a place for himself, hosting a calisthenic program out of Newark, New Jersey, in 1923. The publisher was often joined on air by five of his daughters, whom he had formed into a hard-practicing sibling dance troupe called the Macfaddenettes. Quickly thereafter, Macfadden Publications created the magazine *Radio Stories* (1924). With articles like "How Radio Will Soon Save the World," "Revelations of an Announcer," and "Love and Romance of Radio Stars," this magazine illustrates the company's early premonition of the important role that radio would play in Americans' lives during the interwar era. Later in the decade, Macfadden Publications debuted the hour-long *True Story Hour* on CBS, which dramatized stories from its most popular periodical. Other "radio magazines" it would create include the thirty-minute prime-time dramas *True Romances* and *True Detective Mysteries*.

In addition to serving as "one of radio's overlooked innovators," Macfadden linked his publishing company to new trends in dance.[51] As the decade of the 1920s was earning its "jazz age" moniker, dance trends swept the nation and the world, from the Tango, the Charleston, and the Fox Trot to

Fig.5.3 An announcement for Macfadden Publications' new magazine, *Radio Stories*. Reproduced from the author's personal collection

the Black Bottom, the Samba, and many others. Young people, especially, showed an insatiable passion for this pastime, which they pursued in night-clubs, school gymnasiums, living room parlors, and anywhere else they could find space to congregate. Meanwhile, a modern dance movement, with some linkages to physical culture, was growing in the United States, propelling practitioners such as Isadora Duncan to celebrity status. Responding to the popularity of dance, Macfadden Publications created *Dance Lovers Maga-zine* (later retitled *The Dance*). Employing the talents of the bohemian writer Vera Caspary, this periodical featured educational articles on dance history, concert reviews, dancer biographies, and, to Caspary's continual dismay, the company's signature confessional melodrama and coverage of the Macfad-denettes.[52] Also on the staff was Byrne Macfadden, the publisher's estranged daughter from his second marriage, who came from Canada to New York to work for her father's company until her untimely death from illness in 1926.[53] Helen Macfadden, now a young woman studying dance and gym-nastics, modeled for the magazine and appeared on its cover.

On top of his forays into the worlds of radio and dance, Macfadden showed an enduring interest in connecting Macfadden Publications to the film industry. To bring melodramatic confessions to the big screen, the production company True Story Pictures was launched. Its first feature was *The Wrongdoers* (1925), starring the stage and screen actor Lionel Barrymore, who was simultaneously featured in articles in several of the company's periodicals, including *Physical Culture*. The next year, the com-pany released eight more *True Story*–branded films, including *Broken Homes, Men Women Love, The Virgin Wife, Things Wives Tell,* and *Wives at Auction*. For a few years, those who read and wrote true stories had the chance to see their literary works become major motion pictures.[54]

Beginning in 1924, Macfadden Publications also embarked on what would become a legendary foray into the newspaper business. The idea of running a newspaper had been on Macfadden's mind for a while. Under the guidance of famous newspapermen like Pulitzer and Hearst, the pop-ular press had long combined entertainment with new modes of reportage, amassing enormous urban audiences. Now, Macfadden envisioned cre-ating an illustrated newspaper dedicated to human interest reporting whose articles would be narrated whenever possible in the first-person style common in the publisher's magazines. No concessions whatsoever would be made to middlebrow tastes or snobby notions of journalistic objectivity, which Macfadden called "out of date policies of aloofness and superiority."[55]

To edit this new publication, Macfadden chose an investigative reporter named Emile Gauvreau. A French Canadian–American high school dropout who read *Physical Culture* as a boy, Gauvreau had recently been the managing editor of the *Hartford Courant,* a job he lost after publishing an exposé on medical school diploma mills that angered local politicians with skin in the game. When he showed up in New York in 1924, the unemployed editor was hoping to secure a position with the *New York Times*; instead, he impulsively inquired at Macfadden Publications when he saw its headquarters near his hotel. Macfadden hired him on the spot, and the two men got to work on what would become one of the strangest newspapers in history: the *New York Evening Graphic.*[56]

Advertised as the most revolutionary printed page since Gutenberg, the *Graphic* was a tabloid-style newspaper, conveniently sized for porting around town. Headlined with the motto "Nothing but the Truth," it featured a mix of illustrated human interest and news stories with an emphasis on sex, celebrities, crime, and physical culture. And for added oomph, every issue was published on eye-catching pink paper. In a city accustomed to newspaper sensationalism, Macfadden and Gauvreau's product still managed to shock.[57] In addition to updating readers on its publisher's various health crusades, the *Graphic* provided breathless coverage of murderous love triangles, high-profile kidnapping cases, suicides, and sex scandals of all kinds. For instance, one wildly successful series reported on the marriage between the sixteen-year-old actress Peaches Heenan and Edward "Daddy" Browning, a fifty-one-year-old New York real estate mogul. When the tabloid published the underage bride's "honeymoon diary," the issue sold over half a million copies; it only added to the paper's publicity when, as a result, Macfadden was arrested and charged with obscenity by the Society for the Suppression of Vice. The *Graphic* was not in circulation long before critics began calling it the "New York Evening Porno-Graphic."[58]

To compete with other new tabloids, including the illustrated *Daily News* and Hearst's *Daily Mirror,* the *Graphic* constantly pushed the envelope, attracting a string of costly libel suits along the way. The newspaper's most distinctive and talked-about feature was its "composographs," doctored composite photographs that allowed the paper to print images of events that had not been photographed (or had not even happened). This involved creating studio portraits depicting recent news stories and then superimposing images of the real subjects' heads onto the studio models' bodies. The first composograph illustrated the divorce trial between the prominent American socialite Leonard "Kip" Rhinelander and Alice Jones, a biracial woman who had worked for his family. The proceedings, initiated by Rhinelander after he was threatened with disinheritance, hinged on whether the couple had had sex and therefore whether the groom knew his wife's racial identity when they married. During the trial, Jones exhibited parts of her upper torso and legs to the jury to prove that her husband had known that she was not white. No photographs were allowed in the courtroom, so the *Graphic*'s art editor created a composograph depicting a topless woman being ogled in court to accompany its coverage. The result was, according to one trade journal, "the most shocking news picture ever published in New York journalism."[59] Another famous *Graphic* composograph appeared after Rudy Valentino's tragic 1926 death from appendicitis. The star, who had been friendly with Macfadden and deeply beloved by his readers, was shown being welcomed to heaven by the popular Italian tenor Enrico Caruso.[60]

In keeping with the emphasis on promoting audience interaction, the *Graphic* held frequent contests. Easy crossword puzzles appeared in every issue, tempting those who solved them with large cash prizes, with one $25,000 contest leading to near-riot conditions at Madison Square Garden when thousands turned out for the announcement of winners. Of course, *Graphic* readers were also invited to share their ideas for stories, and the phone rang at all hours with tips and suggestions. One especially juicy call came from a woman who claimed that her daughter had been fathered by William Harding. While other editors refused this story, Gauvreau—struck by the daughter's resemblance to the former US president—printed the scandalous tale under giant headlines.

The *Graphic*, clearly, showed a real knack for satiating the public's growing thirst for celebrity news and gossip. Driving the paper's achievements in this area were the talents of a young entertainment journalist named Walter Winchell, who began working for the *Graphic* in 1924. In his column "Your Broadway and Mine," Winchell chatted about the personal lives of actors and other prominent society figures, using tongue-in-cheek innuendo and what Gauvreau called "slanguage" to amuse readers while deflecting libel suits. Winchell, of course, would go on to become America's most powerful gossip columnist.[61] Another soon-famous figure who got his start at the *Graphic* was Ed Sullivan, who penned the features "Ed Sullivan's Sports Whirl" and "Ed Sullivan Sees Broadway."[62] Such talent helped make Macfadden's tabloid the talk of the New York newspaper world in the 1920s, when "hot news became the wild, blazing, delirious symptom of the time."[63]

Yet perhaps the most sensational thing of all about the *Graphic* was how much the paper hemorrhaged money. The most lurid issues achieved huge sales, but novelty and notoriety were never enough to secure a base of readers and advertisers large enough to cover mounting operating costs, which included not only legal fees, libel settlements, and contest payouts, but also an ever-ballooning payroll as other publishers competed for its most talented personnel. Losing staff to Hearst especially incensed Macfadden, who retaliated by printing gossip about the rival publisher's mistress, but he mostly seemed nonplussed about the paper's finances. For him, the *Graphic* was an interesting experiment and yet another useful platform for communicating with the public, one that also contributed to his growing celebrity as a media mogul. Indeed, Mary sometimes suspected that the paper's spectacular insolvency, which would mount for eight years, was a point of pride for her husband, who had always deemed notoriety to be worth investing in.

In any case, while the *Graphic* was churning out all the news unfit to print, Macfadden was making money hand over fist in the magazine business. At the Macfadden Building, the company's six-story office building located on Broadway and 64th Street, the company maintained its signature approach to producing content by developing new periodicals and seeing if they caught on. As usual, some concepts were more successful than others, but the way Macfadden and Oursler saw things, every release provided the company with valuable information about its readers and their preferences. In terms of confessional content, the midpoint of the decade saw the debut of *True Lovers, True Proposals,* and *Modern Marriage Problems,* the latter of which was meant to appeal to maturing readers who had entered a new stage in their lives. *True Detective Mysteries,* an increasingly strong seller, was joined by *Midnight Mystery Stories* in 1925 as well, with *Master Detective* (1929) following a few years later. *Ghost Stories* (1926), which provided illustrated tales of supposedly true occult encounters, fed into the era's broader fascination with spiritualism and the paranormal. From another direction, *Your Car* (1925), "A Magazine of Romance, Fact, and Fiction," acknowledged the rising importance of the automobile in American life, but this title only lasted five months, perhaps because most of Macfadden's readers did not yet have cars. *Own Your Own Home* (1925) featured articles and stories related to home economics, house and garden maintenance, building, and cooking. In response to public interest in aviation, which Macfadden shared, the company created *Air Stories* (1927), which would later be joined by *Flying Stories* (1928) and then *Model Airplane News* (1929).

Meanwhile, *True Story* continued growing at an astounding rate. In 1925, the magazine's national circulation topped 1.5 million. The next year, Brennan was succeeded by William Jourdan Rapp, who would remain editor of *True Story* for the next sixteen years. The son of a Jewish cigar maker, Rapp was a freelance journalist and playwright who possessed a flair for collaboration and a keen sense of how to tell a good story.[64] Under his leadership, *True Story*'s circulation passed the two million mark in

1927. This meant that Macfadden Publications' signature confession magazine was now vying with the veritable *Ladies' Home Journal* and *McCall's* for the title of most popular periodical in America. Indeed, these circulation figures were especially impressive, the company constantly reminded the public, because its magazines were not mailed to passive subscribers; instead, they were purchased every month at a relatively dear price by enthusiastic consumers who were likely to share their purchase with family, friends, and coworkers. Emphasizing this point, the publishing house had a huge billboard constructed on the roof of its headquarters to mark a milestone that would also become the new company motto. Macfadden Publications, the sign boasted, had achieved "THE LARGEST NEWS STAND SALE IN THE WORLD."

The Only Magazine They Read

The meteoric rise of Macfadden Publications Inc. sparked extensive debate and controversy. True, Macfadden's personal obsession with the human body and iconoclastic health creed had long attracted criticism, but the rise of his postwar media empire elicited unprecedented vitriol. As it started "gaining and holding circulations that are an eighth wonder in the publishing world," a broad range of intellectuals, journalists, literary critics, cultural commentators, educators, and other publishers lambasted its success.[65]

At the head of the crowded pack of detractors was *Time* magazine, America's first newsweekly, which was headed by Henry Luce. Born in 1898 to missionaries in China, Luce was a young and ambitious Yale graduate when he cofounded Time Inc. in New York in 1923. Dedicated to telling "the news through people," Luce's magazine covered Macfadden Publications and its founder with a persistence bordering on obsession. Derisively referring to Macfadden as "Body Love," *Time* criticized the simplistic prose of his publications while painting his company's customer base as a "little educated, barely literate mass" of "[g]um-chewers, shop girls, taxi drivers, street sheiks, bummers, [and] idlers."[66] Through such characterizations, *Time* depicted the competing publishing house as the domain of American society's undesirables, associating it especially with unskilled laborers and the heterosocial, multiethnic youth culture that flourished in heavily immigrant urban neighborhoods. Here and in other outlets, Macfadden Publications' readers were portrayed through recurring tropes of idiocy, degeneracy, irrationality, and animality. Commenting on the "Bare Torso King's" "stable" of "shoddy sex magazines," the *Detroit Saturday Night* averred,

"There may be worse magazines in the world . . . but if there are, intelligent people would rather be burned at the stake than be forced to read them."[67] Discussing Macfadden's "lower-class periodicals," the *English Journal* breezily conflated a descriptor of socioeconomic status with a negative judgment about its readers' moral or evolutionary worth.[68] "Primitive human nature likes to indulge itself in confidences," this author declared, fretting in the same breath over the influence of Macfadden's confession magazines on the "foreign-born who have just learned English" and "the hosts of adult fourteen-year-old minds that the army draft tests found."[69] *Time* classified *Physical Culture* as a "livestock publication," while the general magazine *Life* (not yet owned by Luce) defined "a practically complete idiot" as anyone who believed *True Story*'s stories were real.[70]

Condemnation of Macfadden Publications built on a deep history of complaints about the corrosive effects of popular culture that came to a head in the 1920s. Notably, many of the arguments used to denigrate the dime novels that Bernard McFadden read as a boy attached themselves to Macfadden's publishing house now, needing only minimal refashioning to speak to concerns of the 1920s. Hypothesizing about why Macfadden Publications' media was so popular, many opined that the company's mix of sensationalism, corporeality, and sex titillated emotional and impressionable readers by catering to the lowest common denominator in an undiscerning lowbrow marketplace. As *Time* concluded, Body Love's "published dejecta" spoke to "all the sensations below the zone."[71] Arguments about how Macfadden's media catered to embodied base instincts—rather than to intellectual or cultural sensibilities—were given additional traction by the publisher's background in physical culture.

Ultimately, the ubiquitous criticism that accompanied the growth of Macfadden Publications in the 1920s propagated a racialized and gendered xenophobic discourse that envisioned consumers of mass culture as an overly fertile, less evolved, and overwhelmingly foreign and feminine underclass whose promiscuous purchases were eroding the integrity of US public culture. In these eugenics-inflected pronouncements, there was a circular logic at play. The popularity of the company's media among non-elite readers served as evidence of its artlessness, while such artlessness pointed to the masses' deficiencies as American consumers and citizens.

This discourse, while revealing little about Macfadden Publications' actual readers, throws into relief the social hierarchies and various dynamics of exclusion and marginalization that confronted the company's target audiences. Circulation figures attest that such aspersions did not keep purchasers away; indeed, they may have helped drive more readers into Macfadden's welcoming arms. But it is the case that these negative portrayals contributed to the trouble the company faced attracting major advertisers. Except for a few national accounts carried over from *Physical Culture* for things like juices and cereals, Macfadden Publications was largely ignored by Madison Avenue for much of the 1920s, when "For a time it looked as though *True Story Magazine* was all dressed up and had nowhere to go in the advertising world."[72]

The company's initial response to this hurdle was to try attracting wealthier readers. For instance, in 1923, the year it purchased *Metropolitan,* the company began promoting *True Story* in the *New York Times* with an illustrated full-page ad campaign. Its ad "The First Story Ever Told Was True" attributed the magazine's climbing sales to its capacity to capture universal truths. Likening each issue of the publication to a fascinating dinner party, *Times* readers were told that "the guests who sit" at this "well-laden table" would be rewarded with "narratives that bless and burn," narratives "told with the strength of severity and purpose—so that, seeing how others rise or fall, your life too may be made kinder, nobler, or better."[73] To emphasize this message, and counter negative coverage of *True Story,* Macfadden Publications inaugurated an advisory board containing members of the clergy, whose stamp of approval was meant to communicate the underlying morality of *True Story's* contents. Meanwhile, prominent businessmen and other highly regarded public figures were invited to contribute to the company's various other titles, including *Physical Culture.*

The next promotional advertising campaign Macfadden Publications created took a different tack. Titled "The Lives We Elbow But Can Never Touch," it asked, "Would it startle you to know that the waiter once killed a man in a lover's quarrel in far off Czecko-Slovakia; that the messenger boy is planning to avenge a sister's honor?" Touting it foreign and working-class reader-contributors, Macfadden Publications promised an intimate look at the lives and experiences of America's "other half," thereby riffing on the pastime of "slumming," a form of entertainment based on the pursuit of thrilling yet temporary cross-class (and often cross-racial) experiences.[74] Just as Macfadden had played on elite fears of decline in marketing his physical culture media, Macfadden Publications presented its products as revitalizing material. "Webster defines life as a continuous possibility of sensation," this ad continued, explaining that those "who possess this possibility are alive; those who don't possess it are nearing dissolution."[75] A cure for such dissolution was available at local newsstands.

As his company attempted to woo more elite and middlebrow readers, Macfadden worked on elevating his standing as a health authority, publisher, and businessman. His tactics were frenetic. From one angle, the publisher and Oursler decided that Macfadden should try to secure some kind of health-related political appointment, which soon morphed into the idea that Macfadden might even want to run for office himself. To this end, they organized meetings and public appearances that placed the publisher in the proximity of politicians and other power brokers. In 1924, for instance, the Physical Culture Family visited Washington, DC, where Macfadden delivered a lecture to Congress, offering "absolutely non-partisan" advice about eating, sleeping, and exercising, which was followed by "an exhibition of rhythmic dancing interpreting diet, health and exercises" starring his six daughters.[76] Like sharks smelling blood in the water, politicians began inviting the publisher to events and visiting him at home, correctly sensing that a wealthy media mogul with a desire for status and power could be tapped for campaign donations, endorsements, and favorable coverage.

Another thing Macfadden did was to hire the consulting services of Edward Bernays, the pioneer of corporate public relations. The nephew of Sigmund Freud and an expert in psychology in his own right, Bernays was a master propagandist who, for the massive sum of $12,000, was hired to attend weekly meetings with the publisher and his associates to advise them on managing the Macfadden brand.[77] Bernays found Macfadden perplexing: "He had almost complete illiteracy, almost complet[e] ignorance, and yet he had a canny awareness of what to do about certain things" but total "non-awareness about what not to do about others," he would recall.[78] As it turned out, much of Bernays's work would involve talking his client out of various publicity stunts the publisher had come up with on his own. Still, there were two major successes. First, Bernays helped Macfadden establish a foundation in the United States dedicated to promoting physical education curricula in schools. And second, he used his contacts in England to arrange for the House of Parliament to host a gala for Macfadden in recognition of his contributions to physical culture. Understanding how accolades from abroad could boost his standing at home, the publisher spared no expense in self-funding this event, where he would acquire the epithet "The Father of American Physical Culture." Ultimately, however, working with Macfadden fostered in Bernays the realization that "[c]lients often follow only such advice as they would have acted on without an advisor, and reject other recommendations." Against his adviser's suggestions, the president of Macfadden Publications continued orchestrating his own publicity stunts, such as walking twenty miles barefoot to work because, as reporters were told, wearing shoes impeded one's ability to absorb energy from the earth. His closest associates, especially Oursler, knew better than to challenge their boss's instincts, which had, after all, built Macfadden Publications.

Fortunately for everyone involved in the uphill battle of making Macfadden appear more respectable, in the second half of the decade, Macfadden Publications switched its focus from trying to draw in elite and middle-class readers to wooing advertisers. It did this by promoting the growing purchasing power of its actual primary audience. This change of direction reflected US economic trends. Over the course of the decade, the real gross national product grew 4.2 percent, with a per capita increase of 2.7 percent. Real wages for many workers grew during the 1920s, albeit at different rates between demographic groups and economic sectors, which affected consumption and spending patterns. The proportion of the population who could acquire big-ticket items like automobiles, furniture, radios, and even houses increased with these higher wages and the growing availability of consumer credit. Dropping prices for everyday goods meant that growing numbers of Americans could afford new entertainments, services, and products.[79] Macfadden Publications tasked itself with convincing advertisers that its media empire was in an unprecedented position to help corporations tap new markets and thereby dramatically expand their customer bases.

This change is indicated in the next major ad campaign Macfadden Publications launched, which was conducted in several major newspapers. Instead of addressing these newspapers' readers as potential consumers of its media, the company designed this campaign to speak to the advertising industry and its clients. One ad, accompanied by an illustration of a young woman in an apron with a basket of groceries, explained that while Macfadden Publications' readers "may not ride in a Rolls Royce, and perhaps . . . didn't go to college," they still "in the aggregate . . . have five billion dollars to spend" on household goods and services. In the following month's "An Advertisement to the Campbell Soup Company," a young couple reading *True Story* is accompanied by the provocation, "there are more than two million literate families in this country who almost never see [Campbell's] advertisements."[80] The purpose of this campaign was to convince Madison Avenue of two things: first, that working-class readers' purchasing power was too large to be ignored; and second, that advertising in its periodicals offered an unparalleled opportunity to reach this untapped mass market. Hammering home this message, the campaign created a motto for *True Story*: "The Only Magazine They Read." Through this phrase, the publishing house embraced its associations with those whose class, ethnicity, race, national origin, gender, and/or age were different from the imagined community of *Times* readers. At the same time, it was communicating that Macfadden Publications Inc. was itself no longer a dismissible "them"; instead, the publishing house deserved to be recognized by American corporations as a conduit to valuable demographics of new consumers.

Slowly, Madison Avenue began to receive this message. As late as 1926, *True Story* typically contained "less than a dozen full-page or half-page ads for national advertisers."[81] Over the next two years this number rose dramatically as advertising agencies rushed to introduce Macfadden Publications readers to name-brand products such as Camel cigarettes, Kotex feminine hygiene products, and Lysol cleaning supplies. Simultaneously, advertising agencies began adopting the first-person confessional story format in their campaigns. At major agencies, copywriters mimicked the "*True Story* approach," creating text-heavy ads that read like the narratives in Macfadden's magazines. Using brief, emotive sentences, and often speaking from the perspective of a young woman, they wove tales of "morals, marriage, and romance" in which their client's product somehow offered a solution to a personal problem or otherwise saved the day.[82] Before long, it would be difficult to tell from a glance at some of Macfadden's magazines the difference between the text of a true story and an advertising page.

• • •

In 1928, Bernarr Macfadden turned sixty. It would have been a respectable time to retire; instead, the publisher had himself insured for $1 million because, according to him, he was just entering the prime of his life and career. His body, though wrinkled now, was working at maximum efficiency. You could see it in the marathon walks he took, in the calisthenic drills he led at the office, and in the size of his family, which now included another boy named Brewster who had been born in 1925.

Macfadden's mind too, he believed, was more fertile than ever. Ideas for new publications and other business ventures came to him constantly. In the last years of the 1920s alone, he founded a military-style physical training academy for young men in Castle Heights, Tennessee, and laid the plans for a Macfadden-brand health hotel in upstate New York. With the help of the *Graphic*, he had made friends with men in high places, most notably New York's mayor Jimmy Walker, part of the Tammany machine, who feted the Father of American Physical Culture upon his return from London in a pomp-filled ceremony at City Hall. Macfadden had wanted Walker to appoint him health commissioner of New York City, but when this did not happen, he decided to think bigger. Some kind of federal appointment, he and Oursler agreed, would be more appropriate for his talents. Thus, in the lead up to the US presidential election of 1928, Macfadden made a big show of flying in an airplane to both the Democratic and Republican nominating conventions to personally congratulate the winning candidates, Al Smith and Herbert Hoover, wanting to be on the mind of whichever man won.

And through all this, Macfadden maintained firm control over the day-to-day activities of his publishing house, which remained on an upward trajectory. When Oursler left temporarily to travel abroad in 1928, Macfadden filled the role of supervising editor with Oursler's longtime acquaintance Harold Brainerd Hersey. Hersey's memoirs offer a snapshot of the company's operations at this time. Having been a publisher of pulp fiction magazines, most notably *Ranch Romances* (1924), the new supervising editor arrived curious about the workings of Macfadden Publications. The first thing that struck him, he would later recall, was his boss's unwavering "faith in himself" and willingness to make bold decisions. Hersey pinpointed one particular choice Macfadden had made a decade ago as key to his company's astonishing rise: the decision to take *True Story* "out of the pulpwoods" and remake it into a larger, smooth-paper illustrated magazine. "As a pulp it might have gained and held a large following just as some of his imitators have done with the same idea; it could not, however, have won the . . . loyalty of the big advertisers . . . nor a general reading public of over two million every month," he assessed. At the same time, though, Hersey also believed that even as Macfadden had chosen to leave pulp paper and formats behind to create his company's new magazines, Macfadden Publications was successful because it continued to create media that was "pulp at heart." The pulpness of Macfadden Publications' products that Hersey identified emanated not from their literal material properties, but from their superlative accessibility, lack of pretense, and responsiveness to popular desires. While "pulpwood magazines provide an escape from reality by imaginary romance and adventure," Macfadden's "pulp at heart" media provided an exciting "new reality in place of the old."[83] Part of the pleasure of this new reality for the company's reading public was the sense that they had had a hand in creating it and were central to its representations and operations, thanks to the content-sourcing strategies, editorial method, and see-what-sticks ethos of experimentation that Macfadden Publications developed over the decade Mary would later remember as the "Twirling Twenties."[84]

CHAPTER SIX

The Great Depression and the Macfadden Market

I N 1929, MACFADDEN PUBLICATIONS INC. purchased a shiny new Loening C-2C biplane amphibian for company use. Macfadden, who had become enamored with flying and was in the process of getting his pilot's license, christened the plane *Miss True Story*, a fitting tribute to his most popular magazine on its tenth anniversary. For the publishing house and its founder, it seemed the sky was the limit.

The national economic outlook in 1929 appeared similarly promising. A few months earlier, at a ceremony attended by Macfadden, Secretary of Commerce Herbert Hoover had accepted the Republican Party nomination for president, declaring, "We in America today are nearer to the final triumph over poverty than ever before in the history of any land."[1] On Inauguration Day, in phrasing reminiscent of Macfadden's own rhetorical stylings, the president celebrated the "increased virility and strength" of the nation, symbolized by its booming stock market. "We are building a new race—a new civilization," he professed, one "blessed with comfort and opportunity" and "bright with hope."[2] From the White House, Hoover further vowed to promote the expansion of "private enterprise," which he believed would ensure continued prosperity at home while advancing US strategic priorities and capitalist values around the globe. Macfadden heartily approved of this plan.

By this point, the Father of American Physical Culture, as he liked being called, had become astoundingly wealthy. Recently, he and Mary had moved their Physical Culture Family into an elaborate, thirty-room Italianate villa situated on twenty acres in Englewood, New Jersey, across the Hudson River from Macfadden Publications' offices in Manhattan. Surrounded by scenic wetlands, the estate featured nature trails, a swan-filled lake, tennis courts, a miniature golf course, a large swimming pool, and "perhaps the most up-to-date private gymnasium of its day."[3] Increasing his real estate holdings, Macfadden also purchased the former Jackson Sanatorium in the village of Dansville, New York, a capacious hillside retreat that he transformed into his own Physical Culture Hotel.

Meanwhile, the Macfadden publishing house was booming. In addition to its remarkable ability to attract new magazine readers, the company had demonstrated adaptability and staying power, carving out a distinctive identity for its products and itself in a cutthroat industry.[4] Over a decade of economic growth powered by the dramatic expansion of mass-mediated consumer culture, its interactive circulations had become increasingly "popular" in multiple ways; that is, they reached a broad public, responded to the interests and tastes of non-elites, and were widely associated with an imagined community of common folk large in number yet prone to feeling invisible to or misrepresented by other publishers. "The Macfadden publications are not ahead of the People or behind the People; they are of the People," was how *Time* explained it, albeit not without trepidation.[5] Even Macfadden's biggest critics understood that his publishing house had become something special and very valuable: a spectacularly profitable modern corporation with a populist reputation.

As part of their strategy for continued growth, Macfadden and his associates focused on honing the publishing house's identity as an interlocutor between corporate America and "the People." To this end, in the spring of 1929, Macfadden Publications debuted the *New York Daily Investment News*, a tabloid "devoted exclusively to the task of presenting financial news bereft of technicalities and for the 'popular' interest."[6] It also maintained an aggressive corporate relations campaign aimed at persuading advertisers that *True Story* could help them connect with new customers—both physically, via its large circulations, as well as psychologically and emotionally. Meanwhile, Oursler, who had returned to his position as supervising editor, schemed with his boss about how to leverage the company's financial success into greater renown and political clout for Macfadden. And then, just as this frenzy of activity was reaching a fever pitch, the economic shocks began.

The stock market crash in the autumn of 1929 and subsequent global financial meltdown would usher in a brutal time for the publishing industry. As credit evaporated and advertising revenues plunged, many companies would be forced to downsize, or even shut their doors forever. But not Macfadden Publications. Having long preached in its media that improvement and recovery were always possible, the company and its founder would respond to the economic and political upheavals of the 1930s with a characteristic mix of innovation and opportunism.

First, having already been working toward establishing itself as an intermediary between corporate America and "the people" when the crisis started, the publishing house would use the circumstances of financial upheaval to further advance this mission. Through creatively combining the tools of public relations, advertising, and market research, Macfadden Publications would claim to possess unique insights into—and leverage over—the workings of the perplexing modern economy, packaging its readership as a market of Americanized "wage earners" that held the key to US recovery and future global economic growth.

Next, Macfadden Publications would work to extend the reach of its popular media circulations during the 1930s. In part, this would be facilitated by the company's previous specialization in certain genres. Publications about physical culture, with its promises of recovery; true story media, which centered "the people"; and true crime and detective periodicals, in which complex problems were solved and order restored to society—already company staples, these cultural forms would resonate in newly powerful ways during the 1930s, helping to cement the company's standing as a media powerhouse with uncanny insights into popular taste.

Reflecting a broader corporate trend, the company would also act aggressively to acquire on-brand periodicals from other publishers as well. *Liberty,* a general interest weekly it purchased in 1931, would provide the company with a means of commenting on current events. *Photoplay,* acquired in 1934, would strengthen its connections to Hollywood and celebrity fan culture. Because of the publishing house's broad readership and rising corporate profile, media-savvy politicians and other public figures would increasingly seek to utilize the company and its founder to better communicate with the masses, thereby enhancing Macfadden Publications' influence on public discourse and popular culture. The company and its founder would use this power to advance their own financial and ideological interests, which would become increasingly conservative as the decade progressed.

None of these developments would go uncontested. Already controversial, the Macfadden media empire would become a lightning rod for conversations about the effects of America's industrialized mass culture on individuals and various imagined public spheres in the 1930s. Among the chorus of voices spanning ideologically diverse perspectives who would criticize the company and its founder would be newly influential leftist critics excoriating what they saw as the anti-revolutionary and even fascist tendencies of the Macfadden media empire. Macfadden Publications, in contrast, would portray itself as an exceptionally democratic purveyor of economic and cultural uplift, a moral influence on society, and a champion of "the people." But who "the people" were, and what they wanted, would remain up for debate throughout the long Great Depression ahead.

Publicity Blitz

In the months preceding the crash, Macfadden Publications was busy orchestrating a major publicity blitz. The first prong of this campaign focused on elevating Macfadden's personal reputation. Previously, the publisher had shared details about his life through lectures, editorials, and serialized memoirs in *Physical Culture*. Now, the time had come to produce a more comprehensive accounting of his accomplishments. Combining his longtime enthusiasm for self-promotion with his more recent training in the art of public relations, the publisher commissioned not just one but *three* different biographies about himself.

The result, predictably, was a trio of hagiographies. The first, *The True Story of Bernarr Macfadden,* was authored by none other than the publisher's closest associate, Fulton Oursler, who recounted his boss's eventful coming-of-age story, long career, and sterling professional credentials.[7] Next, *Chats with the Macfadden Family,* by Grace Perkins, focused on Macfadden's not-so-private personal life, with an emphasis on how Macfadden kept the Physical Culture Family in such remarkable shape.[8] An actress, novelist, and prolific contributor to the company's magazines, Perkins was "the fastest good-looking writer I've ever seen," according to Macfadden.[9] She was also, conveniently, Oursler's current wife; the couple had met on the job. Penning the third biography, *Bernarr Macfadden: A Study in Success,* was Clement Wood, a lawyer, novelist, and poet from Alabama.[10] Perhaps out of jealousy, Oursler despised Wood, calling him "a foul-mouthed scribbler."[11] But the only thing obscene about *Bernarr Macfadden: A Study in Success* was the amount of praise it heaped upon its subject, and in this regard, Oursler and Perkins gave Wood a run for his money.

From different angles, all three biographers attempted to construct a coherent portrait of Macfadden. The overarching story they communicated was about an Ozark orphan who pulled himself up by his bootstraps, through physical culture, to become a prophet of health, model patriarch, and innovative media mogul whose ideas were always ahead of their time. Yet through all his successes, they emphasized, Macfadden had never lost touch with his humble roots or ideals, which included an innate love of health, beauty, and truth, and an unyielding faith in humankind's capacities for improvement and transformation. Over his long career, the publisher had learned from experience and led by example, scorning prudishness and convention to connect people with their bodies and to each other in new ways, even when it resulted in mockery or persecution. Not despite, but *because of,* his outsider status, he had been able to connect with a mass audience, whose members listened to his advice, and in turn, entrusted the Macfadden publishing company with their precious attention and stories.

The extent to which Macfadden was not just a good businessman but a great one was a major theme. Wood laid it on especially thick in this regard: "Between 1839 and 1870, eight boys were born in America that have since become noted for their achievements. All came from impoverished families. . . . These eight boys have become John D. Rockefeller, Sr.; Thomas A. Edison; Asa G. Candler; Charles Sumner Woolworth; Henry Ford; Harvey S. Firestone; Amadeo Peter Giannini; and Bernarr Macfadden. All are multi-millionaires, or better; and all are among the score of outstanding financial successes in our modern American culture," he rhapsodized. In lavish prose, the three biographers classified Macfadden as a visionary entrepreneur and captain of industry while drawing out qualities that made him unique. Unlike other businessmen, they implied, Macfadden had pursued ideals such as health, fitness, and the truth over profits; his wealth was a mere "byproduct" of the inherent value of his contributions to society.[12]

The True Story of Bernarr Macfadden, Chats with the Macfadden Family, and *Bernarr Macfadden: A Study in Success* were released simultaneously by the same publisher on the same day in the fall of 1929. Observers could barely believe their eyes. "The authors of these brochures do not spare the goose-grease: poor Macfadden chokes and gurgles in it on every one of their 825 pages. I can recall no more passionate anointing of a living man," scoffed the critic H. L. Mencken.[13] Yet Mencken, as his review admits, also found the many twists and turns of the publisher's life story completely fascinating. Even *Time* could not resist summarizing some of these events for its readers, leading to the pronouncement that the man the magazine denigrated as "Body Love" had become "in his own loud, shallow way, a US prophet."[14] To hagiographers and critics alike, Macfadden was a powerful figure, one who commanded the attention of millions via a publishing empire that was simultaneously an honest expression of his life and personality and a sophisticated, multi-million-dollar organization whose imprint was only growing.

Fig.6.1 Macfadden at work, c. 1930. Keystone-France/Gamma-Keystone via Getty Images

The portrait of Macfadden as both a singular genius and an approachable everyman who had risen from rags to riches to command an enormous popular audience meshed with the evolving brand identity of his publishing house. Correspondingly, Macfadden Publications unfurled a sophisticated public relations campaign designed to communicate its own rags-to-riches corporate biography to the business world. According to this campaign, the company had, like its eponymous founder, started off small and risen from obscurity, facing an endless stream of doubters and naysayers who disparaged its products and readership along the way. But by sticking to its principles, and thereby creating a uniquely democratic editorial method, it had transformed into an unparalleled commercial success. Moreover, just as Macfadden's biographers insisted that wealth and power had not changed the man, but merely allowed him to be more himself, Macfadden Publications' authenticity and financial success were coproductive. By giving voice to people and experiences previously marginalized in the literary industry, the company had thrived. And as the company had thrived, it had increased its audience's opportunities for personal expression, self-improvement, and public visibility, which then made its media empire even more popular—and therefore more potentially useful to those wise enough to recognize its value as a medium of inter- and cross-class communication.

Macfadden Publications crafted this story about itself through a campaign of twenty "institutional advertisements" that it placed in major newspapers around the country. Aimed at advertising executives, investors, and other businessmen, these ads provided information about the company's development alongside what might be called a collective biography of its national readership. Building on the previous branding of *True Story* as "The Only Magazine They Read," they explained how the Macfadden publishing house had been flooded ten years earlier by true stories reflecting the many trials and tribulations of a massive conglomeration of American workers—many of them young, poor, or foreign-born— facing challenges related to dislocation, exploitation, and adaptation. Over the ensuing period of national growth, the company claimed, the "great human documents" it collected had changed in tone and content to reflect American economic progress. Increasingly, contributors who were receiving "more money and more leisure for labor" narrated experiences of economic and cultural advancement, a change Macfadden Publications attributed to the increasingly expert organization of industry. Indexed in the "personal expression from a cross-section of hundreds of thousands of individuals," and thus reflected in the contents of the company's various magazines, were smoother relations between laborers and employers, rising living standards, growing access to education, and the appearance of new "cultural wants" among the masses—wants described specifically as "intelligent" ones.[15]

Alas, according to this story, previous norms of class conflict, along with the social gulf that separated the denizens of Madison Avenue from regular Americans, had caused many to miss the fact that such a "friendly revolution" had taken place. But not the tuned-in Macfadden firm: "What we can do when we see a great mass of folk-literature, as in True Story Magazine, coming from tens of thousands of unknown and unsung recorders of their own emotions, is to lay our ear very humbly and very gently to the pages," and "try to understand the spirit of this great surge of humanity," one of its ads explained. Casting itself as a uniquely positioned interpreter of mass behaviors and desires, Macfadden Publications claimed that "the rumble of threats and mutterings" had been replaced in recent years by "the high, clear voice of those who are now able to gather and garner a full share of the good things of life."[16] A large segment of society, one that in aggregate controlled half of the nation's wages, had been moving collectively forward and upward, coming into its own as an economic and cultural force—and Macfadden Publications was the only large-scale magazine publisher that had been along for the ride, rising in tandem with its customers while retaining an intimate window onto their changing lives.

Attributing rising standards of living and personal wealth to the growth of private enterprise, rather than labor activism or consumer movements, Macfadden Publications was distancing itself from radical politics while making a bid for its own inclusion within a comity of American business elites.[17] Simultaneously, however, the company's corporate relations campaign validated the promise and worthiness of non-elite demographics who made up its readership, portraying them not as foreign interlopers but as "the folk" essential to the future of national prosperity and growth. In making this argument, the company did not deny that its readers had identities and experiences that made them distinct from other Americans; instead, it selectively emphasized some of these differences, while minimizing others.

Consider, for example, "Mainly on the Subject of Women." The text of this ad begins by describing a scenario that happened frequently in real life and therefore appeared often in confessional stories sent to Macfadden Publications: a young, foreign-born, unwed mother shows up at a Court of Domestic Relations, attempting to gain support for her baby from its father. Such cases, the ad explains, "came literally by thousands, until the puzzled judiciary began wondering whether all the young female immigrants were without morals." Macfadden Publications, however, saw a different story in this data, which was that America's recent "large influx of peasantry from certain sections of Europe" consisted of many young women who came from societies where motherhood was respected and familial obligations honored. Unlike men, who absorbed a carelessness that freed them from their previous moral code, women tended to cling to traditional mores by striving to create families and homes. Over time, this impulse helped turn young, foreign-born women into engines of homemaking and domestic consumption in the United States. "A rather interesting woman—this modern wife of the modern worker. Ultra-modern when it comes to buying those innumerable things . . . but mighty conservative when it comes to any change in the moral code," concludes the text.[18]

In this and other installments of its promotional campaign, Macfadden Publications was working to counter advertising industry stereotypes that characterized the working class as lacking the personal qualities and financial means necessary to consume in modern ways. By highlighting the morality and rationality of *True Story* readers, along with their growing ability and willingness to make discretionary purchases, the company drummed the message that its multiethnic mass audience represented a profitable new frontier for advertisers. With native fluency in the language and experiences of the masses, with whom the corporation remained in constant contact, Macfadden's publishing house could help corporate America reconceptualize how it thought about working-class consumers and adapt its strategies to begin reaching them more efficiently and systematically.

Through this argument, the company was confronting the fact that even among advertisers and other publishers in the late 1920s who realized the value of the mass market Macfadden Publications represented, it was widely assumed that as disposable income levels rose and immigrant populations assimilated, middle-class values and behaviors would naturally spread throughout the population.[19] In this imagined scenario, advertisers only needed to pitch themselves to the native-born, white middle class. While affirming that "rising tides lift all boats," Macfadden Publications contested a central assumption of this prevailing "embourgeoisement" thesis by insisting that working-class readers' patterns of consumption were shaped by their own distinct values, tastes, and drives.[20] Furthermore, the company argued, this was a good thing, as these distinct values, tastes, and drives—if properly understood and managed—were especially conducive to the continued expansion of US consumer capitalism. In its campaign, the publishing house was depicting its collective audience— even, and perhaps especially, its female and foreign-born members—as an engine of a superlatively American brand of economic and cultural progress.

This argument was made by drawing parallels between the nation's historical maturation and Macfadden's readers' collective journey from estranged producers to consumers who embodied central elements of American modernity. Just as the United States had started off as rural and revolutionary with a relatively weak sense of collective identity before evolving into its current form, so had the masses undergone a similar transformation. Over the course of the 1920s—the very period of Macfadden Publications' rise—the workers who produced the goods and services that expanded the American economy had made enormous forward strides, gaining the wages—and necessary intelligent cultural wants—to become good national consumers. In a national economic system that was increasingly reliant on mass purchasing, their economic and cultural progress made possible the fulfillment of a core American promise, namely the democratization of economic and social mobility. Their experiences, therefore, provided insight into, and a model for achieving, future progress in this arena, both at home *and* abroad. Calling attention to the relationship between domestic mass consumption and the growth of US financial power, Macfadden Publications argued that its audience was "not only responsible for the conditions of our own America, but is pretty much sponsoring the attitude of the rest of the world."[21]

More than a simple ploy to sell advertising space, Macfadden Publications' institutional advertising campaign at the end of the 1920s broadcasted the pro-capitalist, American identity of the company and its readers while demonstrating its unique capacities to intermediate between the nation's business elites and a diverse working class these elites did not yet properly understand. Highlighting its simultaneous possession of authenticity and expertise, the publishing house identified itself as singularly equipped to midwife the arrival of a more democratic domestic consumer culture, which would naturally provide a model for the future expansion of markets for US products. As one ad proclaimed, "It is a new world, gentlemen, and it might be well to get ready for it."[22]

Economic Chaos and the Search for Stabilization

A new world was coming all right, but not the one Macfadden Publications, or almost anyone else, was anticipating. In the fall of 1929, a stock market surge gave way to a period of instability and contraction, which triggered a series of foreign financial crises. There was a period of dramatic price gyrations, accompanied by more speculation, and then the market crashed on the twenty-ninth of October, sending investors into a panic and placing enormous strains on banks. Within a few weeks, the Dow lost nearly half its value. These events threatened to throw a wrench in Macfadden Publications' promotional strategy, based as it was on the premise that a "new world" of mass prosperity had arrived; at the same time, they made its mission—to attract investment and ad dollars—even more pressing.

As this crisis was unfolding, Macfadden Publications was adjusting its corporate relations materials in real time. During the middle two weeks of October, its ads told "The Amazing True Story of Personal Credit." Combining broader economic data with insights from its magazines about how personal credit was being used by the laboring class, the two installments on this theme argued that "in this new economic set-up where both the money and the credit have come down to the masses America has already become far more sound on personal credits than it ever was on its credits in the business world."[23] In other words, *True Story*'s writers and readers were not overextended; when they did use credit, they did so judiciously, buying things such as cars, homes, furnishings, and other possessions that tended to beget further wealth acquisition and consumer spending. Compared to the wealthier classes, "labor, because of its sad experience in the past" was also "more cautious of its *personal credit standing* than any other group," as "personal pride in stability is a thing so newly acquired as to be rather precious, and therefore to be guarded extra well."[24] Corporate America needed to remain focused on the big picture, which was simply this: "Never before in all recorded history have you ever had a mass of millions of people climbing to a position of cultural wants, and with the cultural capacity for expressing those wants, and the economic capacity for obtaining them."[25] The final ads of 1929 supported this argument with optimistic statistics regarding *True Story* readers' plans for Christmas shopping and holiday celebrations.

Entering the new decade, Macfadden Publications became less Pollyanna-ish yet would maintain its confident tone. Admitting that a difficult period of "adjustment" was happening, the company characterized its readers, who had not been financial risk-takers, as constituting a "balance wheel" and "stabilizing force" on the economy.[26] Running with the themes of balance and adjustment, its ads attributed the current recession, which was not obviously a depression yet, to a mismatch between supply and demand, a situation both temporary and fixable. "The problem is purely one of readjustment. Nothing more. *Adjustment of mass to mass. Mass production to mass consumption,*" it declared reassuringly.[27] Recovery was a matter of achieving better understanding and communication between producers and consumers, which the Macfadden corporation was now claiming as its arena of expertise. To support its arguments, the publishing house emphasized the similarities between its unique editorial practices, the discipline of sociology, and the emergent field of market research.[28] "Are You Clamoring for Case Histories?" asked one ad, which promised that the company was assembling case histories drawn from readers' submissions about the lives and desires of wage-earning Americans "in basketfuls."[29] Another announced, "Certainly no sociologist has ever had such a sweep of humanity passing like a panorama before his eyes."[30] Through insights gained from its pioneering "research" methodologies, Macfadden Publications could help corporations identify and reach new markets, which would be necessary to rectify economic inefficiencies that were behind the current pain, its ads stressed.

Concurrently, the company also encouraged certain forms of mass consumption through its editorial content. An example can be seen in *True Story's* "Home Problems Forum," a running feature in which readers looking for solutions to personal problems asked the magazine's audience for advice, with the editor publishing the best response letters. One "personal problem" from the spring of 1930 concerns whether an engaged couple currently residing with the fiancé's parents need their own home. The resounding response is, yes, of course they do! "This is Nature's law:" the second-place response proclaims, "Each pair of young things must build their own home and live in it, master and mistress of their castle," even if the "castle" may only be a small, humble abode.[31] Also in this issue, "Beth Reveals Her Romantic Adventure in Creating a Modern Kitchen" describes a woman with the opposite problem—her boyfriend's mother does not want her to move into their family home. Investigating the house, Beth finds an ancient kitchen whose inefficient design has been unnecessarily wearing down the mother. After Beth renovates the kitchen, it is decided that she would be an excellent addition to the household, so the couple can finally marry.[32] Here and in other editorial features, the company's contemporary true story magazines emphasized connections between participating in modern consumer culture and romantic and familial fulfillment.

In tone, Macfadden Publications, response to the financial crisis harmonized with broader efforts among businesses and the government to achieve recovery through deploying expertise and orchestrating cooperation between interconnected segments of society. With his "modern technical mind," Hoover was exploring ways for his administration to respond to the problems of economic instability and growing poverty without overstepping what he saw as bounds of government power.[33] In addition to undertaking public infrastructure projects, the president focused on coordinating voluntary efforts by private entities to maintain investment, employment, and production. If corporate America acted in "the spirit of voluntary service," and laborers embraced hard work and "rugged individualism," suffering could be mitigated without undermining organic processes of economic restabilization.[34] Macfadden Publications and its founder were in sync with this approach ideologically, yet the company maintained that those at the top needed to cultivate better connections with the masses whose behavior could make or break any recovery plan.

As 1930 brought worsening domestic conditions and international financial disorder, public confidence in Hoover's abilities to fix the crisis diminished. Some complained he was interfering too much in the economy, or in the wrong ways; others believed his administration was not doing enough.[35] While differences between political parties inflected these debates, it was not a simple matter of laissez-faire Republicans versus interventionist Democrats, as both parties had conservative and liberal wings, and the issues at stake were complex. Points of convergence emerged between pro-capitalist, anti-communist political formations and populist ones, as Americans looked for alternatives to the status quo. It was in this context that Macfadden and his publishing house began cultivating relationships with other prominent political figures of this era. One of these was Benito Mussolini.

The sequence of events that brought Macfadden and Mussolini together in 1930 began the previous year, when President Hoover announced he would be commencing a White House Conference on Child Health and Protection.[36] Likely in recognition of his campaign contributions, but perhaps also due to the efficacy of the biography blitz and his company's ongoing public relations campaign, Macfadden received an invitation to participate in the proceedings. He was to put together a report on the state of child welfare in Europe. Under the auspices of fulfilling this public duty, the publisher planned a fact-finding trip abroad. In the fall of 1930, he traveled across the Atlantic, accompanied by Mary, who had been required to shed thirty pounds for the occasion.

Macfadden's personal impetus for undertaking this journey was not to find facts for the US government but to acquire international recognition, which would be useful if he decided to run for political office. He was particularly eager to visit Italy and meet Mussolini. Since leading the Fascist coalition that overtook the nation's government back in 1922, the dictator had pursued a close relationship with the United States, where he became much admired. Skilled at diplomacy and the arts of propaganda and self-promotion, by 1930 Mussolini had established a global reputation as a strong and effective modernizer, one whose regime appeared to be "bring[ing] order and progress to Italy while holding at bay the menace from the left."[37] Importantly to Macfadden, "Il Duce" was also renowned for his exceptional virility, athleticism, and even glamour. Through Oursler's consular contacts, the publisher arranged a visit.

Upon arriving in Italy, Macfadden was provided with an escort, General Renato Ricci, the Italian Under-Secretary of State for Physical Education. Reflecting his belief that the political project of building up a strong and modern nation went hand in hand with the development of strong and healthy bodies, Mussolini had "blanketed the whole of [the country] with a smooth-working physical culture organization."[38] Ricci led a tour of new facilities designed to mold the minds and muscles of Italy's future citizens and leaders, and Macfadden was smitten. Having long advocated for the development of state-sponsored physical education and training programs in the United States, Fascist Italy seemed a dream come true.[39] Finally, Macfadden was brought to meet with Il Duce himself. "I have followed your work with keen interest and can tell you that I, too, am a physical culturalist," Mussolini greeted his guest. In response, the publisher complimented his host's achievements in building up the nation, and especially its youth. For the rest of their meeting, the men discussed physical education, bodybuilding, diet and exercise, and the theme of building national vitality.[40] Inspired, Macfadden made a diplomatic proposition to his host, suggesting that a cadre of Italian cadets travel to the United States to undergo additional training under his tutelage. In making this offer, Macfadden perhaps hoped to demonstrate the viability of state-sponsored physical culture reforms that he envisioned himself leading in the United States, which might resonate strongly during the contemporary moment of decline and crisis. Mussolini likely saw an opportunity for cultural diplomacy that had the added benefit of connection to a wealthy American ally who happened to own an enormous media company.

While her husband was mingling with dignitaries, Mary was left back at the hotel. One day, she watched as her husband set off for the Vatican for a meeting with Pope Pius XI, lugging an oversized photographic portrait of the Physical Culture Family. In addition to feeling embarrassed by this gesture, she was concerned because her husband had recently informed her that he intended on having two more sons to balance out the family's sex ratio. Mary responded, with finality, that she was finished bearing children. Macfadden's response was immediate and dramatic. His exact phrasing, she would later claim, was, "Woman, you are no longer necessary to my success."[41] After hearing this, Mary sailed home alone, beginning a separation that would become permanent.

Amid the tumult in the Macfaddens' personal lives, the Italian Physical Culture Demonstration, as it would come to be called, went on as planned. On February 23, 1931, the luxury liner *Conte Biancamano* arrived in New York Harbor bearing a group of forty smartly uniformed Italian cadets, aged eighteen to thirty-two, from L'Accademia Fascista Maschile di Educazione Fisica. After meeting their host at Quarantine, the cadets posed for pictures, exchanged salutes and salutations with friends and relatives who had come to meet their ship, and were finally ushered into a fleet of waiting cars. Over the next few weeks, the Italian cadets were taken on a whirlwind sightseeing tour of New York and Washington, DC, attending receptions held in their honor at New York's City Hall, the Italian Embassy, the Annapolis Naval Academy, and Georgetown University. Hoover, who valued cordial relations with Mussolini, then received the cadets at the White House. Relatives back home could follow the cadets' trip in the Roman daily *Il Giornale d'Italia*.

Next up was getting down to the business of fitness. In accordance with Macfadden's instructions, each cadet posed shirtless from multiple angles for a photographer, with measurements of necks, arms, flexed arms, waists, chests expanded and contracted, hips, thighs, and calves scrupulously recorded. At Macfadden's Physical Culture Hotel in Dansville, New York, and subsequently at his Castle Heights Military Academy in Tennessee, they followed an intensive physical training course. Under this extensive exercise regime, and a diet prohibiting wine and pasta, biceps swelled, waists grew more defined, and backs straightened. At the end of five months, each man's body was again photographed and measured to document all the positive changes. Finally, the Italians returned to New York for a farewell dinner at the Hotel Astor, where Macfadden presented each cadet with a certificate of achievement and an eight-volume set of his *Encyclopedia* to lug back to Rome.

The Italian Physical Culture Demonstration was publicized in Macfadden Publications' media. Reporting on events, the *New York Evening Graphic* blared, "Mussolini and Macfadden Try a Noble Experiment to Prevent War," framing the event as a display of international brotherhood. The Father of American Physical Culture, the paper explained, was performing a grand diplomatic and philanthropic gesture by helping to revitalize the Italian nation. Describing the cadets as "bronzed boys" impressed by the largesse and splendor of their trip—and referring to Mussolini, preposterously, as "the Italian Bernarr Macfadden"—this coverage communicated paternalism and American exceptionalism. At the same time, it also highlighted Il Duce's personal strengths and the efficacy of his regime in implementing nationwide physical culture reform.[42] These themes were expounded upon in a book Macfadden Publications subsequently released. Authored by Thomas B. Morgan, the head of the United Press bureau in Rome, with a forward by Macfadden and an introduction by Ricci, *Italian Physical Culture Demonstration* (1932) characterized the events it documented as "the nucleus of a stronger bond" between the United States and Italy.[43] Attentive to two national audiences at once, Morgan praised Macfadden's singular expertise in scientific physical culture methods and Mussolini's unparalleled ability to implement physical culture reforms through his government. Italians had been aroused by Il Duce "to the individual responsibility of keeping the body sound," and then the Father of American Physical Culture had revealed to them new steps forward toward more perfect individual and national health, as evidenced in the book's many pages of before-and-after photos.[44]

The Italian Physical Culture Demonstration and subsequent book about this event communicated several messages at once: the progressiveness of Mussolini's Italy, the genius of Macfadden, the bounty of America, and the good that could be accomplished through US-Italian cooperation. For Il Duce, participating in this event brought the benefits of positive coverage in a vast American publishing empire. Macfadden, meanwhile, was able to demonstrate his international renown as a health and fitness expert while also tapping into the widespread fascination with Mussolini that already existed in the United States, including among Italian Americans, an important demographic for his company.[45] He also signaled the scope of his philanthropic aspirations, which would be manifested at an even greater scale with the creation of the Macfadden Foundation in the fall of 1931, a charity for the promotion of health and fitness that received an initial endowment of $5 million from the publisher.[46]

Significantly, the demonstration also provided a forum for the publisher to articulate his views about what constituted the optimal relationship between the state and the individual in society—a long-standing ideological debate in US political discourse that was becoming even more central within the context of the current depression. Ideally, Macfadden's Italian Demonstration showed, state capacity should be built up by a strong leader in ways that would facilitate individual striving among the masses. Expansions of the powers of a central government were justified to the extent that they promoted strong citizens and collective national progress without undermining the sanctity of individualism or private enterprise. Honed by the possibilities Macfadden witnessed unfolding under Fascism in Italy, this ideological orientation would shape the relationship the publisher and his company began building with another ascending political leader, Franklin Delano Roosevelt, in 1931, as the economic crisis was growing deeper.

The Election of 1932 and the First New Deal

When Macfadden first met Franklin Roosevelt in 1931, Roosevelt was still only the governor of New York. However, widespread disillusionment with the Hoover administration's inability to reverse the economic downturn had made it apparent that the Republican Party's hold on the presidency might be coming to an end. The governor was one of several politicians hoping to be his replacement. But first, Roosevelt would need to secure the Democratic nomination. This is where Macfadden Publications came in.

Back in 1921, Roosevelt's political ambitions had almost been derailed permanently when he contracted a paralytic illness at the age of thirty-nine that left him paralyzed from the waist down. Only after years of treatments aimed at rehabilitation, which helped him learn to move through space without the use of his legs, did he return to his political career, winning the governorship of New York in 1928 and 1930. By this point, Roosevelt had become adept at managing his public appearances to convey strength and capability, and one of the ways in which he did so was by participating in a feature in *Physical Culture*, "Governor Franklin D. Roosevelt on 'How I

Came Back.'" Structured as an interview, this article describes how polio (it was believed at the time) left Roosevelt a "wholly helpless invalid" imprisoned in a "palsied body" who would "never walk again." It then describes how the combination of hydrotherapy treatment in Warm Springs, Georgia, and strenuous physiotherapy and exercise regimens led to a miraculous "recovery."[47] Through optimism and an unwavering commitment to physical training, Roosevelt had, according to this article, regained use of his legs, allowing him to return to the political work to which he was so well suited.

Going forward, Roosevelt would continue to counter criticisms that he was physically unfit to hold political office with an array of different tactics. At times, these tactics included hiding or minimizing his dependence on a wheelchair to move from place to place and downplaying the permanency of his paralysis. But more consequential was Roosevelt's crafting of narratives about his physical condition that communicated his remarkable *abilities*. These included the ability to endure pain and overcome hardship; the ability to diagnose and address seemingly incurable problems; and the ability to achieve recovery, and even new levels of mastery, against all odds. This constellation of qualities came to seem ever more valuable in the context of the worsening economic crisis of the early 1930s. Roosevelt and his supporters used mass media to not only counter discriminatory public perceptions of his disability but also to "construct a bodily understanding of the Great Depression" that made him seem like the candidate best able to put the crippled nation on a path back to health and strength.[48]

Fortuitously for the governor, as he was campaigning for the Democratic nomination, Macfadden Publications was levelling up its position in the media landscape through the acquisition of *Liberty,* a popular weekly magazine. Established in 1924, *Liberty* was a general interest magazine containing a mix of fiction, news, opinion, illustrations and cartoons, and reviews. Priced at five cents, it was known by its slogan, "A Weekly for Everybody," as well as for its practice of printing an estimated "reading time" at the beginning of its articles. When it was announced on April 1, 1931, that Macfadden Publications had finalized a deal to purchase such a mainstream publication, "many thought it was an April Fool's Day joke," for after the *Saturday Evening Post* and *Collier's, Liberty* was the third most popular weekly newsmagazine in the United States, typically selling over two million copies per week.[49] However, it was also the case that the periodical was in dire financial straits. When the opportunity arose to buy *Liberty,* Macfadden and Oursler jumped at the chance to acquire an established general magazine. And Roosevelt, in turn, saw an opportunity to get friendly media coverage in a high-circulation national weekly. Oursler, who became editor of *Liberty*, would later recall Roosevelt calculating that "[t]he *Saturday Evening Post* and *Collier's*, being wealthy in advertising, were bound to support the Republican order. The same was true of newspapers and the radio. But *Liberty* had immense circulation—the largest single-copy sale of all magazines—and very little advertising. We might, [Roosevelt] figured, have the wit to hitch our wagon to his star."[50]

A two-way wooing animated by mutual interest ensued. In late April, *Liberty* published dueling opinion pieces assessing the pros and cons of Hoover and Roosevelt as candidates. Beforehand, Oursler had sent drafts to each politician, and Roosevelt had responded by inviting the editor to his home for a visit, where he merely requested that a sentence stating he had "never fully recovered" from his illness be changed to read, "he had never fully recovered *the use of the muscles in his legs*."[51] Following this friendly encounter, the governor met with Macfadden, charming the publisher by describing his own dedication to physical culture. Invitations for *Liberty*'s publisher and editor to socialize with the elite Roosevelt family soon followed, as did several collaborations.

In the summer of 1931, in response to a whispering campaign among other Democrats that Roosevelt might be too handicapped to deserve the party's nomination, *Liberty* asked the governor: what if the magazine sent a reporter to Albany to live with him for a while to observe how he managed, who would then publish his findings, as well as reports from a panel of physicians, no matter what? "Name your time and send your man," Roosevelt purportedly responded. In the resulting *Liberty* feature, correspondent Earle Looker, a self-described Republican who had previously written about Theodore Roosevelt, answered the question "Is Franklin D. Roosevelt Physically Fit to Be President?" with a resounding yes. After beginning with, "It is an amazing fact that the next President of the United States may be a cripple," the article provided details of Roosevelt's mental acuity, openness to investigation, thrice-daily swimming routine, indefatigable work ethic, strapping good looks, and obvious vigor. "[E]very rumor of Franklin Roosevelt's physical incapacity can be unqualifiably denied as false," it concluded.[52] So effective was this *Liberty* article that Roosevelt's campaign manager Louis Howe himself distributed thousands of copies.

Next, Oursler and Howe negotiated an arrangement in which *Liberty* would run a "New Series of Articles on Matters of State" authored by Roosevelt every other week. Composed with the help of ghostwriters, including Looker, these "terse, professional pieces on taxes, crime, and relief" helped familiarize the public with his candidacy and general agenda, which included a stronger federal government that would address unemployment, utilities monopolies, crime, and other problems plaguing everyday

Americans.[53] Meanwhile, to demonstrate *Liberty*'s value as a mass outlet, Macfadden hired an up-and-coming academic named George Gallup. Deploying pioneering statistical sampling and survey methods, Gallup's study— "the first time anyone had conducted a national survey comparing the readership of major weekly magazines"—showed that the punchy prose style and ample color illustrations of *Liberty* made its content more interesting and memorable to readers than that of other periodicals.[54] Indeed, Gallup found "Is Franklin D. Roosevelt Physically Fit to Be President?" to be "America's Best Read Article."[55] In addition to jump-starting Gallup's legendary polling career, this widely read study (and a follow-up conducted in 1932) helped Macfadden Publications further demonstrate its efficacy in public communications, which enhanced the company's profile among advertisers and savvy politicians like Roosevelt.

Eleanor Roosevelt struck a deal with the publishing house as well. In addition to penning articles for *Liberty,* she worked with Macfadden to develop a new magazine focused on children and parenting, which she would edit assisted by her daughter Anna Roosevelt Dall. A mother of five children and grandmother to three, Eleanor Roosevelt generated story ideas, hired contributors, wrote features, and exerted the right to vet all advertisements. The final product, *Babies—Just Babies,* hit newsstands a month before the election. Stocked with photographs of cherubic infants, it was like *Physical Culture* with "cuddle appeal."[56] Some of Eleanor Roosevelt's high society friends made fun of the publication, ribbing her for working for Macfadden's lowbrow media empire. But *Babies—Just Babies* helped her to project a multifaceted public identity as a dutiful maternal figure, professional reformer, and working woman, a mix of qualities that showed how electing Roosevelt would offer Americans a new kind of first lady.

When Americans went to the polls in 1932 and voted for Roosevelt in a landslide, then, both the next president of the United States and his wife were under contract with Macfadden's publishing house. Reminding the leader-elect that "the pied piper who got rid of the rats who said he wasn't physically fit to be President now wants to get paid," Oursler secured for *Liberty,* exclusively, Roosevelt's first article telling the nation what he intended to do in the White House.[57] "We are about to enter upon a new period of liberalism and of sane reform in the United States," FDR told the magazine's readers, promising to "without injury to the proper rights of any individual and without conflict with the spirit of American institutions" give the people "a new deal in their political and economic life."[58]

As what would become FDR's legislative agenda was taking shape and being shared with the public, Macfadden took a special interest in areas of proposed reform he saw as compatible with his own ideas about how the government could help the "forgotten man," a tellingly gendered figure of speech used by Roosevelt to describe Americans facing unemployment and growing economic insecurity, to whom he promised relief. One reform idea associated with FDR that resonated with the publisher was the possibility of creating an expansive back-to-the-land movement in which unemployed industrial workers could engage in subsistence farming to support themselves and their families.[59] Collaboration between Roosevelt and Macfadden Publications around this issue can be seen in adviser Howe's September 1932 article, "The Fight for the Forgotten Man," which touted Roosevelt's plan for placing unemployed men on abandoned farms so they could "make an honest living." More than half of this article was devoted to a case study of one individual worker's story, a city blacksmith named Fred whose large family had been restored to happiness and security through rural life. Ultimately, *Liberty* would publish more than a dozen articles and editorials promoting the back-to-the-land reform movement between 1932 and 1933.

Simultaneously, Macfadden lobbied Congress in support of a subsistence-homestead program. "Gentleman," he testified, "I think that unless something is done to relieve the serious unemployment we have everywhere we do not know what will happen to us. Firebrands of some kind may start most anything." To help him, he hired a writer and public relations specialist named Edith Radford Lumsden, who stayed in Washington to fight for this legislation. Eventually Macfadden's bill would be passed as the Subsistence Homestead Act of 1933, which comprised a tiny part of the National Industrial Recovery Act whose enactment capped off the first hundred days of FDR's inaugural term.

In a similar campaign, Macfadden presented his own penny restaurants as the kind of relief-providing enterprise the government should support, as he informed Harry L. Hopkins, chair of New York's Temporary Emergency Relief Administration and one of the architects of the New Deal, in 1933. Macfadden then built his biggest penny restaurant yet on West 44th Street in New York, which was four-stories high and capable of serving thousands of hearty, unprocessed meals per day. When its doors opened in June 1933, Anna Roosevelt Dall was on hand at the ceremony to praise Macfadden's efforts to aid "the honest hungry."[60]

Once the Roosevelts were finally settled down in the White House, with FDR now enjoying broad support that allowed him to rollout fifteen major pieces of legislation in his legendary first hundred days, the relationship between the First Family and the Macfadden firm became more perfunctory. Following disagreements about money and whether more controversial topics such as birth control had a place in *Babies—Just Babies,*

Fig.6.2 A March 1933 issue of *Liberty* featuring the newly inaugurated president of the United States, Franklin Delano Roosevelt. © 2021 The Liberty Library Corporation. All Rights Reserved.

Eleanor Roosevelt resigned her editorship, causing the periodical to fold.[61] Meanwhile, the Father of American Physical Culture began to chafe at what he saw as government overreach in the New Deal. For instance, only one year after FDR's daughter had presided over his penny restaurant opening, Macfadden was complaining to the press that the National Recovery Administration's labor policies were interfering with his ability to keep his eateries running.[62] While the publisher had liked the idea of having a charismatic leader with a bold vision for mitigating banking crises, mass unemployment, and extreme poverty through temporary measures, he strongly opposed economic policies that expanded federal control over the operations of private businesses, especially his own.[63] Quickly, he became increasingly critical of both FDR and the New Deal, a position he would publicize in editorials in *Liberty* and speeches to Republican political organizations and other businessmen.

Still, the relationship of mutual interest built between Macfadden Publications, the White House, and the federal government would continue along several avenues. For one, *Liberty* remained a conduit for FDR and members of his administration to communicate with the public and shape popular narratives about New Deal programs and policies. Invitations continued to be issued to Oursler and his wife to visit the Roosevelts in Washington and Hyde Park, where the president flattered the editor by discussing matters of state with him in his private quarters.[64]

Another avenue of collaboration occurred through *True Detective Mysteries*. As the Roosevelt administration was coming to power, the sense of crisis linked to economic depression coexisted alongside a perceived national crime wave. Gangster films such as *The Public Enemy* (1931) and *Scarface* (1932) painted a picture of a society thoroughly corrupted by an organized criminal underworld. Reflecting broader disillusionment with government failures, agents of the state were often no match for this genre's supervillain outlaws, who tended to be portrayed more sympathetically than the police and other state officials who struggled to bring them down. In response, J. Edgar Hoover, the ambitious director of the Bureau of Investigation (renamed the FBI in 1935), launched a "war on crime" that aimed to dramatically raise the profile of the agency he headed and expand its purview. An anti-crime campaign, he intuited, would find favor from both Republicans and Democrats. From Roosevelt's perspective, a successful "war on crime" by the Bureau of Investigation, especially one focused on thieves and racketeers, could help to legitimize other expansions of government resources and federal power designed to rein in white-collar "racketeers." Both Hoover and Roosevelt understood that this "war on crime" would be "won" not on the streets or at the courts but in the media.[65]

While the Bureau of Investigation focused on hunting down high-profile "public enemies" like George "Machine Gun" Kelly, Bonnie and Clyde, and John Dillinger, Hoover developed a sophisticated public relations operation. This operation worked by "leveraging access to its in-demand crime stories to create close relations with dozens of reporters, broadcasters, and editors," while simultaneously blacklisting unfriendly media outlets.[66] As the editor of the third-most-popular American weekly and the supervising editor of *True Detective Mysteries* and *Master Detective,* Oursler was a particularly high-value collaborator, and Macfadden Publications had a proven record of making itself useful.

There was a natural synergy between priorities in Washington and the concept of *True Detective Mysteries,* which merged pulp fiction narrative styles with an emphasis on actual crimes and investigations. Hoover's Bureau wanted to portray criminals as larger-than-life villains, thoroughly evil types with dramatic arcs that ended in their downfall and destruction. At the same time, rather than emphasizing the figure of the singular hero-detective working outside the system, it promoted the idea that such criminals could only be countered by a well-resourced federal agency possessing broad jurisdiction and unparalleled professional skill. *True Detective Mysteries* combined a capacity for sensational storytelling with extensive, realistic coverage of how experts investigated crimes and prosecuted criminals. Furthermore, in keeping with the ethos of Macfadden's other publications, the magazine developed avenues of audience participation that cultivated a sense of connection between readers and broader crime-fighting systems. From the start of the magazine, this included invitations for workaday police officers and detectives to submit their experiences. In 1931, it introduced "The Line-up," which asked audiences for help locating persons wanted by law enforcement agencies (*Master Detective*'s similar feature was called "Wanted"). With access to materials provided by Bureau of Investigation officials, the magazine was also able to give readers the "inside story" of famous cases. "You read many columns in the daily newspapers about John Dillinger; some fact and some fiction. But the complete inside details . . . will be revealed to the public for the first time in our next issue," a typical *True Detective Mysteries* from 1934 promised.[67]

Liberty too played an important role in shaping popular understandings of the federal government's "war on crime." Beginning in the early 1930s, the magazine covered organized crime regularly. In 1933, "How You Can Prevent Crime," a long article ("Reading time: 18 minutes 20 seconds") conveyed Hoover's vision to the public. Authored by Attorney General Homer S. Cummings, it explains that fighting the modern big-time criminal requires acquiring "the same or better weapons and better organization than his own," which could only really happen through an infusion of resources and coordination at the federal level.[68] Subsequently, when the National Conference on Crime was convened by the Attorney General in December 1934, Oursler, representing Macfadden Publications, was the only editor invited to address the gathering.[69] During the conference, Oursler made "a plan to start a sustained campaign of stories" in *Liberty* "which would present in dramatic detail the quiet efficiency and startling achievements" of Hoover's Bureau of Investigation.[70] A few weeks later, the magazine published the first installment of "Our New Civil War," a multipart serial about "How Uncle Sam's Mysterious 'G-Men' Destroy Public Enemies."

Written by the investigative journalist Will Irwin, "Our New Civil War" praises "superpoliceman" Hoover and his cadre of physically and mentally superior "G-Men" who pursue criminals with military discipline. It also explains how the Department of Justice "has built up a scientific laboratory of crime unexcelled in this country and rapidly becoming the best in the world," before providing a breathless account of how the bureau has tracked down notorious kidnappers.[71] The following week's installment focused on the tracking of bank robbers, specifically Bonnie and Clyde, while the third narrated the downfall of the Dillinger gang, and the fourth offered an in-depth look at the Bureau of Investigation's latest technologies and investigation methods. Through this series, and many other collaborative articles in *Liberty* and *True Detective Mysteries* that followed, Macfadden Publications became "a leading voice in the successful crusade to make the G-man a national hero."[72] Expressing his appreciation to Macfadden, Hoover declared, "I regard Fulton Oursler as one of our truly great editors."[73]

In summary, during Roosevelt's first term in office, a period of fast-moving political restructuring that dramatically expanded the size and scope of the federal government in response to the Great Depression, a complicated relationship took shape between the administration and the publishing house that boasted the "Largest News Stand Sale in the World." On the one hand, Macfadden and his supervising editor hitched their wagon to FDR's rising star, encouraged by the politician's personal charisma and media savvy, and no doubt influenced by his popularity among working-class Americans who constituted the bulk of Macfadden Publications' readers. The mutual benefits of this relationship brought the company valuable access to the Roosevelt family and the nation's corridors of power more generally, while the president and others in Washington gained access to a valuable constellation of media outlets. On the other hand, the implementation of the New Deal, particularly legislation that empowered

Fig.6.3 The "war on crime" featured in the June 1934 issue of True *Detective Mysteries*. Reproduced from the author's personal collection

the government to regulate private corporations, threw into relief ideological differences that put Macfadden and his publishing corporation increasingly at odds with the administration and its supporters. With its long-standing dynamic of participatory pastiche allowing for such tensions, Macfadden Publications supported the legitimacy of expansive executive power wielded by exceptional individuals and selectively promoted the growth of government influence in certain areas, especially unemployment relief and the war on crime. Meanwhile, it increasingly circulated conservative viewpoints, including those voiced personally by Macfadden.

The Macfadden Market

In late 1934, when many companies were gasping for life, Macfadden Publications purchased two more periodicals, the film fan magazines *Photoplay* and *Shadowplay,* quickly scrapping the latter to combine readerships. With a history stretching back to the 1910s, *Photoplay* was known

for providing intimate coverage of the film industry and its stars, its reviews of popular movies, and for its annual Medal of Honor contest in
which voting fans—rather than industry professionals or critics—got to
decide the year's best picture. It thus was suited to slot easily into the offerings of Macfadden Publications where it was edited by Ruth Waterbury,
an experienced writer and critic who had previously headed the company's
Movie Mirror.

Taking over *Photoplay* brought increased opportunities to Macfadden
Publications. Over the course of the 1930s, Americans averaged purchasing sixty to eighty million movie tickets *per week.* Furthermore, the
major film studios' 1934 enactment of a set of self-censorship guidelines
known as the Motion Picture Production Code increased the respectability
of cinema across demographics. These factors meant more potential customers as well as advertiser interest in movie magazines. Through becoming the publisher of the nation's most popular film fan periodical,
Macfadden Publications reaped the benefits of increased circulation and
ad revenue while also cementing a mutually beneficial two-way relationship with film studios and stars during Hollywood's Golden Age.[74]

Concurrently, Macfadden Publications continued to spin off its magazines into radio programs, which became a ubiquitous medium of national
entertainment in the 1930s.[75] One popular program was the *True Detective
Mysteries* radio show. Another was the *True Story*–affiliated *The Court of
Human Relations,* which started on NBC and then moved to CBS, becoming one of the network's first corporate-sponsored programs.[76] *The
Court of Human Relations,* in turn, provided material for the company to
produce a series of short films, which were shown in more than one hundred towns and cities and, of course, promoted in the company's radio,
film, true story, and physical culture magazines. Another radio show that
Macfadden Publications created during the Depression was *Forum of Liberty.* In this program, Macfadden was joined on air by business leaders
who presented engaging histories—or true stories—of their industries,
often with the goal of countering popular anti-business sentiments. As remembered by the eminent historian of broadcasting Eric Barnouw—who
himself produced and directed this program in the mid-1930s—the show's
guests would purchase advertising space in *Liberty* for the privilege of communicating their informational content to Macfadden's listeners on this
program.[77]

In keeping with this high pace of media production, Macfadden Publications continued refining its advertising and marketing techniques. To
streamline how it sold space in its magazines, the company packaged together *True Romances, True Experiences, Dream World, Movie Mirror,*

and *Radio Mirror* into the Macfadden "Women's Group." *True Detective Mysteries* and *Master Detective* made up the "Detective Group," which was aimed at men. Separate operations were maintained for *Photoplay, Liberty, True Story,* and *Physical Culture.* This allowed for better targeting of clients and customers. In late 1935, the company also revived its institutional advertising campaign, announcing, "Macfadden Publications Emerges From America's Six Year Debacle with the Largest Voluntary Magazine Circulation in the World."[78] To further contextualize this claim, the company developed a portrait of what it called the Macfadden Market over the next year. In January 1936, its campaign asked, cheekily, "When Does a Market Really Become a Market and Not Merely the Topic of an Advertising Solicitation?" Grabbing attention with a self-reflective acknowledgment that markets were often tautological constructions, this ad assured readers that Macfadden's market represented a "real" social entity rather than a "theoretical" abstraction. What connected Macfadden's readers was that they had been turned into a mass market by the company. "For fifteen years . . . the conditioning of the mind to a desire to buy has been fostered consciously and constantly" by its magazines, as "the cooperative job we have undertaken" has been "to keep the faith of a great mass of people in the new American idea of a *participating* mass." In other words, the message was that Macfadden Publications' interactive media had cultivated among working-class readers a sense of personal investment in a consumer capitalist system that not only allowed, but relied upon, their active and enthusiastic participation. And continuing, the company mused, "You know, you can do a lot with a circulation of six million readers. You can create either a market or a revolution, depending entirely upon the condition of your own mind and your own faith in your own America." Macfadden Publications, the company claimed, was converting the masses into the "largest single market that has ever been developed," and it was doing so with their enthusiastic participation.[79]

Such ads conveyed a powerful subtext. In the absence of continued collaboration between Macfadden Publications and corporate America, might six million readers look elsewhere for ideas, somewhere with less "faith in America," and become more inclined toward revolution? Indeed, there were many signs pointing toward the possibility of a leftist revolutionary uprising. In 1934, the socialist Upton Sinclair, who had penned many articles for Macfadden's early twentieth-century magazines, had launched a wildly popular campaign to become governor of California, terrifying the state's major industries, including Hollywood, and putting pressure on the Roosevelt administration. Although Sinclair lost, his campaign showed the growing enthusiasm for democratic socialism and leftist ideologies.[80]

Meanwhile, the Communist Party had been making major strides in the United States through its Popular Front strategy, which encouraged coalition-building between different leftist and liberal groups, and its concrete support for civil rights and antiracism work. While official membership was never large, the party's political and economic principles, as well as its organizing strategies, had become influential enough to cause bipartisan anxieties.[81]

Partly in response to populist pressures from the left, the Roosevelt administration had asked Congress in 1935 to implement a "Second New Deal," which established the Social Security Act, the Works Progress Administration, and the pro-union National Labor Relations Act (a.k.a. the Wagner Act). Critics of the Second New Deal from the right, including Macfadden, saw it as an unconstitutional betrayal of American capitalism. As he put it in *Liberty*, Roosevelt's "introduction of socialistic activities" was now leading to the "enslavement of labor through rules and regulations," while the New Deal's "restriction of business" was likely to "bring menacing situations of great consequences."[82] Macfadden also charged the New Deal "with direct responsibility for stopping the greatest surge toward unprecedented prosperity that any country has ever experienced."[83] In his estimation, the inefficiencies that had caused the Depression had been close to working themselves out with a little help from the administration in 1933, but subsequent legislation had sabotaged recovery. So loud was Macfadden's surging activism against FDR that onlookers began to speculate that he might be launching a political career in the Republican Party. As rumors began to circulate to this effect, the publisher coyly responded that he would not refuse the party's nomination for president.[84] When a fifty-cent pamphlet appeared on newsstands titled "Bernarr Macfadden: Highlights of 50 Years of Service for His Country," observers could not help but note that the pamphlet "looked like campaign literature."[85]

Meanwhile, Macfadden Publications' ongoing corporate relations campaign portrayed the publishing empire as an entity that had, even within the constraints of the Depression, optimally realized American economic and political ideals. It emphasized that its "largest voluntary circulation in the world" was an explicitly "free flowing" one, which produced entirely "new fields" of magazine consumers.[86] Not coincidentally, this promotional language paralleled common talking points of the conservative anti–New Deal movement, which operationalized freedom rhetoric to valorize laissez-faire economic policies. Indeed, this was the moment in which the phrase "free enterprise" began taking off in the American lexicon, thanks to the wider business community's growing investment in public relations.[87]

Macfadden Publications also claimed that it took non-elite readers and "weld[ed] them into a cohesive, coherent, articulate buying market." This market was then framed as constituting the keystone of the modern US political economy, whose operations were dependent on voluntary mass participation. Notably, it was not the government or its New Deal programs that had brought this market of voluntary participants in the American economic system into being, but rather private industry and especially the Macfadden corporation itself, whose media had long "inspire[d] in [its] readers the American ideal so that their minds would be conditioned, not only to the desires themselves but to the desire to fulfill these desires," specifically through mass-mediated practices of mass consumption.[88]

According to Macfadden Publications, the political economy of the modern United States was rightly premised upon the growing participation of the masses, yet mass politics was threatening to derail the very system that had empowered the masses in the first place. The solution to this problem, the company maintained, required the mass cultivation of subjectivities and behaviors through which diverse individuals would, collectively, come to feel empowered and actualized by and within corporate and consumer capitalism. Only mass media could accomplish this, but not just any mass media was capable. The scale, skills, and resources of a large media corporation that had the right pro-business ideological orientation were needed; yet so too were popular credibility, established connections to marginalized communities, and the capacity to connect forgotten men *and women* to the broader corporate-driven consumer culture while making that consumer culture more responsive to them. Macfadden Publications, of course, possessed all these qualities in spades, as demonstrated through the Macfadden Market and the sophisticated institutional advertising media through which this concept was being conveyed.

Ultimately, Macfadden Publications' campaign, along with Macfadden's own politicking against the New Deal, made the publishing house an important part of a growing movement to combat leftist ideologies by rehabilitating the reputation of business leaders and promoting corporate capitalism itself. By the mid-1930s, it had become accepted wisdom within conservative circles that corporate America needed to do a better job "tell[ing] its story" to the public, as the president of the National Association of Manufacturers put it.[89] Macfadden Publications was already highly adept at this mission, having been working to position itself as an intermediary between corporate America and the masses since even before the onset of the Great Depression.

The increasing prominence of the Macfadden company and Macfadden himself as a source of anti–New Deal, pro-capitalist political discourse was noted by the left. This can be seen in the mid-decade coverage of the publisher and his media empire by the *New Masses* magazine. Since its establishment in 1926 by a group that included members of the Communist Party, *New Masses* had worked to establish a proletarian literary culture in the United States. As the historian Michael Denning has detailed, in this process, the magazine utilized the confession periodical format pioneered by Macfadden's publishing house to offer a "radical mutation of *True Story*" that put "the stories and confessions of ordinary workers" to work in service of its own radical political vision.[90] During the Great Depression, *New Masses* expanded its political commentary, attracting more readers and becoming "the principal organ of the American cultural left."[91] Perhaps because it so well understood the popularity of Macfadden Publications' formats and styles among working-class audiences, the magazine responded with alarm to Macfadden's growing political influence and the company's corporate propaganda.

This can be seen in the May 19, 1936, *New Masses* feature story, "Bernarr Macfadden: From Pornography to Politics." On the cover of this issue, a caricature depicts the publisher's head atop a scantily clad body with large breasts, smooth legs, and polished nails, clutching a tennis racket. The corresponding article, written by frequent contributor John Stuart, describes Macfadden's hold over "Millions of working-class and lower middle-class citizens" who "absorb" his "reactionary editorials and wallow in the politely-dressed filth of his confessionals," because "Macfadden primarily appeals to those whose lack of education or political understanding makes them vulnerable targets for his vicious demagoguery."[92] Continuing, Stuart glosses the publisher's now-familiar rags-to-riches biography to emphasize his lack of training and education, escalating his criticism to emphasize Macfadden's affection for strongmen. Reminding readers of the Italian Physical Culture Demonstration, the author exclaims that Macfadden's promotion of physical culture, nationalism, and military preparedness must "delight the hearts of Hitler and Mussolini," the latter of whom had just announced Italy's annexation of Ethiopia. An accompanying full-page cartoon reinforces the analogy between Macfadden and his brand of mass culture and capitalist totalitarianism. The publisher, wearing a top hat and leopard-print sling, executes a Nazi salute, as the cry "Hiel!" gives way to a parade of beefy, stupid-looking readers depositing coins into Macfadden Publications Inc.'s bulging sacks of money.

New Masses' coverage of Macfadden and his media company is indicative of a broader project among intellectuals in the 1930s to theorize the workings of mass culture with the intent of strengthening leftist political and social movements. Beyond merely disparaging its subject's turn toward the Republican Party, "Bernarr Macfadden: From Pornography to Politics"

Fig.6.4 An editorial cartoon criticizing Macfadden and his publishing company's readership that appeared in a 1936 issue of the *New Masses*. Riazanov Library Digital Archive

draws a direct line between one of America's largest purveyors of mass-market media and a corporate capitalist system that operated through the economic exploitation and political disempowerment of the masses while disingenuously pretending to represent their interests. Moreover, subsequent issues covered the Macfadden corporation's in-house efforts to reduce employee benefits and stymie union participation, countering the company's professed reputation as a democratic operation.[93]

At the same time, it is also the case that the *New Masses,* and other leftist commentators, couched their criticism of Macfadden Publications in terms that echoed critiques that had been leveled at the company for many years by social conservatives. This is apparent in the monstrous depiction of Macfadden as a blowsy woman, a caricature denigrating the thoughtlessness of shallow women consumers while coding as queer the publisher's obsession with the body, which was extended in the article to his fondness for foreign authoritarians. It is also evident in portrayals of the company's readership as an easily penetrable, self-absorbed, and mentally unfit mass, susceptible to pernicious foreign influences and the machinations of homegrown enemies of the people. Ironically, of course, Macfadden's publishing house had long cultivated its populist reputation through articulating solidarities with non-elite readers based on shared experiences of outsider-ness and suspicion of intellectuals and experts who treated them like this. One *New Masses* contributor who grasped this dynamic, and sought to interrupt it, was the African American novelist Richard Wright. When Wright published his manifesto "A Blueprint for Negro Literature" the following year, he prodded fellow writers to more sympathetically consider figures such as "that sixteen-year-old Negro girl reading the *True Story Magazine*" when creating their works.[94]

There are noteworthy structural similarities as well between how *New Masses* and the Macfadden corporation represented the Macfadden Market. Both framed the company's readership as a coherent, singular unit, already optimally primed to want to support a corporate consumer capitalist system dependent on their participation. In other words, even amid the political polarization of this era, the ideological construct of Macfadden's audience as an undifferentiated mass of impressionable, body-conscious, and feminized consumers was shared between Marxist critics of corporate capitalism and the system's staunchest defenders. Yet, while direct evidence about how audiences received and responded to Macfadden's media in the 1930s is fragmentary, there are many indications that the participants in the so-called Macfadden Market were neither being "welded" into a homogenized market of consumer-citizens nor mindlessly abetting the political and economic exploitation of workers by domestic and foreign demagogues.

Multiple sources point to wide variability among the Macfadden company's readership in terms of age, gender identity, race, ethnicity, location, and personal circumstances. These variations provide essential context for understanding how individuals would have consumed its mass media, which like other realms of popular culture likely brought dispersed audiences closer together in some ways while simultaneously allowing for new modes of expressing and "delineating differences."[95] Moreover, considering the demographics, plural, of the company's readership shows its popularity among groups that overwhelmingly tended to: support New Deal programs, oppose the excesses of corporate capitalism, contribute to movements such as industrial unionism and agricultural labor organizing, and articulate complex identities in relationship to US consumer citizenship.

One kind of source offering indirect insights into the Macfadden Market is anthropological and sociological research conducted by academics and educators who fixed their gaze on working-class and non-white communities. Studies published during the Depression note the popularity of Macfadden-brand publications in places and spaces where Americans from southern and eastern European immigrant backgrounds lived, worked, and studied, and thus among communities that provided the backbone for industrial unionism and its support for pro-worker legislation.[96] These include Harvey Warren Zorbaugh's *The Gold Coast and the Slum* (1929), W. C. Haygood's "The Magazine and the Reader in South Chicago" (1935), and William F. Rasche's "The Reading Interests of Young Workers" (1936). In his 1939 work *The Negro Family in the United States,* eminent Howard University sociologist E. Franklin Frazier discusses the popularity of confession magazines among African Americans he interviewed, noting the particular appeal of magazines like *True Story* to single female parents, one of whom "recounted in her life-history a story from one of these magazines that centered around the romantic career of an unmarried mother."[97] Working-class Black women were at the vanguard of multiple intersecting radical political movements in the 1930s, often using their worker and consumer power strategically to advance causes of social, racial, and economic justice.[98] Scholars writing about Indigenous nations and peoples recorded observing similar reading material. Margaret Mead's *The Changing Culture of an Indian Tribe* (1932) notes the popularity of Macfadden's periodicals among members of an anonymized nation living on a reservation in the rural Great Plains.[99] In his study of the Fort Belknap Assiniboine reservation in northern Montana, anthropologist David Rodnick observed that "[t]he reading matter of the young was mainly confined to *True Story Magazine, True Romances, True Detective Stories*" and other similar titles, "all of which are sold at the Lodgepole store."[100] M. Inez Hilger's study of Chippewa families living on the White Earth reservation in Minnesota catalogs that *True Story, True Romances,* and *True Experiences* were among the most popular magazines purchased at reservation stores.[101] Elisabeth Colson's 1941–1942 study among the Makah of Neah Bay, Washington, documents a number of women and girls "obtain[ing] the *True Story* magazine and other 'confessional periodicals' each month" as well as a trend of reading true detective stories.[102] Importantly, these were nations and communities whose memberships often focused on survivance and the maintenance of sovereignty throughout the Depression, not assimilation into a homogenized American mass market.[103]

Biographies and oral histories provide another window onto the social realities of the so-called Macfadden Market. The historian Vicki L. Ruiz's interviews with Mexican Americans who came of age between the world wars reveal the popularity of film fan and confession magazines, including *Photoplay* and *True Story,* in the Southwest, particularly among young women trying to navigate youth culture and dating.[104] In his memoirs about picking cotton as an itinerant worker in the mid-1930s, Alvin Clement recalled the racially segregated reading groups that formed after the workday was over. One group, led by an elderly Black woman, read newspapers and pulp magazines aloud, including *True Detective* and *True*

Romances.[105] In her interview of a young African American woman named Bernice Reid in Virginia a few years later, an employee for the Works Progress Administration's Federal Writers' Project, which supported the collection of oral histories, noted that Mrs. Reid classified reading material, including *True Story* magazine, as her only luxury.[106] Again, these were readers from demographics who overwhelmingly supported challenges to conservative ideologies during the Depression.

Then there are records from those who tried to raise money by submitting stories to Macfadden Publications. After Beatrice Sears, a young woman living in Arkansas, had a narrative accepted, she wrote in expressing her gratitude: "I can find no words to tell you how overjoyed I was. . . . I have been helping my sister, her five small children and her husband, who has been out of work for nearly three years. . . . And when I add that my widowed sister and her family have been living with me . . . you will know that your check helped not only one person, but at least twelve."[107] Maybe Mrs. L. S. Whitehead, the hardworking proprietor of a laundry in Georgia, had the same goal in mind of obtaining money for basic subsistence when she told a government oral historian, perhaps cheekily, "I have always thought I would write my life history and send it to the *True Story* magazine."[108] In the dusty Texas Panhandle, a poor musician named Woody Guthrie tried his hand at writing confessions for *True Story* before becoming a folk icon.[109] Out West, labor activist Julia Ruuttila, a founder of the International Woodworkers of America, sent off writing to *True Story* when money got tight during a lockout. For a story that took her less than four hours to write, she received "a fortune" of $165, which helped her support a soup kitchen for workers.[110]

Alfonso G. Hernandez, a young Mexican American man living in New Mexico, took a different approach, combining handwritten stories about his life in the pages of a scholastic composition book he then titled *Hernandez' True Story*.[111] On the title page of this faux magazine, which ended up being preserved in an archive, the author explains his intent to submit his writing to Macfadden Publications, to be considered for inclusion in *True Story, True Experiences,* or *True Romances*. Then, in installments such as "My Smashed-up Marriage" and "The Self I Left Behind," Hernandez narrates various economic hardships, romantic entanglements, and domestic dramas from his experiences. All these stories mirror stylistic conventions associated with Macfadden's publications, including snappy prose, short sentences, compelling titles, and a melodramatic tone. For instance, "My Smashed-up Marriage" begins, "I thought it would be easy to tell my story. The story of young love turned into a long[,] long hate that burns like a fire in my heart." The rest of the story narrates his poverty in the early 1930s, his luck getting employment from a "government project," and the sadness of his wife leaving him for another man in Mexico. Interestingly, Hernandez explicitly models other aspects of Macfadden-brand periodicals as well, penning announcements for upcoming issues of "outstanding stories from real life" and drawing fake advertisements, including one that publicizes the services of "Alfonso Hernandez, Advisor to Youth," who is depicted as his community's own Macfadden-like advice-giver. In addition, there is poetry in English and Spanish, jokes, and local news stories with a "A.H. Press" (rather than A.P. Press) byline. Solicitations for readers to participate by writing in also appear. "Can you help me??" Hernandez implores in the story "Let Fate Decide," asking, "Which will I take,—Minnie Lucero . . . in her full bloom of her youth or will I take Juanita, a widowed wife who knows life like a copybook????" Like many true story protagonists, as a narrator Hernandez overcomes economic and emotional strife and atones for his indiscretions, emerging a better and wiser person who helps others by sharing his story.

Whether Hernandez ever sent his work to Macfadden Publications would be hard to know. This is especially the case because, in keeping with the tendency in the company's magazines to center Anglo- and Euro-American appearing characters, Hernandez chose to Anglicize the names of his characters. As the key to pseudonyms at the beginning of *Hernandez' True Story* shows (a featured that Macfadden Publications required submissions to include), the author calls himself "Albert Madison," while his wife Aurora is renamed "Helen." Similarly, Alfredo Nuanez is "Fred Nelson," and baby Eduardo, "Eddie." Considering Hernandez's close familiarity with and skill at imitating Macfadden's periodicals, it is sensible to hypothesize that this was a strategic choice crafted in response to the author's perception of the limits of Macfadden Publications' promises of inclusion to readers. At the same time, the very existence of this document suggests how cultural forms commercialized by Macfadden Publications' media empire, especially the popular confession, offered a particularly attractive and accessible mode of expression for some located at the peripheries of economic, political, and cultural power, which was likely the case for a border-crossing agricultural worker living in a period of heightened anti-Mexican discrimination and exploitation in the US Southwest in the Depression.[112] Notably, *Hernandez' True Story* ends with the author expressing his dual-consciousness of both facing and being able to resist oppression. "Like a flower in the desert, I was trampled underfoot, crushed and cast aside. Yet I am smiling bravely on," Hernandez concludes, imagining future success for himself as a popular writer.

• • •

On October 10, 1936, Macfadden was in San Antonio, Texas, where he had traveled to give a speech in support of Kansas governor Alf Landon, the Republican candidate for US president. As late as that summer, Macfadden had remained evasive about whether he might run for the highest office himself, fanning the hopes of fans who formed Macfadden for President Clubs. After the nominating convention, though, he had turned to stumping for Landon in person and via his publications. After his speech, the publisher, now the oldest licensed pilot in the country, was taking off in his personal airplane when something went wrong and the aircraft smashed into a fence. Despite his age, Macfadden emerged from the wreckage completely unscathed, flying back to New York in another plane.

Following the election a few weeks later, when Roosevelt won with the highest share of the popular and electoral votes in over a century, a similar dynamic unfolded. While Landon crashed and burned, the publisher moved on unfazed, reminding readers in that week's *Liberty* that while he had criticized many of the president's policies, he had done so without animus, in a spirit of conscientiousness and American patriotism. "We should cement our forces, put our shoulders to the wheel and work together as a common unit," Macfadden now pronounced.[113]

The remainder of this issue of *Liberty* featured a crowded mélange of content typical to Macfadden Publications' media. There are stories related to: Americans' victory in the Great War, in recognition of Armistice Day; the continuing successes of the FBI's "war on crime"; and the looming threat of "Europe's Coming Conflict," discussed in an article about Stalin and Hitler written by a German American named George Sylvester Viereck. Rounding out the contents is a feature on college football; a Wild West love story; a profile of actress Carole Lombard's love life; film reviews; letters from readers; and color ads for Ethyl gasoline, Lucky Strike cigarettes, and many name-brand home goods. This mixture of topics and formats reflects the multifaceted Macfadden media empire's main areas of emphasis in the late 1930s—news, physical culture, popular entertainment, and stories about everyday people and celebrities—as well as its elevated corporate standing and influence on public affairs.

On this latter point, while Macfadden proved unable to get a Republican (or himself) installed in the Oval Office in the 1936, it is also true that he and his publishing company had been enormously successful in establishing relationships with powerful political actors, from Herbert Hoover, Mussolini, the Roosevelts and the Roosevelt administration, members of the Republican Party, and J. Edgar Hoover's FBI to innumerable business and industry leaders, including those in Hollywood and radio broadcasting, all while extending the popular reach of Macfadden-brand media products.

Through such connections, Macfadden Publications had strengthened its position as an interlocutor between "the people" and the powerful. In other words, it had figured out how to use its mass circulations to claim space and authority within the corporate and political worlds while delivering to the "forgotten man" and woman attractive and entertaining media content—content that promised venues for self-expression as well as intimate access to politicians, celebrities, and business leaders eager to share their own stories with the masses whose support and understanding was a valuable commodity.

Going forward, Macfadden Publications would continue to build upon the political and economic worldview and business tactics it developed during the 1930s, focusing on growing its circulations, packaging its diverse domestic readers as a singular market, and strategically operationalizing discourses of economic revolution, citizenship, and freedom. Through these methods, the company would promote a US political economy based on mass consumption; consumer citizenship; and the valorization of capitalism, individualism, and limitations on government power in some capacities but not others. Utilizing its identity as a publishing house of and for the people, an identity honed during the Great Depression, it would project its corporate vision as a reflection and manifestation of popular desires.

CHAPTER SEVEN

International Issues, Foreign Editions, and the Global Popular

THE RISE OF MACFADDEN PUBLICATIONS in the 1920s and its transformation into a corporate behemoth in the following decade turned Macfadden and his publishing empire into potent symbols of America's sensational and expansive mass media and culture industries. News outlets as well as advertising, film, and radio trade publications closely followed developments with the company and its president, whose business instincts were a source of fascination across multiple industries. Ambitious as ever, Macfadden would spend the second half of the 1930s weighing in on politics, renovating a physical culture resort in Miami, leading epic walking expeditions, and fighting with Mary over their finances as he sought a divorce and she accused him of diverting their shared assets into the supposedly charitable Macfadden Foundation. And through all this, he would remain at the helm of Macfadden Publications, directing the operations of his publishing firm on its quest for greater influence and higher circulations.

To an extent heretofore under-recognized, some of Macfadden Publications' interwar-era revenue and circulation growth during this time came from overseas. Having courted international readers since its earliest days as a purveyor of physical culture media, the publishing house's dramatic expansion following *True Story*'s success was centered in the United States but uncontained by its borders. Starting in the late 1920s and continuing through the Great Depression, local versions of Macfadden Publications' confession magazines appeared in Great Britain, Sweden, Norway, Germany, France, and Holland, in addition to Canada. Furthermore, copies of the company's true story, fitness, film, and other periodicals reached an even wider world of consumers via mail-order subscriptions, local magazine importers and sellers, and a bourgeoning international trade in back issues.

To appreciate the story of Macfadden Publications' global expansion in this period requires looking away from Macfadden himself for a bit. This story can be brought into view better through a "connective comparison" of three foreign markets—Great Britain, Germany, and Australia.[1] These were not the only places where Macfadden's publications obtained noteworthy sales, but they do appear to have constituted his company's largest markets outside North America. Separately, each of these locations provides information about the processes of production, distribution, and reception that shaped Macfadden Publications' international reach. Together, they show how the company and its print media influenced and was influenced by broader trends of media globalization as it contributed to the United States' new role as the world's foremost exporter of mass culture.

The phenomenon of US media globalization, in which Macfadden Publications played a part, resulted from many factors. Especially important was the scale of American mass production combined with the policies of a "promotional state" that viewed cultural exports as a means of bolstering geopolitical, economic, and cultural power.[2] Additionally, growing local demands for cheap popular entertainments and consumer goods in other countries were being stoked by an advertising industry whose clients were always seeking new markets for their products.[3] Actively shaped by various state and non-state actors, transnational economic and cultural brokers, and foreign consumers, the global circulation of American mass-market media and other cultural forms remained a complex and multidirectional process that contributed to the ascendency of the United States as a world power while also generating friction and alternative impacts.[4] Macfadden Publications was one player in this story, and its participation influenced the company's overarching trajectory.

Analyzing Macfadden Publications' overseas expansion in the interwar era reveals several trends relevant to the history of the publishing house and to broader phenomena of US media globalization. First, it shows how patterns of empire, migration, and trade established in earlier decades laid the groundwork for post-WWI international growth. The Physical Culture Publishing Company's early twentieth-century circulations of body-centric books and magazines, and the networks they helped shape, initiated demand for, and facilitated the material mobility of, a broader range of

Macfadden-brand publications across borders in later decades. Next, by elucidating connections between America in the world and the world in America, it shows how Macfadden Publications' catering to a multiethnic, working-class domestic readership in the transformative post-WWI era helped facilitate international growth. Modes of production and editorial methods that cultivated a feedback loop between itself and diverse readers allowed Macfadden Publications to continually fine-tune its products to achieve growing appeal among non-elite readers from many different backgrounds and circumstances. Through this process, media genres and products developed for a diverse and often immigrant mass readership at home came to possess qualities that rendered them more likely to be "culturally translatable to the maximum degree" across numerous international borders.[5]

Furthermore, this analysis throws into relief how the Macfadden corporation's evolution into a US periodical powerhouse—one whose capitalization and broader influence was tied to the ever-growing volume of its circulations—worked to incentivize international expansion and shape its forms. While Macfadden Publications started off in the business of selling magazines to readers, in its pursuit of advertising revenue it moved into the business of selling stories about the centrality of the Macfadden Market to the political economy and future operations of consumer capitalism, which the company, like many others, theorized as requiring constant, unfettered expansion. From the early 1930s onward, then, the non-elite readership of Macfadden Publications at home was understood and represented by the company as an analog for a wider world market whose experiences and sensibilities resembled those of this domestic market, and could be molded in similar ways. Domestic expansion, in this story, was linked to international expansion, for, as the company's corporate relations materials stressed, "This world of ours has definitely started on a new economic era which, beginning here in America, will ultimately encompass the globe."[6] What spread through the Macfadden Market, the company predicted, was likely to spread abroad, and rising international circulation statistics strengthened this message.

This prediction would, to an extent, become a self-fulfilling prophesy. Since Macfadden Publications' business model relied on ever-increasing circulation, the products it churned out needed to circulate somewhere, and foreign markets came to provide an obvious means of increasing sales as well as an outlet for back issues that might otherwise require pulping. Yet at the same time, Macfadden Publications' reach also stemmed from its earlier history, as well as the capacities it had built to construct business arrangements and media products that were adaptable to variegated local circumstances across changing social, political, economic, and cultural landscapes.

Pulp Aggregators and Local Producers in Britain

Predictably, the first overseas edition of *True Story* was produced in London. As we have seen, Macfadden's early business enterprises were transatlantic affairs, with his physical culture media pitched to British audiences and traveling through Britain's colonial and neo-imperial geographies. Although the paroxysms of the First World War and the subsequent economic boom in the United States led the company to concentrate on its domestic market, as described in previous chapters, this reorientation by no means represented a severing of its transatlantic connections.

After Macfadden's London office closed, the American edition of *Physical Culture*, along with many of the company's health and fitness books, remained available to British readers via the company's London agent, the Atlas Publishing and Distributing Company. Articles, letters, and snapshots from British health enthusiasts continued to appear regularly in *Physical Culture*, as did articles by British writers who had previously contributed to *Physical Development*. Reader correspondence evidences the continued flow of the company's physical culture media in South Africa, Singapore, and India, where it could serve to publicize the company's newer publications.

Three years after *True Story* first appeared on US newsstands, a British *True Story* debuted. The inaugural issue announced a first prize of one hundred pounds, as well as several smaller awards, for the best "true to life" stories submitted by readers. "We believe that 'truth is stranger than fiction,'" the editors declared, "We want life experiences. We want to serve life as it is—red-hot from the pens of those who have felt its sorrows and its joys."[7] The British *True Story* was, clearly, based on the exact same premise as its American counterpart, and it solicited the same genres of stories from reader-contributors, offering lucrative prizes and repeating the American magazine's enticing catchphrase. However, for most of the 1920s, the British *True Story* did not bear the imprint of Macfadden or his company. Instead, it was edited, published, and distributed by the London-based publishing house Hutchinson's.

Headed by the British businessman Walter Hutchinson, Hutchinson's would soon become known in many parts of the Anglophone World as a prolific distributor of paperback books. But first, the company played an important role in the British periodical market.[8] In the years following the

First World War, Hutchinson's became the "prime mover in Britain" of "American-style" pulp magazines—that is, cheaply made periodicals that were usually packed with genre fiction and true stories.[9] Alongside *True Story*, the company released *Adventure-Story Magazine* (1922), dedicated to "stories of action and adventure the whole world over, [and] packed with plot and local colour." A spin-off called *Mystery-Story* appeared the next year. In 1924, following the release of Macfadden's *True Romances* in the United States, Hutchinson's introduced *True Love Stories,* which advertised "romances taken from actual life." In these instances, Hutchinson's appears to have functioned as a designated British aggregator and distributor for content licensed from Macfadden Publications throughout most of the 1920s. While the origins of this arrangement are unclear (Hutchinson's main offices, and its documents, burned during the 1940–1941 Blitz), it is possible that Macfadden, through his long-standing business interests in Britain, recognized Hutchinson's as the most appropriate outlet for his promising new publications. It is also possible that the enterprising Walter Hutchinson, who was closely attuned to developments in the American periodical market, approached Macfadden Publications with a licensing request. In any case, Hutchinson's *True Story* and *True Love Stories,* as well as the company's mystery and adventure pulps, reprinted material taken from Macfadden's American magazines (as well as from other titles that Macfadden Publications came to distribute). In addition to confession narratives, this included tales that originated in *Midnight Mystery Stories* and *Ghost Stories* as well as Macfadden Publications' distinctive posed photographic illustrations.[10] Significantly, Hutchinson's also appears to have worked out similar arrangements with other American publishing companies, including the dime novel powerhouse Street & Smith which had moved into pulp magazines. Thus, while Macfadden Publications strove to distinguish itself from its many pulp competitors in the United States by publishing larger-format magazines and aggressively promoting a distinctive Macfadden "brand," across the Atlantic its true stories and pulp fiction were presented alongside other companies' pulp products and packaged in a way that obscured the origins of any single contribution.

Hutchinson's periodicals may have exuded an "American style" through their content and packaging, but the company's British versions of Macfadden's periodicals also reflected trends in commercial publishing that were historically transatlantic in nature. Just as Macfadden's health and fitness works had been shaped in dialog with the physical culture movement in England, the company's new periodicals embodied innovations and trends rooted in the British publishing landscape. For instance, in the years surrounding the turn of the century, England's "essential triumvirate of publisher-entrepreneurs," George Newnes, Alfred Harmsworth, and Arthur Pearson had, contemporary with American figures such as Pulitzer, Hearst, and Macfadden, developed mass-market periodicals that featured "human interest" stories, opportunities for audience participation, and an intimate editorial tone.[11] The case has even been made that Newnes's magazines *Tit-Bits* (1881) and *The Wide World* (1895) should be seen as the originators of the true story genre that would become associated with Macfadden during the interwar era.[12] Following the Great War, English publishers also played an important role in identifying and capitalizing on an increasing demand for periodicals that catered to working-class audiences, specifically young women who labored outside the home for wages. For instance, the same year Macfadden debuted *True Story*, Pearson's editor-in-chief and his wife started *Peg's Paper*, a weekly paper in which a chatty editor named Peg entertained and advised other "mill girls" like herself. If Mary Williamson's life had taken a different turn, and she had not met Macfadden, she might have been a target reader of this publication and others like it.

Another shared facet of American and British print culture in the early twentieth century was the "democratization of writing"—that is, the enormous growth of popular interest in the production and consumption of amateur literary output.[13] While the "democratization of writing" in Britain was certainly tied to local conditions, including the growth of a culturally vibrant working-class political movement that utilized mass-market forms of print media, it was affected by two important, related developments in America. First, there was the lucrative amateur writing advice industry (whose advertisements were a staple in Macfadden-brand media) that mushroomed in the United States before crossing the Atlantic.[14] Second, America's postwar magazine boom, in which Macfadden Publications played a large role, opened opportunities for foreign writers to sell their English-language works to content-hungry American publishers. While the postwar mass-market periodical marketplace was headquartered in the United States, it was by no means bounded by the nation's geographic borders. As a result, true story, pulp fiction, and other forms of mass-market media published in America, such as Macfadden's publications, not only influenced the literary productions of foreign contributors but were also shaped by them.

The complex transatlantic linkages involved in creating Macfadden Publications' media in the United States and the company's British circulations sometimes became visible. For instance, British *Physical Culture* subscribers encountered Macfadden Publications' ads soliciting content from writers anywhere in the world. British writing trade journals also provided amateur writers with advice and instructions related to submitting material to the company in New York. For its part, Hutchinson's actively solicited content from locals, both through the pages of its magazines and via various trade journals that catered to British amateur and professional writers, and Hutchison's solicitations then appeared in US-based trade journals. *The Editor,* the "Journal of Information for Literary Workers," described Hutchinson's as "one of the largest and most reliable of the British publishers," noting beginning in 1922 that "[w]riters with fresh ideas would do well to make a note of these people."[15]

Adding even more complexity to Macfadden's circulations in Britain is the fact that American editions of Macfadden's true story and pulp periodicals crossed the Atlantic (and then fanned out through other parts of the Anglophone World). As we have seen, British subscribers to *Physical Development* began receiving the same issues of *Physical Culture* as American subscribers during the Great War. The fitness magazine eagerly promoted each subsequent publication in the Macfadden family, which readers outside North America could obtain for a relatively small additional cost. In 1921, for example, a post-paid subscription to the American *True Story* cost seventy-five cents more for British readers, who received their copies via the London-based distribution agent W. T. Edgar.

Another way in which British audiences could obtain the American versions of Macfadden's magazines was through the trade in back issues, which became a big business in the 1920s. Back-issue trading—or "dumping" as it was perceived in some contexts—was a significant means through which American mass-market print media reached foreign readers, albeit one whose history remains hard to reconstruct. According to several sources, in the 1920s, tons of magazines from the United States traveled to England in the cargo holds of eastward-bound transatlantic merchant ships, where they provided ballast. Once ashore, these magazines then reached British consumers through outlets such as the department store Woolworth's, where "'Yank Magazines: Interesting Reading' . . . [were] remaindered at 3d." As one observer recounted, "[O]f these there [was] presumably a steady sale, as the stock change[d] frequently."[16] Since extant descriptions of these "Yank Mags" focus on the prevalence of adventure, detective, crime, and science fiction pulps, it is unclear whether Macfadden's "smooth" publications such as *True Story* traveled to Britain in this fashion, but at least the company's horror, mystery, and detective genre publications likely reached Britain via this route.

Back issues of American magazines also reached British readers through the enterprising efforts of a Jewish American businessman from the Lower East Side named Irving Samson Manheimer, who would later come to play an important role at Macfadden Publications Inc. A largely unknown historical figure, when Manheimer is remembered, it is for the role he would come to play in the midcentury comic book industry.[17] However, much earlier, in 1927, the businessman founded the Publisher's Surplus Corporation (later renamed Publishers Distributing Company), which sold back issues of cheap American magazines abroad, specializing in "magazines heavily weighted toward the schlock."[18] According to one magazine historian, Manheimer's company "was soon shipping 5,000,000 copies of magazines a month to London and thousands of others to Australia, Egypt, New Zealand, South Africa, and Palestine," and among these were Macfadden-brand publications.[19] Significantly, with the profits he gleaned from this operation, Manheimer began to acquire stock in Macfadden Publications, which would later have important consequences for the company.[20]

As back issues of Macfadden's periodicals entered England, they may have reinforced public perceptions of cheap mass-market print culture forms such as the true story and pulp magazine as invasive American products that were part of a larger, pernicious "entertainment empire" that threatened local economies and cultures.[21] However, the circulation of media created by Macfadden Publications flowed from long-standing connections with British audiences embedded in the company's history as well as local developments like the rise of Hutchinson's and the growth of a transatlantic amateur writing industry. Furthermore, the emergence of local periodicals that imitated but were in no way affiliated with the American firm helped move the type of products the company produced into what has been called, by the cultural theorist Simon During, the realm of the "global popular."[22]

Examining the first issue of the British publication My Story Weekly, founded in 1927, provides an apt example of this process of "parallel media evolution," which contextualizes the circulation of Macfadden Publications' content abroad.[23] My Story Weekly was one of several British true story magazines introduced in the 1920s that catered specifically to modern young women who worked outside the home—an audience that had emerged as the backbone of Macfadden Publications' success in America. Subtitled "Love Romances Told by the Girls Themselves," My Story Weekly was modeled on the romance-centric confession format pioneered by Macfadden in the United States. Its editor, promising "Big Money for Your Story," told readers, "Everyone has a story to tell . . . All I want you to do is write up any incident in your life which you think would be interesting."[24] Yet as much as it was influenced by Macfadden's American true story magazines, My Story Weekly also reflected local print culture trends as well as common features of popular culture circulations that flowed between and beyond national borders during this era. Consider, for instance, *My Story Weekly*'s inaugural feature, "How I Was Loved by a Sheik." As "one of the most popular ... phenomena of the twentieth century," the romantic figure of the sheik, as well as the desert-captive romance genre more broadly, were truly transnational.[25] British writer Edith M. Hull's 1919 novel, *The Sheik*, which drew on various imperial literary and historical traditions, was far and away the largest-selling novel in Britain during the interwar era.[26] The book, released in the United States in 1921, was adapted into a Hollywood motion picture that starred the Italian immigrant Rudolph Valentino in the titular role. Valentino's wildly popular film then helped propel an international "cult of the sheik" that magazines such as *My Story Weekly*, as well as Macfadden's film and physical culture publications in the United States, drew from and helped to sustain for years.[27] Macfadden Publications' use of entertainment genres and tropes drawn from a transnational literary and cinematic marketplace, combined with Britain's own locally grown participatory media and entrepreneurial pulp aggregators and distributors, made the company's confession media circulations in Great Britain only sometimes recognizable as cultural imports.

Regarding *True Story,* after years of selling content to Hutchinson's, Macfadden Publications introduced a British version of its most popular periodical sometime around 1931.[28] While the Macfaddens' marriage had reached a nadir by this point, the publisher's family ties came in handy, as Mary's brother became the company's representative in England. The British *True Story* contained British advertising and editorial content, but it mostly reprinted articles and illustrations from the American magazine, changing names and locations to reflect local settings. In the United States in the 1930s, Macfadden Publications pointed to its British edition of *True Story* as evidence of its global influence. However, in Britian, *True Story* was characterized as part of the local publishing landscape. Tellingly, by 1934, newspaper ads for the magazine were promoting it with the tagline, "*True Story*—An All-British Production."[29]

Imitation, Opposition, and Appeasement in Australia

Continuing a pattern started earlier in the century, Australia remained a robust market for both the American and British editions of Macfadden's publications throughout the interwar years. During this era, magazines and other mass media came to play an increasingly important role in modern formulations of Australia's national and regional identity.[30] Within this context, the Macfadden publishing empire's physical culture, true story, and film fan media was consumed, imitated, adapted, and appropriated, as well as criticized and even censored.

As we have seen, Macfadden's health and fitness publications reached readers in the Pacific since the Physical Culture Publishing Company's early days. Macfadden's books and the American edition of *Physical Culture* continued to circulate widely around Australia after the war, with Macfadden remaining well known there as a publishing entrepreneur and health authority. Then, following the Great War, two trends converged to reshape the place of Macfadden's physical culture media in the Australian publishing landscape. The first of these trends was the growing centrality of health and athleticism, particularly as manifested through white bodies and outdoor sports, to popular conceptualizations of Australian national identity.[31] The second was a conscious movement among Australians to create more homegrown periodicals, a trend shaped by the creative energies of local writers and publishers as well as by swelling concerns about the detrimental economic impacts and cultural consequences of imported media.[32] Responding to these trends, Australian entrepreneurs created homegrown physical culture periodicals that circulated alongside Macfadden's media, influencing how it was read and received. The two most important publications that resulted were Walter Withrow's *Withrow's Physical Culture* (1920) and Alfred J. Briton's *Vivid Health and Physical Culture* (1929).

Like Macfadden, Withrow and Briton were physical culture instructors before becoming publishers. Based in Sydney, both men promoted an expansive version of physical culture that encompassed various aspects of exercise, sports, diet, natural healing, and interpersonal relationships. They also cultivated accessible editorial personas, made ample use of their own bodies to illustrate their ideas, and encouraged reader participation, for as Withrow often explained, "Co-operation means a better magazine." *Withrow's* and *Vivid Health* were designed to appeal to men and women as well; the first article published in *Withrow's* discussed "Health Exercises for Women," and *Vivid Health* contained "A Complete Women's Section" and a feature called "Our Girls' Club Page." In addition to articles, physique pictorials, and editorials, there were also advertisements for clothing, books, foods, and self-improvement products that could be found in local stores or ordered by mail.

Withrow's and Briton's magazines commonly paraphrased or reprinted features that had originally appeared in Macfadden's American publications. For instance, Withrow's "Physical Culture for the Eyes" echoed Macfadden's book *Strong Eyes*. Similarly, in 1930, *Vivid Health* ran "The

Revolt of Youth," a popular serial that had first appeared in *Physical Culture* a few years earlier. The Australian editors also promoted physical culture by binding it to wider social and cultural preoccupations with matters of sexuality and heterosexual romance via the cultural forms of the intimate editorial and true story—a tried and true Macfadden formula. Often, they echoed Macfadden's phrasing. In his debut editorial in 1920, for example, Withrow declared, "Health is what gives manhood to man; womanhood to women. It is the chief bond in the attractiveness that holds men and women together."[33] Briton's magazine, which appeared a decade after *True Story,* adopted a confessional tone, combining informational articles with personal true stories; in the March 1930 issue, for instance, "T.B. Cured by Natural Methods" appeared alongside "Gripping Serials" and "Several Real-Life Stories." "Readers! You know true stories of yourself or your friends. . . . Write these stories and send them to the Editor," the Australian implored.

These Australian physical culture magazines adopted visual styles associated with Macfadden's periodicals as well. This is most apparent when comparing their covers, which usually featured colorful, dynamic illustrations of muscular men and sporty young women that were strikingly similar aesthetically to Macfadden's covers, to the point of sometimes appearing to be outright copies. Furthermore, the typographic styles chosen by both Australian editors directly copied styles used by Macfadden's media. In the case of *Withrow's Physical Culture,* over time, the size of the editor's name was reduced while the phrase "Physical Culture" grew. By the mid-1920s, when the magazine transformed from an annual into a monthly, many issues of the publication were virtually indistinguishable in outward appearance from the American magazine. *Vivid Health and Physical Culture* went through a similar transformation, shedding the word "Vivid" in 1931 and enlarging the phrase "Physical Culture." Furthermore, inside his magazine, Briton constructed physical culture collages of images culled from both other forms of mass media and reader submissions—the resultant pastiche was often almost identical in appearance to Macfadden's long-running "The Body Beautiful" pictorials.

In content and appearance, *Withrow's* and *Health and Physical Culture* channeled elements of a globalized physique culture that had been profoundly shaped by Macfadden Publications' periodicals, which had themselves long included the contributions of Australasian physical culturalists. Yet, while doing so, they also mediated a distinctive national and regional identity that was sometimes defined in opposition to that of the United States. Both Withrow and Briton positioned their periodicals as expressions of a culturally distinct body politic that possessed exceptional beauty

and vitality, an unmatched spirit of competition, and a uniquely independent attitude. *Health and Physical Culture* even billed itself as "Australia's
National Magazine," with Briton editorializing: "We want to be the link
between every health-lover in the Southern Hemisphere . . . Our magazine
is forming a great Brotherhood of Health . . . Australia and New Zealand
are already setting the standard of physical perfection to the rest of the
civilized world. . . . Health is our heritage. Let us cherish it."[34] Naming
Australia and New Zealand as the world's leaders in physical culture,
Briton challenged portrayals of American physical culture leadership and
US exceptionalism, themes common in Macfadden's media in the 1920s.
When comparing Australian and American bodies, his magazine commonly found the latter wanting. For instance, a 1933 article about a sculpture of the Average American Man asserted, "It is doubtful if this poor
specimen would come anywhere near the Australian average."[35] Representations of beautiful American movie stars were often held up as foils to
rather than models of modern fitness for Australians, with Briton charac-
terizing Hollywood stars as inferior "robot beauties" who embodied the
enervating impacts of America's ubiquitous mass culture.[36] While drawing
liberally from content and visual tropes associated with Macfadden's long-
running physical culture media, Withrow and Briton selectively composed
distinctively nationalist narratives and regional identities that posed challenges to discourses of American exceptionalism.

Still, readers who compared their local Australian physical culture magazines with Macfadden's imported publications sometimes felt more could
be done. *Withrow's Physical Culture* was issued only annually at first, thus
the quantity of content it provided readers paled in comparison to the
American monthly. Briton's magazine was monthly, but readers faulted its
relative paucity of visuals of Australian physiques. "Do try to get real
dinkum Aussie sports men and women on your front page instead of all
those Yankee 'bosh' stars," one implored.[37] "I read several overseas health
publications and though I lean toward my national magazine . . . I feel
that 'Health and Physical Culture' is sadly neglecting one branch of the
'beauty-through-health gospel'. . . . the printing of photographs of well-
built, gracefully-posed men and women which is so popular in England
and America," another criticized.[38] Comparing Briton's magazine directly
to Macfadden's *Physical Culture,* another lamented the Australian's "very
tame" physique photos: "Say editor, is your camera sparking all right?" he
jibed.[39] The editor responded to criticism by admitting that, despite Australia's possession of "the finest specimens . . . in the world," he had trouble
acquiring enough photographs of them.[40] The United States was an "image
factory" of beautiful bodies, and Macfadden Publications' capabilities and

achievements in this area outstripped local production capacities.[41] Readers of Withrow's and Briton's magazines often consumed Australian physical culture magazines in tandem with imported health and fitness media, with Macfadden's publications offering more images and greater topical coverage that was combined with strategic uncoverage of the desirable bodies in its photographs.

Alongside its physical culture media, versions of Macfadden Publications' confession magazines circulated widely in Australia. First, the English editions of *True Story* and *True Romances* became available in Australia on the heels of their debut in England, with Hutchinson's agents and booksellers in Australia advertising them there from 1923. Later in the 1920s, most issues that circulated in Australia were distributed by the intermediary Gordon and Gotch, the largest book and magazine importer and distributor in Australia. Founded in the nineteenth century, Gordon and Gotch had vast connections throughout the Anglophone World in addition to a domestic network of six thousand outlets and agents. By 1924, this company was distributing 1.75 million publications in Australia every week through urban showrooms, newsstands, and local agents, with *True Story* (likely the British edition) becoming "a staple" of its subscription list.[42]

Via the infrastructure it had built, Gordon and Gotch moved imported publications from British and American companies, such as Hutchinson's, throughout Australasia. Local agents advertising the contents of the "satchel[s] of magazines" they received from the company often listed *True Story*, along with Hutchinson's mystery and adventure titles. These ads noted the confession magazines' "startling life stories told in word and pictures" and repeated the catchphrase "Truth is stranger than fiction."[43] By the midpoint of the 1920s, ads for *True Story* became longer and more prominently placed, suggesting growing interest in or availability of the title. Indeed, as surviving photographs indicate, urban consumers could acquire this title from neighborhood newsstands, where it was prominently displayed.[44] Then, at the end of the 1920s, around the same time Macfadden Publications reasserted itself as *True Story*'s British distributor, the company designated the import company Ayers and James as the official distributor of its American magazines in Australia. Ayers and James operated alongside, rather than replaced, Gordon and Gotch. For the remainder of the interwar era, Australian readers had access to both the British and American editions of Macfadden's magazines, which contained similar content but different advertisements and editorials.

Australians also encountered Macfadden-brand media at the movie theater. At least a couple of True Story Studio productions traveled across the Pacific beginning in 1926, when theaters from Perth to Tasmania featured

The Wrongdoers, starring Lionel Barrymore. Ads for the film promoted its association with Macfadden. Another *True Story* picture, *Sinners in Love*, played from 1929. These screenings led to promotional multimedia tie-ins; for instance, ladies who bought tickets to the Hoyt's Regent in Brisbane in the mid-1930s received free copies of *True Story*. With the acquisition of *Photoplay*, the company further cemented its association with a cinematic global popular headquartered in but not confined to the United States. *Photoplay*'s frequent printing of correspondence from Australia and New Zealand suggests that Australian audiences used the company's popular fan magazine to engage critically with imported film productions at a time when Australian cinema was expanding. For instance, one correspondent from the South wrote, "Traveling about Australia I have often heard the cry 'We're tired of American movie nonsense. It's so childish. Why doesn't America grow up?' . . . America, look to your laurels! There are other countries making pictures now."[45] A more diplomatic writer criticized the ethos of national competition that often framed cinema discourse: "To my mind, all films should be produced to not enhance the position of the producing country and company, but to enhance the film industry as a whole," he opined.[46]

Australians also acquired Macfadden-brand publications through the trade in imported back issues. Following the founding of Manheimer's magazine distribution company in 1927, periodical retailers in Australia increasingly advertised "Back Numbers of American Magazines at Bargain Prices." For instance, for much of 1928, one Brisbane bookseller's entire list of bargain magazines consisted of *Physical Culture, True Romances, True Experiences, Ghost Stories, The Dance, Your Home, True Detective Mysteries*, and *True Story*—all Macfadden titles. While current editions usually cost from one to two shillings, these copies sold at three for a shilling, and they averaged around four to seven months behind the most recent American editions. Local newspapers' exchange and mutual benefit columns provide a window onto the commonality of the practice of buying and trading back issues of Macfadden-brand magazines. For example, in the *Western Mail* (Perth) "Friendly Service" section, a correspondent, Manda, offered to exchange "a number of old film magazines" for the conclusion to the *True Experiences* serial "I Chose the Shadows."[47] Having to scramble to track down the conclusion of a story that had piqued one's interest was a downside to buying back issues, but this was not the only problem Australians saw with this practice.

Cheap back issues of American and British magazines such as Macfadden's, along with the high volume of imported popular culture more generally, exacerbated concerns about magazine imports stifling local cultural production and economic opportunity. Increasing agitation for some form of protective legislation led to the Australian Tariff Board's 1930 "Inquiry into a Proposal of Duty on Books, Magazines, and Fashion Plates."[48] While British periodicals made up the majority of foreign imports at the time, news coverage of the inquiry often singled-out the "dumping" of American magazines "containing undesirable reading matter and illustrations" at prices below their cost in the United States.[49] During the hearings, one witness portrayed cheap American magazines as potentially dangerous contagion, both metaphorically and literally: "It is estimated that one American exporter to this country's back date periodicals is selling upwards of 100,000 copies per month to Australia, and the main source of his supplies is the hotel porter, apartment janitors, railway porters, and others of like ilk, who collect from various sources after more or less use has been made of the publication. In other words, 100,000 periodicals per month come to Australia that ought to go to the garbage tip, and could be full of any disease under the sun," he lamented.[50] It is likely that the American exporter to which this witness referred was Manheimer's Publisher's Surplus Corporation, and that a chunk of these magazines were Macfadden's.

While the Tariff Board Inquiry illustrates the economic and cultural anxieties sparked by the circulation of imported mass culture—a widespread phenomenon in many places around the world during the interwar era—it simultaneously reveals the extent to which Australian periodical agents, import companies, and non-elite consumers relied on imported periodicals for income or entertainment.[51] The participatory dynamic that characterized most of Macfadden's publications seems to have been perceived as attractive and exciting to both Australian readers and Australian writers. Not only local merchants recognized this fact; so too did the Macfadden corporation. In 1937, Mr. J. E. Williamson, export manager for Macfadden Publications (and Mary's brother), was sent to Australia to smooth out tensions. Williamson, who divided his time between the US and British offices of the company, told reporters that Macfadden's Australian circulation was 250,000 periodicals per month. Furthermore, Williamson announced that his company was planning to establish a new edition of *True Story* "using Australian material, and published in Australia." Williamson's wife, who worked as a manuscript reader for *True Story* and *True Romances* and accompanied him on this trip, reported that a whopping 20 percent of manuscripts that the company received came from Australia. Furthermore, she added, "In America, we are rather inclined toward Australian stories: the incidents might happen anywhere in the world, but the setting makes them unique."[52] As it turned out, Australian editions of Macfadden Publications' periodicals were not introduced during the 1930s, perhaps due to Mr. Williamson's untimely death in 1938 while en route from South Africa to Singapore on company business, but they would appear immediately after the Second World War.

In the wake of the Tariff Board Inquiry, objections to the importation of cheap American magazines magnified. While professional organizations such as the Society of Australian Authors and the Australian Institute on Advertising certainly opposed these imports for economic reasons, proponents of tariffs and embargoes employed cultural arguments that called attention to the "highly sensational" nature and poor quality of certain American periodicals.[53] Some concerned citizens singled out confession and true detective magazines as symbols of the perniciousness of imported American print culture. As one Queensland Rotary Club member concerned about the "colossal" growth of this kind of media expressed, "It seems a sorry commentary on our educational system that we have taught people to read and the use they make of their education is to devour 'True Experiences' and 'Love Confessions.'" More troublingly to him, "the three-ring circus" of sport, crime, and sex that dominated imported popular culture seemed to be drawing peoples' attention away from important world events like the rise of foreign dictatorships.[54]

In 1938, Macfadden Publication came under increased state scrutiny with the passing of a new Australian Customs Act. Under section 14a of the law, known as the "dragnet clause," any publication that "in the opinion of the Minister for Trade and Customs unduly emphasizes matters of sex or crime or is calculated to encourage depravity, whether by words or pictures, or partly by words and partly by picture" could be banned.[55] Customs agents at Australian ports were empowered as censors and enforcers of the law. While official lists of banned publications were not made public, the identity of banned magazines quickly became obvious to consumers when they could no longer obtain their preferred titles, thus revealing Macfadden's magazines to be subject to exclusion.[56] In the popular press, debates played out over the Customs Department's expanded powers and whether the magazine ban was really necessary or desirable.[57] Ayers and James, the Australian importer of Macfadden Publications' US editions, directly appealed the inclusion of *True Story, True Romances, True Experiences, True Detective Mysteries,* and *Master Detective,* arguing publicly that the regulations unfairly discriminated against American magazines.

As Ayers and James and Gordon and Gotch were entering thousands of copies at a time of Macfadden-brand magazines at Australian ports, customs officials and the Literature Censorship Board debated whether they fell under section 14a.[58] In general, all parties agreed that Macfadden's detective pulps were in clear violation of the law. As they saw it, the magazines' drawn-out and detailed descriptions of violent crime, focus on members of the criminal underworld, and lurid covers marked them as undesirable and even dangerous in the hands of juvenile readers. Macfadden's popular confession and romance periodicals, however, proved more complicated to classify. Upon appeal, the Literature Censorship Board removed prohibitions against *True Experiences,* but *True Story* and *True Romances/True Love and Romances* remained "borderline cases." Censors objected to both the mercenary true story format itself, which they argued encouraged fabrication and plagiarism, as well as to the subject matter: "'True Story' features unpleasant sex relationships and recounts at great length the emotional experiences of the participants. It unduly emphasizes matters of sex and therefore comes within the terms of Item 14A," one censor ruled. Even though most stories arrived at a "moral" conclusion, they were "dragged out the 10,000 words to describe every lurid detail."[59] However, although most Censorship Board reports commented on the undesirable character and poor literary quality of Macfadden's confession magazines, the fact that they tended to imply sex rather than describe it, and were also viewed as aimed at adult and not juvenile readers, left them in a gray area.

Macfadden Publications responded with alacrity to the Australian ban, showing how important it considered this particular market, as well as foreign markets more generally. According to Australian Customs Department records, the company immediately sought to appease the censorship board by deleting advertisements for prohibited goods found in copies bound for Australia. They also cabled descriptions of endorsements of Macfadden-brand magazines from the YWCA, various church authorities, the Girl Scouts, and Eleanor Roosevelt. It is possible that the company was influenced to alter the content of its publications to avoid censure as well. In the summer of 1939, Australian officials monitoring the company's true story magazines discerned improvement, noting, "It is apparent that the publishers of this magazine [*True Romances*] have endeavoured to conform to the Departmental requirements and to include articles which do not depend for their attraction on the objectionable details of romantic attachments to which exception was taken earlier."[60] Another report, noting the "improved tone" of a Macfadden magazine, concluded, "It is apparent . . . that the prohibition imposed has had a salutary effect."[61] In correspondence with Ayers and James, Macfadden Publications' export manager in New York emphasized that the company had hired a new circulation manager and that additional "improvement" was coming.[62]

In 1939, the company also dispatched Macfadden's public relations counsel, Edith R. Lumsden, to Australia to defend the American corporation and seek a compromise with the Censorship Board and Australian

Customs. Lumsden, a former newspaper writer, was described by one local paper as "gentle-mannered, soft-voiced, and . . . homey," the opposite of the pushy American businessman some Australians may have been expecting, which was perhaps what was intended by Macfadden Publications' unconventional choice to employ a woman to represent the corporation. In regard to Macfadden's detective magazines, Lumsden told reporters, "Your authorities have got us in reverse. . . . Our publications have proved to have a high value in the prevention and detection of crime," and were even admired by President Roosevelt, who contributed many times to Macfadden Publications' media empire. Lumsden continued, "As far as the 'Love and Romance' type of magazine is concerned, while we cannot claim that it is of high intellectual value, it is literature of the people for the people, written in their own words—the very warp and woof of their own lives."[63]

Lumsden's trip seems to have helped Macfadden Publications' cause considerably. With the assistance of the US consul-general in Australia, she met with the assistant minister for customs in Canberra and cemented a deal in which the company forwarded advance copies of Macfadden's confession and detective magazines to Australian officials so that approval could be issued on a case-by-case basis without holding up distribution. While *True Detective Stories* and *True Detective Mysteries* remained prohibited, *True Story* and *True Romances* were repeatedly deemed acceptable (albeit generally undesirable). This system of close scrutiny, with Macfadden Publications apparently meeting Australian agents' demands for cooperation, continued until the Second World War temporarily interrupted the international magazine trade. Thus, the case of Australia, where Macfadden's periodicals were variously consumed, imitated, and opposed by different groups, calls attention to the ways in which the promise of foreign markets may have helped shaped the company's media content as well as public relations strategies, abroad and at home.

Translating True Stories in Modern Germany

As we have already seen, before the First World War, a few of Macfadden's health and fitness publications reached European readers from non-English-speaking nations, in part due to travelers and migrants bringing them back from the United States or through the efforts of local importers and translators. In the interwar era, versions of *True Story* cropped up in Germany, Scandinavia, Holland, and France. Germany, where the first of these foreign-language editions of Macfadden Publications' periodicals was introduced, offers insights into this development.

As in Britain, when Macfadden's *True Story* appeared in Germany in the late 1920s, it was produced under the imprint of a local publishing house—Dr. Selle-Eysler (formerly Selle Presse). In operation since 1905, this company had a previous connection to the publishing house's physical culture media. In 1920, Selle-Eysler published a German-language series called Macfadden's Health Books (*Macfaddens Gesundheitsbücher*), which contained translations of Macfadden's *Manhood and Marriage* (*Männlichkeit und Ehe*) and *Womanhood and Marriage* (*Weiblichkeit und Ehe*). This company then introduced German-language editions of several of Macfadden Publications' most popular American magazines beginning in 1927. These included the *True Story* analogs *Wahre Romane* and *Wahre Geschichten*; the "sister magazine" *Wahre Erzählungen* (*True Experiences*) retitled *Wahre Erzählungen und Romane* in 1932); and *Wahre Detektiv Geschichten* (*True Detective Stories*).[64] Taking a closer look at *Wahre Geschichten* and *Wahre Erzählungen* in particular shows how the German editions of Macfadden's periodicals were fashioned in dialog with an emergent global popular influenced by American cultural forms even as they also helped shape local manifestations of modernity and nationalism in Germany during the Weimer era and into the Third Reich.

Selle-Eysler's magazines joined an array of popular publications that accompanied and helped further the development of commercial entertainment and mass consumption in Germany. Despite the efforts of "the government and local authorities, the churches, the educational system, the political parties, the different kinds of libraries, [and] a variety of cultural and moral associations, [and] organizations set up in more than 33 cities specifically in order to wage war on pulp literature," such reading material proliferated.[65] With their abundant advertisements, emphasis on film stars, sensationalistic prose, and American pedigree, Selle-Eysler's versions of Macfadden's magazines were paragons of the *schund-* and *schmutzschriften* (trash and pulp writings) whose success among women, workers, and young people was seen by German elites across the political spectrum as a sign of national disintegration.[66] For many, however, such magazines represented an entrée into a captivating, globalized modern popular culture that promoted personal expression, self-fashioning, celebrity, and romance. As a research study on German reading habits conducted in 1930 reported, a boy from a small town in Pomerania thus expressed his preference for pulp novels and "exciting tales," including *Wahre Geschichten*: "Love stories are smashing. There's all that kissing and hugging. Great fun to read. [And they] [o]nly cost 50 pfennigs," he explained.[67]

The advertisements placed in Selle-Eysler's periodicals suggest the nonelite social status of the company's readers. Like Macfadden's magazines in the United States, the German editions ran mostly small, black-and-white ads for self-improvement books, toiletries, mail-order physical culture courses, and other Selle-Eysler publications. Only the occasional back cover featured "respectable" advertising of national-brand products—and even these were usually dedicated to promoting low-cost consumer goods such as cigarettes and snack foods.[68] Around sixty pages apiece and roughly seven by ten inches, Selle-Eysler's various true story periodicals were typically sized for pulp magazines, which had appeared in Germany before the First World War. This made them notably smaller and cheaper looking than Macfadden's American magazines. Thus, while Macfadden's magazines in the United States were rendered somewhat distinct from other "low-brow" competitors by their size, in Germany they resembled a range of other imported and local pulp magazines associated with non-elite and juvenile readers.

In addition to their smaller size, Selle-Eysler's editions contained only a fraction of the stories, advice departments, illustrations, and advertisements that greeted American readers. In many other respects, however, these German magazines mimicked their US editions. The most obvious parallel was in cover design. Dastardly villains and gun-toting gangsters peered out from *Wahre Detektiv Geschichten,* while the company's various confession titles featured paintings of attractive Hollywood stars and vivacious "modern girls" wearing conspicuous cosmetics, alluring facial expressions, and short hairstyles. Throughout the Weimar era, these colorful portraits, by artists such as the Romanian American illustrator Jules Cannert, were the same ones that graced American newsstands a few months earlier. The German magazines also shared Macfadden Publications' titular font and bright red first letters, as well as a distinctive red badge that listed the newsstand price of each issue. To anyone familiar with Macfadden's US magazines, Selle-Eysler's offerings would have seemed immediately familiar. Moreover, until 1934, *Wahre Geschichten* identified itself clearly on every cover, in German, as "the German edition of the popular American magazine *True Story.*"

The prevalence of Hollywood stars on the front covers of Selle-Eysler's true story periodicals throughout the Weimar period would also have signaled to German audiences a connection between these magazines and America's expansive mass culture. That a substantial fraction of the stories that appeared inside Selle-Eysler's confession magazines focused on American characters and were set in recognizably American contexts, both contemporary and historical, would have bolstered this impression. "Child of the Sun" (1929), for instance, follows Diana Eagle, a Native American girl attending an Indian boarding school.[69] The protagonist of "When a Woman is Alone" (1930) is forced to fend for herself in the Pacific Northwest Indian Territory after her husband leaves to mine gold in Australia.[70] "With Lies in the Heart" (1929) is narrated by an American girl named Virginia who, after passing out from drinking at a party, finds herself pregnant.[71] "My Art, My Love, and the Radio" (1933) describes a working-class American young woman who is forced to choose between an exciting career playing her violin on the radio and the love of a wealthy suitor who does not want to marry a working artist.[72]

At the same time, the German texts also emphasized that their local audiences could and should participate in shaping their magazine. In September 1932, for example, Selle-Eysler suggested that busy workers make use of the upcoming Christmas holiday to pen their experiences for *True Story*'s next competition. Winners were going to receive thousands of dollars in prizes—so, "Why not You?" the editors asked. Furthermore, the company even promised to assist would-be authors with their entries by establishing a committee dedicated to translating selected submissions into English and forwarding them onward to New York.[73] In this respect, Selle-Eysler was not only operating as a licenser and printer of American content; it was playing an active role in ensuring that the participatory dynamic and ethos of accessibility that was so central to Macfadden's true story media was never lost in translation in Germany.

The abbreviated pulp format of the German publications meant that Selle-Eysler selected and printed only a small fraction of the content produced by the US company in any given month. Thus, it is also useful to consider what kinds of features Selle-Eysler chose to reprint as well as the changes and additions that the German brokers (who also anticipated Swiss-German audiences) made to Macfadden's media. While it is unclear whether any German readers succeeded in winning *True Story*'s contests or having their works printed in Macfadden's American editions, Selle-Eysler maintained an appearance of accessibility and local production. This was accomplished in several ways. First, while all issues of *Wahre Geschichten* and *Wahre Erzählungen* contained tales set in America, at least half the stories in these magazines were narrated by local observers or participants and depicted as having taken place in Germany. In keeping with a larger pattern that also characterized other foreign editions of Macfadden's magazines, most of these stories were reprints, with names and locations Germanicized by the editors. The illustrations that accompanied these stories were selected from the distinctive photographic tableaux that Macfadden's photography studio produced in the United States. This process sometimes produced disjunctive or unlikely images, such as a description of a German driving a Chrysler or an illustration with English words discernible in the background. In most instances, however, the transpositions appear to have been relatively seamless. This was facilitated in part by the transnational proliferation of distinctive fashions and hairstyles, especially those associated with "modern girls." By the time Macfadden's confession media debuted in Germany, the straight silhouettes; cloche hats; and bobbed, short-wavy hairstyles worn by the young women who appeared in many of the American company's photographic tableaux had become widely popular styles in Germany as well.[74]

Many of the translated true stories that Selle-Eysler reprinted in *Wahre Geschichten* and *Wahre Erzählungen* feature non-elite young women protagonists, urban settings, and plots that revolve around work or love (or, commonly, a mixture of both). Cross-class romances, marital troubles, intergenerational strife, children born out of wedlock, and economic hardship are recurring themes. As previously discussed, Macfadden Publications' domestic publications were designed to appeal to—particularly by reflecting the experiences of—a diverse working class that was becoming increasingly urban and progressively more enmeshed in a consumer culture fueled by mass production and centered on leisure and entertainment, self-fashioning, and self-expression. During the interwar era, Germany, along with many other places throughout the world, was experiencing patterns of modernization similar to, and indeed linked with, those in the United States. These included urbanization, new public economic roles for women, changes in attitudes toward sexuality and romance, economic instability, and an ascendant consumer culture fueled by a promotional advertising industry.[75] As in the United States, this constellation of economic, social, and cultural changes dramatically affected—and was shaped by—the working class, particularly young women. Thus, many of the features that had become hallmarks of Macfadden Publications media by the late 1920s lent themselves to easy appropriation and adaptation by Selle-Eysler. As the prelude to one true story explained, "This story contains an experience that developed outside of our German conditions. Though their forms may find different expression, the problems of the world are the same."[76]

The translatability of Macfadden's media becomes especially apparent when one considers that two of the most popular true story settings that reappeared continuously in Selle-Eysler's confession magazines were the department store (*Warenhaus*) and the "big city" (*Großstadt*), specifically Berlin. In many ways, Germany's ethnically and religiously diverse cosmopolitan capital offered a fitting analog for the urban backdrops against which many of Macfadden Publications' magazines' narratives took place. Berlin, more than anywhere else in Germany, cultivated a self-consciously modern and cosmopolitan identity in the interwar era. As a center of

production for both the country's national film industry and its bourgeoning advertising profession, the metropolis was extensively enmeshed
in globalized networks of entertainment and consumer culture.[77] Berlin's
retail and entertainment industries offered a host of new economic roles
for women that, in turn, allowed them to participate avidly in the city's
consumer and entertainment cultures.[78] The department store, as both
scholars and early twentieth-century observers have noted, was just as
much a part of a transnational geography as it was a feature of local urban
landscapes.[79] In terms of the employment opportunities it offered working-
class women, the spaces it constructed that combined leisure with shopping, and the increasingly name-branded goods it displayed for purchase,
it was an important site where "consumption, modernity, and globalization" met in Germany, as in the United States and many other places.[80]
Macfadden Publications' numerous true stories that were set in or around
urban department stores, and the photographic illustrations of fashion-
ably dressed working-class women that often accompanied them, were
thus easily relocated by Selle-Eysler to the *Großstadt* and its shopping em-
poriums, as illustrated by "Two People in the Department Store" (1933);
"The Imaginary Groom" (1930), about a woman who works in the toys
department; and "The Girl from the Department Store" (1933), which
was set in Berlin's Bernheim's department store.[81]

Another type of true story produced by Macfadden Publications that Selle-
Eysler deemed maximally culturally translatable to Germany were narratives
set in the "exotic" American West. Compared to Macfadden's American editions, a larger proportion of the confessions in *Wahre Geschichten* and
Wahre Erzählungen set in the United States feature Indigenous (or occasionally Latinx) characters or Anglo-Americans living on some kind of "frontier"
between cultures. Before Macfadden's true story magazines crossed the Atlantic, the genre of the "Western" had become enormously popular in Germany thanks to dime novels, circuses, and cinema.[82] As scholars who have
studied the long-lasting international popularity of the Western have illustrated, the genre has had particular resonances in different cultures.[83] In Germany, as in many other places, "Western motifs during the 1920s and 1930s
constituted a discursive site at which Germans contested the meaning of
modern culture and society."[84] The above-mentioned "Child of the Sun"
(1929), for example, illustrates why the subgenre of the "true story Western,"
which combined frontier settings with a focus on women's personal and romantic experiences, might have resonated with German audiences.

The narrative of "Child of the Sun" describes a love triangle between the
Native American Diana Eagle, a young Anglo-American man who loves
her but not her people, and an older Native American doctor who also

wants to marry Diana. At first, the protagonist is tempted by her handsome young suitor's dashing manners, romantic overtures, and red sports car. Finally, however, she realizes that it is best to marry someone of her own race. This story, which reflected eugenic discourse and the "vanishing Indian" myth prevalent in the United States, also meshed well with debates over modernization occurring in interwar era Germany. For some German audiences, Diana's flashy young suitor, with his disregard for her familial and cultural heritage, might have provided an apt symbol for larger forces of modernization, and particularly "Americanization," that were perceived as threatening the future of German cultural identity. At the same time, the story's cautionary portrayal of "racial mixing" fit in with an ascendant strain of racial politics that would come to fruition, horrifically, during the Third Reich.[85]

In addition to selecting, translating, and adapting true stories and related photographs from Macfadden's American magazines, Selle-Eysler also devoted space in *Wahre Geschichten* and *Wahre Erzählungen* to coverage of physical culture and film, longtime staple topics of Macfadden's publications that connected with working-class audiences. Selle-Eysler, like Macfadden Publications, easily incorporated features on fit bodies, sports, recent films, and movie stars into its true story magazines. In addition to the renowned Hollywood actors on most of its covers, *Wahre Geschichten* contained a regular feature called "Film-Spiegel" ("Film Mirror"), which referenced Macfadden Publications' fan magazine *Movie Mirror*. Usually positioned at the front of the magazine, "Film-Spiegel" consisted of a pictorial assemblage of captioned movie stills, actor publicity shots, and other photographs related to filmmaking. Most issues of *Wahre Erzählungen* began with a feature on physical culture or what Macfadden's magazines called "the body beautiful." This ranged from "Luft und Sonne" ("Air and Sun"), which documented people playing sports and practicing gymnastics, to "Wer hat die schönsten Beine?" a collage that invited readers to consider "Who Has the Most Beautiful Legs?" Unlike most of Selle-Eysler's true stories, these features on film and physical culture were produced locally for German readers rather than imported from the United States. As such, they functioned to highlight German contributions to, and modernity within, global popular culture.

In contrast to Macfadden's Hollywood-focused American magazines, Selle-Eysler's "Film-Spiegel" often documented and celebrated current German cinema. An important center of filmmaking since the medium's invention, Germany constituted Europe's largest film industry in the years between the world wars. Universum Film AG (better known as Ufa), founded with state support in 1917, was its most prolific studio. Also important were the companies Terra and Tobis (the first producer of sound films in Germany), as well as subsidiaries of Hollywood studios, such as Deutsche Universal-Film.[86] While the "American star system, performing styles, flair for publicity and increasing standardization of production elicited enormous attention and imitation in Germany," German film studios also developed their own genres, such as the alpine-adventure *bergfilm*, and cultivated a distinctive avant-garde aesthetic that proved widely influential.[87]

The photographic montages, captions, and text of *Wahre Geschichten's* "Film-Spiegel" emphasized the vitality and excitement of the local industry. For instance, the April 1930 issue presented stills from Ufa's *Die Letzte Kompanie* and Deutsche Universal-Film's adaptation of Erich Maria Remarque's *All Quiet on the Western Front*. These were arranged next to moody, atmospheric publicity shots from Ufa of director Joseph Von Sternberg, the new "film darling" Gustav Fröhlich, and the popular German character actor Heinrich George posing in their homes in moments of leisure. In July of the same year, readers were treated to a montage of stills from a new Ufa film shot in the exotic Sahara, while the December issue offered a glimpse of upcoming releases from German production companies. Featured alongside these films was Paramount studio's *Morocco*, which starred the famous German export Marlene Dietrich. Indeed, throughout the late 1920s and early 1930s, *Wahre Geschichten's* Hollywood coverage often focused on directors and stars who were from (or were popular in) Germany. For instance, when "Film-Spiegel" introduced readers to the American actress Louise Brooks, they printed a film still of a scene in which she appeared on camera with the German character actor Gustaf von Seyfferitz. The April 1931 article "Greta Garbo Speaks German" celebrates the wildly popular Swedish-born actress's performance in MGM's German-language reshoot of *Anna Christie*. An accompanying article, written by the German actor Theo Shall, offers an intimate, first-person account of what it was like to work with the "divine Garbo."[88]

Wahre Erzählungen's physical culture features followed a similar pattern. While Macfadden's American magazines offered an endless array of body beautiful pictorials that featured Hollywood stars as well as "regular" Americans and the occasional foreign reader or performer, Selle-Eysler constructed its own physical culture sections illustrated by photographs from German photographers. "Luft und Sonne" focused on displaying healthy German men, women, and children engaged in sport and exercise. "Let the Children do Gymnastics" (1930), for instance, shows various boys and girls performing gymnastic stretches, which the accompanying text explains are beneficial to the public health of the nation

(*Volkshygiene*).[89] Such *Körperkultur* features, particularly those that showed mass gymnastic displays or German athletes participating in international competitions, reinforced discursive connections between public health, strong bodies, and the German state.[90]

Interspersed among its translated true stories, Selle-Eysler also included additional material produced by and for local audiences. For instance, "Hearing With One's Eyes" (1930) presents an overview of deaf-mute (Taubstumme) education in Germany. The accompanying photographs show young German students practicing rhythmic gymnastics, reading, and elocution.[91] "The Fountain of Youth of the Cosmopolitan City" (1930) describes and pictures beachgoers, some of them modeling bathing fashions, enjoying the beach of Berlin's Lake Wannsee.[92] Taking a cue from publishers like Macfadden, Selle-Eysler also sponsored a beauty contest that it encouraged its readers to enter. "Who will be Miss Germany 1931?" it asked, instructing women to take advantage of "the chance of a lifetime" and enter its competition, which offered not only two thousand Reichsmarks, but also the chance to become a world-traveling star of stage and screen. The final pages of both *Wahre Geschichten* and *Wahre Erzählungen* were also devoted to reader correspondence sections ("The Readers Have Their Say" and "True Teachings," respectively). In these features, readers were encouraged to advise others on their problems regarding love, work, and family. Often, the advice solicited and received in these sections was very specific to German audiences (Would it be hard to enter the shoemaking industry as an older woman? What were the pros and cons of immigrating to America? Be very careful when grinding meat!). Through these features, Selle-Eysler's editions of Macfadden's media made full use of the participatory format to cultivate a sense of local community and connection within the cultural form of the imported true story magazine.

The "cultural translatability" of Macfadden Publications' locally adapted periodicals in Germany is perhaps best illustrated by considering the fate of Selle-Eysler's editions of the American magazines as the Weimar Republic gave way to the Third Reich. At a time when German mass culture, including the publishing industry, was experiencing dramatic flux in the wake of new restrictions, German editions of Macfadden's magazines continued to be published in the country until at least 1941.[93] Comparing issues of *Wahre Geschichten* from the late 1930s to those from earlier in the decade reveals a few noticeable differences. First, the publisher of record changed from Dr. Selle-Eysler to Erich Zander. Sources suggest that Erich Zander became head of Selle-Eysler and took over the company sometime in the mid-1930s. Second, the total length of *Wahre Geschichten* decreased by about a third, likely due to budget constraints. Under Zander, the magazine

also modified elements of its visual aesthetic. Along with the occasional
Hollywood star, the Third Reich–era issues feature cover portraits of recognizably local figures, such as ruddy-cheeked *bergfilm* characters.[94] Such
covers depict both young German (heterosexual) couples as well as glamorous female movie stars and film figures. In keeping with larger trends in
both American and German art, the covers from the late 1930s were more
realistic than illustrations from previous years. The description "The
German Edition of the Popular American Magazine *True Story*" disappeared after the Nazis took power. Finally, under its new imprint, the
typeface of the German edition of *True Story* was changed from the Latin-
style, rounded Antiqua font to the ornate, Gothic-style Fraktur, the official
national typeface between 1933 and 1941.[95] As these changes illustrate,
the issues of *Wahre Geschichten* published by Erich Zander adopted an
overtly Germanicized visual style. Through this style, the publisher signaled accommodation with an increasingly nationalistic (and state-regu-
lated) popular culture that was closely connected to the political ideologies
of the National Socialist regime. The company's transition to a Fraktur
typeface and its use of archetypal characters from German folk culture
and cinema on its covers, along with the continued inclusion of true stories relocated to Germany and locally produced content, helped mark the
publications as a more explicitly German product rather than an American import.

Still, perhaps the most noticeable feature of the post-1933 issues of the
magazine is the extent to which similarities to their Weimar-era predeces-
sors remained. The tenth-year anniversary issue of *Wahre Geschichten,*
from December 1937, provides a useful point of comparison. This issue
features a painting of a handsome young couple against a snowy mountain backdrop. The man, whose yellow and green sweater and bow tie
mark him as distinctively German, holds a pair of ice skates. The headline
story, however, is about Hollywood actor "Clark Gable's Adventurous
Path" from rural obscurity to international stardom. Accompanying illustrations show Gable in formal dress clothes, Gable shirtless and chopping
wood, and Gable romancing various on-screen costars. This detailed look
at Gable's story (and body) reflects the intimate tone, celebration of Hollywood stars and romantic relationships, and themes of self-transformation
and upward mobility that had long characterized Macfadden's publications and their German editions. The remainder of this issue presents
readers with an assortment of romance-centric confessions, a listing of recent films released in Germany (including German, British, and American
titles), a reader advice column, and local advertisements. Like Selle-Eysler's
earlier versions, the images and text represent a mix of translated stories

set in the United States, tales adapted to a German context, and locally produced material. The main stories include "People on a Plane," the final installment of an adventure-romance about a group of passengers stuck in an
aircraft that has crashed somewhere on the frozen North American tundra.
"The Story of the Abandoned," narrated from the perspective of a private
detective hired by the protagonist, describes the death of a woman's first love
in the Great War, her subsequent move from the country to the big city to
find work and forget her past, a marriage of convenience, and the mysterious
disappearance of her husband. While this tale ostensibly takes place in Berlin,
its bluntly sketched urban environs and themes of love, loss, and mystery
might easily have been translated from a US context. "Maybe" tells the story
of a struggling artist who meets a beautiful woman named Hilde Schwarz
while hiking in the mountains. She agrees to model for him, and he falls in
love with her, believing her to be a humble country lass. Soon, however, the
artist discovers that "Hilde" is really a countess who has been concealing her
identity. Based on its references to nobility, alpine setting, and accompanying
realist-style photograph depicting the artist and Hilde skiing together,
"Maybe" seems to have been a local production. Alongside these confession
narratives appeared the usual ads for products such as Kaloderma-brand
hand lotion, blond hair dye, mail-order art and dancing classes, toothpaste,
dishware, and other inexpensive consumer goods.

In Nazi Germany, mass media that promoted political mobilization and
National Socialist values coexisted with a self-consciously modern leisure
and entertainment industry that continuously incorporated elements of a
global popular shaped in dialog with American patterns of consumption
and US cultural exports. As historians have emphasized, these two aspects
of German culture were by no means mutually exclusive or contradictory,
and the Nazi regime well understood the valuable role that a fun and lively
entertainment and consumer culture could play in communicating ideas to
the public and furthering National Socialist political imaginaries.[96] While
many imported US products disappeared from the German landscape
during the 1930s, Macfadden Publications' media, like Hollywood-
inspired cinema forms and the ethos of mass consumption promoted by
advertising and US popular culture, proved easily adaptable to the new
political context of the Third Reich.[97] In particular, the imported true
story magazine's participatory ethos, as well as its emphasis on themes of
modernity and mobility, celebration of film culture, and representations of
fit bodies, ensured cultural translatability in Germany, where media created by Macfadden Publications was made to appear simultaneously
German *and* American, local *and* cosmopolitan.

• • •

Fig. 7.1 German-language editions of Macfadden Publications' true story magazines, 1930s. Reproduced from the author's personal collection

Reporting on the popularity of Macfadden Publications, confession media in a 1938 *Scribner's* magazine article called "True Stories," the journalist Harland Manchester wrote, "What is significant, and what has escaped general attention, is the true-story book's vigorous permeation of foreign countries." "Like our dime novels, our gangster movies, and our jazz music," he continued, "the Great American Purge Story has become an important cultural export." On how and why this had happened, Manchester did not come to a firm conclusion. Readers were told that whether this mass cultural form "speaks with the folk-voice of America . . . or whether its appeal is due to an unlocalized need for catharsis is a matter for pondering."[98]

A connective comparison of Macfadden Publications' foreign editions in Britain, Australia, and Germany undermines the binary assumptions of Manchester's question while elucidating the dynamics of "vigorous permeation." The so-called folk voice of America that Macfadden Publications' media purportedly represented really encapsulated a multiplicity of voices, many of which belonged to working-class, immigrant, and otherwise marginalized readers in the United States. It also reflected the company's projections of the interests and desires of this diverse domestic market, which were linked to its perceptions of the sensibilities of foreign audiences. In catering to a transnational domestic audience that included newly urbanized populations and working-class women, and in seeking to package them as America's new engine of consumption, the company developed widely attractive, accessible, and adaptable magazines that blurred traditional boundaries between producers and consumers; promoted self-expression through mass consumption; and linked audiences with celebrities as well as with other readers with whom they shared common life experiences, interests, and concerns. These qualities made them interesting abroad across a variety of national contexts in the interwar era.

Examining Macfadden Publications' foreign editions and international issues also demonstrates how a constellation of transnational economic, cultural, and political developments, as well as the company's own expansionist goals, helped render Macfadden's formulas superlatively culturally translatable beyond the borders of the United States. Among the most important of these developments were urbanization, changing gender roles for women (including the transnational phenomenon of the "modern girl"), the democratization of reading and writing, the international growth of film and advertising industries, and the mounting importance of mass-market media to the construction of cosmopolitan imaginaries *and* various nationalist projects. Distributed and adapted to foreign audiences via a range of entrepreneurial transnational cultural brokers, Macfadden Publications' interwar-era media slotted into multiple local media environments as well as a capacious, globalized popular culture as the company was working toward building up the "Largest News Stand Sale in the World."

CHAPTER EIGHT

From the World of Tomorrow to the American Century

ON DECEMBER 20, 1937, Bernarr Macfadden, now approaching his seventieth birthday, donned a business suit and ran a comb through the unruly mane that kept his book *Hair Culture* in print. Outfitted in his most respectable attire, he headed to the Empire State Building office of Grover A. Whalen, president of the 1939 New York's World Fair, to sign a contract leasing a $50,000 space at the event. Macfadden Publications Inc., he announced, was planning an "elaborate exhibit."[1]

The decision to participate in this international exhibition was probably an easy one. Macfadden's publishing house had been headquartered in New York for nearly four decades, and the city's residents had long contributed to its success. A World's Fair, with its larger-than-life displays wedding education, entertainment, and commerce, would offer an optimal venue for promoting the Macfadden corporation and its products. Moreover, the simultaneously national and global scope of the event, and the far-flung visitors it might attract, dovetailed nicely with the company's profile and ambitions.

For Macfadden, putting on an elaborate exhibit at the New York World's Fair offered testimony to his success. Over the five decades since his first world's fair, the publisher had grown from a virtually unknown Ozark orphan, bodybuilder, and exercise apparatus demonstrator into a muscular millionaire media mogul. The new exhibit would call attention to just how far he had come. And in doing so, it would remind audiences of his company's similarly astonishing trajectory, as what had once been a small purveyor of health and fitness publications operating on the fringes of mainstream acceptability was now widely recognized as an iconic American media corporation with impressive global reach.

Yet, as it would turn out, the Macfadden Exhibit at the New York World's Fair would also foreshadow an immanent turning point for Macfadden, his publishing company, and their relationship to one another. Nine years deep into the Great Depression, with the world on the brink of another world war, tensions that had been brewing for years between the corporation and its founder would rise to the surface in the late 1930s. When they finally erupted, in 1941, Macfadden would find himself ousted from the publishing house he had led for over four decades, leaving Macfadden Publications to chart a new course forward for itself in unstable times.

Constitutionally resistant to the very idea of retirement, Macfadden would remain active in the worlds of physical culture and publishing for another decade and half, but with a diminishing profile. In the face of growing financial difficulties, some related to the finalization of his divorce from Mary, he would fall back on tried-and-true methods of making a living by promoting physical culture, lecturing, and courting both media attention and a younger woman. In the end, however, none of these activities would reverse the Father of American Physical Culture's unambiguous trajectory toward decline.

Macfadden Publications, meanwhile, would have to navigate another national and global crisis, the Second World War, which brought a sharp fall in international trade and threats of resources shortages and censorship. Yet the war would also offer new opportunities for private corporations and media industries to connect with the government, influence popular culture and public opinion, and participate in shaping domestic and foreign affairs. Throughout the conflict, Macfadden Publications would pursue profits through patriotism while streamlining its operations and working out strategies for future expansion in the new domestic and international landscapes being created by the war and its aftermaths.

Following the end of the war in 1945, the working-class consumer power Macfadden Publications had for so many years been promoting and attempting to harness would mushroom, regenerating formulations of consumer citizenship and an American Dream now centered in the nation's booming suburbs. Simultaneously, the United States would continue its transformation from a world power into a superpower intent on spreading its goods and ideologies (and ideologies through goods) around the globe. In these contexts, the publishing company would ramp up its investments in market research at home, seeking to concretize its role as the mouthpiece of, and channel to, the nation's largest consumer market. It would also, simultaneously, create the Macfadden Publications Foreign Sales Corporation, a new subsidiary focused on international distribution whose emergence coincided with the dawn of what many believed would be an American Century.

The Macfadden Exhibit in the World of Tomorrow

Staged at the close of a decade of widespread economic depression, political strife, and deteriorating international stability, the 1939 World's Fair enticed participants to imagine "The Dawn of a New Day." Covering over 1,200 acres in Flushing Meadows, Queens, its exhibits radiated outward from the Trylon and Perisphere, modernist monuments built for the event. Inside the Perisphere, the world's largest escalator brought visitors to Democracity, a model utopian community set in the year 2039 that articulated the event's central theme: the United States as architect of an amazing future.[2] Private corporations played a major role in molding this message. For instance, the fair's most popular exhibit was the General Motors Pavilion's Futurama, an imagined future suburban utopia traversed by delighted visitors via a conveyance of moving chairs. In addition to offering an exciting redesign of the nation's built environment, which it showed as being entirely dependent on cars, Futurama emphasized the central role American corporations, such as GM, should play in "Building the World of Tomorrow."[3] Positioning the United States as a land of innovation and abundance that would lead the way to an improved future for humanity, this attraction attempted to convey, through immersive entertainment, a political message about the wonders of mass production and corporate capitalism.

Adjacent to both the Trylon and Perisphere and the Transportation Zone was the Communications and Business Zone. Dedicated to advancements in communications technology and media, this area showcased RCA's demonstrations of television broadcasting, AT&T's interactive displays of person-to-person and long-distance telephone calling, and the imposing Hall of Communications. Flanked by a pair of 150-foot-tall red pylons, the Hall of Communications housed exhibitions sponsored by individual publishing, printing, and camera-manufacturing corporations. An inscription on the southern side of the building proclaimed: "MODERN MEANS OF COMMUNICATION SPAN CONTINENTS BRIDGE OCEANS ANNIHILATE TIME AND SPACE SERVANTS OF FREEDOM OF THOUGHT AND ACTION THEY OFFER TO ALL MEN THE WISDOM OF THE AGES TO FREE THEM FROM TYRANNIES AND

ESTABLISH COOPERATION AMONG THE PEOPLES OF THE EARTH." Of course, this optimistic message clashed with the increasingly grim realities of global politics in 1939. Modern means of communication had been easily wedded to nationalist and authoritarian political projects, and on the cusp of a Second World War, they represented strategic military and propaganda assets. However, at this fair hosted by the United States— an innovator in communications technology and the world's foremost producer of mass media—a more utopian perspective was intended. Located inside the Communications Building, Macfadden Publications' exhibit would emphasize the importance of mass-market media to creating a coherent national identity and furthering visions of harmonious internationalism that could come to fruition through the spread of American media and consumer and corporate capitalist values.[4]

The 3,553-square-foot Macfadden Exhibit promoted itself to fairgoers as "A Place to Meet Your Friends" that was restful, entertaining, and instructive. Visitors to the exhibition could browse issues of the company's numerous periodicals, including *Liberty, Photoplay, True Story,* and *Physical Culture.* Magazines were less novel than television and other new technologies on display at the fair, yet the massive scale of the company's publishing empire served as its own modern marvel. Publicity materials presented visitors with the astounding (and unsourced) information that "People Buy 201,339,820 Copies of Macfadden Magazines a Year," a statistic meant to communicate the sheer vastness of the company's combined domestic and foreign markets.[5]

Another of the exhibit's attractions was the air-conditioned Macfadden Theater, a 226-seat movie theater whose exterior architecture echoed the shape of a white ocean liner. *Business Screen* magazine, a trade publication for the commercial and educational film industry, praised the theater's "dynamic modern design" that "provided an irresistible lure to the picture within."[6] Adding to this allure were young women hostesses wearing wide smiles and slim-fitting, sailor-inspired uniforms, who were positioned at the entrance. Inside the theater, a short film titled *I'll Tell the World* played on a loop. Admission to the theater was free, and afterward audiences could meet one of the movie's leads, up-and-coming star Patricia Murray, who had, as the program explained, been cast in the "leading ingénue role" after winning a "Beauty and Brains" contest sponsored by the publishing house.

I'll Tell the World is "a home-spun comedy" centered on "a typical American family" named the Burtons. When the story opens, Mr. Burton's button business has fallen into decline due to his failure to utilize advertising. His wife is frumpy and unhappy. Their daughter wants to marry a young advertising executive but worries that she should remain at home to

Fig.8.1 Program for the Macfadden Exhibit at the 1939 New York World's Fair.
Reproduced from the author's personal collection.

supplement her family's meager income. Things are, in other words, de-
pressed and depressing. To improve this situation, Mr. Burton's family, with
the advertising executive beau, all attempt to convince him of the powers of
modern marketing. Along the way, the film traces the various ways in which
modern advertising, as well as affordable name-brand products that reach
consumers through advertising, enhance the average wage-earning family's
standard of living and ability to prosper. The story concludes with a happy
ending, as the Burtons are "restored to happiness and security when the father discovers the miraculous powers of advertising."[7]

Produced by Macfadden Publications for the fair, *I'll Tell the World* was
a dramatized adaptation of the ten-part series "The American Way of
Life," which appeared in the company's *Liberty* magazine in 1938–1939.
The author of this series was George E. Sokolsky, a well-known public
commentator who had recently become known for his conservative political views. The child of Russian Jewish immigrants who grew up on the
Lower East Side at the turn of the century, Sokolsky had begun his journalism career reporting on the February Revolution in Russia, which
sparked his disillusionment with radical politics. Next, he had worked as
a businessman and foreign correspondent in China before returning to the

United States in the 1930s to become a political columnist, industrial consultant, and spokesperson for NAM, the increasingly powerful trade group dedicated to defending and furthering the interests of American corporations. It was in this capacity that Sokolsky had teamed up with Macfadden Publications.

In the series on which *I'll Tell the World* was based, Sokolsky and *Liberty* contributed to an ongoing, contentious, and multifaceted public conversation about the meaning of "The American Way of Life," an expression that had become a catalyst for debates about the legitimacy of the New Deal and the relationship between capitalism and Americanism.[8] As Oursler told *Liberty*'s readers in his preface to the first installment, the idea for the feature had come to him in response to Congress's years-long campaign to assert the federal government's authority to regulate the advertising industry, which resulted in the 1938 passage of the Wheeler-Lea Amendment to the Federal Trade Commission Act.[9] Believing that "American people would welcome the other side of the story"—the side of business and advertisers—Macfadden Publications hired Sokolsky to produce a sympathetic history of American advertising that would connect with its readers.

The ten installments of "The American Way of Life" trace the development of specific industries, types of products, and places of consumption that had contributed to making a nation whose "lowest earnings group," even after nine straight years of depression, "has more things" than the average person "in any other country."[10] To support his claims, Sokolsky combines extensive statistical data, procured with the help of Macfadden Publications' pioneering in-house research director Everett R. Smith, with colorful narratives about figures ranging from humble homemakers to men and women who became rich entrepreneurs. Arguing that "[e]very great American industry is the dramatization of the life of a forceful, aggressive, often wise individual who set out to do a good job and did it," Sokolsky's true stories function to humanize corporations, which are depicted, along with the advertising industry, as fundamentally American institutions. Throughout, the author references his own biography as well, describing improvements in US living standards he has witnessed in his lifetime and favorably comparing these trends to conditions he experienced living abroad. To Oursler's delight, Sokolsky's series attributing Americans' resiliency and supposed freedom from want to entrepreneurs, corporations, and advertisers "read to us [at the firm] like a romance, a story of adventure, of hazard, and of achievement."[11] It read, in other words, like the kind of not-pulp yet pulp-at-heart true story in which Macfadden Publications had come to specialize.

Turning Sokolsky's *Liberty* essays into a movie for exhibition at the World's Fair was a strategic choice, for as *Business Week* noted, the medium of film "was the ideal vehicle for the exhibitor who has something intangible to sell."[12] In the Macfadden Theater, as through its magazine displays, the company showcased its skill in crafting attractive and accessible media that combined literary and cinematic conventions with an intimate tone. Through these strategies, it connected with popular audiences while advocating for policies and worldviews associated with anti–New Deal conservatives and American corporations.[13] Indeed, the Macfadden Exhibit's program claimed that the company's media could transmit messages that were "absorbed unconsciously" by engrossed audiences.[14] With its aptly titled *I'll Tell the World*, Macfadden Publications was exemplifying how media expertly tailored to non-elites, epitomized by its own participatory and therefore "democratic" magazines and other cultural products, could unlock lucrative new markets while harmonizing populist tensions that tended to accompany structural transformations associated with the expansion of corporate capitalism at home and the promotion of American consumer goods and tastes abroad.[15] The best part was, there was no need to wait for fancy new communications technologies to be invented to achieve this goal. The cultural forms, media circulations, and business organization Macfadden Publications had already developed provided an apparatus for realizing this vision today.

Like any text the company ever created, the Macfadden Exhibit in the World of Tomorrow did not contain a singular set of meanings, however. Audiences who perused the company's magazines on display may certainly have responded positively to their contents, appreciating their accessible content, participatory ethos, intimate tone, and running motifs of health and fitness, beautiful bodies, romance, interpersonal drama, crime and crime-solving, films and celebrity, biography, and political editorializing. Perhaps some may also have developed insight into the advertising industry and consumer capitalism's contributions to an American Way of Life defined by relative consumer abundance while sitting in the Macfadden Theater, which filled to capacity in nice weather. Many visitors probably just sat around enjoying some rest and air-conditioning, though. Furthermore, the exhibit's corporatist messaging portraying corporate-led mass consumption as the cornerstone of American life, US influence, and modern self-fulfillment existed alongside other messages available in Macfadden-brand media and even the space of the exhibition itself. This becomes most evident when considering July 7, 1939, when the Macfadden Exhibit transformed, albeit briefly, into a very different scene.

On this summer afternoon, the seventy-year-old Macfadden arrived at the World's Fair. He was accompanied on this occasion not by businessmen or politicians, but by a contingent of eighty-one fitness enthusiasts ranging in age between fourteen and eighty, all participants in the Fifth Annual Macfadden Health Walk, organized through *Physical Culture*. The group, which at its peak contained 150 people, had started a 617-mile hike over four weeks earlier in Philadelphia. After picking up Macfadden at his health home in Dansville, New York, the walkers had wound their way through the Finger Lakes District and down to New Jersey before eventually reaching their destination in Flushing Meadows. Except for a few cases of blisters and sunburn, the delegation was in good condition when it arrived at its final destination: the Macfadden Exhibit.[16]

The appearance of this motley walking brigade at the center of such a sleek corporate space, in a fair celebrating technological advancements, may have seemed disjunctive to some; yet it also aptly captured important aspects of Macfadden Publications' history and identity. Over many decades, both the company and its founder had produced a range of participatory and multivocal mass media that championed the physical culture life and the experiences and achievements of regular people, ultimately creating an iconic modern media corporation known for maintaining populist sensibilities along with popular appeal. This was evidenced in the two versions of Macfadden on display this day. The exhibit's official publicity materials depicted the publisher as a suit-clad health-expert, millionaire media mogul, and philanthropist with serious political clout and a reputation as a corporate visionary. Yet the wiry, wild-haired showboat leading the Fifth Annual Health Walk was the persona many associated with the company's president—an iconoclast who had been publicly challenging middle-class morality and conventional wisdom about fitness and health, the periodical industry, working-class culture, aging—and more recently, liberal politics—for decades. Here, the "guiding mind behind the mammoth Macfadden publishing organization" exuded an aura of sincerity and simplicity as the figurehead of a group that cost nothing to join besides sweat. The material accoutrements and conveniences that, according to most displays at the 1939 World's Fair, signaled success and advancement paled in comparison to simpler things, namely the marvel of the human body and everyday people's capabilities for mobility and transformation through accessible means like exercise or self-narration. Running alongside the celebrations of consumer abundance and corporate capitalism, this message too was what Macfadden Publications ended up "telling the world" at the World's Fair and through its media empire.

Another alternative representation of Macfadden Publications produced during the period of the fair also bears mentioning here. While the Macfadden Exhibit was going on in New York, 500 miles south, in Durham, North Carolina, Jack Delano, a Russian Jewish émigré employed as a photographer by the New Deal's Farm Security Administration, took a picture at a city bus station whose wall featured an ad for one of Macfadden's products. In the resulting photo, a Black traveler, waiting for his bus beneath signs reading "Colored Waiting Room" and "Private Property," looks over his shoulder toward a poster for *True Story*, specifically an issue promising "Hitler's Love Life Revealed" by "his former maid."[17] Occupying a "central panel of meaning" in the photograph's composition, the *True Story* ad works to suggest parallels between the segregation at the bus terminal and the Nazi's racial regime while also calling attention to the inherent ambiguity of the power dynamics on display in the social and cultural worlds depicted in this scene.[18] A lowly maid is the one who reveals Hitler's private life; this Black traveler could presumably buy this purportedly written-from-below national magazine to read on the segregated platform. But there is no sense that either of these transactions could produce any form of destabilization of the structures of violence and oppression represented by Hitler and Jim Crow. Instead, the potentially empowering cultural form highlighted through this image is the photograph itself, and the New Deal program that produced it outside the parameters of commercialized mass culture, which is being critiqued in its

Fig.8.2 Jack Delano's now-iconic 1940 photograph, *At the Bus Station in Durham, North Carolina.* Prints and Photograph Collection, Library of Congress, LC-DIG-ppmsc-00199

composition. In various ways, then, this iconic photograph, seemingly ephemeral at the time, but more permanent in the long run than the Macfadden Exhibit in the World of Tomorrow, illustrates another permutation of what Macfadden Publications' media, and its advertising, was "tell[ing] the world" in the late 1930s.

Reorganization, Mobilization, and the Postwar Era

Despite the impressive and well-reviewed show Macfadden Publications put on through the Macfadden Exhibit at the World's Fair, by 1939, the company was heading toward a potentially catastrophic financial crisis of its own making. Years earlier, in response to the Great Depression, the company had lowered the prices of its publications, offsetting these price reductions with increasing ad revenue, which it secured through guaranteeing advertising clients higher and higher circulations. This operating model was not, it turned out, infinitely sustainable. Compounding matters, the outbreak of the Second World War in Europe in 1939 interrupted the company's efforts to make deals abroad and thereby increase its circulations in foreign markets. Growth hit a limit, and in 1940, Macfadden Publications Inc. reported over half a million dollars in losses.

Next, there was a circulation scandal. To incentivize sales, Macfadden Publications had been offering bonuses to distributors. Eventually, these payments became high enough that it began to make more sense for sellers to destroy unsold copies of *Liberty*, but report them as sold, to collect the bonuses. This put the publishing house in breach of contract with its advertisers, who had been guaranteed actual circulation for their ads. When the *Liberty* scandal broke in the spring of 1941, prompting a reaudit from the Audit Bureau of Circulation, the company had to reimburse advertisers and face distrust and scrutiny.[19] Making matters even worse, also in 1941, one of *Liberty*'s regular contributors on international relations, George Sylvester Viereck, who had also set up his own small publishing house, was charged with operating as a foreign agent and propagandist for Nazi Germany. The first person to be subpoenaed by the newly established House Special Committee on Un-American Activities, Viereck would be convicted and sent to prison.[20] His growing infamy at such a sensitive time reflected poorly on Macfadden Publications.

Meanwhile, tensions between Macfadden and some of the executives and shareholders of Macfadden Publications, which had been building for years, began coming to a head. These tensions concerned how the president of the company, who was the majority owner of its stock, had been spending company money. Since 1935, Macfadden had been throwing cash from the publishing side of his business at his Dansville and Miami health hotels and various charitable enterprises of the Macfadden Foundation. He had also been bankrolling his own recurrent political campaigning, which in 1940 came to include entering the Senate race in Florida.[21] A further point of contention was the publisher's $50,000 salary (close to $1 million today). As the biographer Robert Ernst details, a small cabal of executives and shareholders at the company, calling themselves a "protective committee," filed four simultaneous suits against Macfadden in New York Federal Court in 1940.[22] Behind the scenes, this group had the support of Macfadden's long-standing business manager and company vice president Orr J. Elder, who had apparently had enough. While the publisher denied the charges against him, arguing that his actions had always been good for the company—believing that he essentially *was* the company—the "protective committee" ultimately prevailed.

In 1941, Macfadden announced that he "had decided to relinquish control of Macfadden Publications, Inc." to spend more time focusing on his philanthropic activities.[23] The reality was that he had been removed from power. As part of his settlement, he sold his stock to the corporation's new managers, paid back $300,000, and agreed not to compete with Macfadden Publications for five years.[24] As *Newsweek* reported, "The retirement of the bushy-haired health faddist from the direction of the $12,000,000 firm . . . came as a surprise to the public but not to a publishing world rife with Macfadden rumors."[25] Ousting Macfadden was the quickest and most effective way for the company to quash these rumors, and it quickly went about restructuring its operations, promoting Elder to the role of president. While this was happening, two of the company's most important figures resigned. William Jourdan Rapp, who had edited *True Story* for sixteen years, left in March 1941; one year later, he would die from a heart attack. Fulton Oursler quit Macfadden Publications the following February; over the next decade, he would write many books, including the best-selling *The Greatest Story Ever Told* series, a trio of true stories about Jesus Christ and other biblical figures, and work as an editor for *Reader's Digest* before his death in 1952. The departures of Macfadden, Rapp, and Oursler marked the end of an era at Macfadden Publications.

Personally and financially, Macfadden would never get over his removal from the publishing house he founded and that still bore his name. Refusing to fade away, however, he presented a strong face (and body) to the public by immediately throwing himself into new business ventures. In 1941, he started a syndicated column devoted to matters of health, fitness, and politics, frequently providing unsolicited advice to national leaders, including the Roosevelt White House, which kept tabs on his musings. Two years later, Macfadden bought back *Physical Culture,* always his favorite magazine, which he would continue to publish under various titles (*Bernarr Macfadden's Health Review,* then *Physical Culture* again, then *Bernarr Macfadden's Vitalized Physical Culture*) for the next ten years. Also in 1943, he established a Health Services Bureau in New York offering naturopathic health advice. This venture was quickly criticized by the AMA, fined, and shut down.[26] Macfadden was furious at this interference. In "An Open Letter to President Roosevelt" published in his fitness magazine and distributed as a stand-alone pamphlet, he claimed that the "allopathic medical health authorities are to blame" for the United States' failure to more quickly trounce Germany in the current war.[27]

During this period, Macfadden also threw himself into improving the physical culture hotel in Miami Beach he had bought in 1935, which was briefly used by the US Army in 1942. While the resort's facilities were impressive and the setting picturesque, it was expensive to promote and maintain, especially as he no longer had access to unlimited free advertising space for his ventures in a spate of popular magazines. Another financial pressure Macfadden faced was the prolonged and acrimonious court proceedings that following his split with Mary. Even after the divorce of the World's Most Perfectly Developed Man and Woman was finalized in 1946, obligatory payments to Mary's trust would remain a source of conflict and strain for him.

With his once legendary fortune draining quickly, Macfadden returned to a money-raising tactic from earlier in his career, booking speaking engagements. Soon, he was proselytizing a new creed he called "Cosmotarianism," which was part health and fitness advocacy, part self-help, and part religion (Weakness is a Sin—Don't be a Sinner!). One successful "service," part of a six-part series, brought 2,000 congregants to Carnegie Hall to hear the Father of American Physical Culture preach on "The Joyous Life—How to Live It." As Macfadden was busy "merg[ing] health and heaven," there was another physical culture enthusiast drawing large crowds to hear her speak at Carnegie Hall.[28] Johnnie Lee McKinney (formerly Hattie Frances Dean McKinney), born in 1904 in Waco, Texas, had been obsessed with health and fitness since she was a teenager, when her favorite magazine was *Physical Culture.* As an adult, she had developed "Cosmo-Dynamics," a philosophy celebrating "personal magnetism, love, and youthfulness," which promised audiences salvation through fitness, positivity, and personal striving.[29] When Macfadden met Johnnie Lee, an attractive and shapely strawberry blonde decades his junior, he pursued her aggressively, first trying to have sex with her, then flying her in his personal plane to Miami, where she discovered that her suitor was about to begin campaigning for the governorship of Florida.[30] Macfadden proposed, Johnnie Lee said yes, and the wedding took place on April 24, 1948, in front of a crowd of 1,500 people.

After Macfadden, unsurprisingly, did not become governor of Florida, the newlyweds returned to New York, where they planned to build up a joint health and fitness business. To Johnnie Lee's surprise, Macfadden insisted they keep separate apartments, meeting only by appointment; it was not long before the latest Mrs. Macfadden discovered that her husband was not spending their nights apart alone. Over the next few years, the couple fought often about Macfadden's infidelity as well as his financial secrecy and controlling personality. Johnnie Lee would later claim, "Life with Bernarr . . . had its ups and downs, but the high spots more than made up for the dips."[31] Really though, it seems that the "dips" prevailed. Their relationship ended for good when Macfadden, after skydiving in New York to celebrate his eighty-second and eighty-third birthdays, insisted that his wife accompany him on his next jump, which would take place in France. When Johnnie Lee refused, Macfadden stormed off to Paris alone, and the couple filed for separation soon after. This left Macfadden, who was now in his mid-eighties, on the hook for alimony in addition to his trust payments to Mary.

After the separation of Macfadden Publications Inc. from Bernarr Macfadden in 1941, the ensuing years proceeded less tumultuously for the company than they did for its founder. As the new head of the company, Elder, a businessman who had always eschewed the public spotlight in proportion to the degree Macfadden chased it, would focus on restoring the company's financial health. As one reporter quipped, instead of physical culture, Elder provided the organization with a "strong dose" of "fiscal culture."[32] He consolidated some of the company's operations and oversaw the move of many of its departments into a 125,000-square-foot office space on East 42nd Street, near Grand Central Station. The same year, the company expanded its book publishing and distributing business, creating a paperback publishing subsidiary, Bartholomew House ("Bart House" for short), which was named after the new building.

Macfadden Publications would also continue to invest heavily in corporate relations. In 1941, it published an oversized book, *History and Magazines*, "in recognition of the 200th anniversary of magazines in America." This handsome publicity tome emphasized the firm's important role in this history. "It has been said that the greatest assurance of American Democracy lies in the understanding of its people. America's great magazines have done much to advance this understanding and thus to protect the system of free enterprise in which we live," it begins. Covering 1776 to the present, subsequent chapters narrate the evolution of magazines: they started as revolutionary broadsheets for the elite, helped to create a prosperous nineteenth-century middle class, fused immigrant and native-born Americans together during the First World War, spread the benefits of mass production in the 1920s, and fostered cooperation during the Great Depression, when "Americans were ready to accept any social system which would seem to offer them security. . . . Right or wrong." Now, in the "Era of Defense Economy," magazines were fostering "understanding" among the Wage Earner Group—the group upon which rests the numerical control of the nation's future."[33] More than any of its competitors, *History and Magazines* implied, Macfadden Publications had incubated both unity and individualism as well as American progress and patriotism.

By this point, burnishing the publishing company's patriotic credentials had become a company priority. With Macfadden's history of editorializing against the Roosevelt administration, plus the recent scandals with *Liberty* and Viereck, the company occupied a relatively precarious position when the United States entered the Second World War at the end of 1941. Quickly, its various periodicals began printing reams of features supporting the war effort. *True Story* described women waiting for letters from lovers in the army, families making due under wartime rationing, soldiers persevering under fire, and romances forged between men and women in the line of duty. Similarly, *True Detective* serials described life under the Nazi police state the United States was battling, the government's pursuit of foreign agents, and how codebreakers cracked enemy secrets. *Photoplay* (now merged with *Movie Mirror*) showed what film celebrities were doing to support the troops and promoted Hollywood films valorizing the United States and its war aims. *Liberty* inaugurated an "America Fights" section in each issue, printed biographies like "MacArthur—Hero and Husband," and ran contests to reward war heroes.[34] Notably, *Liberty* also published more critical articles, though never too critical. For instance, the 1943 feature "My Only Crime is My Face," by the Japanese American journalist Mary Oyama, discusses the trauma and injustice of Executive Order 9066, which forced Oyama's family into incarceration at the Heart Mountain Relocation Center; ultimately, this author concludes that "although we still feel that the basis on which we were evacuated (because of racial extraction) was unjust, and although we believe our incarceration was illegal . . . we have decided that the fullest cooperation with the government is the very best way to prove our loyalty to our country."[35] Just as it had during the prewar period, *Liberty*'s signature practice of discussing political issues from "both sides" helped it assert a reputation for

Fig.8.3 Features from *True Story* during the Second World War, as depicted in Macfadden Publications' 1941 self-promotional book *History and Magazines*. Reproduced from the author's personal collection

inclusivity and objectivity. In practice, though, the inclusion of minority opinions frequently worked to amplify the voices of conservatives and anti–New Dealers, thereby helping the magazine to shape the window of popular discourse in its publishing firm's preferred directions.

Macfadden Publications provided more direct aid to the US government as well. Most obviously, this included advertising war bonds. Like other media companies and the broader entertainment industry, the publishing house also offered its services to government agencies such as the Office of War Information (OWI) and the War Production Board (WPB). One place this can be seen is in *True Story*'s cooperation with government efforts to recruit American women to work in war industries. As confession magazines were popular among working-class women, and *True Story* was the best-selling title in this genre, the OWI viewed Macfadden Publications as a very useful partner in this recruitment effort. The head of the Office's Magazine Bureau met numerous times with Henry Lieferant, a writer, originally from Austria before he had immigrated to the United States, who had replaced Rapp as editor of *True Story*. Lieferant depicted the Macfadden company as eager to lend its services. Issues of *True Story* thereafter incorporated themes and plot suggestions the Magazine Bureau communicated as desirable. For example, one of these suggestions was to de-emphasize sex and violence to make wartime workplaces seem less dangerous and more respectable; as sex and violence, especially in the workplace, had been long-running themes in Macfadden's confession media, the conspicuous reduction in frequency of such topics can be seen as consistent with collaboration with the OWI.[36] Importantly, other messages the OWI wanted women's magazines to emphasize, such as the dignity of being a female worker, were already central to the fabric of *True Story* and its sibling publications.

Macfadden Publications also took on an active role in helping the government more effectively communicate and collaborate with private industry to market its aims to the public.[37] Leading this charge were Everett R. Smith, the company's research director and marketing guru, and the company's in-house advertising expert Carroll Rheinstrom, both of whom took leaves to work for the WPB. This was not just patriotism or altruism. There were concerns about paper rationing, censorship, and distribution interruptions, and working with the WPB offered a way to advocate for their company and the wider mass-market publishing industry.[38] Macfadden Publications, which was still operating in the red in 1942, began declaring profits again in 1943.[39]

Macfadden Publications inaugurated a public service campaign "designed to dramatize the importance of advertising as a postwar planning weapon" in 1943 as well.[40] Likely masterminded by Smith, this extensive campaign simultaneously worked to communicate messages about the organization of postwar society, especially regarding the importance of reemploying male war workers and service personnel, and to educate other industries and government officials about the critical importance of using advertising and mass-market media outlets, especially those attuned to the working class, to realize their goals.[41] Responding to widespread concerns that demobilization would bring a toxic mix of postwar male unemployment, labor strife, and a return to depression, Macfadden Publications injected newspapers with ads. These ads blared the message that the pent-up buying power of the "wage-earner class," and this class's future buying power, held the key to postwar stability and prosperity. In this campaign, images of sturdy men performing a range of blue-collar occupations are accompanied by eye-catching headlines describing the enormous cumulative spending power of such workers. "The Only Man Rich Enough to Keep 55 Million Men at Work," one proclaims, "If Your Advertising Can Get To Him," or better yet, "If Your Advertising Can Influence Him." Constantly reiterating the point that "As the Wage-Earner Goes, So Does America," this public messaging campaign promoted Macfadden Publications, whose magazines "enjoy reader confidence, loyalty, and respect," as a crucial intermediary in the process of peacetime readjustment and postwar economic expansion.[42]

This message was further conveyed in a set of *True Story* editorials dedicated to "talking over" the "American way of life," which were then reprinted and distributed as standalone pamphlets. For instance, amid rising concerns about labor strikes at home and communism abroad in February 1946, editor Lieferant pontificated on the virtues of the "Middle of the Road," making connections between the importance of moderation in personal behavior, a common-sense theme often promoted in its confessions, and moderation in political behavior.[43] The two different formats in which this editorial circulated—as chatty front matter to a popular confession magazine and as slick public relations materials—reified Macfadden Publications' capabilities as an intermediating force in popular culture and industrial and public affairs. Such efforts were paired with emphasis on the company's purported role as a megaphone for the ideas, perceptions, and desires of its masses of readers. This dynamic would be further solidified through its sponsorship of pioneering sociological research, which would lead to the creation of an influential vehicle for the collecting and reporting of public opinion.

Perhaps the most consequential investment Macfadden Publications made in sociological research began in the early 1940s, when Smith connected with the Columbia University–affiliated social researcher Dr. Paul A. Lazarsfeld, a Jewish émigré from Austria who had recently conducted a survey on the 1940 election funded in part by *Liberty* magazine.[44] Later published in 1944 as *The People's Choice,* this study identified mass-market magazine readers as "opinion leaders" in their respective communities. How Lazarsfeld's research might enhance the publishing house's constant uphill battle to sell the Macfadden Market to advertisers was intriguing to the company, especially as the social scientist offered data to back up "the idea that low-income women who read movie and true-story magazines might 'multiply' the effect of advertising in those magazines and therefore [were] more valuable advertising targets than their low income would imply."[45] Smith arranged for Macfadden Publications to award Columbia University's Bureau of Applied Social Research a $30,000 grant to support Lazarsfeld's next study of "personal influence," which took place in Decatur, Illinois, under the direction of a colleague Lazarsfeld hired, the sociologist C. Wright Mills.[46]

Seeking to determine how people, especially women (the demographic of greatest interest to its sponsor), made decisions—from how to vote, to what to buy, to which movies to see—the study was "[c]omplex in design, ingenious in its procedures, [and] laborious in its execution," requiring the "arranging, recording, and coding of approximately 2,000 interviews" over seventeen months.[47] Based on the study's findings, Lazarsfeld and his associates theorized a "two-step flow" of communication and influence; instead of asserting that media penetrated communities, they showed how individuals who were connected to media themselves dispersed information horizontally through interpersonal connections. While the full results would take years to be disseminated, the study's findings were quickly relayed to its sponsor, where they influenced the publishing house's marketing strategies and operations, just as the publishing house's priorities influenced how the sociologists designed and interpreted the study.[48] For Macfadden Publications, this work had several applications. First, it bolstered models of class differentiation and female influence that were used to sell the Macfadden Market to advertisers. Second, it demonstrated the social influence of the type of publications (especially true story and fan magazines) the company sold. And third, it could be used to validate the company's internally generated sociological findings and theories, which it had long been circulating in its corporate relations materials. When finally published in 1955 as *Personal Influence,* this study had an immediate and enormous impact, ultimately becoming a seminal text in the fields of applied sociology and mass communications.[49]

While investing in the research that would eventually become *Personal Influence,* Macfadden Publications was also building up its own in-house surveying capacities. Again under the direction of Smith, the company engineered a method to repeatedly survey a large sample of working-class American households by mail and then convert their survey results into statistical data. With this data, Macfadden Publications would not only know more about its own readers; it could also package this information and pass it on to sectors of business, industry, and the government interested in the thoughts and behaviors of non-elites. The company called this innovation the Wage Earner Forum.[50] To get data from the Wage Earner Forum, the company would send questionnaires to a fixed set of 1,500 households, defined as a married heterosexual couple living together, spread across the United States "in proportion to the wage earner employment concentration," with each man and woman receiving their own form to fill out and mail back to the company. Accessibly worded, and guaranteeing anonymity, the surveys would arrive approximately every six weeks, asking participants to share aspects of their lives, including their opinions on topics such as inflation and price control policies, tax rates, labor conditions and labor-capital relations, foreign relations, socialized medicine, monopolies, political candidates, health insurance, and other weighty topics of national importance.[51]

A successful endeavor, the Wage Earner Forum's findings were widely reported and cited by journalists, policy makers, and others looking to understand or predict public attitudes about a range of issues during the postwar era. The kinds of findings the company shared included information about the importance of women as home goods purchasers, evidence that "lower-middle stratum" voters predicted the outcome of the 1948 presidential election, and discussions about what workers wanted from their employers. As the next decade approached, respondents reported rising living standards manifested through home furnishings and home ownership, work conditions, and leisure time; declining support for some government programs and forms of taxation; and growing concerns about communism. Interrupting any neat ideological binary, they also expressed hesitancy over militarization; less resistance to income tax than sales tax; high price consciousness; and rising expectations, not unrelated to contemporaneous union efforts, for employers to share profits and offer more generous benefits, such as life and health insurance.

Though eliciting and brokering such information, Macfadden Publications institutionalized its long-touted role as a political, economic, social, and cultural intermediary with direct access to "the people" whose voices it reached and disseminated. In doing so, it continued a process begun long before the war of consolidating and distinguishing the non-elite mass market it purported to represent. Externally, this "lower-middle stratum" market was differentiated from the upper and middle classes by income, occupation, culture, and (some) political opinions; internally, it was segmented most markedly by gender, with the company emphasizing how women exerted the greatest influence on the consumption patterns of their households and communities. Focusing its research and communications efforts on white working-class female consumers, especially the wives of blue-collar workers, the company showed that these Americans differed markedly from middle-class and elite women in terms of their preferences in reading material, home furnishings, appliances, fashions, and so on. These differences, it emphasized, were harmonious with practices of mass consumption and ideals of consumer citizenship, as Macfadden Publications' female readership tended to embrace a "more is better" aesthetic through which their rising standard of living could be overtly displayed.[52] In tandem with these activities, Macfadden Publications restructured its advertising operations by adding *True Story* to its preexisting Women's Group of magazines to create the True Story Women's Group in 1949. With this move, the company now offered advertisers a guaranteed circulation of 5,250,000—the largest total guaranteed circulation of any periodical company in the business, geared toward "a market different from any other in its actions and reactions" that constituted most advertisers' "principal prospects" for future growth.[53] When the company developed new magazines, it targeted its offerings to this category, introducing *Good Cooking* (1950) and *TV-Radio Mirror* (1952).

Among the new titles Macfadden Publications introduced, a few were directed at male members of the households of the True Story Women's Group's readers, which along with the company's long-popular detective magazines, came to constitute the Macfadden's Men's Group. These included *Sport* (1946), which was aimed at sports fans, and the adventure-themed *Saga* (1950) and *Climax* (1953), pulp-style magazines that catered especially to GIs and veterans. Notably, the hard-bodied aesthetic and pulp qualities of these latter two publications also hailed gay men. As we have seen, the company had attracted a queer readership since its earliest physical culture days, and queer readers over time had become increasingly networked through consuming and participating in mass media, especially physique publications.[54] In the post-WWII era, amid the rise of a visible homophile movement, reaching a gay readership offered opportunities for profit, which appears to have led the Macfadden publishing corporation to implicitly target gay male consumers. Its strategy for doing so involved signaling that queer pleasures might be found in its media without positively representing same-sex romantic or sexual relationships—a strategy better known today as "queer-baiting."[55] For instance, issues of *Climax,* subtitled "Exciting Stories for Men," feature exaggeratedly muscular male physiques on their covers and contain stories set within homosocial spaces such as the Western frontier or the modern US military (which was deployed around the world in the postwar era of foreign occupations and interventions). The brand of masculinity featured in this title was ostensibly heterosexual and even stridently anti-queer at times. Yet the pulp visual and textual elements selected for *Climax* communicated readiness to be read through a "queer aesthetic sensibility" attuned to "the potentialities that hide beneath the routine and expected."[56] Over time, these potentialities became less hidden and more barely-contained, much like the fantastically bulging muscles beneath the unbuttoned shirts and tight pants favored by *Climax*'s alluring cover men.

Through all these efforts, Macfadden Publications not only operated within but continually made important contributions to an evolving postwar "landscape of mass consumption" in which the empowerment of some previously marginalized consumer citizens proceeded in tandem with the gendered and racialized marginalization of other citizens and their desires and preferences.[57] For instance, with the Wage Earner Forum, Macfadden Publications had control over which and whose data it would collect, and how and to whom it would be reported and interpreted.[58] The architecture of the company's research centered those formerly urban workers, often descended from European "new immigrants," who moved to the newly erected suburbs, constructed heterosexual couplings and nuclear families, and formed personal and political experiences and identities in this milieu, which they inflected with their own worldviews and tastes. By practice and design, this environment excluded Black, Latinx, Asian, and Indigenous Americans; unmarried people; renters; and those deemed politically subversive or otherwise nonnormative.[59] In other words, while groups that had historically been consumers of Macfadden Publications' media were being excluded structurally from many forms of postwar political power, economic mobility, and cultural visibility, Macfadden Publications' representations of the normative (white) Wage Earner and "his wife" further contributed to their marginalization. A different version of this process played out with the company's men's magazines, which acknowledged some gay men's greater purchasing power compared to other groups but only within highly constrained formats that were simultaneously conducive to anti-queer identities and ideologies. As Macfadden Publications invested varying levels and types of resources into cultivating customer bases among some marginalized individuals and groups more than others, different kinds of consumers were rendered unequally visible as distinct or self-representing markets in the corporation's influential research activities, marketing publications, and popular media. Meanwhile, when the company's vision for further expanding its "mass" market of mass consumers, to which it promised to connect advertisers, businesses, and even policy makers, did cause it to see beyond working-class white American suburbia, it tended to look not to other communities of underserved readers in the United States but rather to potential markets overseas.

The American Century?

The ousting of Macfadden and the reorganization of Macfadden Publications without him in 1941 coincided with the rival *Time* publisher Henry Luce's declaration of the arrival of an "American Century" of US international expansion and influence. In a now-famous *Life* magazine editorial, the editor envisioned "an immense American internationalism" created by the spread of American commodities, institutions, and ideals. In phrasing that would have seemed right at home in an article penned by Macfadden for *Physical Culture,* Luce argued, "[T]he world of the 20th century, if it is to come to life in any nobility of health and vigor, must be to a significant degree an American Century," a cause to which readers were encouraged to devote themselves in "joy and gladness and vigor and enthusiasm."[60]

The Macfadden publishing house, which had been pursuing international expansion aggressively before 1941, participated in this mission. While the war made it hard to close international deals or circulate its publications overseas in any serious volume, laying the groundwork to ensure future access to foreign markets would remain a priority for the company. To accomplish this goal, it would seek to foster friendly ties with wartime and postwar government agencies while representing its media and distribution capacities as uniquely conducive to a broader US project of Americanization that was undergoing expansion at this time. This trend can be seen most vividly through the work of the Macfadden Publications executive Carroll Rheinstrom. An expert in advertising and the author of several books on the subject, Rheinstrom worked as director of advertising services for the publishing house throughout the 1920s and 1930s. After leaving briefly in 1940, he returned after the reorganization to assume the position of executive vice president.[61] In addition to providing services to the WPB in 1942, Rheinstrom, a young man still in his thirties, would use his mastery of the arts of persuasion and public relations to lobby for Macfadden Publications' value as a strategic asset to the United States.

In spring and summer of 1945, Rheinstrom petitioned Assistant Secretary of State for Latin American Affairs Nelson Rockefeller for assistance in reestablishing editions of the company's foreign magazines and founding

new ones. In particular, Rheinstrom requested help expediting international travel arrangements to conduct business in Mexico, Argentina, and
Brazil, in addition to Great Britain, France, Sweden, Egypt, Turkey, Italy,
and Spain—a list that hints at the company's ambitions for the postwar
era. Rheinstrom argued, "Any action taken by the State Dept . . . would be
relatively unobtrusive, since [Macfadden Publications] licensed the publication of many foreign editions before the war, and resumption post war
is logical and hardly newsworthy." Evidencing his claims, Rheinstrom explained, "Our magazine *True Story* (also *True Romances*)—which inci-
dentally is the favorite magazine of the American Wage Earner housewives,
and for that reason is supported by practically every important American
advertiser—still enjoys one of the largest women's magazine circulations
in Great Britain." He also cited the company's successes in other countries
before the interruption of the war: "*True Story* in Sweden was highly successful. *True Story* in Germany . . . rolled up one of the largest circulations
there. *True Story* in France sold a million copies a week, and was taken
over and published for a time by the Germans. Our plan is to negotiate in
these countries again for *True Story,* as well as *Photoplay,*" he wrote.[62]

Importantly, Rheinstrom focused on emphasizing the benefits to the government of helping an American company with established circulations
among non-elites. "Because of *True Story's* quarter-century proved appeal
for the masses of the people less likely to be reached by publications such as
Reader's Digest," he argued, "we feel that its function in the subtle dissemination of American ideologies may be most important."[63] In the phrasing of
this appeal, Rheinstrom was making a reference to the State Department's
expanding informational diplomacy efforts at the time. The OWI had backed
international distribution of some US magazines during the war, and in the
OWI's wake, the Office of International Information and Cultural Affairs
(OII) would be continuing these efforts.[64] But, as Rheinstrom understood,
the favored participants in and beneficiaries of the State Department's information diplomacy efforts focused on print culture were middlebrow periodicals; indeed, by 1947, one journalist would remark that "it has come to the
point where magazines like *Reader's Digest* are accepted as the official expression of the voice of" the United States abroad.[65] What Macfadden Publications was trying to interest US officials in was something else: good
relations with an empire of entertaining and participatory mass-market magazines aimed at non-elite readers that would more easily slot (or better yet,
re-slot) into local contexts and therefore not elicit the suspicion or criticality
evoked by materials associated with American propaganda.

Rheinstrom also took special care to spell out the linkages between Macfadden's magazines and the more centralized Hollywood film industry,

which had expanded rapidly in Europe in the wake of the First World War and had developed an especially close relationship with the US government in the latest one. As he described it, his company's globalized prewar circulation networks, combined with its history of cultivating a participatory film fan culture, offered a unique opportunity to "unobtrusively" promote popular enthusiasm for US films abroad in ways that would bolster Hollywood's efficacy as a tool of US economic and cultural power, a lesson the government had learned throughout the war as it coordinated with the studios. "On the premise that the [State] Department is interested in the widest possible dissemination of American motion pictures abroad, the early establishment of American 'fan' magazine readership abroad offers a quick, costless (to the taxpayer) and unobtrusive step to stimulate and sustain the interest of the foreign public," he explained. Continuing, Rheinstrom sermonized:

> Few, unconnected with the motion picture industry, realize the power and influence of a publication like our *Photoplay Magazine*, the oldest and leading magazine in its field. . . . We believe that *Photoplay* . . . carrying glamorous pictures and stories of American movie stars, would have an immediate and widespread acceptance in any language. The current applications to us from publishers in many parts of the world, for publishing rights, would seem to confirm this judgment. If *Photoplay* would be QUICKLY established in the leading countries, enough public opinion and taste to American motion pictures might be established to forestall hostile local legislation. Foreign competition might quickly find the field pre-empted.[66]

In this correspondence, the executive also mentioned that negotiations had been completed for foreign editions of *Photoplay* in Great Britain, Australia, and the Philippines, and that more such deals were underway.

Rheinstrom's appeals did not fall on deaf ears. Rockefeller passed Macfadden Publications' requests for airplane priority clearances and diplomatic contacts on to the Department of State. However, these initial requests appear to have never panned out, and the end of the war found the company still lobbying for help restarting its overseas operations.[67] In addition to the obvious challenges presented by war-related disruptions and scarcity, the company was facing more ideologically driven anxieties on the part of government officials related to which kinds of businesses, products, and consumers deserved additional support. True story and fan magazines were not likely to be seen as optimal ambassadors for American culture abroad, associated as they were with sensation, sex, the working class, women, youth, and the uneducated. Plus, the kinds of periodicals Macfadden Publications produced also fell outside of the areas of arts, education, and culture in which the United States was invested in projecting global leadership. The company would need to keep pressing.

In 1946, the Macfadden company announced the inauguration of the Macfadden Publications Foreign Sales Corporation, a wholly owned subsidiary with Rheinstrom as its president focused on "develop[ing] overseas editions and export trade."[68] In this position, Rheinstrom worked to establish international trade and distribution deals as well as to advocate for the political, cultural, and economic desirability of the foreign circulation of Macfadden's media and commercial mass culture more generally. For instance, after meeting in New York with representatives of Poland, Czechoslovakia, Italy, Greece, and Turkey in 1947, Rheinstrom told the press that foreign governments would be receptive to greater advertising of US products, which might boost morale in a period of "uneasy" political conditions.[69] Relatedly, the following year, he penned an "Open Letter" to George V. Allen, assistant secretary of state for public affairs (and future director of the US Information Agency), in the leading advertising trade magazine, *Printer's Ink*. Titled "Our Public Relations Abroad," the missive lamented that "most men heading up" US Information Offices abroad, which Rheinstrom had visited in his travels as head of the Macfadden Publications Foreign Sales Corporation, "don't even know the names of more than a fraction of the leading publications in their countries."[70] Government officials clearly considered this letter. When Rheinstrom finally embarked on a survey of publishing conditions in the Near and Far East in 1948, the State Department posted a circular to diplomatic and consular representatives in China, Japan, Singapore, India, and Thailand recommending that they provide any possible assistance to him.[71]

Significantly, on this trip, Rheinstrom was not just selling Macfadden Publications' periodicals. In 1948, the Macfadden Publications Foreign Sales Corporation signed a contract with the New York–based National Comics Publications, soon to become known as DC Comics, which designated Rheinstrom the official international licensor and distributor for its publications everywhere in the world besides Great Britain and Canada.[72] Most famous for its superheroes—especially Superman and Batman—DC faced the challenge of not only getting its products to international markets but also battling anti-comic campaigns, or even having to sell "the very idea of the comic book itself to countries that had little or no direct experience" with it.[73] As comics scholar Kevin Patrick has noted, the process of globalizing DC Comics came with a host of obstacles, as "a combination of economic, regulatory, and cultural factors meant that American-style comic books had to be modified in order to meet the unique conditions" of other countries.[74] Macfadden Publications had already been meeting these kinds of challenges before the war, and with Rheinstrom's leadership, its Foreign Sales Corporation offered a natural fit for the American comic publishing giant in the postwar period.

Macfadden Publications was ultimately quite successful in rebuilding and expanding on its prewar media in a relatively short amount of time during and after the Second World War, despite the relative lack of state support for its operations compared to that afforded *Reader's Digest*, published by DeWitt Wallace, and Henry Luce's *Time* and *Life* magazines. In 1943, Macfadden Publications had launched a Mexican version of *True Story* (*Confidencias*). In 1946, it established British and Australian editions of its confession and film magazines, fulfilling promises made before the war. Other foreign deals quickly followed. By the end of 1947, local editions of Macfadden Publications' American magazines had been established or reintroduced in Sweden (*Hela Världen*), France (*Confidences*, which also circulated in Belgium and in French colonies), Argentina (*Cuéntame*), Italy (*Storie Vere*), and the Netherlands (*Ware Verhalen*). In January 1948, a Japanese version of *True Story* (*Jitsuwa to shinsō*) appeared in occupied Japan.[75] In late 1948, thanks in part to lobbying by Macfadden Publications, it was announced that "American comic books, detective stories and true love novelettes will be made available to the Germans with funds guaranteed by the Economic Cooperation Act"; *Wahre Geschichten* resumed circulation soon after in Germany and Switzerland.[76] These international versions of *True Story*, which in many markets were joined by *Photoplay* and *True Romances*, came to constitute what the company dubbed its International True Story Group.

Building on Macfadden Publication's pre-WWII business model, the International True Story Group relied on local publishers who bought limited rights to Macfadden Publications' periodicals and content. These publishers then edited, translated, found advertisers for, printed, and distributed magazines targeted to specific national audiences. For instance, *Storie Vere* was presented to Italian readers by Editoriale Domus, a well-established local publishing house. The company advertised its new magazine as "Different from the Others," while using its pages to promote its own expanding catalog of Italian lifestyle and design magazines. Australia's versions of *Photoplay* and *True Story*, each promoted as "An Australian Production," were published by K. G. Murray and distributed by Gordon and Gotch, the same company that had imported prewar British editions of Macfadden's confession magazines into Australia. According to records kept by the Supreme Command of Allied Powers in occupied Japan, Macfadden Publications sold its content there to the Tokyo-based Romance Sha (The Romance Company), who then translated and repackaged it for Japanese audiences.

For those who knew English, including US occupiers, tens of thousands of copies of Macfadden Publications' American magazines (mostly *Photoplay* and *Sport*) were also shipped to Japan where they were then sold by the Maruzen Co., a longtime Japanese importer of Western products and media.[77]

Subsequently, Rheinstrom and the acting director of the OII arranged for State Department–produced "Americana" featurettes and statistical data about the United States to appear in some of Macfadden Publications' foreign film and confession magazines in Italy, Australia, Japan, and India.[78] Extant issues of the Italian *Storie Vere* from 1949 offer a glimpse of the content of these features and the context in which they appeared. Placed as back covers of *Storie Vere,* a prominent position but one that was also separate from the main content, were full-page, text-heavy informational ads that discuss elements of the European Recovery Program (better known as the Marshall Plan) in Italy. In simple language, these ads advocate industrial modernization, peaceful labor relations, and the removal of national trade and emigration barriers, making arguments such as "International economic cooperation is the revolution of the twentieth century."[79] The resource-strapped OII was pleased with Macfadden Publications' cooperation and assistance. "This is one of the ways—at almost no cost to us—that we can reach the masses who remain little touched by our present official program," the OII director excitedly informed George Allen in July 1949. "Excellent," Allen responded, "I . . . am delighted that our material pleased him [Rheinstrom]."[80] This episode of Macfadden Publications' cooperation with the OII hints that at least some members of the State Department, generally eager to counter negative stereotypes of American mass culture abroad, had come to recognize significant benefits to utilizing mass-market print media tailored specifically for non-elite and women audiences, especially as they faced major budget constraints. With its long history of reaching foreign audiences in the United States and overseas, and its very public embrace of consumer capitalism and anti-leftist politics, Macfadden Publications perhaps represented the best-positioned US periodical company to bring representations of the American Way of Life, and related romances of mass consumer citizenship, to the segments of foreign "masses" who remained "little touched" by the OII's other propaganda efforts.

On the other hand, however, the structure of Macfadden Publications' international publication and distribution arrangements show that the company's overseas media was easily unmoored from top-down messaging and inherently ungovernable. This can be seen in the examples of *Hela Världen* and the Australian *Photoplay* and *True Story*. In the case of the

Swedish *True Story,* the Stockholm-based publisher Åhlén & Åkerlund appears to have wanted nothing to do with the OII-produced featurettes that Macfadden Publications provided. According to Rheinstrom, the Swedish publisher simply rejected them as "too American."[81] (The same company rejected Rheinstrom's offer to license DC Comics).[82] While licensing its material to foreign publishers had been an important strategy in Macfadden Publications' expansion, this system meant that the company maintained little control over the actual foreign editions of the magazines it developed and licensed. A survey of the company's Australian editions between 1948 and 1950 further implies Macfadden Publications' limitations as a conduit of official messaging. Obviously, US Department of State informational featurettes were not identified as such, but comparing Macfadden's Australian editions with their US counterparts suggests that the statistical information and featurettes on American life that the OII arranged to send Macfadden Publications received minimal to zero airing in Australasia. Notably, however, the Australian version of *True Story* did amass more advertising revenue than any other periodical in the nation, attracting accounts of US brands and companies selling American exports, which was perhaps the exact kind of "subtle dissemination of American ideologies" that Rheinstrom had had in mind when he first approached the US government for help.

To summarize this postwar situation, Macfadden Publications sought government assistance when needed (for access to raw materials, consular contacts, and help with regulations and licensing); meanwhile the State Department sought to take advantage of the company's popular appeal and widespread distribution network, but in contrast to the cases of *Reader's Digest* and Henry Luce's media empire, this sporadic relationship of convenience never materialized into any kind of solid partnership. As the OII's successor the US Information Agency (USIA) conducted informational diplomacy campaigns in the wake of the Second World War, Macfadden Publications never represented the type of mass media that state officials considered most beneficial to national interests or security. No copies of *Photoplay, True Story, True Romances, True Detective Stories,* or *Sport* were placed in USIA overseas libraries, for instance. Furthermore, when the State Department worked with private organizations to arrange mailings of back issues of US periodicals abroad—a campaign that in many ways was similar to the networks through which Macfadden's magazines had traveled in the interwar era—film, pulp, and true story magazines were identified explicitly in official correspondence as undesirable for inclusion.[83] Basically, US officials overseeing propaganda and informational diplomacy during the early Cold War were wary of promoting Macfadden's publications because of their pulp-like nature, but were not averse to trying to place their own propaganda within them because of their demonstrated reach. At the same time, Macfadden Publications' very formulation for success in diverse international markets—the promotion of an ethos of transnational participatory pastiche administered by local brokers—spread the reach of the American media empire yet mitigated against any top-down control of the messages it circulated.

Macfadden Publications' international dealings as an exporter, licenser, and distributor of down-market popular print culture in the postwar era helped determine the future of the company and its media in the 1950s. Most directly, circulation statistics and profits coming from the Macfadden Publications Foreign Sales Corporation and the International True Story Group came to constitute a progressively significant source of revenue for the company, a phenomenon that was followed in the trade press. This is perhaps what inspired the businessman Irving S. Manheimer to make a move on the corporation. As discussed in Chapter 7, Manheimer was the founder of the Publisher's Surplus Corporation, which before the war had distributed back issues of Macfadden-brand magazines (and other periodicals) abroad. In 1950, with the profits from what was now called the Publishers Distributing Company, Manheimer began to quietly buy up shares of Macfadden Publications, using various names. Then, according to an employee's account, when "Orr J. Elder, the dignified president of Macfadden Publications, was sitting in his office one morning . . . his secretary told him a man named Irving S. Manheimer wanted to see him. Elder thought he had heard of Manheimer, but couldn't place him . . . 'Tell him,' Irving said with the full force of his five feet four inches, 'I've just bought his company.'"[84] Immediately following Manheimer's acquisition of majority control of the company, Elder retired, transitioning into a two-year consulting arrangement with the publishing house he had been with since the beginning of the century.

With Manheimer now at the helm of Macfadden Publications, the company was again reorganized. Many of the higher-salaried employees were let go, and editorial and production costs were cut wherever possible for its ten magazines. Rheinstrom left the corporation's foreign sales subsidiary in 1952, with National Comics Publications buying back his contract and naming Carroll Rheinstrom International Editions Inc. its exclusive international distributor. Rheinstrom would spend his subsequent career traversing the globe with his wife selling DC Comics to the world, getting fabulously wealthy in the process.[85] Offsetting this loss, Manheimer, who had been investing in comic books and comic book distribution since the late 1930s and who had cofounded the Association of Comics Magazine

Publishers in 1948, brought his own industry connections and contracts to the firm.[86]

In addition to its domestic magazines, foreign editions, and international licensing and distribution activities, the Macfadden book subsidiary Bartholomew House also contributed to the company's postwar evolution. In the mid-1940s, Bart House published some original books, most importantly movie novelizations and works by the science fiction writer H. P. Lovecraft. But from 1946 forward, it specialized in soft-cover reprints of hardback books and special edition one-off anthologies of magazine articles, usually priced at a mere twenty-five cents. Half its titles were mystery genre fiction, but it occasionally offered more literary works like *The Promise,* Pearl S. Buck's best-selling novel about Chinese soldiers in WWII Burma.[87]

In the mid-1950s, in part due to competition from other mass media forms, particularly television, there were contractions in the periodical industry, leading some to worry about the viability of the magazine as a cultural form. Such concerns were overblown, especially for larger companies with the resources to swallow competition.[88] The Macfadden firm was well positioned to benefit during this period, in which it became the distributor of the company Ziff-Davis's magazines, which included titles such as *Radio & TV News, Popular Electronics, Amazing Stories,* and *Modern Bride.* On the heels of this deal, it became the distributor for Rand McNally's children's books and Pyramid paperbacks as well. Under the leadership of Manheimer, who had begun his career disseminating Macfadden's magazines overseas, distributing other American companies' print media became central to Macfadden Publications' postwar business model.

The dawn of the 1960s brought yet another turning point, which would in some ways be a final one. In early 1961, the public learned that Manheimer was negotiating a merger in which the Macfadden corporation would be acquired by the Bartell Broadcasting Corporation, owner of a chain of radio and television broadcasting stations in the United States and the Caribbean. A newcomer to the publishing world, the Bartell company was seeking to develop a total "communications complex," integrating radio, television, and print, and foregrounding "the mass consumer."[89] As cofounder George Bartell, a former instructor of speech and communications at the University of Wisconsin who left to become a broadcasting industry entrepreneur, told the press, "When I first heard Macfadden was on the market . . . I rushed out and bought copies of all their magazines" to see that "they were aimed at the same people who listen to my radio stations— the wage earner and his wife, who packs the lunch pail." To publicize the merger, Bartell's ad space salesmen fanned out across Madison Avenue carrying lunch pails, "each packed with a profile of the Macfadden reader."[90]

The financial complexities of this merger would take months to finalize, but the reorganized Macfadden-Bartell company immediately took several steps. First, in addition to promoting Macfadden's stable of magazines, it bid aggressively to buy out competitors; soon, it had acquired Fawcett's *True Confessions* and *Motion Picture,* as well as a competitor to *True Detective.* Second, it acquired a soft-cover book line from the magazine and comic book publisher Hillman Periodicals. Under the name Macfadden Books, it expanded what had previously been Bart House's paperback publishing and distribution operations. Reflecting a tried-and-true Macfadden Publications formula, Macfadden Books published on a variety of themes that ranged from genre pulp fiction to writings by well-known politicians. In 1964, for example, the imprint republished Kay Martin's *The Whispered Sex,* a now-canonical work of lesbian pulp fiction, and the best-selling paperback edition of archconservative Arizona senator Barry Goldwater's *The Conscience of a Conservative.* Third, the company continued Macfadden Publications' market research operations, including what was now called the Macfadden-Bartell Wage Earner Forum. And fourthly, Macfadden-Bartell, already an early player in foreign television broadcasting with stations in the Caribbean, made a large investment in Teleglobe Pay-TV System Inc., which was developing a subscription television system that operated through broadcast and cable transmission.

With these activities, the new Macfadden-Bartell built upon and reconfigured elements of the publishing house started by Macfadden in 1899, creating a platform-crossing "communications complex" with transnational ambitions. Across various genres and platforms, its media proved adaptable to a range of normative and subcultural identities while bolstering formulations of *mass* consumer citizenship that seamed together, through participatory media and related promises of market inclusion and expansion, populist structures and sensibilities with corporate capitalist ones. In all these respects, Macfadden-Bartell adapted the central formula of Macfadden's publishing house, carrying its legacy forward into a sixth decade.

• • •

Ultimately, the Macfadden corporation outlived Macfadden the man, but not by very long.

For most of his career, Macfadden had told anyone who would listen that he expected to live until the age 125, thanks to physical culture. After his successful skydiving stunt over Paris in 1952 to celebrate his eighty-fourth birthday, it seemed that if any human was going to reach this benchmark it might be him. The next few years, however, would prove rough ones for his wellbeing. After his separation from Johnnie Lee, Macfadden moved into a small suite at a hotel in Jersey City, where he rarely had visitors. When Fulton Oursler's son came to see him one day, he found "a kind of prisoner in that hotel room, with few friends and little to do, alone there with his tangled, fuzzy memories of grandeur, when he was the head of a group of magazines worth more than $30,000,000."[91] To make matters worse, in 1953, Mary Macfadden, who was still living on the increasingly rundown Englewood estate, published a tell-all account about their marriage. Co-written with Emile Gauvreau, the one-time editor of Macfadden's *Evening Graphic* tabloid, *Dumbbells and Carrot Strips: The Story of Bernarr Macfadden* finally gave Mary the opportunity to share her experiences as a wife and mother and claim her contributions to the making of the Macfadden media empire. Hauntingly, she dedicated the book "To all the wise and patient physicians . . . particularly those merciful doctors ever ready to reduce the pains of childbirth." Though not everyone believed Mary's account, the book took a sledgehammer to the salubrious public image that the Father of American Physical Culture had spent his life constructing.

Then, in December 1954, Macfadden was arrested and thrown in jail. Unlike his previous run-ins with the law for opposing censorship, this time his offense was missing alimony and trust payments to his ex-wives Mary and Johnnie Lee. After the Macfadden Foundation bailed him out, he fled upstate for a while, crossing into Canada for a reprieve before returning to New Jersey. But then the whole episode repeated itself, with Macfadden landing back in jail, where he spent a lonely Christmas.[92] The courts had trouble believing the ex-publishing mogul was really broke; so did Mary and Johnnie Lee, who claimed he had buried a lot of his money to keep it safe. In any case, the stress of the situation exacted a mounting toll. The following autumn, Macfadden became ill with digestive troubles. As was his wont, he refused professional medical attention, instead prescribing himself a fast. When he began to lose consciousness, he was rushed to the Jersey City Medical Center, where doctors diagnosed him with a liver blockage and jaundice. Five days later, on October 12, 1955, the eighty-seven-year-old bodybuilder and ex-media mogul took his last breath in a hospital bed.

Bernarr Macfadden was buried in New York's Woodlawn Cemetery, his grave marked with a bust of his head and the inscription "Father of Physical Culture." In the flood of obituaries that followed, news outlets near and far commemorated his unusual life and many accomplishments. As the *South China Morning Post* in Hong Kong reminded its readers, Macfadden had "Achieved Fame by Muscles, Magazines, and Manly Daring," exerting what the *New York Times* called a "two-fold influence" by pioneering health and fitness ideas and transforming the mass-market periodical industry.[93] *Newsday* included a "Macfadden the Fabulous" photo montage, a feature the memorialized surely would have appreciated. There were also more critical portraits: "colorful, controversial, eccentric and charlatan were among the descriptions hurled" at Macfadden, *Variety* reported in its long goodbye to the publisher.[94] Fittingly, at least one acolyte who found his local paper's obituary inadequately laudatory wrote in to tell the editor so: "The fact is," this fan penned, "that . . . Bernarr Macfadden, a lad with a most unpromising constitutional, physical, environment[al], and economic endowment, was able to live to the age of 87 years a life of exceptional vigor; that he rejected . . . personal enrichment in order that he might make available to his fellow man the fruits of his experience." Following the death of the man it had once teased as "Body Love," *Time* had to admit, "His legacy is with us even now."[95]

Time's statement would remain true for many years. Most visibly, this could be seen in the national and international popularity of bodybuilding and physique competitions, the global proliferation of fitness periodicals, and the many waves of healthy living and alternative medicine movements that kept the publisher's *Encyclopedia of Physical Culture* and other works in circulation not just in the United States, but around the world.[96] The media forms and genres Macfadden helped pioneer would also remain widely popular, especially true story and true crime magazines, fan magazines, and sensational tabloids willing to take great liberties doctoring photos. Less visibly, Macfadden and the media products and networks his publishing company created would also continue to operate subculturally to foster queer communities formed around practices of bodybuilding, confession and pulp fiction reading and writing, and media fandom.[97]

Ten years after Macfadden's death, the Macfadden publishing company also passed on, albeit in a more metaphorical sense. This event, when it happened, made few waves and was barely noticed in either the corporate world or the popular press. In May 1965, at the Bartell-Macfadden Corporation's annual shareholders' meeting in Milwaukee, executive George Bartell recommended that the "Macfadden" be dropped from the company's name. In business-speak, Bartell explained this change as "more accurately reflecting the expanding scope and operational direction" of the corporation.[98] And that was it. Going forward the company would be known only as the Bartell Media Corporation. There were never any eulogies or obituaries for Macfadden Publications.

Epilogue: Pulp Empire Today

IN THE WINTER OF 2000, construction workers in Manhattan began dismantling a six-story building that had been standing for almost a century on the northeast corner of Broadway and 64th Street. The elegant structure, featuring broad bay windows and white terracotta trim, was erected in 1907 by Richard Goulet, heir to one of Gilded Age New York's wealthiest families, as an automotive showroom. After the First World War, the Goulet Garage became a 154,000-square-foot office building, a perfect fit for a rapidly growing publishing company looking for more space—Macfadden Publications Inc. For the next decade, 1926 Broadway served as the bustling headquarters of the expanding Macfadden publishing empire. Situated in an economically, ethnically, and racially diverse neighborhood heavily dominated by immigrants, workers, and small businesses, the Macfadden Building, as it was then known, rose above streets whose denizens were likely purchasers of its occupant's own colorful periodicals.

Following the Second World War, the area around this building underwent a transformation. Surrounding tenements were demolished and residents displaced to make way for "urban renewal" projects. In the 1960s, on land seized through eminent domain, the performing arts hub Lincoln Center took shape. One by one, the neighborhood's other "Class B" buildings—New York's designation for "workhorse" commercial real estate lacking the size, amenities, and central location of the city's flashier corporate towers—were replaced by high-rises, theaters, chain stores, and upmarket eateries. It appeared the writing was on the wall for the former Macfadden Building, which had come to house an eclectic mix of small businesses, when a large corporation, World Gym, took over the entire second floor in the early 1990s, positioning rows of Stairmasters and Life-cycles in the windows.[1] Predictably, a few years later, 1926 Broadway was slated for redevelopment.

Hearing this news, a group of Upper West Siders tried to save the building, one of the last "Class B" structures still standing around Lincoln Center, and the only remaining low-rise that did not eclipse the view of the sky. Their preservation campaign emphasized the structure's pleasing architectural ele-ments, its links to the city's early automotive culture, and its identity as a "people building" on a block now dominated by large-scale commercial ten-ants and expensive apartments.[2] But the Landmarks Preservation Committee remained unmoved and the redevelopment proceeded as planned. The bay windows were replaced, the decorative cornices and medallions were drilled away, and a twenty-nine-story apartment tower emerged. Old tenants left and new commercial and residential occupants moved in. Currently, the ground floor of 1926 Broadway houses a chain home goods store, a retailer of women's athletic apparel, and a luxury real estate agency.[3] Where once a giant sign on the roof proclaimed Macfadden Publications' "Largest News Stand Sale in the World," no remaining trace proclaims the significance of the media company that operated from this building during its heyday. Per-haps this is fitting, though; for if there was one constant with Macfadden and the business he founded, it was their voracious pursuit of expansion through continuous processes of growth, adaptation, and remaking. In this respect—as well as in the continuing presence of fitness-related commerce in the building and in the nearby newsstands selling magazines to passersby—the history and legacies of Macfadden's pulp empire endure amid twenty-first century redevelopment.

Notably, however, the history and legacies of other forms of culture and media are much easier to see from this vantage point. The shiny, nondescript facade of 1926 Broadway now reflects attention back across the street to Lincoln Center and the impressive suite of cultural and entertainment offerings there. These offerings include the Metropolitan Opera, the New York City Ballet, and the New York Philharmonic Orchestra, bastions of high culture similar to those found in many other world cities. Yet Lincoln Center is also, famously, home to world-renowned venues for jazz and film, forms of glob-ally popular entertainment developed by and for working-class Americans, including those who lived in this neighborhood before urban renewal. Unlike any of Macfadden's cultural contributions, film and jazz obtained the status of Culture—with a capital "C"—during the Cold War. Since then, they have received extensive analysis and commemoration. Jazz concerts and film retrospectives hosted at Lincoln Center testify to the starring role played by popular culture and mass media forms developed by and for non-elites in shaping domestic American history and the expansive role of the United States on the world stage before and beyond the Second World War.[4] American jazz and film are often depicted, to put it simply, as symbols of a dynamic, democratic nation whose outsized influence on globalized popular culture took root in the first half of the twentieth century.

In addition to being preserved in nationally and internationally significant institutional spaces, such as Lincoln Center, music and film—particularly jazz and Hollywood movies—have come to occupy prime real estate in the landscape of US historiography. Here, they feature especially prominently in discussions about the politics of mass culture and the phenomenon of Americanization, a framework that has been used to analyze both the construction and enforcement of certain norms of national identity and behavior at home and extensions of US influence abroad through military, economic, political, and cultural means.[5] Despite their imbrication in similar processes, neither the mass-market periodical publishing industry, nor its products and their purveyors, have been engaged by scholars as thoroughly along these intersecting dimensions. This is particularly true in regard to transnational print cultural networks that predated the Cold War era and for magazines that catered to women, immigrants, and the working class. Yet centering these arenas offers valuable historical insights. Through the case study of the Physical Culture Publishing Company/Macfadden Publications, this book has explored the ways mass-market print media—especially participatory magazine genres in transnational circulation—shaped formations of American culture, identity, and influence during pivotal decades of US ascendency that were also, importantly, globalizing decades of fitness, reform, empire, travel, migration, economic integration, consumerism, corporatization, war, and media industry transformation. In doing so, it has constructed a new history of the Macfadden pulp empire, whose story can help us better understand US mass media expansion; the complexity of processes conceptualized as "globalization" and "Americanization"; and the dynamic relationships between culture, media, and power.

To recap, first, examining an Ozark orphan's coming of age in the physical culture world of the American Midwest showed how yearnings for regenerative impulses, cross-cultural encounters, and developments in print, entertainment, and exhibition cultures combined in the late nineteenth century to set the stage for body-centric mass media and related consumer markets and practices to emerge. This milieu produced a muscular showman and health fanatic eager to evangelize his ideas far and wide through performances, photographs, and the printed word; and this man became Bernarr Macfadden, the purportedly self-made man who presented himself to America and the world as a model for universal emulation.

Next, tracking the rise of the Physical Culture Publishing Company illustrated the central role played by Anglo-American Atlantic crossings, British colonial and neocolonial networks, and widening spheres of US military and market power to the development of Macfadden's publishing empire and to the connections forged at this time between mass media and imperialism more broadly. Furthermore, close examinations of *Physical Culture* evidenced how body-centric popular print circulations achieved widespread salience by mediating formations of race and nation, gender and sexuality, and modernity and consumer capitalism within iterative and interactive cultural formats that were perceived as responsive and accessible to diverse audiences.

This led, we saw, to media that produced a proliferation of messages and meanings. On one hand, the Physical Culture Publishing Company's media bolstered Anglo-Saxon solidarity, male authority, and heterosexual normativity, thereby strengthening gendered ideologies of white supremacy that provided ideological scaffolding for overseas and settler colonial warfare, Jim Crow, the eugenics movement, and other hegemonic and imperial projects. But on the other hand, audience participation and aesthetics of pastiche infused its publications with qualities of polysemy and multivocality. These qualities were amplified by the geographic and identic mobility of individuals, including Macfadden, and of the human body itself, which was presented as a locus for growth and transformation. Significantly, many other forms of domestically and globally popular American mass culture, including Macfadden's subsequent products, would share sensibilities developed in physical culture media in the early twentieth century.

Next, this book situated the debut of *True Story* magazine and the rise of Macfadden Publications within broader economic, social, and demographic transformations in the 1920s, as the United States and the world were being reconstructed after the First World War. The engine of American ascendency during this period was the nation's booming economy, which was powered by the toils of a heavily immigrant industrial workforce (and, less visibly, the racialized and gendered agricultural and reproductive labor that sustained it). Macfadden Publications distinguished itself in this context by catering to non-elites previously marginalized by a periodical industry built for wealthy and middlebrow consumers. It did this with accessible, participatory, cross-platform, intertextual, and sensational publications that were "pulp at heart." The confessional format in which the company specialized, and the related editorial methods it developed, centered readers and writers new to magazine consumption, thereby helping to extend the boundaries of who and what was understood as marketable. This helped Macfadden and his company position themselves from the late 1920s onward as interlocutors between "the people" and entities such as advertisers and politicians. Through popular media and sophisticated public relations campaigns, they crafted romances of individual empowerment, consumer citizenship, and perpetual growth.

In the 1930s, Macfadden Publications took a hard rightward political shift, a position expressed through the anti–New Deal politicking of its president and the ideological content of some of its media. This increasingly placed the corporation directly at odds with leftist popular movements fueled by many of the demographics that constituted its primary readership. Predictably, it also put the publishing house and its founder in the crosshairs of ascendant Marxist-influenced intellectuals and commentators, who saw the Macfadden media empire as the embodiment of fascist tendencies running through commercialized American mass culture that linked the United States to broadening global structures of imperialism and authoritarianism. That this critique tended to be expressed through misogynistic and homophobic formulations that trivialized and villainized already disempowered social groups foreclosed some of its radical potential, however, a dynamic that would persist far into the future. Meanwhile, the company forged new allyships within US corporate culture, working from this position toward harmonizing populist and corporate capitalist ideologies through its media and public relations.

As in its previous iteration as the Physical Culture Publishing Company, Macfadden Publications actively pursued international expansion, distributing its wares abroad and licensing foreign editions. How, where, and why these circulated is complicated to reconstruct, but doing so shows no one-way "vigorous permeation" of US exports, as one commentor at the time claimed. Macfadden Publications' media, created in conversation with a diverse (and frequently immigrant) working class at home, foregrounded visual aesthetics and textual themes that resonated in many social, geographic, and political contexts. The centering of health, fitness, and beautiful bodies, especially youthful and white-appearing ones; the foregrounding of urban and frontier settings, later to be replaced by suburban ones; a persistant thematic focus on individual mobility and self-transformation; the spotlighting of celebrities and celebrity-politicians and their intimate lives; the frequent use of collage and montage formats; and the systematic inclusion of participatory and interactive features—all these qualities propelled the international mobility of Macfadden Publications' products. The superlative international translatability of media already adapted to a diverse domestic audience at home combined with broader structural elements related to empire and hegemony—for example, the transnational salience of building up white-ness, the global presence of Hollywood, post-WWII US occupations—to expand, along with the efforts of myriad individual transnational cultural brokers, the international dimensions of the "Largest News Stand Sale in the World."

With foreign sales contributing, Macfadden Publications' upwardly climbing circulation statistics allowed for Macfadden and his associates to achieve greater influence in politics and public affairs. They also helped the company substantiate its portrayals of a vast domestic Macfadden Market that offered a stand-in for a broader world of mass consumers that the company's products and operations were supposedly optimized to un-derstand and reach. This message was articulated explicitly at the 1939 World's Fair, where the Macfadden Exhibit contributed to a broader cam-paign aimed at countering consumer rights, pro-labor laws, anti-capitalist movements, and government programs that were overwhelmingly popular among non-elites yet threatened the business establishment and its theori-zation of America's, and therefore the world's, ideal political economy. The circular discourse that Macfadden Publications constructed in its public messaging could be interrupted when "the people" it claimed to represent made visible its contradictions or exaggerations. However, with the company exerting greater centralized editorial control, such interrup-tions happened mainly outside the realm of mass mediation.

Looking back at the broad sweep of Macfadden Publications' history, it might seem ironic that Macfadden and the publishing empire he built came to a crisis in 1941, the very year rival publisher Luce predicted the dawn of an American Century built atop decades of less formalized US economic and cultural influence. What happened to the company over the following two decades, however, is instructive for understanding the op-erations of a strain of twentieth-century American transnational cultural influence that is less flashy and more fundamentally unstable than that signified by, for instance, Cold War alliances between the US government and middlebrow magazine powerhouses like Luce's own Time-Life com-pany. In other words, it provides insight into a type of power historically associated with the United States, but not coterminous with it, that is ma-terially and functionally pulp in nature, in that it transits through ephem-eral forms of mass-mediated popular culture and possesses concurrent tendencies toward proliferating, disintegrating, and reconfiguring pro-cesses of Americanization at home and abroad as well as asymmetric rela-tionships of power more broadly.

As evidenced through the company's inability, despite persistent efforts, to form a solid partnership with the Department of State, the Macfadden publishing empire proved a poor fit with the formal apparatuses of US informational diplomacy in the postwar era. Even with the eccentric Macfadden out of the picture, the firm did not embody the image the United States sought to project of itself as a superpower, notwithstanding its literal global representation of none other than Superman. The state saw other popular cultural forms as more optimal vehicles for smoothing military-backed and nonmilitarized extensions of US hegemony during the Cold War. And therefore, it would be these media, including film and jazz, rather than mass-market magazines like Macfadden's, that would come to symbolize in public memory and scholarship the complex roles played by popular culture in shaping the predicted American Century.

Ending this book with a return to the now-unrecognizable headquarters of Macfadden Publications during its heyday provides an opportunity to remember a once-iconic publishing house that has been largely forgotten today despite its contributions to mass media and popular culture during pivotal decades of US ascendency and globalization in the twentieth century. At the same time, considering the ultimate trajectory of the Macfadden publishing empire over the *longue durée* also provides a useful perspective on what its history might suggest about the dawn of the Consumer Century, which can be seen as having replaced the American Century in a new age of national and global transformations.[6] The Macfadden publishing empire that rose in the early twentieth century did not take off in the post-WWII years, but it did not "fall" either. Instead of conforming to a "rise and fall" narrative, the company and its publications proliferated, disintegrated, and got remade into new things, following a pattern typical of paper media and pulp cultural forms—a trajectory also typical, historically speaking, of empires.

Constructed out of cheap materials and built on the principles of sensationalism, popularity, interactivity, transformability, and expandability, Macfadden Publications' physical publications and licensed content flowed easily into—or often, back into—many international markets. This was often helped along by structural factors related to expanding US military, economic, and political power, but in this process, the company's media often became less American, as the types of publications and content in which it specialized in exporting were conducive to being extensively localized, which ended up obviating the need for imports and licensing; tellingly, by the time Macfadden Publications was bought by the Bartell group in the early 1960s, the exporting subsidiary appears to have been broken up completely. Put more simply, in the post-WWII period, Macfadden's true story, film, detective, and sport magazines were subsumed into a globalized commercial milieu from whence they came. Meanwhile, the Macfadden corporation did such a good job creating intertextual and cross-platform media and consolidating a suitably homogenous mass market for national advertisers that it became an attractive acquisition for well-capitalized broadcast corporation that envisioned it as one pillar of an overarching "communications complex." Less than four years later, the distinct identity of Macfadden Publications disappeared, leaving media forms it had pioneered to circulate on as both part of a mainstream commercial "complex" and as available to be appropriated and adapted within subcultural networks that would later themselves become markets.

Ultimately, therefore, the true story of Macfadden's pulp empire of muscles and magazines offers a window onto another story historians have only begun to trace. This story is about how early twentieth-century processes of US media globalization and the making and remaking of interactive mass media circulations, platforms, and markets foreshadowed the transformation of the American Century into a Consumer Century and shaped the cultural politics of the participatory and globalized media landscape we live with today.

Abbreviations

Publishers

PCPC   Physical Culture Publishing Company
MP   Macfadden Publications
USGPO   US Government Printing Office

Periodicals

PC   *Physical Culture*
PD   *Physical Development*
TS   *True Story*
TDM   *True Detective Mysteries*
WG   *Wahre Geschichten*
WPC   *Withrow's Physical Culture*
HPC   *Health and Physical Culture*
WER   *Wahre Erzählungen und Romane*

Newspapers

NYT   *New York Times*
WSJ   *Wall Street Journal*
CDT   *Chicago Daily Tribune*
CT   *Chicago Tribune*
SMH   *Sydney Morning Herald*
WP   *Washington Post*
DFP   *Detroit Free Press*

Archives

NAA   National Archives of Australia, Canberra, AU
NARA National Archives and Records Administration, College Park, MD, USA
LOC   Library of Congress, Washington, DC, USA

Notes

Introduction

1. See Reuters-Gaumont British Newsreel, "McFadden's Parachute Jump," 1952, https://www.britishpathe.com/video/VLVA62RRD5VJI994ED5WEAHF7NC8Z -MCFADDENS-PARACHUTE-JUMP.
2. "Bravo Macfadden," *Newsweek*, September 8, 1952, 46.
3. "Health Cultist B. Macfadden Dies of Stroke," *Long Beach Independent*, Oct. 13, 1955, 1.
4. See Theodore Adorno and Max Horkheimer, "The Culture Industry: Enlightenment as Mass Deception," in Adorno and Horkheimer, *Dialectic of Enlightenment*, trans. John Cumming (New York: Continuum, 1989 [1944]).
5. Ann Fabian, "Making a Commodity of Truth: Speculations on the Career of Bernarr Macfadden," *American Literary History* 5.1 (1993): 51.
6. See William H. Taft, "Bernarr Macfadden: One of a Kind," *Journalism Quarterly* 45.4 (1968): 627–633. Other early studies include Clifford Waugh, "Bernarr Macfadden: The Muscular Prophet" (PhD diss., SUNY-Buffalo, 1973); Alexander Markovich, "The Publishing Empire of Bernarr Macfadden" (MA thesis, Univ. of Missouri, 1958).
7. Ben Yagoda, "The True Story of Bernard Macfadden: Lives and Loves of the Father of the Confession Magazine," *American Heritage*, December 1981, 22–29; Robert Ernst, *Weakness Is a Crime: The Life of Bernarr Macfadden* (Syracuse, NY: Syracuse Univ. Press, 1991); William R. Hunt, *Body Love: The Amazing Career of Bernarr Macfadden* (Bowling Green, OH: Bowling Green State Univ. Popular Press, 1991).

8. Harvey Green, *Fit for America: Health, Fitness, and Sport in American Society* (New York: Pantheon, 1986), 249; Jan Todd, "Bernarr Macfadden: Reformer of the Feminine Form," *Journal of Sport History* 14.1 (Spring 1987): 61–75.

9. See Roland Marchand, *Advertising the American Dream: Making Way for Modernity, 1920–1940* (Berkeley: Univ. of California Press, 1886); Michael Denning, *The Cultural Front: The Laboring of American Culture in the Twentieth Century* (New York: Verso, 1998); Jacqueline A. Hatton, "True Stories: Working Class Mythology, American Confessional Culture, and True Story Magazine, 1919–1929" (PhD diss., Cornell Univ., 1997); Regina Kunzel, *Fallen Women, Problem Girls: Unmarried Mothers and the Professionalization of Social Work, 1890–1945* (Princeton, NJ: Princeton Univ. Press, 1995); David K. Johnson, *Buying Gay: How Physique Entrepreneurs Sparked a Movement* (New York: Columbia Univ. Press, 2019).

10. Fabian, "Making a Commodity of Truth," 67. Also see Fabian, *The Unvarnished Truth: Personal Narratives in Nineteenth-Century America* (Berkeley: Univ. of California Press, 2000). Another important work that engages the confessional aspects of Macfadden's publications is Dave Tell, *Confessional Crises and Cultural Politics in Twentieth-Century America* (State College, PA: Penn State Univ. Press, 2012).

11. Mark Adams, *Mr. America: How Muscular Millionaire Bernarr Macfadden Transformed the Nation Through Sex, Salad, and the Ultimate Starvation Diet* (New York: HarperCollins, 2009).

12. Alva Johnson, "The Great Macfadden," *Saturday Evening Post*, June 21, 1941, 9.

13. See Thomas Bender, *A Nation Among Nations: America's Place in World History* (New York: Hill and Wang, 2006); Emily S. Rosenberg, ed., *A World Connecting, 1870–1945* (Cambridge, MA: Harvard Univ. Press, 2012); Ian R. Tyrell, *Transnational Nation: United States History in Global Perspective Since 1789* (New York: Palgrave, 2007).

14. See Rachel Lee Rubin and Jeffrey Melnick, eds., *Immigrants and American Popular Culture: An Introduction* (New York: NYU Press, 2006); Susan L. Mizruchi, *The Rise of Multicultural America: Economy and Print Culture, 1865–1915* (Chapel Hill: UNC Press, 2008); John Bodnar, *The Transplanted: A History of Immigrants in Urban America* (Bloomington: Indiana Univ. Press, 1985); Donna Gabaccia, *Foreign Relations: American Immigration in Global Perspective* (Princeton, NJ: Princeton Univ. Press, 2015).

15. See Amy Kaplan, *The Anarchy of Empire in the Making of U.S. Culture* (Cambridge, MA: Harvard Univ. Press, 2005); Kristin L. Hoganson, *Consumer's Imperium: The Global Production of American Domesticity, 1865–1920* (Chapel Hill: UNC Press, 2007); Mary A. Renda, *Taking Haiti: Military Occupation and the Culture of U.S. Imperialism* (Chapel Hill: UNC Press, 2001); Emily S. Rosenberg, *Spreading the American Dream: American Economic and Cultural Expansion, 1890–1945* (New York: Hill and Wang, 1982); Camilla Fojas, *Islands of Empire: Pop Culture and U.S. Power* (Austin: Univ. of Texas Press, 2014); Shelly Streeby, *American Sensations: Class, Empire, and the Production of Popular Culture* (Berkeley: Univ. of California Press, 2002); Tanner

Mirrlees, *Hearts and Mines: The US Empire's Culture Industry* (Vancouver: UBC Press, 2016); Victoria de Grazia, *Irresistible Empire: America's Advance through Twentieth-Century Europe* (Cambridge, MA: Harvard Univ. Press, 2006); Robert M. Pike, *Communication and Empire: Media, Markets, and Globalization, 1860–1930* (Durham, NC: Duke Univ. Press, 2007).

16. See Penny Von Eschen, *Satchmo Blows Up the World: Jazz Ambassadors Play the Cold War* (Cambridge, MA: Harvard Univ. Press, 2006); Jayna Brown, *Babylon Girls: Black Women Performers and the Shaping of the Modern* (Durham, NC: Duke Univ. Press, 2008); Alys Eve Weinbaum et al., *The Modern Girl Around the World: Consumption, Modernity, and Globalization* (Durham, NC: Duke Univ. Press, 2008); de Grazia, *Irresistible Empire.*

17. See Robert W. Rydell and Rob Kroes, *Buffalo Bill in Bologna: The American-ization of the World, 1869–1922* (Chicago: Univ. of Chicago Press, 2005); de Grazia, *Irresistible Empire*; Weinbaum et al., *The Modern Girl Around the World*; Uta G. Poigner, *Jazz, Rock, and Rebels: Cold War Politics and Amer-ican Culture in a Divided Germany* (Berkeley: Univ. of California Press, 2000); Julio Moreno, *Yankee, Don't Go Home: Mexican Nationalism, American Business Culture, and the Shaping of Modern Mexico, 1920–1950* (Chapel Hill: UNC Press, 2003).

18. See Cedric J. Robinson, *Black Marxism: The Making of the Black Radical Tradition*, 3rd ed. (Chapel Hill, UNC Press, 2021 [1983]) on racial capitalism. On consumer and corporate capitalism, see William R. Leach, *Land of Desire: Merchants, Power, and the Rise of a New American Culture* (New York: Vin-tage Books, 1993); Charles Perrow, *Organizing America: Wealth, Power, and the Origins of Corporate Capitalism* (Princeton, NJ: Princeton Univ. Press, 2002); Sven Beckert and Christine Desan, eds., *American Capitalism: New Histories* (New York: Columbia Univ. Press, 2018); Johnathan Levy, *Ages of American Capitalism: A History of the United States* (New York: Random House, 2021); Sven Beckert, *Empire of Cotton: A Global History* (New York: Vintage, 2015).

19. Oxford Dictionaries Online, s.v. "pulp."

20. See Benedict Anderson, *Imagined Communities: Reflections on the Origins and Spread of Nationalism* (New York: Verso, 1983); Michael Warner, *Pub-lics and Counterpublics* (New York: Zone Books, 2005); Mizruchi, *Rise of Multicultural America.*

21. See Pierre Bourdieu, *Distinction: A Social Critique of Taste,* trans. R. Nice (Cambridge, MA: Harvard Univ. Press, 1984); Lawrence W. Levine, *High-brow/Lowbrow: The Emergence of Culture Hierarchy in America* (Cam-bridge, MA: Harvard Univ. Press, 1990).

22. See Michael Denning, *Mechanic Accents: Dime Novels and Working-Class Culture in America* (New York: Verso, 1998); Erin A. Smith, *Hard Boiled: Working-Class Readers and Pulp Magazines* (Philadelphia: Temple Univ. Press, 2000); Nan Estad, *Ladies of Labor, Girls of Adventure: Working Women, Popular Culture, and Labor Politics at the Turn of the Century* (New York: Columbia Univ. Press, 1999); Jeremy Agnew, *The Age of Dimes and Pulps: The History of Sensationalist Literature, 1830–1960* (Jefferson, NC:

McFarland, 2018); David Hajdu, *The Ten Cent Plague: The Great Comic Books Scare and How It Changed America* (New York: Farrar, Straus and Giroux, 2008).

1. Decades of Fitness in the Dynamic Midwest

1. Clement Wood, *Bernarr Macfadden: A Study in Success* (New York: Lewis Copeland, 1929), 44.
2. Wood, *Bernarr Macfadden*, 54.
3. Jonathan Nashel, *Edward Landsdale's Cold War* (Amherst: Univ. of Massachusetts Press, 2005), 11.
4. See Kristin L. Hoganson, *The Heartland: An American History* (New York: Penguin Press, 2019).
5. Jackson Lears, *Rebirth of a Nation: The Making of Modern America, 1877–1920* (New York: Harper, 2010), 1.
6. Ronald L. Numbers, *Prophetess of Health: A Study of Ellen G. White* (New York: Harper & Row, 1976).
7. See Harold B. Segel, *Body Ascendant: Modernism and the Physical Imperative* (Baltimore, MD: Johns Hopkins Univ. Press, 1998); Mary Lynn Stewart, *For Health and Beauty: Physical Culture for French Women, 1880s–1930s* (Baltimore, MD: Johns Hopkins Univ. Press, 2001); Roland Naul and Ken Hardman, eds., *Sport and Physical Education in Germany* (London: Routledge, 2002); Wilson Chako Jacob, *Working-Out Egypt: Effendi Masculinity and Subject Formation in Colonial Modernity, 1870–1940* (Durham, NC: Duke Univ. Press, 2011).
8. Mark Jackson, ed., *The Oxford Handbook of the History of Medicine* (Oxford: Oxford Univ. Press, 2011).
9. Paul Starr, *The Social Transformation of American Medicine: The Rise of a Sovereign Profession and the Making of a Vast Industry* (New York: Basic Books, 2017); John S. Haller, *American Medicine in Transition, 1840–1910* (Urbana-Champaign: Univ. of Illinois Press, 1981).
10. Wood, *Bernarr Macfadden*, 44.
11. See Sheldon J. Watts, *Disease and Medicine in World History* (New York: Routledge, 2003).
12. Anita Clair Fellman and Michael Fellman, *Making Sense of Self: Medical Advice Literature in Nineteenth Century America* (Philadelphia: Univ. of Pennsylvania Press, 1981), 5.
13. See Harvey Green, *Fit for America: Health, Fitness, Sport, and American Society* (Baltimore, MD: Johns Hopkins Univ. Press, 1986); James B. Salazar, *Bodies of Reform: The Rhetoric of Character in Gilded Age America* (New York: NYU Press, 2010); Ruth C. Engs, *Clean Living Movements: American Cycles of Health Reform* (Westport, CT: Praeger, 2001).
14. Herbert Edgar Douglass, *Dramatic Prophecies of Ellen White: Stories of World Events Divinely Foretold* (Nampa, ID: Pacific Press, 2007), 61. Also see Numbers, *Prophetess of Health*; Malcolm Bull and Keith Lockhart, *Seeking a*

Sanctuary: Seventh-day Adventism and the American Dream (New York: Harper & Row, 1989).

15. See Lears, *Rebirth of a Nation*; David G. Schuster, *Neurasthenic Nation: America's Search for Health, Happiness, and Comfort, 1869–1920* (New Brunswick, NJ: Rutgers Univ. Press, 2011).

16. See Leo Marx, *The Machine in the Garden: Technology and the Pastoral Ideal in America* (Oxford Univ. Press, 1964); Stephen J. Mexal, *The Conservative Aesthetic: Theodore Roosevelt, Popular Darwinism, and the American Literary West* (Lanham, MD: Lexington Books, 2021).

17. See Katherine Bjork, *Prairie Imperialists: The Indian Country Origins of American Empire* (Philadelphia: Univ. of Pennsylvania Press, 2018).

18. See Richard Slotkin, *Regeneration Through Violence: The Mythology of the American Frontier* (Norman, OK: Univ. of Oklahoma Press, 1975); John Higham, *Strangers in the Land: Patterns of American Nativism, 1860–1925* (New Brunswick, NJ: Rutgers Univ. Press, 2002); Henry Louis Gates Jr., *Stony the Road: Reconstruction, White Supremacy, and the Rise of Jim Crow* (New York: Penguin Press, 2020).

19. See Lears, *Rebirth of a Nation*.

20. Wood, *Bernarr Macfadden*, 45, 47–48.

21. "120 Years of Literacy," National Center for Education Statistics, http://nces .ed.gov/naal/lit_history.asp.

22. Paul Starr, *The Creation of the Media: Political Origins of Modern Communications* (New York: Basic Books, 2004); Cathy N. Davidson, ed., *Reading in America: Literature and Social History* (Baltimore, MD: Johns Hopkins, 1989); Richard H. Brodhead, *Cultures of Letters: Scenes of Reading and Writing in Nineteenth-Century America* (Chicago: Univ. of Chicago Press, 1993).

23. Bernarr Macfadden, "My Life Story," *PC*, April 1914.

24. Thomas Kent, *Interpretation and Genre: The Role of Generic Perception in the Study of Texts* (Lewisburg, PA: Bucknell Univ. Press, 1987), 82.

25. See J. Randolph Cox, *The Dime Novel Companion: A Source Book* (Westport, CT: Greenwood, 2000); Shelley Streebey, "Dime Novels and the Rise of Mass-Market Genres," in *The Cambridge History of the American Novel*, ed. Leonard Cassuto et al. (Cambridge: Cambridge Univ. Press, 2011), 586–599. Michael Denning, *Mechanic Accents: Dime Novels and Working-class Culture in America*, 2nd ed. (New York: Verso, 1998).

26. J. A. Mangan and James Walvin, *Manliness and Morality: Middle-class Masculinity in Britain and America* (Manchester: Manchester Univ. Press, 1987), 4. See also Ryan K. Anderson, *Frank Merriwell and the Fiction of All-American Boyhood: The Progressive Era Creation of the Schoolboy Sports Story* (Fayetteville: Univ. of Arkansas Press, 2015).

27. William Graham Sumner, "What Our Boys are Reading," *Century Magazine*, March 1878, 681–684.

28. Anthony Comstock, *Traps for the Young* (New York: Funk and Wagnalls, 1883), chap. 3.

29. See Quentin Reynolds, *The Fiction Factory: From Pulp Row to Quality Street* (New York: Random House, 1955).

30. "Literary Notices," *Godey's Lady's Book*, February 1871, 193, quoted in Green, *Fit for America*, 183.

31. William Blaikie, *How to Get Strong and Stay So* (New York: Harper and Bros., 1879), 97. Also see Doug Bryant, "William Blaikie and Physical Fitness in Late Nineteenth Century America," *Iron Game History* 2.3 (1992): 3–6.

32. Amandus Johnson, *Swedish Contributions to American National Life, 1638–1921* (New York: Committee of the Swedish Section of America's Making Inc., 1921), 35–36.

33. Joseph Alter, "Indian Clubs and Colonialism: Hindu Masculinity and Muscular Christianity," *Comparative Studies in Society and History* 46.3 (2004): 497–534.

34. See Alter, "Indian Clubs"; Green, *Fit for America*, 183–193.

35. Elliot J. Gorn, *The Manly Art: Bare-Knuckle Prize Fighting in America* (Ithaca, NY: Cornell Univ. Press, 1986), 180. Also see Guy Reel, *The National Police Gazette and the Making of the American Man* (New York: Palgrave Macmillan, 2006); John Rickards Betts, "Sporting Journalism in Nineteenth-Century America," *American Quarterly* 5.1 (Spring 1953): 39–56.

36. See Janet M. Davis, *The Circus Age: Culture and Society Under the America Big Top* (Chapel Hill: UNC Press, 2002); Adria L. Imada, *Aloha America: Hula Circuits through U.S. Empire* (Durham, NC: Duke Univ. Press, 2012); Emily S. Rosenberg, *Transnational Currents in a Shrinking World, 1870–1945* (Cambridge, MA: Harvard Univ. Press, 2014).

37. John Springhall, *The Genesis of Mass Culture: The Show Business Live in America, 1840–1940* (New York: Palgrave Macmillan, 2008).

38. Wood, *Bernarr Macfadden*, 46.

39. Louis Warren, *Buffalo Bill's America: William Cody and the Wild West Show* (New York: Vintage, 2005).

40. A. B. Stewart, "My Diary or Route Book of P.T. Barnum's Greatest Show on Earth and the Great London Circus for the Season of 1883," http://www.circushistory.org/History/PTB1883.htm.

41. See Bluford Adams, *E Pluribus Barnum: The Great Showman and the Making of U.S. Popular Culture* (Minneapolis: Univ. of Minnesota Press, 1997), 185.

42. See Rachel Adams, *Sideshow USA: Freaks and the American Cultural Imagination* (Chicago: Univ. of Chicago Press, 2002); Rosemarie Garland Thomson, ed., *Freakery: Cultural Spectacles of the Extraordinary Body* (New York: NYU Press, 1996).

43. See Jane Goodall, *Performance and Evolution in the Age of Darwin* (New York: Routledge, 2002); Robert Rydell, *All the Worlds a Fair: Visions of Empire at American International Expositions, 1876–1916* (Chicago: Univ. of Chicago Press, 1987); Elazar Barkan and Ronald Bush, eds., *Prehistories of the Future: The Primitivist Project and the Culture of Modernism* (Palo Alto, CA: Stanford Univ. Press, 1995).

44. See Peta Tait, *Circus Bodies: Cultural Identity in Aeriel Performance* (New York: Routledge, 2005); M. Alison Kibler, *Rank Women: Gender and Cultural*

Hierarchy in American Vaudeville (Chapel Hill: UNC Press, 1999); Jennifer Putzi, *Identifying Marks: Race, Gender, and the Marked Body in Nineteenth-Century America* (Athens: Univ. of Georgia Press, 2006).

45. See Roger Daniels, *Coming to America: A History of Immigration and Ethnicity in American Life,* 2nd ed. (New York: Harper, 2002), 148–157.

46. See James M. Bergquist, "German Communities in American Cities: An Interpretation of the Nineteenth-Century Experience," *Journal of American Ethnic History* 4.1 (1984): 9–30.

47. Bergquist, "German Communities," 12.

48. See Eric Pumroy and Katja Rampelmann, eds., *Research Guide to the Turner Movement in the United States* (Westport, CT: Greenwood Press, 1996), xvii.

49. See Annette R. Hoffman, ed., *Turnen and Sport: Transatlantic Transfers* (Münster: Waxmann Verlag, 2004).

50. See Hoffman, *Turnen and Sport.*

51. Pumroy and Rampelmann, *Research Guide,* xxiii.

52. Wood, *Bernarr Macfadden,* 56.

53. "George Baptiste, Noted Wrestler," *St. Louis Star and Times,* Dec. 2, 1938, 25.

54. Wood, *Bernarr Macfadden,* 61.

55. Gerald W. Morton and George M. O'Brien, *Wrestling to Rasslin': Ancient Sport to American Spectacle* (Bowling Green, OH: Bowling Green State Univ. Press, 1985), 32. Also see Alex Bundgaard, *Muscle and Manliness: The Rise of Sport in American Boarding Schools* (Syracuse, NY: Syracuse Univ. Press, 2005); Elliot Gorn, *The Manly Art: Bare-Knuckle Prize Fighting in America* (Ithaca, NY: Cornell Univ. Press, 1986); J. A. Mangan, ed., *Reformers, Sport, Modernizers: Middle-Class Revolutions* (Portland, OR: Frank Cass, 2002).

56. Wood, *Bernarr Macfadden,* 75.

57. See Morton and O'Brien, *Wrestling to Rasslin';* Scott Beekman, *Ringside: A History of Professional Wrestling* (Westport, CT: Praeger, 2006).

58. Wood, *Bernarr Macfadden,* 68. Wood erroneously identifies this man as "Matsado Sirikitchi." See "Matsada Sorakichi, The Wonderful Japanese Wrestler," *Police Gazette,* May 3, 1984, 44.

59. "A Plucky Jap," *CT,* March 11, 1884, 5.

60. Wood, *Bernarr Macfadden,* 65.

61. See "Homeopathy, Hydrotherapy, and Kinesitherapy," *American Magazine,* May 1852, 238.

62. On Columbian Exhibition scholarship, see David J. Bertuca, Donald K. Hartman, and Susan M. Neumeister, eds., *The World's Columbian Exposition: A Centennial Bibliographic Guide* (Westport, CT: Greenwood Press, 1996). More recently, see Dennis B. Downey, *A Season of Renewal: The Columbian Exposition and Victorian America* (Westport, CT: Praeger, 2001); Chaim M. Rosenberg, *America at the Fair: Chicago's 1893 World's Columbian Exposition* (Charleston, SC: Arcadia, 2008); Robert W. Rydell, John E. Findling, and Kimberly D. Pelle, *Fair America: World's Fairs in the United States* (Washington, DC: Smithsonian, 2000).

63. David Stone, *Chicago's Classical Architecture: The Legacy of the White City* (Charleston, SC: Arcadia, 2005); Stanley Applebaum, ed., *The Chicago*

World's Fair of 1893: A Photographic Record (Mineola, NY: Dover, 1980); Carolyn Kinder Carr, *Revisiting the White City: American Art at the 1893 World's Fair* (Washington, DC: National Museum of American Art, 1993).

64. Robert W. Rydell, *All the World's a Fair: Visions of Empire at American International Expositions, 1876–1916* (Chicago: Univ. of Chicago Press, 1984).

65. See Rydell, *All the World's a Fair*; Goodall, *Performance and Evolution*; Micaela di Leonardo, *Exotics at Home: Anthropologies, Others, and American Modernity* (Chicago: Univ. of Chicago Press, 1998); Bridget R. Cooks, "Fixing Race: Visual Representations of African Americans at the World's Columbian Exposition, Chicago, 1893," *Patterns of Prejudice* 41.5 (2007): 435–465.

66. Donna Carlton, *Looking for Little Egypt* (Bloomington, IN: IDD, 1995).

67. Christopher Robert Reed, *"All the World is Here!": The Black Presence at the White City* (Bloomington: Indiana Univ. Press, 2000).

68. See James Gilbert, *Whose Fair? Experience, Memory, and the History of the Great St. Louis Exposition* (Chicago: Univ. of Chicago Press, 2009).

69. See Lears, *Rebirth of a Nation*.

70. Nancy Tomes, *The Gospel of Germs: Men, Women, and the Microbe in American Life* (Cambridge, MA: Harvard Univ. Press, 1998); Priscilla Wald, Nancy Tomes, and Lisa Lync, "Contagion and Culture," *American Literary History* 14.4 (2002): 617–624.

71. David L. Chapman, *Sandow the Magnificent: Eugen Sandow and the Beginnings of Bodybuilding* (Urbana-Champaign: Univ. of Illinois Press, 1994); David Waller, *The Perfect Man: The Muscular Life and Times of Eugen Sandow, Victorian Strongman* (Brighton: Victorian Secrets, Ltd., 2011).

72. See John Kasson, *Houdini, Tarzan, and the Perfect Man: The White Male Body and the Challenge of Modernity in America* (New York: Hill and Wang, 2002), 53–57; Constance Crompton, "Staging Gentility at the Columbian Exposition: Masculinity On and Off the Midway," in *Meet Me at the Fair: A World's Fair Reader*, ed. Lauren Hollengreen et al. (Pittsburgh, PA: ETC Press, 2014), 113–126.

73. Chapman, *Sandow the Magnificent*, 61. Also see Ethan Mordden, *Ziegfeld: The Man Who Invented Show Business* (New York: St. Martin's Press, 2008).

2. The Transatlantic Birth of the Physical Culture Publishing Company

1. See "Map of the City of New York," in F. E. Pierce, *The Tenement-House Committee Maps* (New York: Harper & Bros., 1895).

2. See Richard Hofstadter, *The Age of Reform* (New York: Vintage, 1960); Daniel T. Rodgers, *Atlantic Crossings: Social Politics in a Progressive Age* (Cambridge, MA: Harvard Univ. Press, 1998).

3. See Stephen Fox, *Transatlantic: Samuel Cunard, Isambard Brunel, and the Great Atlantic Steamship* (New York: HarperCollins, 2003).

4. See Richard Holt, *Sport and the British: A Modern History* (Oxford: Oxford Univ. Press, 1989); Bruce Haley, *The Healthy Body and Victorian Culture* (Cambridge, MA: Harvard Univ. Press, 1978); John Hargreaves, *Sport, Power,*

Culture: A Social and Historical Analysis of Popular Sports in Britain (New York: St. Martins, 1986).

5. Graham Dawson, *Soldier Heroes: British Adventure, Empire, and the Imagining of Masculinities* (London: Routledge, 1994); Beau Riffenburgh, *The Myth of the Explorer: The Press, Sensationalism, and Geographical Discovery* (London: Belhaven, 1993); John J. Macaloo, *Muscular Christianity and the Colonial and Post-Colonial World* (New York: Taylor and Francis, 2007).

6. John C. Mitcham, *Race and Imperial Defense in the British World, 1870–1914* (Cambridge: Cambridge Univ. Press, 2016); Mrinalini Sinha, *Colonial Masculinity: The 'Manly Englishman' and the 'Effeminate Bengali' in the Late 19th Century* (Manchester: Manchester Univ. Press, 1995).

7. See Clifford Putney, *Muscular Christianity: Manhood and Sports in Protestant America, 1880–1920* (Cambridge, MA: Harvard Univ. Press, 2003); Donald E. Hall, *Muscular Christianity: Embodying the Victorian Age* (Cambridge: Cambridge Univ. Press, 1994); Martin Polley, ed., *The History of Sport in Britain, 1880–1914* (London: Routledge, 2004).

8. For example, see Tony Collins, *A Social History of the English Rugby Union* (New York and London: Routledge, 2009).

9. See Allen Guttmann, *The Olympics: A History of the Modern Games,* 2nd ed. (Urbana-Champaign: Univ. of Illinois Press, 2002).

10. See Catriona Parratt, *"More Than Mere Amusement": Working Class Women's Leisure in England, 1750–1914* (Boston: Northeastern Univ. Press, 2001); Tracy J. R. Collins, "Physical Fitness, Sports, Athletics, and the Rise of the New Woman" (PhD diss., Purdue Univ., 2007); Kathleen E. McCrone, *Sport and the Physical Emancipation of English Women, 1870–1914* (Lexington: Univ. Press of Kentucky, 1988).

11. "Club Chatter," *Today,* January 30, 1897, 432.

12. Michael Anton Budd, *The Sculpture Machine: Physical Culture and Body Politics in the Age of Empire* (New York: NYU Press, 1997), 43.

13. Budd, *Sculpture Machine,* 29–30.

14. Clement Wood, *Bernarr Macfadden: A Study in Success* (New York: Lewis Copeland, 1929), 86.

15. Macfadden tells this story in his 1914 *Physical Culture* memoirs, and it gets repeated in almost every subsequent account of his life.

16. See Daniel Rodgers, "In Search of Progressivism," *Reviews in American History* 10.4 (1982): 113–132.

17. See C. M. Van Stockum, *Sport: An Attempt at Bibliography of Periodicals Published During 1890–1912* (New York: Dood and Livingston, 1914); Jan Todd, Joe Roark, and Terry Todd, "A Briefly Annotated Bibliography of English Language and Serial Publications in the Field of Physical Culture," *Iron Game History* (March 1991): 25–40.

18. See Frank L. Mott, *A History of American Magazines,* vol. IV: 1885–1905 (Cambridge, MA: Harvard Univ. Press, 1957); John Tebbel and Mary Ellen Zuckerman, *The Magazine in America, 1741–1990* (Oxford: Oxford Univ.

Press, 1991); Howard Cox and Simon Mowatt, *Revolutions from Grub Street: A History of Publishing in Britain* (Oxford: Oxford Univ. Press, 1956).

19. Jamie Stoops, *The Thorny Path: Pornography in Early Twentieth-Century Britain* (Montreal: McGill-Queens Univ. Press, 2018); Thomas Waugh, *Hard to Imagine: Gay Male Eroticism in Photography and Film from Their Beginnings to Stonewall* (New York: Columbia Univ. Press, 1996).

20. See David L. Chapman, *Sandow the Magnificent: Eugen Sandow and the Beginnings of Bodybuilding* (Urbana-Champaign: Univ. of Illinois Press, 1994).

21. "Once and Invalid, now an Athlete," *PC*, 1899, at http://archives.starkcenter.org/handle/11048/3693; "The Editor's Special Department," *PC*, 1900, 152, at http://archives.starkcenter.org/handle/11048/3671.

22. See Christian Mair, ed., *The Politics of English as a World Language: New Horizons in Postcolonial Cultural Studies* (Amsterdam: Editions Rodopi, 2003); Jan Blommaert, "Commentary: A Sociolinguistics of Globalization," *Journal of Sociolinguistics* 7.4 (2003): 607–623.

23. See Caroline Daley, *Leisure and Pleasure: Reforming the New Zealand Body* (Auckland: Auckland Univ. Press, 2003), 48; Chapman, *Sandow the Magnificent*; David Walker, "Race Building and the Disciplining of White Australia," in *Legacies of White Australia: Race, Culture, Nation*, ed. Laksiri Jayasuriya, David Walker, and Jan Gothard (Crawley: Univ. of Western Australia Press, 2003), 33–50.

24. Mark Singleton, *Yoga Body: The Origins of Modern Posture Practice* (Oxford: Oxford Univ. Press, 2010), 89.

25. "Talks on Health," *St. Paul Globe*, Nov. 7, 1904, 2.

26. See Perdita Buchan, *Utopia, New Jersey: Travels in the Nearest Eden* (New Brunswick, NJ: Rutgers Univ. Press, 2007), 85–115.

27. See N. W. Ayer and Son, *American Newspaper Annual of 1905* (Philadelphia: Newspaper Advertising Agents, 1905), 609.

28. "Cambridge Letter," *Oxford Magazine*, Feb. 11, 1903, 212.

29. See "The Religion of Health," The American Menu, http://www.theamericanmenu.com/2012/01/religion-of-health.html.

30. Film footage online at http://www.loc.gov/item/96516402/.

31. "England's Representatives in the Madison Square Garden Exhibition," *PD*, March 1904, n.p.; "Likely Competitors from New Zealand," *PC*, November 1903, 347.

32. Chapman, *Sandow the Magnificent*, 161.

33. *PC*, January 1910, 102.

34. Bernarr Macfadden, "Open Letter," *The Adelaide Register*, August 19, 1902, 6.

35. Daley, *Leisure and Pleasure*, 60.

36. *PC*, May 1907, 349; *PC*, August 1914, 222; *PC*, January 1913, 102.

37. See *The Argus* (Melbourne, Australia), December 24, 1904, 4; *The Mercury* (Hobart, Tasmania), July 8, 1902, 4.

38. *See Western Mail* (Perth, Australia), September 12, 1913, 17.

39. Bernarr Macfadden, "My Life Story," *PC*, January 1915, 85.

40. See Friedhelm Kirchfeld and Wade Boyle, *Nature Doctors: Pioneers in Naturopathic Medicine* (Portland, OR: Medicina Biológica, 1994).

41. Tommy Boydell, *My Beloved Country* (Cape Town: Nasionale Boekhandel Bpk, 1959).

42. See Dattatraya Chintaman Mujumdar, ed., *Encyclopedia of Indian Physical Culture* (Baroda: Sree Ram Vijaya Printing Press, 1950); Joseph Alter, "Indian Clubs and Colonialism: Hindu Masculinity and Muscular Christianity," *Comparative Studies in Society and History* 46.3: 497–534; Singleton, *Yoga Body*.

43. *PC,* June 1911, 710.

44. See Barbara Reeves-Ellington, Kathryn Kish-Sklar, Connie Shemo, eds., *Competing Kingdoms: Women, Mission, Nation and the American Protestant Empire, 1812–1960* (Durham, NC: Duke Univ. Press, 2010); Ian Tyrell, *Reforming the World: The Creation of America's Moral Empire* (Princeton, NJ: Princeton Univ. Press, 2010); Emily S. Rosenberg, *Spreading the American Dream: American Economic and Cultural Expansion, 1890–1945* (New York: Hill and Wang, 1982); Victoria de Grazia, *Irresistible Empire: America's Advance Through Twentieth-Century Europe* (Cambridge, MA: Harvard Univ. Press, 2006); Robert W. Rydell and Rob Kroes, *Buffalo Bill in Bologna: The Americanization of the World, 1969–1922* (Chicago: Univ. of Chicago, 2005); Jonathan Zimmerman, *Innocents Abroad: American Teachers in the American Century* (Cambridge, MA: Harvard Univ. Press, 2008).

45. See especially Paul A. Kramer, *The Blood of Government: Race, Empire, the United States, and the Philippines* (Chapel Hill: UNC Press, 2006).

46. R. A. Holman, "Comstock vs. Macfadden," *Tomorrow,* February 1908, 44.

47. Tyrell, *Reforming the World.*

48. See Ian Tyrell, *Woman's World/Woman's Empire* (Chapel Hill: UNC Press, 2010).

49. Bernarr Macfadden, "Prosecution of the Editor," *PC,* February 1910, 135.

50. See Putney, *Muscular Christianity,* 19; Nina Mjagkij, *Light in the Darkness, African Americans and the YMCA, 1852–1946* (Lexington: Univ. Press of Kentucky, 2003).

51. *PC,* May 1907, 409; *PC,* July 1910, 104–105. For corroborating evidence that Collins was a real person, see American Bureau of Shipping, *1905 Record of American and Foreign Shipping* (New York, Pohlemus Print Company, 1905), 507.

52. See Amy Werbel, *Lust on Trial: Censorship and the Rise of American Obscenity in the Age of Anthony Comstock* (New York: Columbia Univ. Press, 2018).

53. See *Macfadden v. United States,* 213 U.S. 288 (1909).

54. See Anthony Arthur, *Radical Innocent: Upton Sinclair* (New York: Random House, 2008), 119–129.

55. See Robert Ernst, *Weakness Is a Crime: The Life of Bernarr Macfadden* (Syracuse, NY: Syracuse Univ. Press, 1991) on the AMA's campaign against Macfadden.

3. Circulating Physiques in an Age of Imperialism and Migration

1. Mary Williamson Macfadden and Emile Gauvreau, *Dumbbells and Carrot Strips: The Story of Benarr Macfadden* (New York: Holt, 1953), 20.

2. Benedict Anderson, *Imagined Communities: Reflections on the Origin and Spread of Nationalism* (London: Verso, 2006). Also see Marilyn Lake and

Henry Reynolds, *Drawing the Global Colour Line: White Men's Countries and the International Challenge of Racial Equality* (Cambridge: Cambridge Univ. Press, 2008).

3. *PD*, March 1913, 41.

4. W. E. B. Du Bois, *The Souls of Black Folk* (Chicago: A.C. McClurg, 1903), vii.

5. W. E. B. Du Bois, "The Souls of White Folk," *The Independent*, August 10, 1910, 339. See Lake and Reynolds, *Drawing the Global Colour Line*, 2, 248.

6. Lake and Reynolds, *Drawing the Global Colour Line*, 4.

7. See Shawn Michelle Smith, *American Archives: Gender, Race, and Class in Visual Culture* (Princeton, NJ: Princeton Univ. Press, 1999), chap. 6.

8. See Martin Summers, *Manliness and Its Discontents: The Black Middle Class and the Transformation of Masculinity* (Chapel Hill: UNC Press 2004).

9. Lake and Reynolds, *Drawing the Global Colour Line*, 6–7.

10. See Thomas D. Pendergast, *Creating the Modern Man: American Magazines and Consumer Culture, 1900–1950* (Columbia: Univ. of Missouri Press, 2000).

11. Bernarr Macfadden, *The Virile Powers of Superb Manhood: How Developed, How Lost, How Regained* (New York: PCPC, 1900), 13.

12. See Gail Bederman, *Manliness and Civilization: A Cultural History of Gender and Race in the United States* (Chicago: Univ. of Chicago Press, 1995), 24; Kristin L. Hoganson, *Fighting for American Manhood: How Gender Politics Provoked the Spanish-American and Philippine-American Wars* (New Haven, CT: Yale Univ. Press, 2000).

13. Macfadden, *Virile Powers*, 6.

14. See Richard Dyer, "White Man's Muscles," in *Race and the Subject of Masculinities*, ed. Harry Stecopoulos and Michael Uebel (Durham, NC: Duke Univ. Press, 1997), 286–314; Michael Anton Budd, *The Sculpture Machine: Physical Culture and Body Politics in the Age of Empire* (New York: NYU Press, 1997).

15. Bernarr Macfadden, "The Japanese Will Whip Us," *PC*, February 1907, 105.

16. See especially Matthew Frye Jacobson, *Barbarian Virtues: The United States Encounters Foreign Peoples at Home and Abroad, 1876–1917* (New York: Hill and Wang, 2001); Kent Fedorowich and Andrew S. Thompson, eds., *Empire, Migration and Identity in the British World* (Manchester: Manchester Univ. Press, 2015).

17. Bernarr Macfadden, "My Lecture Tour Through England," *PC*, March 1907, 263.

18. A. O. Opperman, "Physical Culture Our Only Hope for Regeneration," *PC*, September 1902, 321.

19. Theodore Roosevelt to G. Stanley Hall, Nov. 29, 1899, quoted in Jacobson, *Barbarian Virtues*, 3.

20. Benarr Macfadden, "Editor's Viewpoint," *PC*, July 1908, 1.

21. E. P. Tape, "The Remarkable Powers of Endurance of Primitive People," *PC*, August 1902, 258.

22. See Stephanie L. Hawkins, *American Iconographic: National Geographic, Global Culture, and the Visual Imagination* (Charlottesville: UVA Press, 2010).

23. See Hawkins, *American Iconographic*; Laura Wexler, *Tender Violence: Domestic Visions in an Age of U.S. Imperialism* (Chapel Hill: UNC Press, 2000);

Anne Maxwell, *Colonial Photography and Exhibitions: Representations of the Native and the Making of European Identities* (Leicester: Leiscester Univ. Press, 2000); Tanya Sheehan, *Photography, History, Difference* (Hanover, NH: Dartmouth College Press, 2014); Steve Clark, ed., *Travel Writing and Empire: Postcolonial Theory in Transit* (London: Zed Books, 1999).

24. Jacobson, *Barbarian Virtues*, 102–103.

25. See especially Paul A. Kramer, *The Blood of Government: Race, Empire, the United States, and the Philippines* (Chapel Hill: UNC Press, 2006).

26. Wesley Atkins, "The Igorrotes, a Hardy, Vigorous People," *PC*, April 1910, 367.

27. *PC*, October 1902, 32.

28. Robert H. Macdonald, *Sons of the Empire: The Frontier and the Boy Scout Movement, 1890–1918* (Toronto: Univ. of Toronto Press, 1993).

29. *PC*, June 1914, 30a.

30. See Moses A. Dirk, *Frontier Violence and Stolen Indigenous Children in Australian History* (Oxford: Bergham, 2004); Timothy Bottoms, *Conspiracy of Silence: Queensland's Frontier Killing Times* (Sydney: Allen and Unwin, 2013).

31. Jan Todd, "Bernarr Macfadden: Reformer of Feminine Form," *Journal of Sport History* 14.1 (1987): 61–75.

32. See Gillian Sutherland, *In Search of the New Woman: Middle Class Women and Work in Britain, 1870–1914* (Cambridge: Cambridge Univ. Press, 2015); Martha H. Patterson, ed., *The American New Woman Revisited: A Reader, 1894–1930* (New Brunswick, NJ: Rutgers, 2008); Martha Banta, *Imaging American Women: Idea and Ideals in Cultural History* (New York: Columbia Univ. Press, 1987).

33. See Bederman, *Manliness and Civilization*, chap. 4.

34. Henry Winston Hardwick, "The Corset Exposed," *PC*, July 1908, 60.

35. See Mary K. Bloodsworth-Lugo, *In-between Bodies, Sexual Difference, Race, and Sexuality* (Albany: SUNY Press, 2007); Evelleen Richards, *Darwin and the Making of Sexual Selection* (Chicago: Univ. of Chicago Press, 2017).

36. See Katherine Endres, "The Feminism of Bernarr Macfadden," *Media History Monographs* 13.2 (2011): 1–14; Ian R. Tyrell, *Woman's World/Woman's Empire* (Chapel Hill, UNC Press, 1991).

37. "Indian Body Building," *PC*, June 1901, 105.

38. Charles Merriles, "The Average Woman," *PC*, July 1908, 19.

39. Bernarr Macfadden, "The Unshapely Anglo-Saxon Leg," *PC*, May 1905, 319. On race motherhood, see Ina Zweiniger-Bargielowska, *Managing the Body: Beauty, Health, and Fitness in Britain, 1800–1839* (Oxford: Oxford Univ. Press, 2010).

40. Allison Bashford and Philippa Levine, eds., *The Oxford Handbook of the History of Eugenics* (Oxford: Oxford Univ. Press, 2010); Alexandra Minna Stern, *Eugenic Nation: Faults and Frontiers of Better Breeding in Modern America* (Berkeley: Univ. of California Press, 2005).

41. See Shannon L. Walsh, *Eugenics and Physical Culture in the Progressive Era: Watch Whiteness Workout* (London: Palgrave Macmillan, 2020).

42. Christina Cogdell and Susan Currell, eds., *Popular Eugenics: National Efficiency and American Mass Culture in the 1930s* (Athens: Ohio Univ. Press, 2006); Budd, *Sculpture Machine*; Edwin Black, *War Against the Weak: Eugenics and America's Campaign to Create a Master Race* (New York: Four Walls Eight Windows, 2004).

43. Carl Easton Williams and Bernarr Macfadden, *The Olympian System of Physical and Mental Development* (Chicago: Hammond Press, 1919), 9. On disability and eugenics, see Sharon L. Snyder and David T. Mitchell, *Cultural Locations of Disability* (Chicago: Univ. of Chicago Press, 2006).

44. David M. Kennedy, *Birth Control in America: The Career of Margaret Sanger* (New Haven, CT: Yale Univ. Press, 1970); Linda Gordon, *The Politics of Population: Birth Control and the Eugenics Movement* (Urbana-Champaign: Univ. of Illinois Press, 2002).

45. See Patricia Vertinsky, "A Militant Madonna: Charlotte Perkins Gilman, Feminism, and Physical Culture" *History of Sport* 18.1 (2001): 55–72; Dana Seitler, "Unnatural Selection" *American Quarterly* 55.1 (2003): 61–88; Bederman, *Manliness and Civilization*, chap. 4.

46. Carl Easton Williams, "What Shall We Do With the Unfit," *PC*, 1913. Also see Stern, *Eugenic America*; Walsh, *Eugenics and Physical Culture*.

47. Budd, *Sculpture Machine*.

48. See Paul A. Kramer, *The Blood of Government*, 196–241; James Gilbert, *Whose Fair? Experience, Memory, and the History of the Great St. Louis Exhibition* (Chicago: Univ. of Chicago Press, 2009).

49. Liz Conor, *The Spectacular Modern Woman: Feminine Visibility in the 1920s* (Bloomington: Indiana Univ. Press, 2004), usefully defines spectacular visibility as a form of "modern subjectivity" generated via interaction with visual mass-media and characterized by fluidity between self-image, public image, and identity. Also see Andrew Thacker, *Moving through Modernity* (Manchester: Manchester Univ. Press, 2003).

50. Booker T. Washington, "Keeping Tuskegee Students in Physical Repair," *PC*, March 1910, 223.

51. Bederman, *Manliness and Civilization*, 2.

52. See Theresa Runstedtler, *Jack Johnson, Rebel Soujourner: Boxing in the Shadow of the Global Color Line* (Berkeley: Univ. of California Press, 2012); Geofrey C. Ward, *Unforgivable Blackness: The Rise and Fall of Jack Johnson* (New York: Alfred A. Knopf, 2004).

53. See Bederman, *Manliness and Civilization*.

54. See Frederick Jameson, *Postmodernism, or the Cultural Logic of Late Capitalism* (Durham, NC: Duke Univ. Press, 1991). Whereas Jameson uses phrases such as *imitative, blank,* and *dead* to criticize mass-cultural pastiche's lack of political power, here, the term is intended to evoke the generative dimensions of sequential and juxtapositional media forms.

55. See Lutz Koepnick, *Walter Benjamin and the Aesthetics of Power,* 2nd ed. (Lincoln: Univ. of Nebraska Press, 1999), 132; Sergei Eisenstein, "A Dialectical Approach to Film Form," in *Film Form: Essays in Film Form,* ed. and trans. Jay Leyda (New York: Harcourt, Brace & World, 1949); Roland Barthes,

Camera Lucinda: Reflections on Photography, trans. Richard Howard (New York: Hill and Wang, 1981); Miriam Silverberg, *Erotic Grotesque Nonsense: The Mass Culture of Japanese Modern Times* (Berkeley: Univ. of California Press, 2009); Conor, *Spectacular Modern Woman.*

56. See Edward W. Soja, *Third Space: Journeys to Los Angeles and Other Real-and-Imagined Places* (New York: Blackwell, 1996); Rob Shields, *Places on the Margin: Alternative Geographies of Modernity* (London: Routledge, 1991). Thacker, *Moving through Modernity.*

57. F. A. Hornibrook, "The Fijians and Physical Culture," *PC,* September 1907, 151.

58. L. E. Eubanks, "Hints on Posing the Physique Beautiful," *PC,* May 1913, 420.

59. *PC,* June 1910, 617.

60. *PC,* June 1911, 712.

61. See Jeffrey Lehman, ed., *Gale Encyclopedia of Multicultural America,* 2nd ed. (New York: Gale Group, 2000); Roger Daniels, *Coming to America: A History of Immigration and Ethnicity in American Life* (New York: HarperCollins, 2002) 232–235.

62. Mark Wyman, *Round-trip to America: The Immigrants Return to Europe, 1880–1930* (Ithaca, NY: Cornell Univ. Press, 1993).

63. *PC,* June 1911, 712.

64. *PC,* December 1908, 581.

65. See Jan Todd, "Portrait of a Strongman: The Circus Career of Ottley Russell Coulter: 1912–1916," *Iron Game History* 7.1 (2001): 4–21.

66. See Ralph Weber, *Notre Dame's John Zahm* (South Bend, IN: Univ. of Notre Dame Press, 1961).

67. William White, "South American Library Presented to Notre Dame," *Library Journal* (June 1917): 455.

68. Todd, "Portrait of a Strongman," 11. Also see Ottley R. Coulter Collection, HJLSC.

69. *PC,* October 1910, 533.

70. See Wendy Ross, "Jiu-Jitsuing Uncle Sam: The Unmanly Art of Jiu-Jitsu and the Yellow Peril Threat in the Progressive Era United States," *Pacific Historical Review* 84.4 (2015): 448–477.

71. *PC,* August 1914, 170–171.

72. Letter from G. Y. Manikrau, *Physical Culture,* n.d. (c. 1912). Folder: Ottley R. Coulter Clippings, Ottley R. Coulter Collection, HJLSC.

73. See Budd, *Sculpture Machine.* On muscular nationalism's implications for women, see Sikata Banarjee, *Muscular Nationalism: Gender, Violence, and Empire in India and Ireland, 1914–2004* (New York: NYU Press, 2012).

74. Wilson Chacko Jacob, *Working Out Egypt: Effendi Masculinity and Subject Formation in Colonial Modernity, 1870–1940* (Durham, NC: Duke Univ. Press, 2011), 6, 15, 66.

75. See Upton Sinclair, *The Autobiography of Upton Sinclair* (New York: Harcourt, 1962).

76. Macfadden and Gauvreau, *Dumbbells and Carrot Strips,* 143. On France, see Mary Lynn Stewart, *For Health and Beauty: Physical Culture for French Women, 1880s–1930* (Baltimore, MD: Johns Hopkins Univ. Press, 2000); Christopher E.

Forth, *The Dreyfus Affair and the Crisis of French Manhood* (Baltimore, MD: Johns Hopkins Univ. Press, 2006).

77. Macfadden and Gauvreau, *Dumbbells and Carrot Strips,* 143.

78. Macfadden and Gauvreau, *Dumbbells and Carrot Strips,* 172.

4. Building Up the Nation during the First World War

1. Mary Williamson Macfadden and Emile Gauvreau, *Dumbbells and Carrot Strips: The Story of Bernarr Macfadden* (New York: Holt, 1953), 178.

2. See testimony in Macfadden v. Macfadden, 46 N.J. Super. 242, 134 A.2d 531 (1957).

3. Macfadden and Gauvreau, *Dumbbells and Carrot Strips,* 181.

4. Macfadden and Gauvreau, *Dumbbells and Carrot Strips,* 192.

5. See William Mulligan, *The Great War for Peace* (New Haven, CT: Yale Univ. Press, 2014).

6. Michael Kazin, *War Against War: The American Fight for Peace, 1914–1918* (New York: Simon and Schuster, 2017).

7. Ross Kennedy, *The Will to Believe: Woodrow Wilson, World War I, and America's Strategy for Peace and Security* (Kent, OH: Kent State Univ. Press, 2009).

8. See Daniel T. Rodgers, *Atlantic Crossings: Social Politics in a Progressive Age* (Cambridge, MA: Belknap Press, 2000); Michael McGerr, *A Fierce Discontent: The Rise and Fall of the Progressive Movement in America* (New York: Simon and Schuster, 2005); Kazin, *War Against War.*

9. Bernarr Macfadden, "My Life Story," *PC,* Mar. 1914, 235.

10. See T. J. Jackson Lears, "From Salvation to Self-realization: Advertising and the Therapeutic Roots of the Consumer Society," in *The Culture of Consumption,* ed. Richard Wightman Fox and T. J. Jackson Lears (New York: Pantheon Books, 1983); Ellen Gruber Garvey, *The Adman in the Parlor: Magazines and the Gendering of Consumer Culture, 1880s–1910s* (Oxford: Oxford Univ. Press, 1996).

11. Bernarr Macfadden, *Vitality Supreme* (New York: PCPC, 1915), preface.

12. See especially Thomas Waugh, *Hard to Imagine: Gay Male Eroticism in Photography and Film from Their Beginnings to Stonewall* (New York: Columbia Univ. Press, 1996); George Chauncey, *Gay New York: Gender, Urban Culture, and the Making of the Gay Male World* (New York: Basic Books, 1994).

13. "Anthony Comstock Dies in His Crusade," *NYT,* Sept. 2, 1915, 1, 6.

14. See Zachary Smith, *Age of Fear: Othering and American Identity During WWI* (Baltimore, MD: Johns Hopkins Univ. Press, 2019).

15. Woodrow Wilson, Address to the Senate of the United States: "A World League for Peace" (1917), online by the American Presidency Project, eds. Gerhard Peters and John T. Woolley, https://www.presidency.ucsb.edu/node/206603.

16. George Creel, *How We Advertised America* (New York: Harper and Brothers, 1920), 4.

17. Alan Axelrod, *Selling the Great War: The Making of American Propaganda* (New York: Palgrave, 2009); Gary Gerstle, *American Crucible: Race and Nation in the Twentieth Century* (Princeton, NJ: Princeton Univ. Press, 2001).

18. See examples in Pearl James, ed., *Picture This: World War I Posters and Visual Culture* (Lincoln: Univ. of Nebraska Press, 2009).

19. "Bernarr Macfadden Proposes a Defense League," *PC,* Mar. 1916, 88.

20. See Christopher Capozzola, *Uncle Sam Wants You: World War I and the Making of the Modern American Citizen* (Oxford: Oxford Univ. Press, 2008); Jennifer D. Keene, *Doughboys, the Great War, and the Remaking of America* (Baltimore, MD: Johns Hopkins Univ. Press, 2003).

21. William J. Lee, "Playgrounds and Physical Preparedness," *PC,* Oct. 1917, 93.

22. Raymond Fosdick, "How Can We Have Universal Military Training," *PC,* Aug. 1918, 25.

23. See Capozzolla, *Uncle Sam Wants You.*

24. *PC,* Oct. 1917, 24a–26.

25. Achille Mbembe, *Necropolitics* (Durham, NC: Duke Univ. Press, 2019).

26. Creel, *How We Advertised America.*

27. Michael Kazin, *War Against War.*

28. Woodrow Wilson, "Final Address in Support of the League of Nations," Sept. 25, 1919.

29. Nancy Gentile Ford, *Americans All! Foreign-Born Soldiers in WWI* (College Station: Texas A&M Press, 2001).

30. See Chad L. Williams, *Torchbearers of Democracy: African American Soldiers in the World War I Era* (Chapel Hill: UNC Press, 2010); Emily S. Rosenberg, "World War One, Wilsonianism, and Challenges to U.S. Empire," *Diplomatic History* 38.4 (2014): 852–863.

31. "Regeneration of a Coward," *PC,* Aug. 1918, 9.

32. "Bernarr Macfadden's Viewpoint," *PC,* Oct. 1918, 8.

33. See David Roediger, *Working Toward Whiteness: How America's Immigrants Became White* (New York: Basic Books, 2005); Matthew Frye Jacobsen, *Whiteness of a Different Color: European Immigrants and the Alchemy of Race* (Cambridge, MA: Harvard Univ. Press, 1999).

34. Budd, *Sculpture Machine,* 47.

35. See Edwin L. Battistella, *Do You Make These Mistakes in English? The Story of Sherwin Cody's Famous Language School* (Oxford: Oxford Univ. Press, 2009).

36. Budd, *Sculpture Machine,* 47.

37. See Michael Denning, *Mechanic Accents: Dime Novels and Working-Class Culture in America,* 2nd ed. (New York: Verso, 1998); Nan Enstad, *Ladies of Labor, Girls of Adventure: Working Women, Popular Culture, and Labor Politics in the Turn of the Twentieth Century* (New York: Columbia Univ. Press, 1999); Kathy Peiss, *Cheap Amusements and Leisure in Turn-of-the-Century New York* (Philadelphia: Temple Univ. Press, 1986); Vicki Ruiz, *From Out of the Shadows: Mexican Women in Twentieth-Century America,* 10th ed. (Oxford: Oxford Univ. Press, 2008).

38. Kazin, *War Against War.*

39. See Stephen H. Norwood, *Strikebreaking and Intimidation: Mercenaries and Masculinity in Twentieth-Century America* (Chapel Hill: UNC Press, 2002); Joseph A. McCartin, *Labor's Great War: The Struggle for Industrial Democracy*

and the Origins of Modern American Labor Relations, 1912–1921 (Chapel Hill: Univ. of North Carolina Press, 1997).

40. Jacobsen, *Whiteness of a Different Color.*

41. Dominique Padurano, "Consuming La Bella Figura: Charles Atlas and American Masculinity, 1910–40," in *Making Italian America: Consumer Culture and the Production of Ethnic Identities,* ed. Simone Cinotto (New York: Fordham Univ. Press), 105–106.

42. Angelo Siciliano, "Building the Physique of a Greek God," *PC,* Nov. 1921, 36.

43. Padurano, "La Bella Figura," 106.

44. Siciliano, "Building the Physique," 36.

45. See Christopher Breu, *Hard-Boiled Masculinities* (Minneapolis: Univ. of Minnesota Press, 2005); Jacqueline Reich, "'The World's Most Perfectly Developed Man': Charles Atlas, Physical Culture, and the Inscription of American Masculinity," *Men and Masculinities* 12.4 (2012): http://jmm.sagepub.com/content/12/4/444; Dominique Padurano, "Making American Men: Charles Atlas and the Business of Bodies, 1892–1945" (PhD diss., Rutgers Univ., 2007).

46. J. Anthony Guillory, "The Physical Uplift of the Race: The Emergence of the African American Physical Culture Movement, 1900–1930" (PhD diss., 2015).

47. "Physical Culture for July," *Baltimore Afro-American,* Jul. 29, 1911, 6.

48. Davarian L. Baldwin, *Chicago's New Negroes: Modernity, the Great Migration, and Black Urban Life* (Chapel Hill: UNC Press, 2007), 195. In addition to Baldwin, also see Henry Louis Gates Jr. and Gene Andrew Jarrett, eds., *The New Negro: Readings on Race, Representation, and African American Culture, 1892–1938* (Princeton, NJ: Princeton Univ. Press, 2007).

49. See Williams, *Torch-bearers of Democracy*; Arthur E. Barbeau and Florette Henri, *The Unknown Soldiers: African-American Troops in WWI* (New York: Hachette Books, 1996); Mark Whalen, *The Great War and the Culture of the New Negro* (Gainesville, FL: Univ. Press of Florida, 2008).

50. See Kinshasha Holman Conwill, ed., *We Return Fighting: World War I and the Shaping of Modern Black Identity* (Washington, DC: Smithsonian Books, 2019); Martin Summers, *Manliness and Its Discontents: The Black Middle Class and the Transformation of Masculinity, 1900–1930* (Chapel Hill: Univ. of North Carolina Press, 2004); Gates and Jarrett, *New Negro.*

51. Jacqueline Najuma Stewart, "Negroes Laughing at Themselves: Black Spectatorship and the Performance of Urban Modernity" *Critical Inquiry* 29.4 (Summer 2003): 653. Also see Stewart, *Migrating to the Movies: Cinema and Black Urban Modernity* (Berkeley: Univ. of California Press, 2005).

52. Davarian L. Baldwin and Minkah Makalani, eds., *Escape from New York: The "Harlem Renaissance" Reconsidered* (Minneapolis: Univ. of Minnesota Press, 2013); Daniel Anderson, *The Culture of Sports in the Harlem Renaissance* (Jefferson, NC: McFarland, 2017).

53. Jean Toomer, *The Wayward and the Seeking: A Collection of Writings by Jean Toomer,* ed. Darwin T. Turner (Washington DC: Howard Univ. Press, 1983), 89.

54. Jean Toomer, autobiographical manuscript written around 1935, Folder 362, Box 11, Jean Toomer Papers, Beinecke Rare Book and Manuscript Library, Yale Univ., New Haven, CT.

55. Jean Toomer Scrapbook, Folder 1505, Box 66, Jean Toomer Papers.

56. For a more extensive analysis, see Mark Whalan, "'Taking Myself in Hand:' Jean Toomer and Physical Culture," *Modernism/modernity* 10.4 (2003): 597–615.

57. Margaret Rose Vendryes, *Barthé: A Life in Sculpture* (Jackson: Univ. Press of Mississippi, 2008).

58. Vendryes, *Barthé: A Life in Sculpture*, 15.

59. See Randolph P. Byrd and Henry Louis Gates Jr., "Jean Toomer's Conflicted Racial Identity," *The Chronicle of Higher Education*, Feb. 6, 2011, and the resultant online discussion, "The Complicated Racial Identity of Jean Toomer," Mar. 6, 2011, http://chronicle.com/article/The-Complicated-Racial/126554/. Also see Tania Friedel, *Racial Discourse and Cosmopolitanism in Twentieth-Century African American Writing* (New York: Taylor and Francis Group, 2008).

60. Whalan, "Taking Myself in Hand," 598.

61. James Smalls, "Sculpting Black Queer Bodies and Desires: The Case of Richmond Barthé," in *Understanding Blackness through Performance*, ed. Anne Crémieux, Xavier Lemoine, and Jean-Paul Rocchi (New York: Palgrave, 2013), 199–220.

62. Smalls, "Sculpting Black Queer Bodies," 200.

63. Macfadden and Gauvreau, *Dumbbells and Carrot Strips*, 392.

5. The Sensational Rise of Macfadden Publications Inc.

1. Ann Hagedorn, *Savage Peace: Hope and Fear in America, 1919* (New York: Simon and Schuster, 2007).

2. Henry F. May, *The End of American Innocence: The First Years of Our Own Time, 1912–1917* (New York: Albert Knopf, 1959).

3. Adam Tooze, *The Deluge: The Great War, America, and the Remaking of the World Order, 1916–1931* (New York: Penguin, 2014).

4. Charles F. McGovern, *Sold American: Consumption and Citizenship, 1890–1945* (Chapel Hill: UNC Press, 2009).

5. See Frank Luther Mott, *A History of American Magazines, Vol. V: 1905–1930* (Cambridge, MA: Belknap, 1968); Vand D. E. Summer, *The Magazine Century: American Magazines Since 1900* (New York: Peter Lang, 2010); Theodore Peterson, *Magazines in the Twentieth Century* (Urbana-Champaign: University of Illinois Press, 1964).

6. Ellen Gruber Garvey, *Adman in the Parlor: Magazines and the Gendering of Consumer Culture, 1880s–1910s* (Oxford: Oxford University Press, 1996); Richard Ohman, *Selling Culture: Magazines, Markets, and Class at the Turn of the Century* (New York: Verso, 1996).

7. See Suzanne W. Churchill and Adam McKible, *Little Magazines and Modernism: New Approaches* (New York: Routledge, 2016).

8. Peter Haining, *The Classic Era of Pulp Magazines* (Chicago: Chicago Review Press, 2001); Erin A. Smith, "How the Other Half Read: Advertising, Working-Class Readers, and Pulp Magazines," *Book History* 3 (2000): 204–230.

9. Peterson, *Magazines in the Twentieth Century*, 283.

10. See Gerard Jones, *Men of Tomorrow: Geeks, Gangsters, and the Birth of the Comic Book* (New York: Basic Books, 2008).

11. Mary Williamson Macfadden and Emile Gauvreau, *Dumbbells and Carrot Strips: The Story of Bernarr Macfadden* (New York: Holt, 1953), 222.

12. Warren Harding, "Inaugural Address," March 4, 1921.

13. *TS*, February 1926, 65, quoted in Ann Fabian, "Making a Commodity of Truth: Speculations on the Career of Bernarr Macfadden," *American Literary History* 5.1 (1993): 64.

14. Harold Brainerd Hersey, *Pulpwood Editor: The Amazing World of the Thriller Magazines* (New York: Frederick A. Stokes, 1938), 214.

15. Macfadden and Gauvreau, *Dumbbells and Carrot Strips*, 223.

16. See Roland Marchand, *Advertising the American Dream: Making Way for Modernity, 1920–1940* (Berkeley: University of California Press, 1986), 54.

17. Bernarr Macfadden, "Do You Read Pictures," *TS*, March 1920, 11.

18. See Josephus V. Higgenbothem, "The Truth about Rotogravure," *The Printing Art*, Sept. 1921–Feb. 1922, 424–436.

19. "The Heart of a Hunchback," *TS*, March 1924, 56; Hersey, *Pulpwood Editor*, 214.

20. Macfadden and Gauvreau, *Dumbbells and Carrot Strips*, 269.

21. See Anthony Slide, *Inside the Hollywood Fan Magazine: A History of Star Makers, Fabricators, and Gossip Mongers* (Jackson: University Press of Mississippi, 2010).

22. "Our New Sister," *TS*, June 1921, 2.

23. Nan Enstad, *Ladies of Labor, Girls of Adventure: Working Women, Popular Culture, and Labor Politics in the Turn of the Twentieth Century* (New York: Columbia Univ. Press, 1999).

24. Tony Goodstone, ed., *The Pulps: Fifty Years of American Pop Culture* (New York: Chelsea House, 1976), 89. Erin A. Smith, *Hard Boiled: Working-Class Readers and Pulp Magazines* (Philadelphia: Temple University Press, 2000); E. R. Hagemann, *A Comprehensive Index to* Black Mask, *1920–51* (Bowling Green, OH: Bowling Green State University Popular Press, 1982).

25. See Don Herron, "Up and Down these Mean Streets," http://www.donherron.com/hammett-who-killed-bob-teal/.

26. All from *PC*, March 1920.

27. "Bernarr Macfadden's Viewpoint," *PC*, October 1924, 27.

28. See Heather Addison, *Hollywood and the Rise of Physical Culture* (New York: Routledge, 2003).

29. Macfadden and Gauvreau, *Dumbbells and Carrot Strips*; William R. Hunt, *Body Love: The Amazing Career of Bernarr Macfadden* (Bowling Green, OH: Bowling Green State Univ. Popular Press, 1991), 170.

30. See Bernarr Macfadden, *Predetermine Your Baby's Sex* (New York: Macfadden Publications, 1926).

31. See Macfadden Publications Inc., *Statistical and Financial Analysis of Macfadden Publications Inc.* (New York: MP, 1929).

32. Allene Talmey, "Millions from Dumb-bells," *Outlook and Independent*, July 4, 1930, 163–166.

33. Ann Fabian, *The Unvarnished Truth: Personal Narratives in Nineteenth-Century America* (Berkeley: University of California Press, 2000), 160.

34. Fabian, *Unvarnished Truth,* 7.

35. For a guide to scholarship on "Confessional Discourse," see James Jasinski, *Sourcebook on Rhetoric* (Los Angeles: SAGE, 2001), 100–102. Also see Dave Tell, *Confessional Crises and Cultural Politics in Twentieth-Century America* (State College: Penn State Univ. Press, 2012).

36. "New Macfadden Publications," *Bookseller and Stationer,* Aug. 15, 1922, 30.

37. Hersey, *Pulpwood Editor,* 214.

38. Adam McKeogh, "The Truth About the True Story Magazine," *English Journal* 16.6 (1927): 421.

39. The Modern Girl Around the World Research Group, *The Modern Girl Around the World: Consumption, Identity, and Globalization* (Durham, NC: Duke University Press, 2008).

40. See Catherine Gourley, *Flappers and the New American Woman: Perceptions of Women from 1918 through the 1920s* (Minneapolis, MN: Twenty-First Century Books, 2008).

41. "The Chorus Girl Speaks," *TS,* April 1921, 21.

42. Anzia Yezierska, "Salome of the Tenements," *Beautiful Womanhood,* 1922–1923.

43. "Cinderella Story of a Servant Girl," *Cedar Rapids Evening Gazette,* March 5, 1921.

44. Gordon Hunter, *What America Read: Taste, Class, and the Novel, 1920–1960* (Chapel Hill: University of North Carolina Press, 2008), 98.

45. Melanie Leninson, "'To Make Myself for a Person': Passing Narratives and the Divided Self in the Work of Anzia Yezierska," *Studies in American Jewish Literature* 13 (1994): 2–9; Catherine Rottenberg, "Salome of the Tenements, the American Dream and Class Performativity," *American Studies* 45.1 (2004): 65–83.

46. "Out of the Melting Pot," *TS,* June 1921, 10.

47. "Suzanne of the Studios," *TS,* March 1920, 56.

48. See Roseann Mandziuk, "Confessional Discourse and Modern Desires: Power and Pleasure in True Story Magazine," *Critical Studies in Media Communication* 18.2 (2001): 174–193.

49. "Under Sentence of Marriage," *TS,* February 1920, 38.

50. See Adrienne L. McLean, "'New Films in Story Form': Movie Story Magazines and Spectatorship," *Cinema Journal* 42.3 (2003): 3–26.

51. Michele Hilmes, *Radio Voices: American Broadcasting, 1922–1952* (Minneapolis: University of Minnesota Press, 1997), 100.

52. Vera Caspary, *The Secrets of Grown-Ups: An Autobiography* (New York: McGraw-Hill, 1979).

53. Joan Wiegers, "The Macfadden Connection," *Dance Magazine,* June 2002.

54. McLean, "'New Films in Story Form'"; Kathryn H. Fuller, *At the Picture Show: Small-Town Audiences and the Creation of Movie Fan Culture* (Washington, DC: Smithsonian Institution Press, 1996).

55. John F. Roche, "Bernarr Macfadden Tells Philosophy Behind His Newspaper Enterprises," *Editor and Publisher,* Aug. 21, 1929, 1.

56. See Emile Gauvreau, *My Last Million Readers* (New York: E. P. Dutton, 1941), 114.

57. John D. Stevens, *Sensationalism and the New York Press* (New York: Columbia University Press, 1991).

58. See Lester Cohen, *The New York Graphic: The World's Zaniest Newspaper* (Philadelphia: Chilton Books, 1964); Scott Corbett, *Sauce for the Gander* (White Plains, NY: Baldwin Books, 1954).

59. Quoted in Mia Fineman, *Faking It: Manipulated Photography Before Photoshop* (New York: Metropolitan Museum of Art, 2012), 144.

60. "Composographs," *Life*, Jan. 2, 1950, 95.

61. Neal Gabler, *Winchell: Gossip, Power, and the Culture of Celebrity* (Vintage: New York, 1994).

62. James Maguire, *Impresario: The Life and Times of Ed Sullivan* (New York: Billboard, 2011).

63. Gauvreau, *My Last Million Readers*, 114.

64. Rapp collaborated with the Harlem Renaissance writer Wallace Thurman on three plays, including *Harlem: A Melodrama of Negro Life* (1929).

65. Hersey, *Pulpwood Editor*, 214.

66. "The Press: Below the Zone," *Time*, November 1, 1926; "The Press: Teeth, Fingernails," *Time*, September 22, 1924.

67. N. H. Bowen, "Macfadden, The Bare Torso King, and his Shoddy Sex Magazines," *Detroit Saturday Night*, May 3, 1924, quoted in Hunt, *Body Love*, 108.

68. McKeogh, "The Truth," 421.

69. McKeogh, "The Truth," 418.

70. Tip Bliss, "The Practically Complete Idiot," *Life*, April 30, 1925, 9.

71. "The Press: Below the Zone," *Time*, November 1, 1926.

72. Hersey, *Pulpwood Editor*, 215.

73. "The First Story Ever Told Was True," *NYT*, Oct. 10, 1923, 15.

74. See Chad C. Heap, *Slumming: Sexual and Racial Encounters in American Nightlife, 1885–1940* (Chicago: University of Chicago Press, 2009); Robert M. Dowling, *Slumming in New York: From the Waterfront to Mythic Harlem* (Urbana-Champaign: University of Illinois Press, 2008).

75. "The Lives We Elbow But Can Never Touch," *NYT*, Nov. 15, 1923, 15.

76. "Congress to Be Told How to Keep Healthy," *WP*, April 18, 1924, 3; "Laughter Advised as Help to Health," *WP*, April 24, 1924, 3.

77. Larry Tye, *The Father of Spin: Edward L. Bernays and the Birth of Public Relations* (New York: Henry Holt, 2002); Roland Marchand, *Creating the Corporate Soul: The Rise of Public Relations and the Corporate Imagery in American Big Business*, 2nd ed. (Berkeley: University of California Press, 2001).

78. Edward L. Bernays, "Typescripts on Publicizing the Physical Culture Movement, 1927," LOC, Thrift and Prosperity, http://hdl.loc.gov/loc.mss/amrlm.meo.

79. See Gene Smiley, "US Economy in the 1920s," *EH.Net Encyclopedia*, ed. Robert Whaples, June 29, 2004, http://eh.net/encyclopedia/the-u-s-economy-in-the-1920s/.

80. "5 Billion Dollars to Spend," *CT*, March 8, 1927, 22; "An Advertisement to the Campbell's Soup Company," *NYT*, April 5, 1927, 19.

81. Marchand, *Advertising the American Dream*, 56.

82. Barbara Olsen, "Sourcing Elitist Attitudes in Early Advertising From the Archives," in *NA-Advances in Consumer Research Volume*, vol. 27, ed. Stephen J. Hoch and Robert J. Meyer (Provo, UT: Association for Consumer Research), 295–300.

83. Hersey, *Pulpwood Editor*, 205–207.

84. Macfadden and Gauvreau, *Dumbbells and Carrot Strips*, 382.

6. The Great Depression and the Macfadden Market

1. Herbert Hoover, "Address of Acceptance," August 11, 1928, in *The New Day: Campaign Speeches of Herbert Hoover* (Palo Alto, CA: Stanford University Press, 1928), 7–44.

2. Herbert Hoover, "Inaugural Speech," March 4, 1929, https://avalon.law.yale.edu/20th_century/hoover.asp.

3. Mary Williamson Macfadden and Emile Gauvreau, *Dumbbells and Carrot Strips: The Story of Bernarr Macfadden* (New York: Holt, 1953), 391.

4. On the company's aggressive attempts to reduce competition, see Sam Moskowitz, "Amazing Encounter: MacFadden's Takeover of Gernsback's Co." *Fantasy Review* 9.2 (1986): 8; Moskowitz, "Amazing Encounter: MacFadden's Takeover of Gernsback's Co. Pt. II" *Fantasy Review* 9.3 (1986): 8.

5. *Time*, May 27, 1929, 74.

6. "Plans Financial Tabloid," *NYT*, Mar. 28, 1929, 46.

7. Fulton Oursler, *The True Story of Bernarr Macfadden* (New York: Lewis Copeland, 1929).

8. Grace Perkins, *Chats with the Macfadden Family* (New York: Lewis Copeland, 1929).

9. Macfadden and Gauvreau, *Dumbbells and Carrot Strips*, 322–323.

10. Clement Wood, *Bernarr Macfadden: A Study in Success* (New York: Lewis Copeland, 1929).

11. Fulton Oursler, *Behold This Dreamer: An Autobiography* (New York: Little, Brown, 1964), 270.

12. Wood, *Bernarr Macfadden*, 2–3.

13. H. L. Mencken, "An American Idealist," *The American Mercury*, May 1930, 124.

14. "Physcultopathist" *Time*, Jan. 13, 1930, 70–71.

15. "True Mirrors for Reflection," *NYT*, July 23, 1929, 13.

16. "Well—What Are Keats," *NYT*, Sept. 3, 1929, 15.

17. See Charles F. McGovern, *Sold American: Consumption and Citizenship, 1890–1945* (Chapel Hill: UNC Press, 2006).

18. "Mainly on the Subject of Women," *NYT*, Oct. 1, 1929, 15.

19. See Roland Marchand, *Advertising the American Dream: Making Way for Modernity, 1920–1940* (Berkeley: University of California Press, 1986); Stuart Ewen and Elizabeth Ewen, *Channels of Desire: Mass Images and the Shaping of American Consciousness* (Minneapolis, University of Minnesota Press, 1992); Lizabeth Cohen, "Encountering Mass Culture at the Grassroots: The

Experience of Chicago Workers in the 1920s," *American Quarterly* 41.1 (Mar. 1989): 6–33.

20. See John H. Goldthorpe et al., "The Affluent Worker and the Thesis of 'Embourgeoisement': Some Preliminary Research Findings," *Sociology* 1.1 (1967): 11–31.

21. "Well—What Are Keats," *NYT*, Sept. 3, 1929, 15.

22. "The Great Experiment," *DFP*, June 11, 1929, 9.

23. "The Amazing True Story of Personal Credit," *DFP*, Oct. 15, 1929; "Concluding the Story on Personal Credit," *DFP*, Oct. 29, 1929, 9.

24. "When the Gods Fall Down," *CDT*, Nov. 12, 1929, 17.

25. "The True Story of the Pee-pul," *DFP*, Nov. 26, 1929, 9.

26. "The True Story of the Masses in the Long Roll of History," *CDT*, Jan. 14, 1930, 13.

27. "The True Story of American Business Affairs," *CDT*, Dec. 2, 1930, 9.

28. See Douglas B. Ward, *A New Brand of Business: Curtis Publishing Company and the Origins of Market Research, 1911–1930* (Philadelphia: Temple University Press, 2010); Daniel J. Robinson, *The Measure of Democracy: Polling, Market Research, and Public Life, 1930–1945* (Toronto: University of Toronto Press, 1999).

29. "Are You Clamoring for Case Histories?" *CDT*, Mar. 25, 1930, 13.

30. "The True Story of American Business Affairs," *NYT*, Dec. 2, 1930, 21.

31. "Home Problems Forum," *TS*, April 1930, 8.

32. "The True Story Home Maker Forum," *TS*, April 1930, 117.

33. Quoted in Nicolas Lemann, "Hating on Herbert Hoover," *New Yorker*, October 23, 2017.

34. Herbert Hoover, "Response to the Press," Oct. 4, 1940, https://iowaculture.gov /history/education/educator-resources/primary-source-sets/great-depression -and-herbert-hoover/herbert; also see Herbert Hoover, *American Individualism* (New York: Doubleday, 1922).

35. See Eric Rauchway, *Winter War: Hoover, Roosevelt, and the First Clash Over the New Deal* (New York: Basic Books, 2018).

36. Herbert Hoover, "Statement on Plans for a White House Conference on Child Health and Protection," *The American Presidency Project*, ed. Gerhard Peters and John T. Woolley, https://www.presidency.ucsb.edu/node/211106.

37. See Adam Tooze, "Why We Loved Mussolini," *NYRB*, Aug. 18, 2016; Giacamo Migone, *The United States and Fascist Italy: The Rise of American Finance in Europe*, trans. Molly Tamor (Cambridge: Cambridge University Press: 2016); Katy Hull, *The Machine Has a Soul: American Sympathy with Italian Fascism* (Princeton, NJ: Princeton University Press, 2021).

38. Thomas B. Morgan, *Italian Physical Culture Demonstration* (New York: Macfadden Books, 1932), 13.

39. See Benito Mussolini, *Fascism: Doctrine and Institutions* (Rome: Ardita, 1935); Allesio Ponzio, *Shaping the New Man: Youth Training Regimes in Fascist Italy and Nazi Germany* (Madison: University of Wisconsin Press, 2015).

40. Morgan, *Italian Physical Culture Demonstration*, 24–35.

41. Macfadden and Gauvreau, *Dumbbells and Carrot Strips*, 405.

42. See Benito Mussolini, "Building a Nation's Health," *PC*, July 1932, 14.

43. Morgan, *Italian Physical Culture Demonstration*, 10. Also see Thomas B. Morgan, *The Listening Post: Eighteen Years on Vatican Hill* (New York: G. P. Putnam, 1944).

44. Morgan, *Italian Physical Culture Demonstration*, 18.

45. See Giorgio Bertellini, *The Divo and the Duce* (Berkeley: University of California Press, 2019); Michael Jospeh Roberto, *The Coming of the American Behemoth: The Origins of Fascism in the United States, 1920–1940* (New York: Monthly Review Press, 2018).

46. On Macfadden's subsequent international endeavor, see Thomas Dixon, *A Dreamer in Portugal: The True Story of Bernarr Macfadden's Mission to Continental Europe* (New York: Covici-Friede, 1934).

47. William H. Crawford, "Governor Franklin D. Roosevelt on 'How I Came Back,'" *PC*, Sept. 1930, 14.

48. See Davis W. Houck and Amos Kiewe, *FDR's Body Politics: The Rhetoric of Disability* (College Station: Texas A&M University Press), 10; Frank Costigliola, "Roosevelt's Body and National Power," in *Body and Nation: The Global Realm of U.S. Body Politics in the Twentieth Century,* ed. Emily S. Rosenberg and Shanon Fitzpatrick (Durham, NC: Duke University Press, 2014), 125–146.

49. Oursler, *Behold This Dreamer*, 267.

50. Oursler, *Behold This Dreamer*, 370.

51. Jay Franklin, "Another Roosevelt in the White House?" *Liberty,* April 30, 1931, 22. Emphasis added.

52. Earle Looker, "Is Franklin D. Roosevelt Physically Fit to Be President," *Liberty,* July 25, 1931, 10. See Houck and Kiewe, *FDR's Body Politics,* chap. 5.

53. Betty Houchin Winfield, *FDR and the News Media* (Urbana-Champaign: University of Illinois Press, 1990), 20. Also see correspondence in Franklin D. Roosevelt, Papers as Governor, Series 1, Box 51, Folder: Macfadden, Bernarr, FDRPL.

54. Susan Ohmer, *George Gallup in Hollywood* (New York: Columbia University Press, 2006), 34–35.

55. *Advertising and Selling*, Feb. 1932, 70. Also see Ohmer, *George Gallup in Hollywood,* 37.

56. "The Press: Cuddle Appeal," *Time,* October 3, 1932, http://content.time.com/time/subscriber/article/0,33009,744529-1,00.html.

57. Oursler, *Behold This Dreamer*.

58. Franklin D. Roosevelt, "The Election: An Interpretation," *Liberty,* Dec. 10, 1932, 6–7.

59. Gertrude Almy Slichter, "Franklin D. Roosevelt's Farm Policy as Governor of New York," *Agricultural History* 33.4 (1959): 167–177.

60. "Mrs. Dall Opens Penny Restaurant," *NYT,* June 22, 1933, 17.

61. Maureen Hoffman Beasley, *Eleanor Roosevelt and the Media* (Urbana-Champaign: University of Illinois Press, 1987), 69–70. For E. Roosevelt's communications with Macfadden from White House, see Eleanor Roosevelt Papers, White House Correspondence, 1933–45, Personal Letters, 1935, Box 616, Folder: Macfadden, Bernarr, FDRPL.

62. "Will End Penny Meals," *NYT,* July 12, 1934, 8.

63. See Rauchway, *Winter War.*

64. Oursler, *Behold This Dreamer.*

65. See Franklin D. Roosevelt, "Help Them Go Straight!" *TDM,* July 1930, 19; Joseph B. Keenan, "Roosevelt Puts Crime on the Spot," *Liberty,* August 1934.

66. Claire Bond Potter, *War on Crime: Bandits, G-Men, and the Politics of Mass Culture* (New Brunswick, NJ: Rutgers, 1998); Matthew Cecil, "Friends of the Bureau: Personal Correspondence and the Cultivation of Journalist-Adjuncts by J. Edgar Hoover's FBI," *Journalism and Mass Communication Quarterly* 88.2 (2001): 267–284.

67. "The Inside Story of Dillinger at Last," *TDM,* Nov. 1934, 3.

68. Homer S. Cummings, "How You Can Prevent Crime," *Liberty,* Dec. 23, 1933, 12.

69. Fulton Oursler, "The Opportunities of the Press in the War Against Crime," in *Proceedings of the Attorney General's Conference on Crime* (Washington, DC: Department of Justice, 1934), 110.

70. Oursler, *Behold This Dreamer,* 317–318.

71. Will Irwin, "Our New Civil War," *Liberty,* Jan. 5, 1935, 5–6.

72. Oursler, *Behold This Dreamer,* 318. Also see Sean McCann, *Gumshoe America: Hard-Boiled Crime Fiction and the Rise and Fall of New Deal Liberalism* (Durham, NC: Duke University Press, 2000).

73. Oursler, *Behold This Dreamer,* 319.

74. See Iwan Morgan and Philip John Davies, eds., *Hollywood and the Great Depression: American Film, Politics, and Society in the 1930s* (Edinburgh: Edinburgh University Press, 2016); Samantha Barbas, *Movie Crazy: Stars, Fans, and the Cult of Celebrity* (New York: Palgrave, 2001).

75. See Bruce Lenthall, *Radio's America: The Great Depression and the Rise of Modern Mass Culture* (Chicago: University of Chicago Press, 2007).

76. "True Story Returns," *Broadcasting,* May 1, 1934, 14.

77. Eric Barnouw, *Media Marathon: A Twentieth-Century Memoir* (Durham, NC: Duke University Press, 1996), 47.

78. "Macfadden Publications Emerges," *NYT,* Nov. 19, 1935, 15.

79. "When Does a Market Really Become a Market," *CDT,* Jan. 21, 1936, 11.

80. Greg Mitchell, *The Campaign of the Century: Upton Sinclair's Race for Governor of California and the Birth of Media Politics* (San Francisco: Polipoint Press, 2010).

81. Rhonda Levine, *Class Struggle and the New Deal: Industrial Labor, Industrial Capital, and the State* (Lawrence: University Press of Kansas, 1988); Robin D. G. Kelly, *Hammer and Hoe: Alabama Communists During the Great Depression* (Chapel Hill: UNC Press, 1990).

82. Bernarr Macfadden, "Publisher of Liberty Accused of 'Muscling In' on the Republican Presidential Nomination," *Liberty,* Dec. 14, 1935, 4.

83. "'New Depression' Laid to New Deal," *NYT,* April 9, 1936, 9.

84. "MACFADDEN: Publisher Won't Refuse to Run for President," *Newsweek,* Sept. 28, 1935, 11.

85. "MACFADDEN: A Lonely Crusader Reviews His Life in Two Parts," *Newsweek,* Dec. 14, 1935.

86. "An Extemporaneous Sermon that Took Sixty Years to Prepare," *CDT*, Feb. 18, 1936, 18.

87. See Warren Susman, *Culture as History: The Transformation of American Society in the Twentieth Century* (Washington, DC: Smithsonian Books, 2003); Wendy Wall, *Inventing the "American Way": The Politics of Consensus from the New Deal to the Civil Rights Movement* (Oxford: Oxford University Press, 2008); Lawrence B. Glickman, *Free Enterprise: An American History* (New Haven, CT: Yale University Press, 2019).

88. "The Macfadden Market," *CDT*, Mar. 17, 1936, 13.

89. Wall, *Inventing the American Way*, 50.

90. Michael Denning, *The Cultural Front: The Laboring of American Culture in the Twentieth Century* (New York: Verso, 1998), 204.

91. Barbara Foley, *Radical Presentations: Politics and Form in U.S. Proletarian Fiction, 1929–1941* (Durham, NC: Duke University Press, 1993), 65.

92. John Stuart, "Bernarr Macfadden: From Pornography to Politics," *New Masses*, May 19, 1936, 9.

93. "From a Macfadden Employe[e]," *New Masses*, June 16, 1936, 22.

94. Richard Wright, "A Blueprint for Negro Literature," *New Challenge*, Fall 1937, 53.

95. See Lizabeth Cohen, *Making a New Deal: Industrial Workers in Chicago, 1919–1939*, 2nd ed. (Cambridge: Cambridge University Press, 2008), 331.

96. See Cohen, "Encountering Mass Culture" and *Making a New Deal*; Nelson Lichtenstein, *State of the Union: A Century of American Labor* (Princeton, NJ: Princeton University Press, 2002).

97. E. Franklin Frazier, *The Negro Family in the United States* (Chicago: University of Chicago Press, 1939).

98. LaShawn D. Harris, "Running with the Reds: African American Women and the Communist Party during the Great Depression," *Journal of African American History* 94.1 (2009): 21–40.

99. Margaret Mead, *The Changing Culture of an Indian Tribe* (New York: Columbia University Press, 1932).

100. David Belknap, *The Fort Belknap Assiniboine of Northern Montana* (Philadelphia: University of Pennsylvania, 1938).

101. M. Inez Hilger, *Chippewa Families: A Social Study of White Earth Reservation, 1938* (St. Paul, MN: Borealis Books, 1938).

102. Elisabeth Colson, *The Makah Indians: A Study of an Indian Tribe in Modern American Society* (Westport, CT: Greenwood Press, 1974).

103. Gerald Vizenor, *Manifest Manners: Narratives on Postindian Survivance* (Lincoln: University of Nebraska Press, 1999).

104. Vicki Ruiz, *From Out of the Shadows: Mexican Women in Twentieth-Century America*, 10th ed. (Oxford: Oxford Univ. Press, 2008), 52, 81.

105. Alvin H. Clement, *Cotton Picking Boy: 1932 through 1936* (Lincoln: Writers' Club Press, 2002), 31.

106. See interview of Bernice Reid in Nancy J. Martin-Perdue and Charles L. Perdue Jr., eds., *Talk About Trouble: A New Deal Portrait of Virginians in the Great Depression* (Chapel Hill: University of North Carolina Press, 1996), 197.

107. "How it Feels to Win a Prize," *TS*, August 1933, 13. This family can be found in the 1940 US Census.

108. "New Way Dry Cleaning and Laundry," in *Life Histories: Manuscripts from the Federal Writers Project, 1936–1940*, LOC, *American Memory*, https://www.loc.gov/item/wpalh000517/.

109. Ed Cray, *Ramblin' Man: The Life and Times of Woody Guthrie* (New York: W. W. Norton, 2010), 418.

110. Sandy Polishuk, *Sticking to the Union: The Life and Times of Julia Ruuttila* (New York: Palgrave Macmillan, 2003).

111. Manuscript of "Hernandez' True Story Magazine," 1935, MSS 648 SC, Center for Southwest Research, University Libraries, University of New Mexico, Albuquerque, NM, USA.

112. See Francisco Balderrama and Raymond Rodríguez, *Decade of Betrayal: Mexican Repatriation in the 1930s* (Albuquerque: University of New Mexico Press, 2006); Zaragosa Vargas, *Labor Rights Are Civil Rights: Mexican American Workers in Twentieth-Century America* (Princeton, NJ: Princeton University Press, 2005).

113. Bernarr Macfadden, "May the Best Man Win!" *Liberty*, Nov. 14, 1936, 4.

7. International Issues, Foreign Editions, and the Global Popular

1. On the methodology of "connective comparison," see the Modern Girl Around the World Research Group, *The Modern Girl Around the World: Consumption, Modernity, and Globalization* (Durham, NC: Duke Univ. Press, 2008), 2–8.

2. See Emily S. Rosenberg, *Spreading the American Dream: American Economic and Cultural Expansion, 1890–1945* (New York: Hill and Wang, 1982). Film scholarship has best documented this trend—for example, Kristen Thompson, *Exporting Entertainment: America in the World Film Market, 1907–1934* (London: BFI, 1985); Melvin Stokes and Richard Maltby, eds., *Hollywood Abroad: Audiences and Cultural Exchange* (London: BFI, 2008); John Trumpbour, *Selling Hollywood to the World: U.S. and European Struggles for Mastery of the Global Film Industry, 1920–1950* (Cambridge: Cambridge Univ. Press, 2002).

3. See Mark Tungate, *Ad Land: A Global History of Advertising* (London: Kogan Page, 2007); Bartow J. Elmore, *Citizen Coke: The Making of Coca-Cola Capitalism* (New York: Norton, 2016); Stefan Schwarkopf, "Who Said 'Americanization'?: The Case of Twentieth-Century Advertising and Mass Marketing from a British Perspective," in *Decentering America*, ed. Jessica C. E. Gienow-Hecht (New York: Berghan Books, 2007).

4. See Anna Lowenhaupt Tsing, *Friction: An Ethnography of Global Connection* (Princeton, NJ: Princeton Univ. Press, 2004); Victoria de Grazia, *Irresistible Empire: America's Advance through Twentieth-Century Europe* (Cambridge, MA: Harvard Univ. Press, 2006); Robert W. Rydell and Rob Kroes, *Buffalo Bill in Bologna: The Americanization of the World, 1869–1922* (Chicago: Univ. of

Chicago Press, 2005); Amanda Ciafone, *Counter-Cola: A Multinational History of the Global Corporation* (Berkeley: Univ. of California Press, 2019).

5. On the "global popular," used throughout this chapter, see Simon During, "Popular Culture on a Global Scale: A Challenge for Cultural Studies?" *Critical Inquiry* 23.4 (1997): 808–833.

6. "No Companionate Marriage!" *NYT,* January 6, 1931, 22.

7. "The Literary Market," *The Editor,* November 18, 1922, 2.

8. See Iain Stevenson, *Book Makers: British Publishing in the Twentieth Century* (London: British Library, 2010).

9. Mike Ashley and Robert A. W. Lowndes, *The Gernsback Days: A Study of the Evolution of Modern Science Fiction from 1911 to 1936* (Holicong, PA: Wildside Press, 2004), 231; Mike Ashley, *The Age of the Storytellers: British Popular Fiction Magazines: 1880–1950* (London: British Library Publishing Division, 2006), 40–41.

10. Mike Ashley, *Age of the Storytellers,* 41, 127. Also see Joseph McAleer, *Popular Reading and Publishing in Britain, 1914–1950* (Oxford: Claredon Press, 1992).

11. Ashley, *Age of Storytellers,* 7; Martin Conboy, *Tabloid Britain: Constructing Community Through Language* (London: Taylor and Francis, 2006), 4; Joel H. Wiener, *The Americanization of the British Press, 1830s–1914* (New York: Palgrave Macmillan, 2011).

12. Kate Jackson, *George Newnes and the New Journalism in Britain, 1880–1910: Culture and Profit* (Surrey: Ashgate, 2001), 174. Also see Joel H. Wiener, *Papers for the Millions: The New Journalism in Britain, 1850s–1914* (Westport, CT: Greenwood Press, 1988); Bridget Griffin-Foley, "From Tit-Bits to Big Brother: A Century of Audience Participation in the Media," *Media, Culture, and Society* 26.4 (2006): 533–538.

13. See Christopher Hilliard, *To Exercise Our Talents: The Democratization of Writing in Britain* (Cambridge, MA: Harvard Univ. Press, 2006).

14. See Hilliard, *To Exercise Our Talents.*

15. *The Editor,* October 7, 1922, 11.

16. Q. D. Leavis, *Fiction and the Reading Public* (London: Chatto and Windus, 1939), 14.

17. Joe Simon and Jim Simon, *The Comic Book Makers* (New York: Vanguard, 2003).

18. Ed Fitzgerald, *A Nickel an Inch: A Memoir* (New York: Athenaeum, 1985).

19. Theodore Peterson, *Magazines in the Twentieth Century* (Urbana-Champaign: Univ. of Illinois Press, 1956), 107.

20. See Chapter 8.

21. See Genevieve Abravanal, *Americanizing Britain: The Rise of Modernism in the Age of the Entertainment Empire* (Oxford: Oxford Univ. Press, 2012); David Ellwood, *The Shock of America: Europe and the Challenge of the Century* (Oxford: Oxford Univ. Press, 2012); Matthew Hilton, *Consumerism in Twentieth-Century Britain: The Search for a Historical Movement* (Cambridge: Cambridge Univ. Press, 2003).

22. See During, "Popular Culture."

23. The term *parallel media evolution* is borrowed from communications studies. See Rudolf Stöber, "What Media Evolution Is," *European Journal of Communication* 19.4 (2004): 483–505.

24. Quoted in Hilliard, *To Exercise Our Talents*, 198. On *My Story Weekly* and similar periodicals, see Billie Melman, *Women and Popular Imagination in the 1920s: Flappers and Nymphs* (London: Macmillan, 2002).

25. David Hansen-Miller, *Civilized Violence: Subjectivity, Gender and Popular Cinema* (Burlington, VT: Ashgate, 2011), 66; Susan Nance, *How the Arabian Nights Inspired the American Dream, 1790–1935* (Chapel Hill: Univ. of North Carolina Press, 2009).

26. Alison Light, *Forever England: Femininity, Literature, and Conservatism Between the Wars* (London: Routledge, 1991), 175. On *My Story Weekly*'s first issue, see Laura Frost, "The Romance of Cliché: E. M. Hull, D. H. Lawrence, and Interwar Erotic Fiction," in *Bad Modernisms*, ed. Douglas Mao and Rebecca L. Walkowitz (Durham, NC: Duke Univ. Press, 2006), 94–118.

27. Liz Conor, *Spectacular Modern Woman: Feminine Visibility in the 1920s* (Bloomington: Indiana Univ. Press, 2004), 334. On the sheik, see Amy Lawrence, "Rudolph Valentino," in *Idols of Modernity: Movie Stars of the 1920s*, ed. Patrice Petro (New Brunswick, NJ: Rutgers Univ. Press, 2010), 87–107; Mica Nava, *Visceral Cosmopolitanism: Gender, Culture and the Normalisation of Difference* (Oxford: Oxford Univ. Press, 2007), 35–40.

28. The *British Newspaper Directory* puts the start of the British edition of *True Story* at 1931, published by Illustrated Publications, Ltd.

29. See "If I *Must* Choose," *Hull Daily Mail*, November 21, 1934, 8. This ad features an excerpt from a true story that begins, "I, an ordinary English mother . . ."

30. Catriona Elder, *Being Australian, Narratives of National Identity* (Crow's Nest, NSW: Allen and Unwin, 2007).

31. See J. A. Mangan and John Nauright, eds., *Sport in Australasian Society: Past and Present* (London: Frank Cass, 2000); Charlotte Macdonald, *Strong, Beautiful, and Modern: National Fitness in New Britain, New Zealand, Australia, and Canada, 1935–1960* (Wellington, NZ: Bridget Williams Books, 2011); Jill Julius Matthews, "Building the Body Beautiful," *Australian Feminist Studies* 5 (1987): 17–34; Kay Saunders, "'Specimens of Superb Manhood': The Lifesaver as National Icon," *Journal of Australian Studies* 22.56 (1998): 96–105; Caroline Daley, *Leisure and Pleasure* (Auckland: Auckland Univ. Press, 2003).

32. Roger Osborne, "A National Interest in an International Market: The Circulation of Magazines in Australia in the 1920s," *History Australia* 5.3 (2008): 75.1–75.16. Also see Martin Lyons and John Arnold, eds., *A History of the Book in Australia, 1891–1945: A National Culture in a Colonised Market* (Queensland: Univ. of Queensland Press, 2001); Bob Catley, *Globalising Australian Capitalism* (Cambridge: Cambridge Univ. Press, 1996).

33. Walter Withrow, "The Editor's Forward," *WPC*, 1920 (annual), 5.

34. Alfred J. Briton, *HPC*, January 1930, 4.

35. "The Average American Man," *HPC*, February 1933, 32.

36. Alfred J. Briton, "Greta—Garbler of Girls," *HPC*, February 1933, 51.

37. *HPC*, July 1934, n.p.

38. "Well-Wisher," *HPC*, September 1934, n.p.

39. *HPC*, September 1933, 47; *HPC*, September 1934, n.p.

40. "Well-Wisher," *HPC*, September 1934, n.p.

41. Paul Frosh, *The Image Factory: Consumer Culture, Photography, and the Visual Content Industry* (Oxford: Berg Publishers, 2003).

42. See Denis Cryle, "Culture and Commerce: Gordon and Gotch in Australia 1890–1940," http://hass.unsw.adfa.edu.au/ASEC/HOBA96_Papers/cryle.html. (Accessed November 18, 2012); Osborne, "A National Interest," 75.7.

43. "Publications Received," *Guardian* (Portland, Victoria), March 15, 1923, 2.

44. See "News and Tobacconist Stand (1930)," in *Great Australian Book of Nostalgia,* ed. John Larkins (Adelaide: Rigby, 1976).

45. *Photoplay,* January 1935, 47.

46. *Photoplay,* March 1935, 11.

47. "Friendly Service," *Western Mail,* May 27, 1938, 41.

48. See Australian Tariff Board, *Report of Evidence at Tariff Board Inquiries into Proposal of Duty on Books, Magazines, and Fashion Plates* (Melbourne: Australian Booksellers' Association, 1930).

49. "American Magazines," *SMH,* May 26, 1931, 6.

50. Australian Tariff Board, *Report of Evidence,* 30.

51. See Osborne, "National Interest."

52. "Reads Romances from Life," *SMH,* March 4, 1937, 18.

53. "Cheap American Magazines," *The Argus,* January 20, 1932, 2.

54. "Revolutions—Mostly Little," *Morning Bulletin,* September 2, 1938, 11.

55. Section 14a expanded previous definitions of obscenity and the powers of the Customs Department. On Australian customs and literature, see Deana Heath, "Literary Censorship, Imperialism and the White Australia Policy," in Lyons and Arnold, *A History of the Book in Australia,* 69–82.

56. See David Day, *Contraband and Controversy: The Customs History of Australia from 1901* (Canberra: AGPS, 1996); Peter Coleman, *Obscenity, Blasphemy and Sedition: The Rise and Fall of Literary Censorship in Australia* (Sydney: Duffy and Snellgrove, 2000).

57. "Trashy Magazines," *The West Australian,* May 12, 1938, 20; "Literary Garbage" *The West Australian,* June 4, 1938, 20; "Magazine Ban: Legality to be Challenged," *SMH,* August 24, 1938, 16; "Stemming the Flood of Pernicious Literature," *The Recorder,* December 29, 1938, 2.

58. These debates are documented in the correspondence and customs forms found in the folios "Prohibited Publications—'Detective Fiction Weekly' . . . 'The Stocking Parade'" (1963/4587) and "Prohibited Publications—'True Romance' and 'True Story'—General Policy on Magazines" (1940/3147), in Central Record Series A425, Correspondence Files, Department of Trade and Customs, Central Office, NAA: A425: 1963/4587 or 1940/3147.

59. Correspondence from Senior Clerk, Customs and Excise Office, to Comptroller-General, Department of Trade and Customs, March 6, 1940. NAA: A425: 1940/3147.

60. Report from Senior Clerk to Comptroller-General, July 11, 1939, NAA; A425: 1940/3147.

61. Report from Senior Clerk to Comptroller-General, October 11, 1939; NAA; A425: 1940/3147.

62. Letter from William L. Lucas (export manager for Macfadden Publications) to E. Abbott (Comptroller-General), September 19, 1939. NAA: A425: 1940/3147.

63. See "Magazine Ban," *SMH*, September 26, 1938, 7; "Crime Stories," *Cairns Post*, September 27, 1938, 7.

64. See Thomas Dietzel and Hans-Otto Hügel, *Deutsche Literarische Zeitschriften 1880–1945: Ein Repertorium* (Munich and New York: de Gruyter Saur, 1988).

65. Gideon Reuveni, *Reading Germany: Literature and Consumer Culture in Germany Before 1933*, trans. Ruth Morris (New York and Oxford: Berghahn Books, 2006), 249–250.

66. See Reuveni, *Reading Germany*; Karin L. Ritzheimer, "Protecting Youth from 'Trash': Anti-Schund Campaigns in Baden, 1900–1933 (PhD diss., SUNY-Binghamton, 2007); Gary D. Stark, *Banned in Berlin: Censorship in Germany, 1871–1918* (Oxford: Berghahn Books, 2009).

67. Willhelm Gensche, "Was liest unsere Jugend?" in *Was liest unsere Jugend?* (Berlin: Decker's Verlag, 1931), 62, 76, quoted in Reuveni, *Reading Germany*, 243. Also see Kerstin Barndt, "Mothers, Citizens, and Consumers: Female Readers in Weimar Germany," in *Weimar Publics/Weimar Subjects: Rethinking the Political Culture of Germany*, ed. Kathleen Canning, Kerstin Barndt, and Kristin Mcguire (New York: Berghahn, 2010), 95–115.

68. See E. Swett, S. Jonathan Wiesen, and Jonathan R. Zatlin, eds., *Selling Modernity: Advertising in Twentieth-Century Germany* (Durham, NC: Duke Univ. Press, 2007).

69. "Das Kind der Sonne," *WG*, April 1929, 5.

70. "Wenn eine Frau Alleine Bleibt," *WG*, Oct. 1930, 16.

71. "Mit der Lüge im Herzen," *WG*, April 1929, 16.

72. "Meine Kunst, Meine Liebe und das Radio," *WER*, March 1933, 29.

73. *WER*, September 1932, 1.

74. See Uta G. Poiger, "Fantasies of Universality? Neue Frauen, Race, and Nation in Weimar and Nazi Germany," in The Modern Girl Around the World Research Group, *The Modern Girl Around the World*, 317–346; Katie Sutton, *The Masculine Women in Weimar Germany* (Oxford: Berghahn, 2011), especially chapter 1; Irene Guenther, *Nazi Chic? Fashioning Women in the Third Reich* (Oxford: Berg, 2004).

75. See Richard W. McCormick, *Gender and Sexuality in Weimar Modernity: Film, Literature, and "New Objectivity"* (New York: Palgrave, 2001); Anthony McElligot, *The German Urban Experience, 1900–1945: Modernity and Crisis* (London: Routledge, 2001); Stefanie Harris, *Mediating Modernity: German Literature and the "New" Media, 1895–1930* (Univ. Park: Pennsylvania State Univ. Press, 2009); Mary Nolan, *Visions of Modernity: American Business and the Modernization of Germany* (Oxford: Oxford Univ. Press, 1994).

76. "Meine Kunst, Meine Liebe und das Radio," 29.

77. See Eric D. Weitz, *Weimar Germany: Promise and Tragedy* (Princeton, NJ: Princeton Univ. Press, 2009), chap. 2; Theo Balderston, *Economics and Politics in the Weimar Republic* (Cambridge: Cambridge Univ. Press, 2002); Canning, Barndt, and McGuire, *Weimar Politics/Weimar Subjects*; Corey Ross, *Media and the Making of Modern Germany: Mass Communications, Society, and Politics from the Empire to The Third Reich* (Oxford: Oxford Univ. Press, 2008).

78. See Katharina von Ankum, ed., *Women in the Metropolis: Gender and Modernity in Weimar Culture* (Berkeley: Univ. of California Press, 1997).

79. See Alexander Sedlmaier, *From Department Store to Shopping Mall: New Research in the Transnational History of Large-Scale Retail* (Berlin: Verlag, 2005), 9–17; Michael K. Goodman, David Goodman, and Michael Redclift, *Consuming Space: Placing Consumption in Perspective* (Burlington, VT: Ashgate, 2010).

80. The phrase "consumption, modernity, and globalization" is from The Modern Girl Around the World Research Group, *The Modern Girl Around the World*. Also see de Grazia, *Irresistible Empire*, chap. 3; Sherman Cochran, *Inventing Nanjing Road: Commercial Culture in Shanghai, 1900–1945* (Ithaca, NY: Cornell Univ. Press, 2000).

81. "Das Mädel aus dem Warenhaus," *Wahre Erzählungen*, December 1930, 51.

82. See Colin G. Calloway, Gerd Gemünden, and Susanne Zantop, eds., *Germans and Indians: Fantasies, Encounters, Projections* (Lincoln: Univ. of Nebraska Press, 2002).

83. See André Bazin, "The Western, or the American Film Par Excellence," in *What Is Cinema?* vol. 2, trans. Hugh Gray (Berkeley: Univ. of California Press, 1971); Christopher Frayling, *Spaghetti Westerns: Cowboys and Europeans from Karl May to Sergio Leone* (London: I. B. Tauris, 2006); Rydell and Kroes, *Buffalo Bill in Bologna*.

84. Lutz P. Koepnick, "Siegfried Rides Again: Westerns, Technology, and the Third Reich," *Cultural Studies* 11.3 (1997): 420.

85. See Paul Weindling, *Health, Race and German Politics Between National Unification and Nazism, 1870–1945* (Cambridge: Cambridge Univ. Press, 1989); Annette F. Timm, *The Politics of Fertility in Twentieth-Century Berlin* (Cambridge: Cambridge Univ. Press, 2010); Cornelie Usbourne, *The Politics of the Body on Weimar Germany: Women's Reproductive Rights and Duties* (Ann Arbor: Univ. of Michigan Press, 1992).

86. See Thomas J. Saunders, *Hollywood in Berlin: American Cinema and Weimar Germany* (Berkeley: Univ. of California Press, 1994).

87. Saunders, *Hollywood in Berlin*, 16.

88. "Greta Garbo spricht deutsch," *WG*, April 1931, 4.

89. "Laßt schon die Kinder Gymnastik treiben," *Wahre Erzählungen*, October 1930, 4–5.

90. See Michael Hau, *The Cult of Health and Beauty in Germany* (Chicago: Univ. of Chicago Press, 2003); Chad Ross, *Naked Germany: Health, Race and the Nation* (London: Berg, 2005); Erik N. Jensen, *Body by Weimar: Athletes, Gender, and German Modernity* (Oxford: Oxford Univ. Press, 2010); Carl

William Westhoff, "The Role of 'Leibesuebung' and Sport in the Third Reich" (PhD diss., Michigan State Univ., 1978).

91. "Mit Den Augen Hören," *WG*, June 1930, 32.

92. "Der Jungbrunnen der Weltstadt," *WG*, July 1930, 31.

93. The latest edition I have seen published during the Second World War is from 1941.

94. See Eric Rentschler, "Mountains and Modernity: Relocating the *Bergfilm*," *New German Critique* 51 (1990): 137–161; Robert C. Reimer, ed., *Cultural History Through a National Socialist Lens: Essays on the Cinema of the Third Reich* (Rochester, NY: Camden House, 2000).

95. See Silvia Hartmann, *Fraktur oder Antiqua: der Schriftstreit von 1881 bis 1941* (Berlin: Lang, 1998); Rueveni, *Reading Germany*, 205–208.

96. See Ross, *Media and the Making of Modern Germany*; Pamela E. Swett, Corey Ross, and Fabrice d'Almeida, eds., *Pleasure and Power in Nazi Germany* (New York: Palgrave Macmillan, 2011); Michael H. Kater, "The Impact of American Popular Culture on German Youth," in *The Arts in Modern Germany: Continuity, Conformity, Change*, ed. Jonathan Huener and Frances R. Nicosia (Oxford: Berghahn, 2006); Shelley Baranowski, *Strength Through Joy: Consumerism and Mass Tourism in the Third Reich* (Cambridge: Cambridge Univ. Press, 2004).

97. See Michael H. Kater, *Different Drummers: Jazz in the Culture of Nazi Germany* (Oxford: Oxford Univ. Press, 2003); David Snowball, "Controlling Degenerate Music: Jazz in the Third Reich," in *Jazz and the Germans*, ed. Michael J. Budd (Hillsdale, NY: Pendragon Press, 2002), 149–166; Lutz Peter Koepnick, *The Dark Mirror: German Cinema Between Hitler and Hollywood* (Berkeley: Univ. of California Press, 2002).

98. Harland Manchester, "True Stories," *Scribner's*, August 1938, 25–29.

8. From the World of Tomorrow to the American Century

1. "Fair Signs Six Companies," *NYT*, Dec. 21, 1937, 21; also see "Bernarr Macfadden and Grover Whalen Sign Contract," Photograph, New York Public Library Digital Archive, https://digitalcollections.nypl.org/items/5e66b3e8-a4d2-d471-e040-e00a180654d7.

2. See Robert Rydell, *World of Fairs: The Century of Progress Expositions* (Chicago: Univ. of Chicago Press, 1993); Marco Duranti, "Utopia, Nostalgia, and World War at the 1939–40 New York World's Fair," *Journal of Contemporary History* 41.4 (2006): 663–668. David E. Nye, "Ritual Tomorrows: The New York World's Fair of 1939," *History and Anthropology* 6.1 (1992): 1–21.

3. See Roland Marchand, "The Designers Go to the Fair II: Norman Bel Geddes, The General Motors 'Futurama,' and the Visit to the Factory Transformed," *Design Issues* 8.2 (Spring 1992): 22–40; Paul Mason Fotsch, "The Building of a Superhighway Future at the New York World's Fair," *Cultural Critique* 48.1 (2001): 65–97.

4. See Herbert Schiller, *Mass Communications and American Empire*, 2nd ed. (Boulder, CO: Westview Press, 1992); Gary S. Messinger, *Battle for the Mind:*

War and Peace in the Era of Mass Communications (Amherst: Univ. of Massachusetts Press, 2011).

5. "McFadden's Amazon Show," *Billboard,* March 25, 1939, 31.

6. *Business Screen* 2.1 (1939), 22–23.

7. "Films for the Fair," *NYT,* March 5, 1939; "Telling the World About Magazines and Advertising," *Business Screen* 1.6 (1939), 12; Rick Prelinger, *The Field Guide to Sponsored Films* (San Francisco: National Film Preservation Foundation, 2006), 46; Charles F. McGovern, *Sold American: Consumption and Citizenship, 1890–1945* (Chapel Hill: UNC Press, 2006), 322.

8. See Warren Susman, *Culture as History: The Transformation of American Society in the Twentieth Century* (Washington, DC: Smithsonian Books, 2003), 154; Wendy Wall, *Inventing the "American Way:" The Politics of Consensus from the New Deal to the Civil Rights Movement* (Oxford: Oxford Univ. Press, 2008); Jackson Lears, *Fables of Abundance: A Cultural History of Advertising in America* (New York: Basic Books, 1995); McGovern, *Sold American.*

9. Inger L. Stole, "Consumer Protection in Historical Perspective: The Five-Year Battle Over Federal Regulation of Advertising, 1933–38," *Mass Communication and Society* 3.4 (2000): 351–372.

10. George E. Sokolsky, "The American Way of Life," *Liberty,* Nov. 5, 1938, 20.

11. Fulton Oursler, "Why These Articles Were Written," *Liberty,* Nov. 5, 1938, 20.

12. Quoted in Helen A. Harrison, ed., *Dawn of a New Day: The New York World's Fair, 1939/40* (New York: NYU Press, 1980), 25.

13. McGovern, *Sold American,* 322.

14. See *Macfadden Exhibit,* Program, New York World's Fair, 1939 (New York: MP, 1939).

15. The descriptor "democratic" comes from Macfadden Publications' program.

16. "617-Mile Walk Ends With Visit to Fair," *NYT,* July 8, 1939, 7.

17. Jack Delano, *At the bus station in Durham, North Carolina,* May 1940, Farm Security Administration. LOC https://lccn.loc.gov/2017747598.

18. See Elizabeth Abel, *The Signs of the Times: The Visual Politics of Jim Crow* (Berkeley: Univ. of California Press, 2010), 83–85.

19. "The Press: Scandal in Circulation," *Time,* May 12, 1941.

20. See "George Sylvester Viereck," US Congress, House, Special Committee on Un-American Activities (1938–44), *Investigation of Un-American Propaganda Activities in the United States, Parts 6–8* (Washington, DC: USGPO, 1942), 39.

21. On the Florida race, see Mark Adams, *Mr. America: How Muscular Millionaire Bernarr Macfadden Transformed the Nation Through Sex, Salad, and the Ultimate Starvation Diet* (New York: HarperCollins, 2009), chap. 15.

22. See Robert Ernst, *Weakness Is a Crime: The Life of Bernarr Macfadden* (Syracuse, NY: Syracuse Univ. Press, 1991), 171–174.

23. "Macfadden Resigns Post," *NYT,* Feb. 28, 1941, 15.

24. "Stockholders Win, Macfadden Must Repay $300,000," *WP,* Aug. 29, 1941, 25; Ernst, *Weakness Is a Crime,* 173–174.

25. "Macfadden Steps Down," *Newsweek,* March 10, 1941, 59.

26. William R. Hunt, *Body Love: The Amazing Career of Bernarr Macfadden* (Bowling Green, OH: Bowling Green State Univ. Popular Press, 1991), 189.

27. Bernarr Macfadden, "An Open Letter to President Roosevelt," *PC*, October 1944. Pamphlet version distributed by the American Editorial Syndicate (New York).

28. "Macfadden's New Heaven," *Newsweek,* June 4, 1945, 93.

29. See Johnnie Lee Macfadden, *Barefoot in Eden: The Macfadden Plan for Health, Charm, and Long-Lasting Youth* (Englewood Cliffs, NJ: Prentice Hall, 1962).

30. Ernst, *Weakness Is a Crime,* 184.

31. Macfadden, *Barefoot in Eden,* 119.

32. "Macfadden Minus Macfadden," *Newsweek,* September 2, 1946, 55–56.

33. MP, *History and Magazines* (New York: MP, 1941).

34. Annalee Whitmore Jacoby, "MacArthur—Hero and Husband," *Liberty,* May 30, 1943, 18–21.

35. Mary Oyama, "My Only Crime is My Face," *Liberty,* Aug. 14, 1943, 11, 57–58. Also see Valerie Matsumoto, *The Nisei Social World of Los Angeles, 1920–1950* (Oxford: Oxford Univ. Press, 2014).

36. See Maureen Honey, *Creating Rosie the Riveter: Class, Gender, and Propaganda during World War II* (Amherst: Univ. of Massachusetts Press, 1984); Inger Stole, *Advertising at War: Business, Consumers and the Government in the 1940s* (Urbana-Champaign: Univ. of Illinois Press, 2012).

37. Alan Brinkley, *The End of Reform: New Deal Liberalism in Recession and War* (New York: Vintage, 1996); Greg Messinger, *Battle for the Mind.*

38. "Smith in WPB Research Post," *NYT,* Aug. 14, 1943, 19.

39. "Minus Macfadden," *Newsweek,* Sept. 2, 1946, 55–56.

40. "Advertising News and Notes," *NYT,* Nov. 6, 1943, 24.

41. Also see Everett R. Smith, *Destiny of Free Enterprise* (New York: MP, 1943) and *What Shall We Do About It?* (New York: MP, 1944).

42. "The Only Man Rich Enough to Keep 55 Million Men At Work," *WSJ,* June 13, 1945, 5.

43. Henry Lieferant, "Middle of the Road," *TS,* February 1946.

44. See David E. Morrison, "The Influences Influencing *Personal Influence*: Scholarship and Entrepreneurship," *Annals of the American Academy of Political and Social Science* 608.1 (2006): 51–75.

45. Morrison, "The Influences Influencing," 71.

46. John H. Summers, "Perpetual Revelations: C. Wright Mills and Paul Lazersfeld," *Annals of the American Academy of Political and Social Science* 608.1 (Nov. 2006): 25–40; Jonathan Sterne, "C. Wright Mills, the Bureau for Applied Social Research, and the Meaning of Critical Scholarship," *Cultural Studies—Critical Methodologies* 5.1 (2005): 65–94.

47. Summers, "Perpetual Revelations," 26.

48. Note the introduction of the word *Influence* in Macfadden Publications' 1945–1946 informational campaigns, discussed above.

49. Elihu Katz and Paul A. Lazarsfeld, *Personal Influence: The Part Played by People in the Flow of Mass Communications* (New York: Free Press, 1955).

50. "Advertising News and Notes," *NYT,* Sept. 21, 1943, 39; See also Everett Smith, "What Does Social Class Mean to Marketers," *Media/scope* 6 (April 1962): 46–48.

51. See James D. Shaffer, "Methodological Bases for the Operation of a Consumer Purchase Panel" (PhD diss., Department of Agricultural Economics, Michigan State College of Agriculture and Applied Science, 1952).

52. See Shelley Nickles, "More Is Better: Mass Consumption, Gender, and Class Identity in Postwar America," *American Quarterly* 54.4 (2002): 581–662; Eung-Sook Kim, "Confession, Control, and Consumption: The Working-Class Market World of *True Story* Magazine" (PhD diss., Univ. of Iowa, 1992).

53. "TSWG," *CDT,* Apr. 11, 1949, 15.

54. See Thomas Waugh, *Hard to Imagine: Gay Male Eroticism in Photography and Film from Their Beginnings to Stonewall* (New York: Columbia Univ. Press, 1996); David K. Johnson, *Buying Gay: How Physique Entrepreneurs Sparked a Movement* (New York: Columbia Univ. Press, 2019); Michael Bronski, *Pulp Friction: Uncovering the Golden Age of Gay Male Pulps* (New York: St. Martin's, 2003).

55. See Joseph Brennan, *Queerbaiting and Fandom: Teasing Fans through Homo-erotic Possibilities* (Iowa City: Univ. of Iowa Press, 2019).

56. See Matthew Isherwood, "Toward a Queer Aesthetic Sensibility: Orientation, Disposition and Desire," *Studies in Art Education* 61.3 (2020): 230–239; José Esteban Muñoz, *Cruising Utopia: The Then and There of Queer Futurity* (New York: NYU Press, 2009).

57. Lizabeth Cohen, *A Consumers' Republic: The Politics of Consumption in Postwar America* (New York: Vintage, 2003), 191.

58. See Sarah E. Igo, *The Averaged American: Surveys, Citizens, and the Making of a Mass Public* (Cambridge, MA: Harvard Univ. Press, 2007).

59. Kenneth T. Jackson, *Crabgrass Frontier: The Suburbanization of the United States* (Oxford: Oxford Univ. Press, 1987); Becky M. Nicolaides and Andrew Wiese, eds., *The Suburb Reader* (New York: Routledge, 2006).

60. Henry R. Luce, "The American Century," *Life,* Feb. 17, 1941.

61. See Hunt, *Body Love,* 173.

62. Letter from Carroll Rheinstrom to Nelson Rockefeller, July 18, 1948, NARA, RG59: General Records of the Department of Stat, Department of State Decimal File, 1945–49, 811.917/7–1848, Box 5024.

63. See Joanne P. Sharp, *Condensing the Cold War: Reader's Digest and American Identity* (Minneapolis: Univ. of Minnesota Press, 2001).

64. See Greg Barnhisel and Catherine Turner, eds., *Pressing the Fight: Print, Propaganda, and the Cold War* (Amherst: Univ. of Massachusetts Press, 2010); Laura A. Belmonte, *Selling the American Way: US Propaganda and the Cold War* (Philadelphia: Univ. of Pennsylvania Press, 2008); Nicholas J. Cull, *The Cold War and the United States Information Agency: American Propaganda and Public Diplomacy* (Cambridge: Cambridge Univ. Press, 2009); Inger Stole, "Advertising America: Official Propaganda and the U.S. Promotional

Industries, 1946–1950," *Journalism and Communication Monographs* 23.1 (2021): 4–63.

65. Nathan, "American Magazines for Export," 11.

66. Letter from Rheinstrom to Rockefeller, July 18, 1948.

67. Letter from Nelson Rockefeller to Carroll Rheinstrom, April 16, 1945, NARA, RG 59: General Records of the Department of State, Department of State Central Decimal File, 111.12 Rockefeller, Nelson, Folder: Macfadden Publications.

68. "Other Company Meetings: Macfadden Publications," *NYT*, May 3, 1946.

69. "Advertising News and Notes," *NYT*, Apr. 21, 1947, 32.

70. Carroll Rheinstrom, "Our Public Relations Abroad," *Printer's Ink*, April 30, 1948, 27.

71. Letter from Carroll Rheinstrom to George Allen, September 15, 1948, and "Travel of Carroll Rheinstrom," Circular from Department of State to American Diplomatic and Consular Officers, October 4, 1948. Both located in NARA, RG 59: General Records of the Department of State, Department of State Decimal File 1945–49, Box 5024, Folder: 032 Rheinstrom, Carroll.

72. On American comics abroad after the Second World War, see John A. Lent, ed., *Pulp Demons: International Dimensions of the Postwar Anti-Comics Campaign* (Cranbury, NJ: Associated Univ. Press, 1999); Paul S. Hirsch, *Pulp Empire: The Secret History of Comic Book Imperialism* (Chicago: Chicago Univ. Press, 2021); Jason Dittmer, *Captain America and the Nationalist Superhero: Metaphors, Narratives, and Geopolitics* (Philadelphia: Temple Univ. Press, 2012).

73. Kevin Patrick, *The Phantom Unmasked: America's First Superhero* (Iowa City: Univ. of Iowa Press, 2017), 78.

74. Patrick, *Phantom Unmasked*, 78.

75. Marc McLelland, *Love, Sex, and Democracy in Japan During the American Occupation* (New York: Palgrave Macmillan, 2012), 110.

76. "ECA Underwrites Laughter for the Germans," *NYT*, Nov. 6, 1948. Also see US Congress, House, Committee on Appropriations, Foreign Aid Appropriation Bill for 1950: Hearings Before the Subcommittee of the Committee On Appropriations, House of Representatives, Eighty-first Congress, First Session (Washington, DC: USGPO, 1949), 43–44.

77. In the first quarter of 1949, Macfadden Publications shipped around 10,000 total issues of its US magazines to Japan. This total would then more than double over the next business quarter. See NARA, RG331, Allied Operational and Occupation Headquarters, WWII, Foreign Business Investment Correspondence Files, 1949–1950, SCAP Legal Division, Folder: "Macfadden Publications" (SCAP license FI-150).

78. Letter from Carroll Rheinstrom to Bartow H. Underhill, July 21, 1949, RG59, General Records of the Department of State Subject Files, 1948–1953, International Information Administration, Private Enterprise Cooperation Staff (IAA/ICO), Box 18, Folder: "Macfadden Publications."

79. "La Tempesta Distrugge Il Lavoro Dell'Uomo," *Storie Vere*, March 21, 1949, back cover. See David Ellwood, "From Re-Education to the Selling of the Marshall Plan in Italy" in *The Political Re-education of Germany and Her*

Allies after World War II, ed. Nicholas Pronay and Keith Wilson (London: Croom Helm, 1985); James E. Miller, *The United States and Italy, 1948–1950: The Politics and Diplomacy of Stabilization* (Chapel Hill: UNC Press, 1986).

80. See memo from Lloyd A. Free (Acting Director of OII) to George Allen, July 25, 1949, and memo from Lloyd A. Free to Mr. Bragg. July 21, 1949. Both located in NARA, RG 59, Subject File, 1941–1953, International Information Administration, Private Enterprise Cooperation Staff (IIA/ICO), Box 18, Folder: "Macfadden Publications."

81. See letter from Carroll Rheinstrom to Bartow H. Underhill, July 21, 1949, NARA, RG 59, Subject File, 1941–1953, International Information Administration, Private Enterprise Cooperation Staff (IIA/ICO), Box 18, Folder: "Macfadden Publications."

82. See "Carroll Rheinstrom" in Barry Marx, ed., *Fifty Who Made DC Great* (New York: DC Comics, 1985).

83. See the USIA pamphlet "How Private Enterprise Can Help Develop a Better Understanding of the United States Throughout the World," NARA, RG 306 Records of the United States Information Agency, Agency History Program Subject Files, Box 14, Folder: Private Industry Cooperation Plan, 1953.

84. Ed Fitzgerald, *Nickel an Inch,* 103; see also, "Group Gains Control of Macfadden Stock," *WSJ,* Feb. 7, 1951, 4.

85. See Howard Blue, "Did You Know Superman's Friend?" *Block Island Times*, April 4, 1919, https://www.blockislandtimes.com/article/did-you-know-superman's-friend/54477.

86. David Hajdu, *The Ten Cent Plague: The Great Comic-Book Scare and How It Changed America* (London: Picador, 2009), 128.

87. Kenneth R. Johnson, "Bart House Books," 2021, http://bookscans.com/Publishers/krjohnson/defunctpages/Bart_House.pdf. On the rise of paperbacks, see Kenneth C. Davis, *Two-Bit Culture: The Paperbacking of America* (Boston: Houghton Mifflin, 1984).

88. "Big Magazine Publishers Rose in '56 Casualties," *NYT,* March 26, 1957, 5.

89. "Surging ahead," *CDT,* May 15, 1961, c6.

90. "Mass Mush," *Newsweek,* Jul. 19, 1961, 54.

91. The details in this paragraph are from Ernst, *Weakness Is a Crime,* 203.

92. "Ex Wife's Suit Jails Macfadden," *WP,* April 19, 1955, 1.

93. "US Publisher Dies in Jersey City," *South China Morning Post,* Oct. 14, 1955, 7; "Macfadden Dead" *NYT,* Oct. 13, 1955, 31.

94. "Macfadden Made Quite an Impact on the U.S. Scene," *Variety,* October 19, 1955, 2–3.

95. "Crazy and In Charge," *Time,* Dec. 7, 1998, 207–208.

96. See John D. Fair, *Mr. America: The Tragic History of a Body Building Icon* (Austin: Univ. of Texas Press, 2015); Mark Adams, *Mr. America*; Susan Bordo, *The Male Body: A New Look at Men in Public and Private* (New York: Farrar, Straus, and Giroux, 2000); Shilipa Dave et al., *Global Asian American Popular Cultures* (New York: NYU Press, 2016).

97. Waugh, *Hard to Imagine*; Johnson, *Buying Gay*; John D. Fair, *Mr. America: The Tragic History of a Bodybuilding Icon* (Austin: Univ. of Texas Press,

2015); Tanya Bunsell, *Strong and Hard Women: An Ethnography of Female Bodybuilding* (New York: Routledge, 2013); Kathryn Bond Stockton, *Beautiful Bottom, Beautiful Shame: Where "Black" Meets "Queer"* (Durham, NC: Duke Univ. Press, 2006); Susan Stryker, *Queer Pulp: Perverted Passions from the Golden Age of the Paperback* (San Francisco: Chronicle Books, 2001); Bronski, *Pulp Friction*; Georges-Claude Guilbert, *Gay Icons: The (Mostly) Female Entertainers Gay Men Love* (Jefferson, NC: McFarland, 2018).

98. "It's Bartell Media Com Now," *Variety*, May 19, 1965, 91.

Epilogue

1. David Dunlap, "Anatomy of a 'People Building,'" *NYT*, Mar. 2, 1997, R1.
2. Dunlap, "Anatomy," R1.
3. Rachalle Garbarine, "264 Apartments in Two Towers Near Lincoln Center," *NYT*, Sept. 19, 2003, B8.
4. See *Winning the Cold War: The US Ideological Offensive*, Hearings, US Congress House Foreign Affairs, Subcommittee on International Organizations and Movements, 1963 (Washington, DC: USGPO, 1963–1964).
5. For example, see Penny M. Von Eschen, *Satchmo Blows Up the World: Jazz Ambassadors Play the Cold War* (Cambridge, MA: Harvard University Press, 2006); Lisa E. Davenport, *Jazz Diplomacy: Promoting America in the Cold War Era* (Jackson: University of Mississippi Press, 2009); Hiroshi Kitamura, *Screening Enlightenment: Hollywood and the Cultural Reconstruction of Defeated Japan* (Ithaca, NY: Cornell University Press, 2002); Kristen Thompson, *Exporting Entertainment: America in the World Film Market, 1907–1934* (London: BFI, 1985); Richard Pells, *Modernist America: Art Music Movies and the Globalization of American Culture* (New Haven, CT: Yale University Press, 2011).
6. See Emily S. Rosenberg, "Consuming the American Century," in *The Short American Century: A Postmortem*, ed. Andrew J. Bacevich (Cambridge, MA: Harvard Univ. Press, 2012).

Acknowledgments

I began this project in the Department of History at the University of California, Irvine (UCI). First and foremost, therefore, I am grateful for the sustained support of Emily S. Rosenberg, who modeled exemplary research, writing, mentoring, and teaching. I would also like to thank the larger intellectual community at UCI, especially Sharon Block, Dan McClure, Emily Sundstrom, Tina Shull, David Wight, Annessa Stagner Stulp, Aubrey Adams, Robert Chase, and Christine Eubank. At UCI, I received much-needed funding from a five-year Chancellor's Fellowship, a Brython Davis Fellowship, and a grant from the UCI International Center for Writing and Translation. Additionally, the Society of Historians of American Foreign Relations (SHAFR) awarded me a travel grant and a full-year fellowship. I am very grateful for SHAFR and the numerous SHAFR members who provided me with professional guidance, commentary on my work, and opportunities for further research and collaboration over the years.

In reconstructing the history of the Macfadden publishing house and its world, I received indispensable help from archivists and librarians at the H. J. Lutcher Stark Center for Physical Culture and Sports at the University of Texas, Austin (especially Cindy Slater and Jan Todd); the US National Archives in College Park, Maryland; the National Library of Australia, in Canberra; the Mitchell Library in Sydney, Australia; the State Library Victoria, in Melbourne, Australia; the Center for Southwest Research at the University of New Mexico; and the Beinecke Rare Book and Manuscript Library at Yale University. Digital archives also played an important role in my research, especially the Media History Digital Library, the US Library of Congress, the Riazanov Library Digital Archive, the Ball State University Digital Media Repository Collections, and the New York Public Library

Digital Collections. Thank you to all whose labor created and organized this wealth of physical and digital materials.

The process of revising and completing this book took place mostly in Montreal, where I had the opportunity to teach countless brilliant, creative, and passionate students for eight years. Teaching and learning from students has been the most rewarding aspect of my career, and I consider myself enormously lucky in this regard. During this time, I was especially fortunate to have had two undergraduate research assistants who worked on projects directly related to this book, David Helps and Ariella Garmaise. I benefited enormously as well from the support of talented friends and colleagues I first met in Montreal. Michelle Cho, Jeremy Tai, Poulami Roychowdhury, Scott Kushner, Dave Meren, and Merve Emre all discussed aspects of this work with me and provided feedback. Additional encouragement came from Julian Nemeth and Tamara Leisser, my first friends in Quebec.

The work of turning the manuscript of *True Story* into an actual book was made possible by the staff of Harvard University Press. Here, I would especially like to thank Andrew Kinney, Mihaela Pacurar, and Brian Distelberg, as well as the two anonymous reviewers who provided me with encouraging feedback amid the COVID-19 pandemic.

Finally, I would like to acknowledge the love and support of my family: my mother, Ruthann Meyer; my father, Christopher Meyer; my siblings, J. B. Fitzpatrick, Connie Meyer, and Kelsey Meyer; and my best friend, Timothy Merlis, who has been with me from the beginning of this project and helped me reach its end. Thank you!

Index